# BIRTHING
# BLACK
# MOTHERS

# BIRTHING BLACK MOTHER

Jennifer C. Nash

DUKE UNIVERSITY PRESS
*Durham and London*
2021

© 2021 Duke University Press
All rights reserved

Designed by Courtney Leigh Richardson
Typeset in Portrait, Helvetica, and Canela by Westchester Publishing Services

Library of Congress Cataloging-in-Publication Data
Names: Nash, Jennifer C., [date] author.
Title: Birthing Black mothers / Jennifer C. Nash.
Description: Durham : Duke University Press, 2021. | Includes bibliographical references and index.
Identifiers: LCCN 2020048999 (print)
LCCN 2020049000 (ebook)
ISBN 9781478013501 (hardcover)
ISBN 9781478014423 (paperback)
ISBN 9781478021728 (ebook)
Subjects: LCSH: African American mothers. | Womanism. | Black lives matter movement. | Doulas—United States. | Reproductive health services—Social aspects—United States. | African American women—Medical care—United States. | Race discrimination—Health aspects—United States.
Classification: LCC E185.86.N35 2021 (print) | LCC E185.86 (ebook) | DDC 306.874/30896073—dc23
LC record available at https://lccn.loc.gov/2020048999
LC ebook record available at https://lccn.loc.gov/2020049000

COVER ART: © LAKISHA COHILL, COURTESY OF THE ARTIST

**FOR YEARS,
I'VE CRIED FOR OTHER
WOMEN'S CHILDREN.**

Valerie Castile

*Contents*

Acknowledgments · ix ·

**INTRODUCTION**
The Afterlives of Malaysia Goodson,
or Black Mothering in Crisis
· 1 ·

ONE. **BLACK GOLD**
Remaking Black Breasts
in an Era of Crisis
· 31 ·

TWO. **IN THE ROOM**
Birthwork by Women of
Color in a State of Emergency
· 69 ·

THREE. **BLACK MATERNAL AESTHETICS**
The Making of a Noncrisis Style
· 103 ·

FOUR. **WRITING BLACK MOTHERHOOD**
Black Maternal Memoirs and
Economies of Grief
· 133 ·

**CONCLUSION**
The Afterlives of Jazmine Headley
· 173 ·

**CODA**
"All Mothers Were Summoned
when George Floyd Called Out
for His Mama"
· 179 ·

Notes · 187 ·
Bibliography · 209 ·
Index · 235 ·

*Acknowledgments*

I have lived much of the last ten years on the move. The question "where are you from?" has become a fraught one as I rattle off the list of cities that have been home—or that have promised the feeling of home. This book has been my traveling companion through Chicago, Cambridge, and Durham, even though it was actually born on a cold January morning in a delivery room in Rockville, Maryland, with the birth of my daughter. I come to this project as Naima Ahmad Nash's mother and as Carolyn Nash's daughter. Our entangled lives are not outside of the terrain this book maps, and so it is no coincidence that I was drawn to this project after my daughter was born, and that it was written with a fierce desire for my mother to hold this book in her hands, and to know that she was in my mind and heart as I worked.

What has remained constant in the long season of change are enduring friendships, especially with my homegirls, my treasured interlocutors, and my most generous readers. My daily conversations with Emily Owens have become as natural and necessary as breathing. I am forever grateful for how she has given me the gift of sisterhood and especially thankful for a year spent as neighbors while I finished this project. Her feedback on many early drafts of this project also helped me find a way forward. Samantha Pinto is my ride or die. The daily doses of real talk and humor, and our many collaborations, have helped me retain my faith in the pleasurable possibilities of academic life. I thank her, always, for her care of this horse, for the millions of times she reminded me that there is something here worth saying, and for her willingness to always read one more draft. Emily Hirsch has become, quite simply, family (part of the bosom, as we say). I am grateful for our ongoing conversation and for her devotion to her role as Auntie.

I owe endless gratitude to my Chicago friends, who kept my heart warm when my body was cold. Mishana Garschi was the keeper of my sanity during our shared years in the tundra as we shared tikel gomen and many cookies and mastered the art of exiting like LeBron. She is also the editorial GOAT, and I am very grateful for the attention she gave to these pages. Meghan Morris and Nate Ela (and Philo and Calix) were our Chicago family. Our dinners, mornings at wiggleworms, and pretzel and hummus feasts were sustaining. Chaunesti Webb and I spent many afternoons talking and enjoying croissants, and those afternoon chats helped make the long Chicago winters warmer and brighter. Her friendship and generous spirit continue to nourish me. Maria Pino Duran showered me with *co-madre* love and taught me—simply by being—the meaning of feminist friendship. My teachers kept my mind and body strong: Jennifer Thornton taught me how to hang upside down and helped me conquer my fears. I remain eternally grateful to Liz Roncka, who helped me continue my practice—first in Boston, and then on-screen during the long season of COVID-19. Paulo Carvalho taught me how to make music and reminded me of the importance of putting feeling into everything I do.

Many thanks to my Northwestern colleagues: Nick Davis, kihana ross, E. Patrick Johnson, Tracy Vaughn-Manley, Nitasha Sharma, Martha Biondi, Celeste Watkins-Hayes, Mary Pattillo, and Mary Dietz. Extra thanks to E. Patrick Johnson, who modeled what a compassionate and visionary chair can make possible. Seth Bernstein made departmental life more cheerful (and very organized). My students showed up with curiosity, openness, and a willingness to think together. They remind me why this is the work that I do. And I have endless gratitude for my new colleagues in Gender, Sexuality, and Feminist Studies at Duke University: thank you for welcoming me into your community with kindness and care.

Many thanks to dear friends because our connections transcend place: Katie Rademacher Kein (for ten years of daily texts), Peter Geller, Amy Hesse Siniscalchi, Justin Mann, Tom Guglielmo, Durba Mitra, Sarah Jane Cervenak, Attiya Ahmad, Ramzi Fawaz, Katie Reiser, Jonathan Evans, and Amber Musser. I treasure you all.

Thanks to Kate Baldwin for her generous reading of the maternal memoir chapter and to Caroline Light for her tremendously thoughtful insights on the breastfeeding chapter. Thanks to Sophie Krensky for sharing her experiences with birthwork and for her indispensable *Maternal Health* newsletters; Julie Morel for her research on race and midwifery and for her tremendously helpful perspectives from the field; Emily Hirsch—again—for reading drafts, brainstorming titles, and offering feedback; and Brock Colyar for insightful comments and the ongoing conversation about everything from governance feminism to Joni Mitchell. Thanks to Lakisha Cohill for sharing her beautiful work and for the time she devoted to talking to me about her political and aesthetic commitments.

Maya Glenn was a research assistant extraordinaire. She is also a deeply brilliant scholar. I am looking forward to the time, a few short years from now, when I am holding her book in my hands. Thanks also to Jaileen Pierre-Louis for her dedicated research assistance and for many wonderful conversations.

Duke University Press has played a critical role in my intellectual life. Early conversations with Elizabeth Ault helped me find my way forward with this project, and her deep support of my work along with her enthusiasm, good humor, and intellectual rigor allowed me to see this project to completion. As always, I am grateful to the anonymous readers for their supportive rigor. Their questions helped me stretch this manuscript and its critical possibilities. Thanks to WSQ and Theory and Event for publishing earlier versions of sections of this work. Portions of chapter 2 were published in "Birthing Black Mothers: Birth Work and the Making of Black Maternal Political Subjects," *Women's Studies Quarterly* 47, nos. 3-4 (2019): 29-50; and portions of chapter 3 appeared in "Black Maternal Aesthetics," *Theory and Event* 22, no. 3 (2019): 551-75.

Endless thanks to the ACLS Burkhardt Fellowship for supporting a year of leave that gave me the time, space, and the necessary calm to finish this project, and to the Radcliffe Institute of Advanced Study for intellectual community. Thanks to the Sexualities Project at Northwestern, Northwestern Provost Fellowship, and Northwestern College Faculty Development Grant for supporting my work.

I wouldn't have written a sentence of this book without the labor and deep kindness of folks who have poured love, time, and energy into Naima. I will always have endless gratitude for Taji, Alma, Deonna, Kevin, and especially Maria.

Finally, to my family:

I stand on the shoulders of my elders, and I feel their presence more profoundly in my life as the years pass. I carry Christine Eastmond, Maurice Eastmond, Alfred Nash, Parthenia Nash, and Mae Thompson in my heart.

Amar (BBD) Ahmad taught me how to stepparent. In the process, he became my dear friend. I will forever appreciate his sense of humor and admire his creative life.

When I asked Naima Ahmad Nash what she wanted me to write about her, she said, "Please write: 'Dear Naima, I love you.' That's it." I will add that she moved to a new city for something called "mama's fellowship" and did it with grace, style, and good humor. She has opened my heart in ways I never imagined possible, and I remain deeply grateful for our ongoing adventure and for every single day of conversation.

Douglas Nash has taught me the importance of humility and generosity, the value of lifelong friendships, and the importance of always being authentically yourself. Carolyn Nash has shown me what it means to practice care. She grows magnificent plants, cares for every cat she meets, and adoringly tends to her granddaughter. Collectively, my parents are my north star. They have showed up for me every time I have asked and even at times when I haven't. I owe them more than I could ever say. What I can offer, again and always, is my endless gratitude for their love.

Like everything in my life, this book was made possible by Amin Ahmad. For the last sixteen years, his steady love has been my anchor. It has become harder to sum up what the many years of being together means to me, harder to account for how much we have shared, and harder to offer a succinct thanks to the person who has been by my side through what I can only call everything. It is certainly the case that the two kids who shared a tea by the Charles River in 2004 could have never anticipated the life we now share. And it is also the case that this life is the thing that I am most grateful for. This book is for Amin, with endless thanks for his unyielding faith in me. He is my home in the world.

# INTRODUCTION

*The Afterlives of Malaysia Goodson,
or Black Mothering in Crisis*

Malaysia Goodson spent a January evening in 2019 shopping in Manhattan. When she and her one-year-old daughter, Rhylee, arrived at the subway station at 53rd Street and 7th Avenue, Goodson discovered that the station, like so many of New York City's subway stations, had no elevator. So when she reached the flight of stairs that would lead her to the crowded platform, she clutched Rhylee in one arm, lifted Rhylee's stroller in her other arm, and began her descent.¹ Goodson's unconscious body was discovered a few minutes later at the bottom of the stairwell, with Rhylee safely resting beneath her. By the time Goodson was transported to the hospital, she was already dead.² In the weeks that followed, her death became a symbol of bureaucratic callousness, a testament to the city's crumbling infrastructure and failure to provide accessible transportation, and an emblem of the invisibility of Black mothers, particularly poor Black mothers, in public spaces.³ If Goodson's daily life was spent navigating invisibility, the very invisibility that could allow others to walk past as she struggled to carry a stroller and a baby down the crowded subway stairs, in death, she was publicly celebrated as a hero, as a mother who transformed

FIGURE I.1. Protesters in New York City in March 2019. Their protest was to honor Malaysia Goodson and to advocate for subway accessibility. Courtesy of Erik McGregor.

her body into a human shield to protect her child. Indeed, the media read Goodson's final moments as a sign of her deep commitment to her daughter, a conception of the heroic labor of the Black maternal as, in Aliyyah Abdur-Rahman's words, "standing at the mouth of a grave with defiant feet and balled fists refusing to let my [child] come or fall in."[4]

Three months later, in April 2019, aspiring Democratic Party presidential nominee Elizabeth Warren participated in "She the People," a forum for women of color voters. Warren, who had developed a reputation for her detailed policy recommendations (her campaign slogan was "I have a plan for that"), unveiled her newest innovation. If Black women are three to four times more likely to die during childbirth, Warren suggested that the state provide hospitals with financial incentives to improve health outcomes for Black mothers specifically. She said, "Doctors and nurses don't hear African American women's issues the same way that they hear things from white women. We gotta change that and we gotta change it fast because people's lives are at stake."[5] Later that week, in an essay published in *Essence* magazine, Warren elaborated on her proposal, noting, "Black women shouldn't have to develop elaborate birth plans or personally shell out thousands of dollars for extra eyes and ears at the hospital to ensure they survive the experience of childbirth."[6] Warren was hailed both for making Black maternal health a campaign issue and for her investment in offering a clear policy intervention designed to safeguard Black maternal life.

Over the course of 2019, Malaysia Goodson's name traveled far from New York City, via national and even international media, as a symbol of Black maternal trauma and heroism. Presidential candidates, including Warren and Kamala Harris, wielded the specter of Black maternal death as a sign of their commitment to the multiply marginalized; as Kirsten Gillibrand reminded viewers during one Democratic debate, "I sat down with Eric Garner's mother, and I can tell you when you've lost your son, when he's begged for breath, when you know because you have a video, when you know he said, 'I can't breathe' so many times, over and over again, when you know he used an illegal chokehold, that person should be fired."[7] Black mothers were figured as the memory-keepers of slain Black children—particularly Black boys—and as always braced for inevitable future violence. They were icons of trauma, grief, heroism, and death "trotted" out by an array of figures on the US Left as "the ultimate example of how bad things are."[8] And Black mothers emphatically placed themselves in the public sphere to speak about the antiBlack conditions that were killing their children and to advocate for their needs, including perhaps the most basic need—for "More Life."[9] In so doing, they rendered motherhood a powerful vehicle for making visible a set of conditions that has long been, and continues to be, wholly unlivable for Black people.

If Black mothers have become politically legible because of their newly visible but long-standing proximity to their dead children, they have also recently entered the public consciousness in a new way. Not simply proximate to their children's anticipated death, Black mothers are now imagined as themselves occupying death-worlds because of their distinct vulnerability to a decidedly not-new condition: medical racism and obstetric violence. For instance, Linda Villarosa's 2018 *New York Times* magazine long-form article, which documented a "life-or-death crisis" facing Black mothers and infants, was picked up by Public Broadcasting Service (PBS), National Public Radio (NPR), *Truthout*, *Mother Jones*, and *Democracy Now*; was cited by state legislatures as they formed task forces to respond to the crisis of Black maternal health; and also inaugurated a year of significant coverage of Black maternal health in nearly every major US newspaper.[10] Collectively, that outpouring of journalistic work amplified a singular point: racism is responsible for the deadly health outcomes that Black mothers and children experience. Writing a year after Villarosa's widely circulated exposé, Amy Roeder starkly noted, "For Black women far more than for white women, giving birth can amount to a death sentence. . . . Their odds of surviving childbirth are comparable to those of women in countries such as Mexico and Uzbekistan, where significant proportions of the population live in poverty."[11] The attention to staggeringly high Black maternal and infant mortality rates led scholars and activists to describe institutionalized medicine as "failing its Black mothers," and politicians and activists devoted sustained rhetorical attention to the plight of Black mothers and their vulnerable children.[12] This journalistic work—often informed by the critical innovations of Black feminists working under the banner of reproductive justice—has amplified a singular point: Black mothers are in crisis.

*Birthing Black Mothers* probes a moment where the long-standing conditions of the ordinary have been newly framed as a crisis and where Black motherhood itself has become a site of cultural interest, empathy, fascination, support, and seemingly benign regulation both by the biopolitical state and by Black feminists as they have collaborated to figure Black mothers as living *in* crisis. This book argues that Black mothers in the United States have become spectacularly and dangerously visible through the frame of crisis, one that insists on their spatial and temporal location in a death-world that is described as reminiscent of the nation's imagined past, even as it is consistent with the conditions of the unfolding present. While crisis has made the precarity of Black mothering newly visible—if not remediable—it has also tethered Black maternal flesh to disorder, even if it is not the disorder of earlier eras, namely pathology and poverty. It is precisely because Black motherhood is now cast as suffering rather than pathological, as tragic rather than self-destructive, as traumatized rather than deviant, that the crisis frame can be both deeply seductive and rhetorically effective. Yet the rhetoric of crisis is part of an enduring and troubling tradition of rendering Black women generally, and Black mothers specifically, into symbols, even if now Black mothers are symbols of tragic heroism rather than deviance.

*Birthing Black Mothers* traces how the crisis frame has transformed Black mothers into a distinct form of Left political currency during the era of Black Lives Matter (BLM). Black mothers become political currency when the category "Black mother" comes to refer not to a form of relationality, a set of practices, a form of labor, or an embodied experience, but instead to a political category that is a synonym for pain. In naming Black mothers as Left currency, I track how Black mothers are invoked by politicians like Warren and Gillibrand and how Black feminists invoke Black mothers to describe the racism inherent to institutionalized medicine. I study how Black feminist ethics—like reproductive justice—have become Left talking points, so that politicians like Warren can make claims like "the women of color who have championed the reproductive justice movement teach us that we must go beyond choice to ensure meaningful access for every woman in America—not just the privileged and wealthy few."[13] Thus the book traces how Black mothers generally, and birthing Black mothers particularly, have become a political category, a woke credential, mobilized by a variety of actors on the US Left. Of course, the relegation of Black mothers to the realm of the symbolic has been inherent to the US project of race-making since the nation's inception. What is distinctive about the political moment that constitutes the backdrop of my analysis is that Black mothers are figured as bodies that warrant compassion, education, and support because of their proximity to death, because they are living *in* crisis.

In describing the rhetoric of crisis as generating a distinctly Left form of currency, I remain acutely conscious of how the US Right has also rendered Black mothers as a kind of political currency, one that secures narratives of Black pathology in a moment where, as Laura Briggs convincingly argues, "All politics have become reproductive politics."[14] I see the work of the US Left's investment in crisis rhetoric as a different kind of political labor, even as it is one that I subject to critical scrutiny. As the US Left "responds" to the antiBlackness, misogyny, and transphobia of the Trump administration and to the sea of nonindictments and nonconvictions of state officials who have slain Black people, Black mothers are a valuable currency that can confer Left bona fides on the speaker who selectively invokes them. When members of Mothers of the Movement appeared onstage at the 2016 Democratic National Convention to confer their support to Hillary Clinton, when Kamala Harris and Kirsten Gillibrand each insisted on recounting the details of their conversations with Eric Garner's mother during a Democratic debate in 2019 (Harris insisted, "Now, I would like to also talk about this conversation about Eric Garner, because I, *too*, met with his mother"), Black mothers—particularly suffering Black mothers—are visibly a kind of political commodity, one that, simply by being referenced, can provide moral authority for those who speak their names.[15]

Black mothers are thus objects of Left political value and symbolic support because of their imagined location at the nexus of dual crises—navigating the intersecting forces of medical racism and state-sanctioned violence that render Black life vulnerable. I use the term *symbolic support* to underscore that I see neither the brief outrage surrounding Goodson's death nor Warren's policy proposals as producing meaningful changes in the lives and experiences of Black mothers. Instead, Black mothers are simply invoked as bodies that signify and inhabit crisis, that are always "standing at the mouth" of their children's graves. The US Left has, then, tethered Black mothers to a new set of "controlling images" that center trauma and injury, bringing Black mothers into view only through their capacity to stand for brokenness of a different kind.[16] Black feminism is not outside the project of rendering Black mothers as symbols, even as it has engaged in that endeavor benignly, in a collective effort to secure Black mothers' bodily autonomy and sexual freedom. Indeed, the labor of making Black motherhood political, making the birthing Black mother a political subject rather than an embodied position, is often forged in the name of Black feminist praxis and its commitments to reproductive justice and birth equity.

*Birthing Black Mothers* defines the moment when Black mothers have been refigured not as pathological but as living in crisis, as a central and undertheorized part of the ongoing BLM era. If it remains the case that Black boys and men are described as the icons of the BLM social movement, this book tells a different story, arguing that Black mothers have come to be the centerpiece of BLM's political project, the primary symbol around which the quest for Black life has been made visible. This book argues that Black mothers' capacity to stand for pain and to engender support rather than condemnation is most visible in two archives—public health and aesthetics—which have both been shaped and remade by the political imperative of BLM. Even as I critically engage the symbolic and rhetorical traffic around Black mothers' lives, I hold on to the material reality of Black mothers' (and children's) disproportionate deaths, the deathly outcomes of antiBlack obstetric violence, which connect Black mothers across class lines. As Dána-Ain Davis notes, "The distance between poor, low-income, and middle-class and professional Black women's birth outcomes is a short one. The class structure in US society is ostensibly a strategy for accessing sets of privilege that supposedly transcend race and racism. Of course, we know that is not the case."[17] What unites Black mothers is an intimate proximity to noncare that can manifest itself in an array of ways, ranging from medical indifference to forced Cesarean sections, from encouragement to *not* reproduce to systemic neglect of Black women's pain. This project is deeply committed to doing justice to that reality outside the realm of the symbolic or the rhetorical. Thus, I document the myriad ways that Black mothers and children experience medicalized violence, and I consider the complex ways Black feminists might envision new forms of freedom for Black mothers, including freedom from the rhetoric of crisis and the weight of the symbolic.

*Black Maternal Politics*

In considering how Black mothers forge political work in, through, and against the rhetoric of crisis, and in studying how actors on the Left take up Black motherhood as a symbol of trauma and brokenness, this book advances the term *Black maternal politics*. I develop my understanding of Black maternal politics mindful of how Black women have strategically and historically used motherhood as a platform for activism, perhaps most spectacularly during the civil rights movement. Françoise Hamlin's call to study the civil rights movement "through the context of mothering and women's empowerment and resistance" and her careful analysis of how "African Americans repositioned and transformed seemingly static stations into weapons of resistance, empowerment, and maneuver, rather than dwelling solely within the four walls of narrow Eurocentric constructions of domestic space," suggest the centrality of maternal politics to Black women's activism.[18] Feminist writers have long developed the term *maternal politics* to describe moments when, as Julia Wells notes, "women . . . are not fighting for their own personal rights as women but for their custodial rights as mothers," or when, as Patricia Hill Collins argues, there is a collective sense that "motherhood could be a symbol of power."[19] I am thus mindful of both the rich historical archive on Black maternal politics and the theoretical effort to define—and, in the case of Collins, defend—the political and affective power of Black maternal politics.

In the context of this project, I consider Black maternal politics in two ways. First, I read Black maternal politics as practices of survival, forms of advocacy, and strategies developed for safeguarding Black maternal and child life, for making visible how obstetric violence *is* a form of state violence that threatens to engulf Black bodies, for making apparent how BLM *is* a Black Mamas Matter movement. These are political projects that are necessarily Black feminist and that stage their work in the service of "More Life" in its varied forms, including the right to live, breathe, eat, drink clean water, move around cities, and traverse public spaces without fear. They use Black maternity as a platform for imagining varied and robust visions of freedom, and they treat Black mothers as the paradigmatic symbol around which to make the vital need for "More Life" visible. And, as I argue in this book, they are political projects that wage their work strategically around certain affects—sorrow, grief, hurt—precisely because these affects authorize Black maternal work in ways that rage, desire, and longing still do not. When I describe *Black maternal politics*, I unearth the various political projects that unfold under the banner of Black motherhood, projects that manifest themselves in myriad ways, ranging from Black peer breastfeeding classes to Black doula trainings, rather than treating Black motherhood as a singular or united space marked by a particular set of political desires. I also use the term *Black maternal politics* to understand Left efforts to expose crisis, to respond to Black death by emphatically naming the crisis as a key political issue, and to secure a claim to speaking for the multiply marginalized by naming Black mothers as bodies that matter. Yet the materiality of Black mothers' bodies, and the urgency of their political needs, often falls out of this iteration of Black maternal politics, even as this form of organizing has been a powerful way for Black women to achieve an ostensibly legitimate platform for staging political dialogue about their needs. In this inflection of Black maternal politics, I study how the birthing Black mother becomes a political category that can garner certain kinds of affective engagement: pity, compassion, encouragement, support.

I construct my conception of Black maternal politics in conversation with Erica S. Lawson's work on "bereaved Black mothers," which reads Black maternal grief as the foundation of certain forms of Black female activism. Lawson treats Black maternal grief as both public and gendered, arguing that "while grief is not exclusively maternal, it is a differently gendered emotion with unique implications for women's activism. . . . By giving and preserving life, Black mothers threaten anti-Black necropolitics in the racial state."[20] For Black mothers, Lawson argues, grief becomes a way of making visible Black male death, and the pain of standing next to—and sometimes for—one's slain Black son is the foundational act of Black maternal political subjectivity. This public grief becomes the basis of political activism, the foundation of a form of political work that enables Black mothers to place critical attention on the antiBlack logics at the heart of the racial state and to connect forms of racial violence from across historical periods. My conception of Black maternal politics is also indebted to Ruth Feldstein's analysis of race and motherhood, particularly her engagement with Mamie Till Bradley's decision to "let the world see" Emmett Till's mutilated body (an analysis that Lawson also centers in her work). For Feldstein, the strategic mobilization of motherhood as a political identity reveals the "radical potential of traditional roles."[21] Feldstein writes, "When Mamie Till Bradley opened her son's casket 'to let the people see,' she exposed more than her dead son's body. She had the courage and the determination to translate her personal pain and her family's tragedy into political terms. In negotiating her private role as a mother into the public and political sphere, she helped change the terms on which her son's death was understood and debated."[22] Like Lawson, Feldstein treats the willingness to place private grief on public view as a form of Black maternal activism strategically waged by Bradley, and thus Feldstein reads Bradley as a political actor who consciously and boldly deployed Till's funeral as a space for making painfully visible the brutality of antiBlack violence.

What Feldstein and Lawson share in their conception of "bereaved Black mothers" is the notion that Black maternal politics are born from private grief *transformed* into public action. Black maternal political subjectivity is thought to emerge from a wound that shifts the Black mother from an apolitical subject to a political one, from a private life to a public one. In this account, there was a Black maternal apolitical past, a rupture constituted by violence, and a present marked by respectable political activism rooted in loss, not anger. I probe the utility of this prevailing frame that attaches righteous and legible Black maternal politics to tragedy, that figures Black maternal activism as a form of politics born from trauma as opposed to already existing. I ask why Black maternal politics garners its currency from the idea that it emerges *only* after grief, and that its respectability and power are made possible because of loss. This book is born from a desire to interrogate and trouble this narrative of Black maternal political life, as well as to understand the political utility of this narrative, recognizing that Black mothers often deploy this narrative to make palatable and actionable their politics even as their own presentations of their histories and political desires often challenge this very narrative.

In probing Black maternal politics, I also consider the Black maternal affects that are culturally authorized—grief, sorrow, mourning—and those that remain relegated to the periphery, including Black maternal rage. As I argue in chapter 4, cultural markets constructed around—and profiting from—both Black male death and Black maternal grief hinge on suturing Black maternal life to respectable performances of sorrow. These are performances imagined to effect change. For example, in the weeks following Ahmaud Arbery's murder in 2020, his mother, Wanda Cooper-Jones, powerfully advocated for hate crime legislation in Georgia—one of four states with no hate crime laws. In her passionate pleas for legal change, she mobilized grief to argue for legislative reform.[23] Her advocacy connected her son's murder to the homophobic murder of Ronald Trey Peters in 2019,[24] to swastikas spray-painted on the walls of a Georgia high school,[25] and to a white teenager's 2019 planned knife attack in a Black church in Georgia.[26] Yet in a cultural milieu that continues—as Robin D. G. Kelley argues—to value white property over Black life, expressions of Black rage continue to be disavowed and treated as excessive, problematic, or counterproductive. In 2017, when Valerie Castile, Philando Castile's mother, stood on the steps of a Minnesota courthouse and spoke about the not guilty verdict in the case against Officer Jeronimo Yanez, she said emphatically, "The system continues to fail Black people, and it will continue to fail you all."[27] Three years later, she responded to the murder of George Floyd and again wielded the language of warning: "I've said it time after time. You cannot keep treating people this way. They're going to rebel. I knew this day would come. George Floyd was the straw that broke the camel's back."[28] Castile voices her sense that "this day would come," that Black rage—sometimes in partnership with white rage—would be the rational response to centuries of uninterrupted white supremacist patriarchal violence. Her warning though suggests the ongoing invisibility of Black maternal rage as a politically efficacious affect. In positing the relative absence of cultural space for Black maternal rage, my impulse is not to place grief and rage in tension. Instead, I probe the kinds of Black maternal affects and performance of Black motherhood that are cast as politically generative, as well as those that are too often dismissed or concealed in the name—the illusion—of a common good.

*Crisis*

The years spanning 2010–20 have been marked by an abundance of journalistic attention to Black maternal and infant health (which is often described as journalistic advocacy on behalf of Black life itself): in a 2017 *Los Angeles Times* article, Ann M. Simmons described Black maternal mortality as "the quiet crisis among African Americans," and ProPublica and NPR began collaborating on their "Lost Mothers" series, which investigated maternal deaths.[29] That same year, Annie Waldman reported that hospitals that are "Black-serving"—the institutions where Black mothers are most likely to deliver their children—are the same hospitals where mothers are more likely to experience postpartum complications, including infections and embolisms. Waldman's article emphasized a single cause for this racial disparity in postpartum health: racism. In her description of public health data from New York City, she writes, "Even when accounting for risk factors like low educational attainment, obesity and neighborhood poverty level, the city's black mothers still face significantly higher rates of harm, the agency found. Of note, black mothers who are college-educated fare worse than women of all other races who never finished high school. Obese women of all races do better than black women who are of normal weight. And black women in the wealthiest neighborhoods do worse than white, Hispanic and Asian mothers in the poorest ones."[30] A year later, Villarosa's article also emphasized that the single cause of differential outcomes for Black and white mothers, for Black and white infants, is racism. She writes, "For black women in America, an inescapable atmosphere of societal and systemic racism can create a kind of toxic physiological stress, resulting in conditions—including hypertension and pre-eclampsia—that lead directly to higher rates of infant and maternal death. And that societal racism is further expressed in a pervasive, longstanding racial bias in health care—including the dismissal of legitimate concerns and symptoms—that can help explain poor birth outcomes even in the case of black women with the most advantages."[31]

In response to the popular coverage of Black maternal health, there have been various local, state, and federal efforts to "respond" to the enduring condition of antiBlack obstetric violence and perinatal neglect newly cast as an urgent crisis. In 2018, the federal government passed the Preventing Maternal Deaths Act, which provided federal grants to states that actively investigate maternal deaths; fifty-seven members of Congress joined the newly formed Black Maternal Health Caucus; and Illinois senator Dick Durbin and representative Robin Kelly introduced the Mothers and Offspring Mortality and Morbidity Awareness Act (MOMMA Act), which would "improve access to culturally-competent care" and extend Medicaid coverage to a full year postpartum.[32] And a few days before Mother's Day in 2019, Senator Cory Booker and Representative Ayanna Pressley introduced a bill called the Maximizing Outcomes for Moms through Medicaid Improvement and Enhancement of Services Act (MOMMIES Act), which extended Medicaid coverage—which was required to last sixty days following birth, though some states had longer periods of coverage—for postpartum women to a year after giving birth and explicitly supported "services that are proven to positively impact maternal health outcomes for black women," including doulas and midwives.[33]

Similar efforts unfolded at state and local levels: in 2018, Governor Andrew Cuomo of New York announced a state response to address Black maternal mortality that would follow Minnesota's and Oregon's leads and expand Medicaid coverage to include doulas.[34] That same year, San Francisco's public health department partnered with SisterWeb to provide doula access for Black mothers,[35] and in 2017 Baltimore launched a program to train city residents to become doulas serving the B'More Healthy Babies Program, a city initiative aimed at reducing infant mortality.[36] In 2019, the city of Washington, DC, formed a maternal mortality commission titled Save Black Women to address the facts that its maternal mortality rates are double the national average and that Wards 7 and 8 in the District lacked maternity wards, which led a representative from the American College of Obstetricians and Gynecologists to declare that "Washington DC is the most dangerous place to give birth in the United States if you are African American."[37]

Despite the proliferation of popular attention and national, state, and local legislative interventions, the Centers for Disease Control's May 2019 report on maternal mortality found that the racial disparity in maternal mortality has not changed and might have even worsened.[38] Danielle Jackson describes this curious intersection of attention and inertia, noting, "The inaction and confusion at the state and federal levels say a lot about gridlock and bureaucratic disorganization, but also, who and what we value in our society."[39] Her work underscores how the discursive explosion marked by temporalities of urgency often stands in for political work designed to ameliorate the very conditions that produce the "crisis." Haile Eshe Cole echoes the sense that the amplification of discourse around Black maternal crisis often replaces actual political labor to improve the lives of Black mothers and children. She writes, "The contemporary urgency around elucidating the dilemma of black maternal and infant death . . . has in many ways become a means of capitalizing on the spectacle of black suffering and death. Specifically, it has become efficacious and newsworthy to center research and programming on black mortality."[40] Cole's notion that the "urgency" around Black maternal life (and death) is about the "spectacle of Black suffering and death"—and even about the currency that adheres to gesturing to that spectacle—resonates with my interest in tracing how Black mothers' mortality has become a key sign around which the US Left has organized itself in the BLM era, even as Black mothers and children continue to suffer. In this moment, simply noticing the racial disparities that mark Black perinatal life is treated *as* political work invested in ameliorating those inequities. We might think of this outpouring of attention alongside political stasis as actually constitutive of the crisis frame.

Crisis—the primary frame through which Black mothers and Black motherhood become visible—has affective, temporal, and aesthetic dimensions that collectively conjure up an image of Black mothers occupying a nontime and nonplace, one that is thought to be qualitatively different from the here and now of the contemporary United States. In other words, crisis renders Black maternal bodies out of time and out of place, as noncitizens, as historical actors who do not fit into the present moment. Crisis often performs its rhetorical labor by describing Black mothers as analogous with non-US women. In Villarosa's celebrated article, for example, she describes the Black maternal death rate as "triple the rate of white New Yorkers, and roughly comparable to complication rates in Sierra Leone."[41] Similarly, Roeder's description of Black maternal death rates reminds readers, "While press and publicity around the push offered harrowing stories, women reading these stories in the U.S. may well have come away believing that it was a problem for mothers in villages in Sierra Leone—but surely not in Atlanta or Washington, D.C."[42] These journalistic exposés on Black maternal health often argue that Black women experience forms of risk and violence that would be imaginable—or even acceptable—only outside the boundaries of the United States. We might also consider how obstetric violence inflicted on mothers "in villages," on mothers in Mexico, Sierra Leone, and Uzbekistan, is treated as normalized and inevitable and thus unremarkable. Black women, though, are imagined to live in a no-nation within a nation, to experience forms of violence that are thought to exist only outside US borders.

Similarly, Black women are figured as living not simply in the "afterlives of slavery" but also in the temporality of enslavement.[43] Villarosa's assessment of Black infant and maternal mortality reports that "Black infants in America are now more than twice as likely to die as white infants—11.3 per 1,000 black babies, compared with 4.9 per 1,000 white babies, according to the most recent government data—a racial disparity that is actually wider than in 1850, 15 years before the end of slavery, when most black women were considered chattel."[44] Villarosa emphasizes the nature of the "life-or-death" situation facing Black mothers by underscoring that the conditions of the present are *worse* than in 1850. In April 2019, aspiring Democratic presidential candidate Beto O'Rourke picked up the 1850 statistic, noting, "We have an infant mortality discrepancy between white and Black America that is worse today than it was in 1850, 15 years before the abolition of slavery."[45] Indeed, this historical statistic has come to be a rhetorical touchstone in the new attention to Black maternal health, widely cited as evidence of the urgency of the conditions of the present and the resemblance of the present to a past that some imagine we have moved beyond or transcended.[46] This conception of the relegation of Black mothers to a no-place, or at least a non-US-place, and to a no-time, or at least to a nonpresent time, works not to mark Black mothers as deviant, but instead to mark them as bodies worthy of compassion, of education, and even of salvation through Left intervention that will enable Black mothers' compliance with edicts of good motherhood. Thus, crisis engenders a certain kind of temporality—urgency—which creates an obligation for swift response, for action to halt the state of emergency.

My understanding of crisis is indebted to Lauren Berlant's work, which calls us to imagine crisis as a genre that "belies the constitutive point that slow death—or the structurally induced attrition of persons keyed to their membership in certain populations—is neither a state of exception nor the opposite, mere banality, but a domain where an upsetting scene of living is revealed to be interwoven with ordinary life after all, like ants discovered scurrying under a thoughtlessly lifted rock."[47] For Berlant, "crisis" constitutes an impasse, not an event, a set of conditions for which there is no ending, even as crisis as a genre is presented as a "state of exception," as a rupture with, rather than a continuation of, the conditions of the ordinary. The genre of crisis, which sounds in the tenor of rupture, amplification, emergency, obscures how crisis actually refers to ongoing conditions of the ordinary and the labor—physical, emotional, psychic, spiritual—that people are forced to perform to endure. As Berlant notes,

> Often when scholars and activists apprehend the phenomenon of slow death in long-term conditions of privation, they choose to misrepresent the duration and scale of the situation by calling a crisis that which is a fact of life and has been a defining fact of life for a given population that lives that crisis in ordinary time. Of course this deployment of crisis is often explicitly and intentionally a redefinitional tactic, an inflationary, distorting, or misdirecting gesture that aspires to make an environmental phenomenon appear suddenly as an event, because as a structural or predictable condition it has not engendered the kinds of historic action we associate with the heroic agency a crisis implicitly calls for.[48]

Black mothers are not the only site of contemporary crisis. Janet Roitman's work reveals that crisis has become the prevailing genre of US political life. Roitman writes, "Crisis texts are a veritable industry. The geography of crisis has come to be world geography CNN-style: crisis in Afghanistan, crisis in Darfur, crisis in Iran, crisis in Iraq, crisis in the Congo, crisis in Cairo, crisis in the Middle East, crisis on Main Street. But beyond global geopolitics, crisis qualifies the very nature of events: humanitarian crisis, environmental crisis, energy crisis, debt crisis, financial crisis, and so forth."[49] For Roitman, "Crisis-claims evoke a moral demand for a difference between the past and the future.... That is, crisis, or the disclosure of epistemological limits occasions critique."[50] Crisis then contains an implicit ethical demand for another kind of future and for immediate intervention to transform the conditions of the present into a different kind of future.[51] Crisis discourse has revealed that Black mothers come into view as nonpathological subjects worthy of compassion only through the temporality of urgency and through an insistence of figuring a future that is imagined as a radical break with the present.

Following Roitman's and Berlant's leads, this book thinks about crisis as a framing device, a "redefinitional tactic," that aspires to make visible long-standing forms of juridical and medical violence. Also, this device exposes these forms of violence in order to do justice to the women and children who experience that violence but, more often than not, perform this labor to confer Left bona fides, to establish the Left credentials of an actor. This project probes both institutional attachments to the logic of Black maternal crisis and Black mothers' deployments of the genre of crisis in the hopes of making evident forms of violence that render hospitals sites of death, violence, coercion, injury, and trauma for Black mothers and children, even as the forms of that violence vary and often unfold under the mantle of protecting Black mothers. I treat contemporary Black maternal politics as performing its work under the banner of crisis, and I view crisis as the primary way that Black mothers are interpellated as political subjects worthy of care and concern. Indeed, I argue that Black mothers have been able to come into political view only through crisis—whether through crises of pathology or crises of lack of support.

My consideration of Black mothers' deployment of the rhetoric of crisis to flag and describe institutionalized violence is indebted to Rebecca Wanzo's work, which notes that "African American women have struggled to gain political currency against narratives that often exclude them from stories about proper victims, and when they are visible, it is often because they powerfully illustrate one or more of the conventions in sentimental political storytelling."[52] Wanzo suggests that "sentimental political storytelling" is a form of narration that mobilizes sympathy for political ends, and that storytelling about suffering, which endeavors to garner sympathy and maybe even political action, must negotiate differing conventions, including "progress narratives that either offer more sympathy for people who are successful enough that they have moved beyond requesting state and institutional intervention" or "the idea that some people who claim to be suffering 'real' pain are only suffering hysterical or phantom pain."[53] Wanzo's notion of the marketplace of narratives suggests the affective and political utility of crisis discourse that treats violence as an interruption and an exception, rather than as the ongoing condition of some people's lives.

I draw on Wanzo's pathbreaking project to study the Left "marketplace" of narratives for Black motherhood, treating them as marketplaces organized entirely by a desire to see grieving, traumatized bodies, and I probe how Black women speak to, in, and through crisis to secure their visibility and to advocate for their needs. Following Wanzo and Berlant, this book thinks about both the institutional construction of crisis in the service of political currency *and* the strategic deployment of crisis rhetoric by Black mothers and by activists allied with Black women's imagined political needs and struggles, carefully tracing how Black mothers both represent themselves and refuse to represent themselves as sites of crisis. I probe the crisis framing as a strategic mode taken up by Black mothers and Black maternal activists, and I interrogate the meanings of the state taking up this mode. Black women are not outside the "social problems marketplace," to borrow the term Wanzo develops.[54] This book is deeply conscious of how Black women are key institutional actors mobilizing the notion of crisis to make visible Black maternal suffering and death and to make apparent the myriad ways that hospitals can be death-worlds for Black mothers and their children. This book, then, remains deeply interested in how Black mothers strategically represent themselves as in, of, and around crisis to secure resources, make visible their needs, and advocate for the enduring importance of attention to Black perinatal life while also, at times, complicating the notion of Black maternal disorganization. In thinking about Black mothers' self-presentation as strategic, I am necessarily in conversation with Darlene Clark Hine's work on dissemblance and Evelyn Brooks Higginbotham's work on the politics of respectability, both of which trace the strategies Black women deploy to maintain the richness and privacy of their interior lives while laboring on behalf of Black women's freedom. I see Black mothers' engagement with crisis as a way to strategically and lovingly advocate for livable lives, even as there are political costs to this approach. Even as I think about crisis as a Black maternal political strategy, I ask whether there are ways for Black mothers to be visible without the temporality of crisis, without the insistence on their bodies as out of place and out of time.

*Histories of Black Motherhood*

Though my project is tethered to a particular moment in the representation and circulation of ideas of Black maternity's political charge, my work is informed by the long tradition of Black feminist theorizing about both Black motherhood's histories and Black motherhood as an institution, a site of antiBlack and misogynistic violence, a form of activism, and a lived, embodied experience.[55] It is also shaped by Black feminist scholarship that has troubled the language of rights as the cornerstone of reproductive freedom, gesturing instead toward an expansive conception of reproductive justice, which includes freedoms to have children and freedoms *not* to have children and which always includes the freedom to have one's child live. Indeed, Black motherhood has been a central site of Black feminist analysis, which has theorized Black mothering in at least a few ways: as a primal site of violence with "unmothering" as central to histories of enslavement and to the "afterlives of slavery," or as a dense site of political, spiritual, and embodied empowerment.[56] While I am indebted to scholarship that has moved the field in both directions, *Birthing Black Mothers* considers Black motherhood differently: I ask how Black mothers are relegated to the realm of the symbolic and how Black mothers work with, through, and against their symbolic currency.

Central to Black feminist engagement with motherhood as a site of violence and trauma has been Black feminist scholarship on slavery, which has emphasized, as Jennifer Morgan notes, the "enormous degree of uncertainty that was manifested in the bodies of children whose future was out of [their mothers'] control."[57] Black feminist historical work has crucially taken up *partus sequitur ventrem* as the cornerstone of forced ruptures in Black maternity, and it centered sexual violence against Black women and the violent control of reproduction as hallmarks of the Black maternal. Morgan reveals how enslaved women "viscerally experienced their embodied contradiction," where their reproductivity was "part of [their] owners' mathematics" and a source of "great anxiety, if not anguish" for the women.[58] As Morgan notes, "Building a system of racial slavery on the notion of heritability did not require the presence of natural population growth among the enslaved, but it did require a clear understanding that enslaved women gave birth to enslaved children. Resituating heritability was key in the practice of an enslavement that systematically alienated the enslaved from their kin and their lineage."[59] Because slavery as an institution was built around "losing your mother," both the motherland and the literal violent tearing apart of families, and because it was constructed around forced breeding and the destruction of Black families, a theory of the Black maternal must contend with the *longue durée* of slavery. Black feminist historiographical work—which is always also Black feminist theoretical work—has, then, centered the violent unmaking of Black motherhood as a crucial technology of racial domination. This work has also argued, as Alys Weinbaum notes, that "in all situations in which human biological life is commodified, processes of commodification must be understood as subtended by the long history of slave breeding as it was practiced in the Americas and Caribbean."[60] This, Weinbaum asserts, is a fundamentally Black feminist conception of history and biocapitalism, one that recognizes the "nexus" between slavery and surrogacy, between slavery and reproductive technologies, that develops a palimpsestic conception of temporality that refuses the allure of racial progress narratives.[61]

Black feminists have also carefully considered the legacies of slavery in shaping contemporary experiences of the Black maternal, highlighting both the ongoing state regulation of Black motherhood and the fundamental devaluation of Black motherhood that continues to shape state policy. Dorothy Roberts's *Killing the Black Body* remains a field-transforming touchstone for considering the legal regulation of Black motherhood, revealing the long history of the US state's commitment to both regulating and foreclosing Black women's reproduction. As Roberts notes, "Regulating Black women's reproductive decisions has been a central aspect of racial oppression in America.... [T]he control of Black women's reproduction has shaped the meaning of reproductive liberty in

America."[62] Roberts's text underscores how control over Black women's reproduction is a central tool of US racial domination, and it captures the variety of state interventions designed to control Black women's fertility, ranging from forced implantation of Norplant to the severe punishment of drug-addicted mothers.

Roberts's work also fundamentally reoriented feminist conversations about reproductive rights from their focus on choice—often a debate about the choice to have or not have an abortion—to one centered on a robust and affirmative conception of liberty. In the years to come, Roberts's scholarship would provide a theoretical scaffolding to the reproductive justice movement, one that was born, in part, because of the limitations of choice as the touchstone of feminist politics around reproductive freedom. Loretta Ross describes reproductive justice as a framework and movement that "goes beyond the pro-choice/pro-life debate and has three primary principles: (1) the right *not* to have a child; (2) the right to *have* a child; and (3) the right to parent children in safe and healthy environments."[63] Reproductive justice projects tether intersectionality theory and human rights frameworks to recognize the varied and multiple experiences of mothering and to demand, as Ross and Solinger note, that "the state (that is, the government) not unduly interfere with women's reproductive decision making, but . . . that the state has an obligation to help create the conditions for women to exercise their decisions without coercion and with social supports. In this way, reproductive justice rests on claims for both negative and positive human rights."[64] Ultimately, reproductive justice movements and projects like the foundational and celebrated SisterSong Women of Color Reproductive Justice Coalition "connect the dots between many social issues that seem unrelated to reproductive rights and to traditional views of reproductive politics."[65] They are, thus, projects fundamentally undergirded by Black feminist theory, deeply committed to centering and honoring Black mothers' experiences. Yet, as Khiara M. Bridges argues, reproductive justice movements have also become institutionalized within feminist political work more generally, rendering "reproductive justice" the primary way that political organizers describe their investments and commitments, even when their investments move far from women of color's bodily autonomy.[66]

While Black feminist historiographical work emphasizes the centrality of reproductive unfreedom and unmothering to an account of Black women's maternal experiences, there remains a considerable scholarly debate on how to account for unmothering—whether the literal ripping apart of enslaved families or the state's ongoing commitment to curtailing Black mothering. Sasha Turner's work offers a strong critique of what she sees as a prevailing Black maternal resilience narrative. Instead, Turner calls for a sustained historical engagement with enslaved women's maternal grief. This engagement would transform interpretations of maternal loss that treat grief as a strategy through which mothers became "the emotional center of the family," shore up ideas of "female frailty and delicacy," or render invisible enslaved women's sorrow.[67] Recent Black feminist work on mothering has been committed to showing how the "afterlives of slavery" continue to affect quotidian experiences of mothering, and it has suggested the centrality of sorrow—particularly sorrow that is not tethered to "grievance" and the pursuit of judicial recourse—to analyses of Black maternal life.[68] Dána-Ain Davis notes, "To be sure Black mothering can be sorrowful when we lose our children but also just the *threat* of losing our children can precipitate an almost constant state of sorrow. We have been losing our children for centuries: through the slave trade, the plantation system, and as a result of infant mortality. We have lost our children as a consequence of the 'war' on drugs, stop and frisk policies, and to the prison industrial complex."[69] Here, loss is constitutive of Black mothering—where loss constitutes both the actual theft of Black children and living with the possibility of Black death. And the labor of engaged Black feminist theory and praxis is to make analytical space for sorrow and to treat it as indicative of a presence we must welcome to get to a greater truth.

Other Black feminist scholarship centers Black mothers' experiences, responding to a feminist canon that has neglected Black mothering entirely. At times, this work has moved in a celebratory register, treating Black motherhood as "a site where [Black women] can develop a belief in their own empowerment. Black women can see motherhood as providing a base for self-actualization, for acquiring status in the Black community and as a catalyst of social activism."[70] This Black feminist work on mothering has often exploded biological conceptions of motherhood, theorizing "othermothers" and "all our kin" to foreground communal styles of mothering, caregiving, and being-together that bind Black women to Black communities, and that even render Black children as what Karla FC Holloway terms "community property."[71] Importantly, for Black feminists, the conceptions of mother and mothering are not tethered to the biological or the reproductive. Black feminist work on community mothering, as well as conceptions of mothering-work as a practice of care that can be engaged in on behalf of others and even on behalf of the self, as Alexis Pauline Gumbs reminds us, gives us a capacious conception of mothering.[72] Collins, for example, celebrates othermothers as "women who assist bloodmothers by sharing mothering responsibilities" and notes that these othermothers "are key not only in supporting children but also in helping bloodmothers who, for whatever reason, lack the preparation or desire for motherhood."[73] Black motherhood, then, is largely described and celebrated as a communal affair marked by a community of women who collectively labor to create radical sanctuary for Black life. Often absent from this Black feminist celebration of Black maternal advocacy and care are a rigorous interrogation of the gendered politics of parenting and a critique of how bloodmothering *and* othermothering largely remain relegated to devalued women's work.

Black feminist historical work on mothering—with its commitment to both exposing enduring violence and the experiential—forms the backdrop of my exploration of the logics and temporalities of crisis and urgency. Yet I explore how data and metrics about Black maternal precarity, and journalistic coverage of Black maternal death, have made Black mothers into symbols of another kind. My project advances a reading rooted neither in romantic resilience nor in trauma and instead probes how and why resilience and trauma seem to be the necessary frames for making visible Black mothers' political agency and visibility. Moreover, I critically interrogate how, for example, frameworks like reproductive justice have become installed, institutionalized, and used to describe myriad forms of feminist activism around reproductive rights, including advocacy that moves apart from Black feminist ethics and investments. Here, like my work on intersectionality, I track the institutional lives (and even afterlives) of Black feminist innovations, reading "reproductive justice" as a framework that has traveled far from its investments in the obstetric violence inflicted on the perinatal Black body to a fundable and politically desirable way of branding various forms of political and programmatic projects. This, then, lets me probe the institutional value and currency of Black feminist innovations and explore their uptake in projects by the US Left.

*Black Lives Matter*

*Birthing Black Mothers* treats BLM not simply as a powerful political project that makes a claim for the value, visibility, and vitality of Black life over and against state-sanctioned antiBlack violence. I also treat it as an aesthetic movement marked by the birth of new markets—including literary and visual markets—that render visible and circulate certain forms of Black cultural production, including certain representations of Black maternity. I also understand BLM to undergird the dramatic uptick of work—academic and activist—on the health effects of both daily racism and physician bias, a new and profound attention to how "racism gets under the skin," and a return to earlier work on the embodied and even molecular effects of discrimination, stigma, and antiBlackness.[74] This shift is visible in interventions like the American Academy of Pediatrics' (AAP) first public statement on racism in 2019, which centers the effects of racism on children's health, noting, "Racism is a core social determinant of health that is a driver of health inequities. . . . These health inequities are not the result of individual behavior choices or genetic predisposition but are caused by economic, political, and social conditions, including racism."[75] The AAP urged pediatricians to assess patients for stressors and "social determinants of health often associated with racism" and to attend to the effects of "vicarious racism" on children's health.[76] The shifts in the political life of public health are also evident in the activist work of groups like White Coats for Black Lives (WC4BL), a national organization of medical students that has called institutional attention to medical racism, asking about the collective responsibility of physicians to combat racism and to develop an expansive conception of patient care that includes examining the health effects of carcerality and poverty.[77]

Yet the shifts in public health discourse—if not practice—engendered by BLM are particularly visible around a sustained public health attention to Black mothers' collective suffering. This is particularly clear in the new and sustained attention to Arline T. Geronimus's work on "weathering," work that was cited extensively in Villarosa's *New York Times Magazine* article.[78] Geronimus coined "weathering" in 1992 to describe the premature health deterioration of Black people as a direct consequence of "the cumulative impact of repeated experience with social or economic adversity and political marginalization."[79] Weathering illustrates how racism literally erodes the body, wearing it away over time, and captures how chronic stress can, over time, render the body vulnerable at a cellular level. Geronimus built her now widely cited concept around Black maternal health. In one of her studies, she found that Black women in their twenties had higher rates of infant mortality than Black teenagers, while the opposite was true for white women. She attributed elevated rates of infant mortality among Black women to the cumulative effects of racism, to the corporeal toll of racial violence.[80] She has also found that racial stress makes itself visible even at the molecular level, with one study showing that Black women in their forties and fifties appear—at a chromosomal level—to be seven and a half years older than a white person of the same age.[81] This "accelerated biological aging," which Geronimus measured through analyzing telomere length, suggests that "social structural processes exert their impact on morbidity and mortality to produce racial health inequality."[82] The attention to Black infant and maternal mortality has made weathering part of a popular, scholarly, and political conversation on the health outcomes of racism, with Black maternal bodies acting as a kind of urtext for understanding the embodied costs of racism.⁸³ Geronimus has recently noted how her work on weathering was initially mocked—some public health scholars treated her work as problematically advocating for inherent genetic differences between Blacks and whites.⁸⁴ If in the 1990s, she was accused of pathologically advocating so-called teenage pregnancy, in a BLM era, one newly attentive to the medical consequences of racial stress, she is celebrated as posing "questions [that were] ahead of their time."⁸⁵

Thus, I treat BLM as a capacious social movement that has performed its work, at least in part, by making the claims that Black *maternal* lives matter, that Black maternal death is an issue of state-sanctioned violence, and that we have come to view Black mothers as the quintessential political Black subject. In making these arguments, I put two timelines in conversation: a set of activist work around state-sanctioned violence against Black men, and a set of activist and aesthetic projects around medical violence against Black women. Part of my endeavor is to trouble the narrative that the symbol of BLM is the slain Black male body; instead, we must consider how the Black mother—whether figured as the guardian of her dead Black son or the pregnant mother battling obstetric violence in her quest to literally birth Black life—has also become a key symbol of the movement.

How might we historicize the movement for Black life? Keeanga-Yamahtta Taylor writes, "Every movement needs a catalyst, an event that captures people's experiences and draws them out from their isolation into a collective force with the power to transform social conditions. Few could have predicted that white police officer Darren Wilson shooting Mike Brown would ignite a rebellion in a small, largely unknown Missouri suburb called Ferguson."⁸⁶ Taylor's vision of BLM roots its histories in Ferguson and the murder of Michael Brown in 2014, and it underscores that normalized and unredressed police violence was the "catalyst" for BLM. I read BLM more broadly, suggesting that it has also been a call to "defend the dead," to "tend to the Black dead and dying" through a concerted practice of lovingly "saying their names," publicly remembering slain Black people, including Philando Castile, George Floyd, Breonna Taylor, Sandra Bland, Tony McDade, Freddie Gray, Riah Milton, Akai Gurley, Laquan McDonald, Alton Sterling, Keith Lamont Scott, Natasha McKenna, Paul O'Neal, Christina Taylor, Tamir Rice, Michael Brown, Aiyana Stanley-Jones, Dominique "Rem'mie" Fells, and Eric Garner.⁸⁷ We might then even think of BLM as a project that asks us to listen to the dead speak, whether in the form of video from Sandra Bland's phone that surfaced four years after her death or in the form of police texts sent minutes after Eric Garner's murder that declared Garner's murder "no big deal."⁸⁸ "Defending the dead" is a capacious project that recognizes the many ways that Black life is curtailed, surveilled, and limited, the host of ways that Black life is constructed as socially disposable. As Alicia Garza notes, "It [BLM] is an acknowledgement that Black poverty and genocide is state violence. It is an acknowledgement that 1 million Black people are locked in cages in this country—one half of all people in prisons or jails—is an act of state violence. It is an acknowledgement that Black women continue to bear the burden of a relentless assault on our children and our families and that assault is an act of state violence."[89] We can understand BLM, like reproductive justice movements, as broad in its conception of violence and harm.

If Taylor's narrative of BLM begins with Ferguson, for other scholars and activists the movement "begins" with Trayvon Martin's murder in 2012. Martin was murdered at the Retreat at Twin Lakes in Sanford, Florida, the gated community where he was visiting his father and his father's girlfriend.[90] George Zimmerman, who imagined himself as a one-man neighborhood watch, claimed he shot Martin in self-defense and was ultimately acquitted of Martin's murder in 2013. Zimmerman's acquittal sparked nationwide protests, oftentimes drawing on the symbol of the hoodie, the now-iconic sweatshirt that Martin was wearing when Zimmerman killed him, a garment that Zimmerman used to describe and rationalize Martin's "suspiciousness." Two years later, Brown was murdered by Ferguson police officer Darren Wilson. The nonindictment of Wilson, the *New York Times'* decision to refer to Brown as "no angel," the militarized response to protesters in Ferguson, and the Ferguson officials' decision to leave Brown's body lying in the summer heat for hours made "Ferguson" a shorthand for a pervasive and routinized antiBlack violence.[91] That same year, in 2014, Eric Garner was murdered by the New York Police Department (NYPD) who placed him in a chokehold—a tactic prohibited by the NYPD in 1993—because Garner was selling single cigarettes without tax stamps.[92] Garner's final words, "I can't breathe, I can't breathe," became a rallying call for BLM for protecting Black life, for safeguarding Black breath. That same year, Akai Gurley was shot by Officer Peter Liang who was patrolling the stairwell in the Louis Pink Houses in Brooklyn, New York (Liang was convicted of manslaughter in 2016—though a judge reduced the conviction to criminally negligent homicide and sentenced Liang to five years of probation and eight hundred hours of community service)—and Tamir Rice, a twelve-year-old child, was shot by a white police officer in Cleveland (the grand jury declined to indict the officer). A year later, in 2015, Sandra Bland was stopped in Prairie View, Texas, for a traffic violation. When the officer ordered Bland to extinguish her cigarette and to get out of her car, she refused, and he pointed his Taser at her and shouted, "I will light you up!" Bland was found hanging in a jail cell three days later (the state ruled it a suicide). I recount some of these deaths not to participate in the all-too-familiar spectacularization of antiBlack violence, but in the spirit of aggregating these cases to read patterns of Black death and white nonindictment, to capture the sheer ordinariness of these deaths. I also recount them to make visible the attention to state-sanctioned death that unfolded in a short period; the intensity of the coverage of each of these stories made the frighteningly routinized experiences of Black death suddenly a national spectacle.

If BLM has made visible both these routinized forms of violence and the sustained grief that surrounds them, it has also been an umbrella under which a variety of forms of protest have been staged, ranging from organized responses to militarized state violence in the streets of Ferguson in 2014 and across the nation in response to George Floyd's murder in 2020; to protests against the murder of Black people attending a Bible study group in a Charleston, South Carolina, church by a white supremacist in 2015; to public actions like National Football League player Colin Kaepernick's decision to kneel during the National Anthem in 2016. These forms of activism have been met by various forms of punishment—including economic punishment as in the case of Kaepernick and sustained practices of violent harassment and surveillance of BLM activists (the FBI, for example, warned of "Black identity extremists" espousing "perceptions of unjust treatment of African-Americans and the perceived unchallenged illegitimate actions of law enforcement will inspire premeditated attacks against law enforcement").[93]

At times, Black maternal politics unfold in distinct ways from BLM's most public activist and advocacy work, often performing their political work through the guise of the *apolitical*, through the promise that politics waged in the name of maternal activism are more akin to a spiritual calling than a politic. In 2016, for example, at the Democratic National Convention, Mothers of the Movement appeared onstage to confer their legitimacy, respectability, and dignified grief on Democratic nominee Hillary Clinton. They also appeared, of course, to provide a reference for Clinton, promising that Black voters could trust Clinton, that Clinton would represent their interests and commitments. The Mothers appeared onstage in an arc that looked like a prayer circle and they testified. Geneva Reed-Veal, Sandra Bland's mother, hailed Clinton as a figure who "will say our children's names," and she assured the audience that "Hillary knows that when a young Black life is cut short, it's not just a personal loss. It is a national loss. It is a loss that diminishes all of us."[94] Lucy McBath declared, "I am still Jordan Davis's mother. His life ended the day he was shot and killed for playing loud music but my job as his mother didn't."⁹⁵ Here, activism is cast not as something chosen but as something thrust on Black mothers who wage their political work on behalf of their dead children. This rhetoric of maternal activism as missionary labor, as given and not chosen, is something McBath deployed in her congressional race in Georgia (which she ultimately won), noting, "Six years ago I went from a Marietta mom to a mother on a mission" and in her insistence that "I have a responsibility to God to walk the path He's laid. In spite of my anger, and my fear that we won't get the verdict that we want, I am still called by the God I serve to walk this out."⁹⁶ Sybrina Fulton, Trayvon Martin's mother, also described her political work as inflected by a higher calling—as a "mission"—describing Mothers of the Movement as "mothers now on a mission in the hope of ensuring that the violence doesn't touch other mothers, other fathers, other families."⁹⁷ The reference to a "mission" suggests that Black maternal activism transcends partisan divides, that it is apolitical in its commitments to family unity, that it is divinely inflected, performed out of a deep commitment to the dead, that it is soul-work.⁹⁸ This, then, is a moment when "a group of mothers who belong to a club no one ever wants to join" can set political agendas and lend political currency to politicians like Clinton and even to artists like Beyoncé Knowles, who included Mothers of the Movement in her visual album *Lemonade* in 2016.⁹⁹ The political task of the Black maternal, then, has become an integral part of BLM, particularly because it performs its stealth political work through seeming apolitical.

Efforts like the Black feminist-spearheaded Black Mamas Bailout also make apparent the overlapping concerns of BLM and Black maternal politics. Black Mamas Bailout has tethered the abolitionist commitments of BLM to a Black feminist investment in reproductive justice. Initiated by the National Bail Out Collective, the campaign began in 2017 in cities including Atlanta, Brooklyn, and Detroit and was an effort to eliminate pretrial detention and to focus on women's particular experiences of carceral violence. While the organizers always insisted on their inclusive conception of "mamas"—"We're talking about more than just birth mothers: caregivers, queer mamas, and the people responsible for taking care of our families and communities"—they also organized the efforts around Mother's Day, arguing that efforts to bail out Black mothers would allow them to celebrate the holiday with their families.¹⁰⁰ Thus, the figure of the Black mother became central to their project's activist work and to the organization's plea that bailout efforts would reunite families. In 2017, the effort's inaugural year, they raised $1 million and bailed out one hundred Black mothers and caregivers all under the simple slogan "Money kept them in. Black love got them out." For Black Mamas Bailout, one of the primary forms of carceral violence is its disintegration of Black familial life, and the "Black mama" stands as the icon of family. To bring Black mamas home is a profound act of family reunification and of supporting Black social life.

While Mothers of the Movement and Black Mamas Bailout are two very different political mobilizations of Black motherhood, they collectively underscore what is a central proposition of the book: Black mothers have become the primary icon of BLM. Even as BLM is often described—and, at times, criticized—for placing Black boys and Black men at the center of its conception of antiBlack violence, this book makes a different argument: Black mothers have become this central icon because they are imagined to stand in for dead Black boys or because they make visible the trauma of losing a child (or the traumatic fear of losing a child). But, as I argue in this book, Black mothers have also become central to BLM because of their position at intersecting forms of state violence. Here, death takes the form not of the police officer's fist, baton, or chokehold, but of the doctor, the hospital, or the delivery room. These spaces of violence—of medicalized violence, which is newly understood to be state violence—are now figured as ground zero in the struggle for Black life. Black mothers are also increasingly understood as productive of Black life itself, as the necessary fleshy beings whose bodies make possible Black life. They have offered a new conceptualization of the meanings and sites of Black death.

*Black Feminist Institution Making*

If this book tracks how the logics of crisis have led Black women to advocate for their place within—often *deeply* within—existing structures, whether through getting trained as peer lactation consultants or through advocating for the state to compensate women of color doulas, it necessarily sits with Black women's complex attachments to institutions, including the state. In thinking about Black women's fraught relationship to institutionality—a relationship that includes both desires for institutionalization and ambivalence around institutionality—I seek to extend a Black feminist conversation that has largely thought about Black feminists' complex institutional entanglements around the space of the university. Scholars including Ann duCille and Barbara Christian have offered rigorous accounts of Black feminism's simultaneous ubiquity in the academy while asking whether Black feminism—and Black feminists—can "survive" the academy.[101] In these accounts, Black feminism is positioned as an anti-institutional form of knowledge that the university has strategically taken up—or even cannibalized. But how might we understand a moment when Black feminists—and Black feminist ideas about reproductive justice and birth equity—are actually incorporated into the state's responses to birth inequity and Black infant and maternal mortality? How might we contend with some women of color doulas' aspirations to be reimbursed by the state for their services, for example, even as they frame their work as paraprofessional and antimedical, as I describe in the book's second chapter? How can we understand Black feminist support of a near-mandate to breastfeed, a mandate that is inflicted most perniciously on poor Black women's bodies? And how might we capture and trouble a Black feminist advocacy of the symbiotic relationship between reproductive justice and the state?

This is a book invested in naming, describing, and analyzing what I call the *feminist birth industry* and in spotlighting both the newfound place of Black motherhood in the construction of that industry and the centrality of Black feminist praxis to that industry. Like my earlier work on feminism's institutional work, my impulse here is not to diagnose or bemoan feminism's institutional iterations and desires but instead to think deeply about the challenges these institutional formations pose for Black feminist theory and practice. I develop the term *feminist birth industry* to describe how feminism has remade birthing in myriad ways, including the installation of the idea that birth is understood as a self-making event, one that can be crafted, tailored, and planned both to safeguard maternal health and to ensure an "experience" that meaningfully marks the transition to motherhood. It is not my contention that hospitals are now feminist spaces or that institutionalized medicine is a site of feminist practice. Indeed, the persistence of unwanted C-sections and obstetric violence reveals that birth remains a crucial site of the patriarchal control of women's bodies. Instead, it is my claim that feminism has remade the desires that birthers bring to birth and the demands they can now make about their births, including desires for unmedicated births, for immediate breastfeeding, and for birthworker-assisted labor. I see the feminist birthing industry as including a wide range of efforts that have been institutionalized to various extents and in differing ways, including the installation of doulas, midwives, lactation consultants, and peer breastfeeding counselors; the growing visibility of breastfeeding activism (what Courtney Jung critiques as "lactivism")[102]; the growth of Baby-Friendly hospitals designed to promote breastfeeding; the state support of breastfeeding through the Special Supplemental Nutrition Program for Women, Infants, and Children (WIC) feeding programs; and the "birth plan," which, at the very least, is a thought-exercise encouraging birthers to imagine or even design a desired birth.

*Birthing Black Mothers* treats Black feminism—and Black women—as at the vanguard of the institutional efforts that are now unfolding to center the transformative and life-affirming work of doulas, to treat breast milk as a technology of Black life, and to treat maternity wards as battlegrounds in the battle for Black life. In other words, I see Black feminism as a crucial force in shaping the feminist birth industry, as central to feminist labor to alter birth and its meanings, aesthetics, politics, and outcomes. I study how Black women's engagement with "crisis"—an engagement that often explicitly mobilizes the language of Black feminist theory (including intersectionality)—often includes an attachment to, rather than a divestment from, institutions like hospitals and an attachment to feminist trainings to enable participation in these institutions. In telling a story about Black feminism's institutional entanglements, I interrupt the conception of Black feminism as an inherently anti-institutional project or, as James Bliss notes, "a practice of critique at, and on, the limits of institutionality."[103] Treating Black feminism not as the uninstitutionalized "nonspace feared by both state power and its most radical critics" but as the vanguard of the feminist birthing industry and its entanglements with the state disrupts one of the primary "stories we tell," one where feminism's institutional logics are the primary terrain of something regularly vilified as hallmarks of white feminism, including governance feminism and carceral feminism.[104] In telling another story about Black feminism, I aspire to interrupt what has become a romantic account of Black feminist theory, one that ultimately hinders our capacity to collectively grasp Black feminism's multiple critical and political desires. In considering Black feminism's own will to institutional embeddedness, my goal is not to demonize a tradition I am deeply invested in. Instead, I seek to do justice to the tradition's complexity by sitting with aspects of it that remain too rarely considered. By considering the institutional ambitions of Black feminist work, my endeavor here—as in all my work—is to trace the complex lives of Black feminist theory and to wholly resist accounts of Black feminist theory and politics, and of Black women, that resort to the romantic, casting Black women exclusively as anti-institutional heroines. I see this as a form of doing justice to Black feminist theoretical complexity and heterogeneity and to Black women's varied and, at times, competing political demands and desires. I see it as a way of doing justice to the material realities of Black mothers' lives—like Malaysia Goodson who comes to be written into the official archive through her "fatal fall," taken up as bureaucratic evidence of Black mothers' willingness to sacrifice their lives for their children.

The book unfolds in two parts; the first is rooted in public health debates and the second is centered on visual culture. The book's first chapter explores a particular iteration of the "crisis" facing Black mothers—the construction of Black mothers as nonbreastfeeders—and grapples with efforts to support, encourage, and bolster Black breastfeeding by making the claim that Black breast milk is *Black gold*, a crucial technology of Black life. In the second chapter, I turn to the labor of women of color doulas in metropolitan Chicago, tracing how they are increasingly positioned—by the state and by their own commitments—as on the "front lines" of the war to preserve Black life. This chapter captures the tremendous physical, affective, and spiritual labor of these doulas while also considering what it means that the state has invested—at least rhetorically—in largely untrained feminist entrepreneurial labor as that which will save Black mothers' lives. In the third chapter, I turn to a trio of Black female celebrities who, I argue, rewrite Black mothers' relationships to crisis. I trace how Serena Williams, Michelle Obama, and Beyoncé Knowles offer Black maternal aesthetics of friendship, abundance, sensuality, and glamour that effectively rescript prevailing conceptions of precarity, scarcity, and crisis. The book's final chapter turns to an archive of Black maternal memoirs, examining how contemporary Black maternal life writing both sits with and against crisis, at times offering visions of the Black maternal that refuse logics of death and tragedy and reframe the figure of the Black mother and her psychic and political capacities. In the coda, I turn to considering the place of Black mothers in the "third pandemic," a term used by activists to describe the intersection of COVID-19, the murders of Black people by the police, and Black maternal mortality.

ONE. **BLACK GOLD**

*Remaking Black Breasts
in an Era of Crisis*

In February 2018, Gap launched its newest advertising campaign on Instagram with a simple slogan: "love your forever favorite." One image featured a Black woman—wearing a weathered Gap T-shirt—breastfeeding her child. While the advertisement was supposed to be for Gap's new intimate-apparel line, the shirt's brand name was hidden, as was the maternal model's face, leaving the viewer to gaze upon the nursing Black child, his mother's hand tenderly resting on his back. In a *Washington Post* article, A. Rochaun Meadows-Fernandez celebrated the advertisement: "It is epic for a multitude of reasons: She is a dark-skinned Black woman, she is a Black woman with a wedding ring, and she is breastfeeding a *toddler*! . . . The crown of curls and coils atop both the mother and child's head symbolize multicultural beauty and is a simple yet powerful reflection of the Black family. Before this image we had very few models of unfiltered Black motherhood."[1] The story behind the advertisement—or at least the one that was rehearsed for the media—only added to the praise showered on the company, which was suddenly cast as both compassionate and progressive. Adaora Akubilo, the maternal model, reported that she needed to nurse during the photo shoot and the photographer encouraged her to simply feed her son.[2] The advertisement was taken as evidence of the corporation's celebration of breastfeeding, and the story surrounding the labor conditions that produced it added legitimacy to the perception that Gap was actually invested in supporting Black women's breastfeeding. In an era when Gap's sales were "dismal," the ad was, as *Forbes* noted, "the kind of win Gap needs right now," evidence of a commitment to "supporting Black women who choose to breastfeed."[3] Gap's representation of Black women's breastfeeding as natural and normal, and the interpretation of the advertisement as representing Black breast milk as a kind of liquid gold—a form of emotional and physical nutrition that could sustain infant life—struck gold.

I begin with this image—and its widespread celebration—to argue that the temporality of crisis has produced a new aesthetic of Black breastfeeding and a new commitment to responding to the "crisis" of Black nonbreastfeeding through visual appeals. This "crisis" is imagined to take the form of a significant numerical gap between white and Black breastfeeding rates, one that has tangible effects on Black maternal and infant health and that is thought to be remediable through efforts to champion Black breastfeeding. Black breastfeeding has been visually transformed into a practice that is deeply political and that is imagined to constitute a sign of resistance to the state, the corporation, and institutionalized medicine, even as all three are foundational to the contemporary visual resignification and recruitment of Black breasts. In a Black Lives Matter (BLM) era where Black life—coded as Black children—is repeatedly described as fragile, where Black people are described as living lives shaped (even at the epidemiological level) by racism, Black breastfeeders are increasingly celebrated for their performances of Left citizenship precisely because the nutrition that breast milk is thought to offer is far more than physical. Black breast milk is celebrated as providing emotional and even political sustenance in the face of Black precarity.[4]

I also read the Gap advertisement—and the enthusiasm around it—as evidence of the largely invisible and deeply powerful collaboration among the state, corporate interests, and a Black feminist missionary effort to create a new representation of the Black breastfeeding subject. One of the central preoccupations of this chapter is considering how various actors with seemingly disparate political investments resignify Black breasts in the name of crisis mitigation, producing an image of a compliant and ethical Black breastfeeder. This Black breastfeeding subject submits to the mandates—which are now rooted both in the state and in a Black feminist praxis—to guard against the imagined myriad health risks of nonbreastfeeding in the service of safeguarding Black life.

FIGURE 1.1. Gap advertisement with a breastfeeding model (2018).

In naming the intersections of state and corporate logics and a Black feminist praxis, my impulse is neither to perform the now-familiar critique of feminism's strange bedfellows nor to suggest that Black feminism was ever wholly outside of the state or the corporation. Instead, I seek to center this collaboration as necessary terrain for Black feminist theorists to grapple with, particularly in an era when Black feminist theory continues to be romantically celebrated as inherently anti-institutional, fugitive, and radical. While this chapter studies the politics of hailing Black breastfeeding—and Black breastfeeders—as central to protecting Black life, it is also interested in what it means to imagine Black feminism as a tradition whose conceptions of life and risk, vulnerability and labor, are formed and branded *both* against and alongside state and corporate logics.

A year before Gap's advertisement, the *New York Times* reported on a Black breastfeeding gap. The article relied on data collected by Chelsea O. McKinney and her colleagues, which found that 61 percent of Black mothers initiated breastfeeding compared to 78 percent of white mothers.[5] McKinney found that the gap was due to multiple forces, including hospitals' practice of offering Black mothers formula at higher rates than white mothers, medical institutions' failure to encourage Black women to breastfeed, and Black women's relative unfamiliarity with breastfeeding since they were more likely to come from families where breastfeeding was not practiced. McKinney warned against the particular danger of formula's ubiquitous presence in maternity wards, noting that "changing hospital relationships with formula companies that relinquish fiscal dependency on free formula is a notorious challenge for many hospitals that strive to improve breastfeeding outcomes."[6] The hailing of formula companies as the genesis of the crisis shored up the notion that corporations—which could be forces for good (as in the case of Gap's imagined promotion of breastfeeding)—could be the source of inequity and even antiBlack misogynistic violence, particularly when they made their presence felt in the space of institutionalized medicine.[7] McKinney's findings underscored that Black breasts were in crisis, and nothing short of a wholesale effort to champion their productive capacities was necessary.

The idea of Black maternal *nonbreastfeeding*—or a Black breastfeeding gap—is repeated as a truism in both scholarly and popular literature, even as some Black breastfeeding activists argue that the rehearsal of this fact obscures long histories and ongoing practices of Black breastfeeding. Jessica Martucci, for example, notes, "Today there remains a considerable gap in the rates of breastfeeding between white and Black mothers in the United States."[8] Andrea Freeman argues, "These disparities in breastfeeding rates correspond with other racial health disparities, including infant mortality, which strikes more than twice as many Black babies as White babies. This ratio has remained consistent since slavery."[9] And Angela Johnson, Rosalind Kirk, Katherine Lisa Rosenblum, and Maria Muzik write, "One group of U.S. women—namely, African American mothers—have persistently lagged behind, showing, by far, the lowest breastfeeding rates. This puts African American mothers and their babies at higher risk for poor postnatal outcomes and may be a substantial contributor to the origins of health disparities among African Americans across the lifetime."[10] Yet some Black feminist birthworkers, peer breastfeeding counselors, and maternal health advocates emphasize that the preoccupation with a Black breastfeeding gap is often built on ignoring Black women's breastfeeding practices. Lauren, a Chicago-based, Black certified midwife, lactation consultant, and doula, narrated her experience participating in a certified lactation consultant training. In the training course, students sat in rows listening to lectures about the mechanics of breastfeeding. The instructor, Lauren noted, emphasized a single fact: Black mothers do not breastfeed. Lauren said, "I wanted to get trained as a certified lactation counselor. My baby was maybe eight months, six or eight months, and so I was pumping. So I've positioned myself close to the front, next to a plug and the whole week they were like, 'Black women don't breastfeed.' And I'm sitting there. The machine is so loud, it was old school and I was like *are you serious*? I'm in the third row, you don't see me with my breast and my pump! You don't hear it? I was just so offended."[11] Lauren's comments suggest the invisibility of Black breastfeeding (and pumping) practices and underscore that the oft-rehearsed refrain that Black women do not breastfeed may reflect a willful unseeing of Black breastfeeding rather than the empirical truth of a gap.

Rather than treating the gap as either rooted in scientific fact or racialized fiction, this chapter probes a moment when Black women's imagined nonbreastfeeding is constructed as a particular kind of crisis, one that warrants public health, activist, and aesthetic intervention in the form of compassion, information, public relations, mentoring, education, and resignification through the realm of the visual. This chapter argues that the current representation of Black women as *unsupported* rather than *unwilling* breastfeeders is a new one that has transformed the conception of breast milk into a technology of Black life that provides physical and emotional nutrition for Black infants and for Black communities. If breast milk, particularly colostrum, has been celebrated as *liquid gold*—as a nutritional superfood deeply responsive to an infant's changing physical needs, as a substance that cannot be replicated by formula companies no matter their effort, and as the gold standard of infant nutrition—this chapter uses the term *Black gold* to describe the benefits that breast milk is thought to confer on Black infants who are more likely to experience precarity, violence, and proximity to trauma even in utero.[12] Kimberly Seals Allers, one of the founders of the national Black Breastfeeding Week project, notes, "Black women disproportionately give birth to babies who are too small, too sick, or they give birth too soon. . . . Because of how Black women actually give birth, and this is regardless of socioeconomics and education, those babies need breastmilk more."[13] For Allers, Black breast milk is a crucial inoculation against vulnerability in its myriad forms, as well as a kind of physical and emotional nurturance that provides far more than physical satiety. This chapter explores how Black breasts, which are regularly figured as hypersexualized sites of "excess flesh," as evidence of Black sexual impulses misdirected, or as reminders of an era when Black women worked as wet nurses, have become newly worthy of support and education.[14] The form of this support often relies on the grammar of the visual to develop and proliferate a celebratory Black lactation aesthetic as a necessary response to the gap.

This chapter unfolds in three parts. First, I analyze the idea of the Black breastfeeding gap, exploring how it is imagined and represented not as a numerical disparity but as a material space that Black women and children inhabit. I study how the gap has been depicted as risky, barren, and desolate, as a deathly space for Black women and their children. And I trace how Black breastfeeding is represented by the state, Black feminists, and even corporations as more than a practice, but a different landscape entirely, one marked by plenitude, health, and nutrition. Second, I turn to public health literature on breastfeeding, examining how, in a relatively short period of time, Black breastfeeding has been refigured from an inoculation against obesity that Black women refuse, to the cure to Black precarity, thus making possible the compassionate reimagining of Black women's breasts. Finally, I conclude by turning to a rich visual archive of images supporting Black women's breastfeeding efforts. I am particularly attuned to how Black women aesthetically respond to the temporalities of crisis. The archive of Black feminist visual rejoinders to crisis suggests both how Black mothers figure Black breasts beyond the temporality of urgency and how the framework of crisis continues to shape and even constrain the visual registers through which Black maternal flesh can be imagined and represented.

*Representing the Gap*

While McKinney's article—and the subsequent popular coverage of her findings—underscored a significant racial gap in infant-feeding practices, the measurement has come to be described as far more than a metric of racial disparity. The gap stands as evidence of racist and sexist violence, pernicious corporate workings in medicalized spaces that particularly burden Black women, and medical indifference to Black life. It is, as Katherine McKittrick terms it, a "mathematics of the unliving" that indexes the organization of institutional medicine around Black nonlife.[15] Increasingly, the gap is figured as literal territory that Black women and their children inhabit, a barren space of unfreedom. It is precisely because the gap is represented as a territorial problem—the geographic segregation of Black women and their children to death-worlds—that the appeal to the visual works as an imagined solution to the gap. The visual is the register that helps envision new landscapes, new topographies, of infant feeding centered on Black vitality.

For some scholars, the gap is best understood as a food desert, a nutritionless site of precarity, and not the result of Black women's imagined refusal to comply with public health recommendations. For example, the geographies—or nongeographies—of Black breastfeeding are marked by the paucity of Black lactation consultants to support Black breastfeeding so that, as Allers notes, "As I traveled the country, asking everyone if they knew of any African American IBCLCs [international board-certified lactation consultants], this story took less journalistic routes and more grapevine and Underground Railroad–like pathways. There were stories and urban legends of Black IBCLCs. At one point, I wondered if I was searching for Black IBCLCs or Big Foot."[16] Allers's analogizing of the "search" for Black lactation expertise to the quest to find "Big Foot" suggests that the territory of the gap is produced by institutionalized nonsupport.

For others, the gap is a landscape created and constituted by forms of entrenched segregation. For example, Baby-Friendly hospitals—a designation given to hospitals by Baby-Friendly USA when they demonstrate a commitment of time and staff training to support breastfeeding mothers and to "influence breastfeeding attitudes"—often entirely "bypass" Black communities, as 45 percent of US Baby-Friendly hospitals are in cities that have Black populations of less than 3 percent.[17] Rita Henley Johnson argues that Baby-Friendly hospitals have effectively created a "geographic segregation of breastfeeding" even as they purport to labor on behalf of breastfeeding.[18] Here, the gap is produced through institutional medicine's practices of medicalized segregation, and even Left efforts to encourage breastfeeding relegate Black mothers and children to spaces where medical staff lack a commitment to breastfeeding.

Other scholars treat the gap as indicative of a particular form of largely unnamed violence, as what Andrea Freeman terms "food oppression." Indeed, Freeman argues that formula is, itself, a "junk or fast food for infants" that is "unequivocally inferior to breast milk" and that breast milk is "active immunity from disease."[19] The analogizing of formula to "junk food," itself a racially marked category often deployed to denigrate the food choices of poor Black women and their children, gets mobilized to argue that the absence of better, more nutritional infant-feeding options consign Black women to formula-filled death-worlds. For Freeman, "food oppression" and its relegation of Black women and children to a space marked not merely by "junk food" but also by immunological deprivation is a direct result of the state's actions—and neglects. This, she argues, is based on three things: the government purchases the majority of formula sold in the United States for distribution through the Special Supplemental Nutrition Program for Women, Infants, and Children (WIC); the United States has refused to ratify the World Health Organization's ban on promoting breast-milk substitutes or to set clear standards for formula labels; and workplace law has failed to create adequate accommodations for breastfeeding at work. Freeman asserts that this constellation of state efforts has a particular effect on Black women who are often interpreted as "choosing" formula when they are actually operating under a set of intense constraints that eviscerate their capacities for "choice and free will."[20] When Freeman describes the gap as a manifestation of food oppression, she captures a fundamental form of violence that shapes every aspect of Black life, from its earliest moments.

Even as scholars advance varied explanations for the Black breastfeeding gap and theorize its landscape differently, their interpretations emphatically avoid the construction of Black mothers as unwilling breastfeeders or as noncompliant patients. Their conception of the gap is not an account of Black women's failure to mitigate medical risk but is instead a narrative focused on a lack of supportive infrastructure to encourage Black women's potentially life-affirming labor of breastfeeding. This is an account of a lack of representations of Black breastfeeding that makes it impossible for Black women to even visualize themselves as breastfeeders. This is a BLM story told through the flesh of Black mothers, one that sees Black maternal breasts as a key site through which Black life is sustained, prompting some activists to see Black breastfeeding itself as a "life-or-death" matter.[21]

In response to the gap, compassion has become the affective valence of the day. Compassion often takes the form of education, which is what undergirds the calls for support, encouragement, and assistance. A collective sense of compassion is visible in the sense that the gap persists because Black women need information about breastfeeding and supportive infrastructure to encourage breastfeeding, even as the construction of Black women's misinformation is steeped in racialized tropes. As Johnson and colleagues argue, what is required to promote Black maternal breastfeeding is "interpersonal and empathetic peer-based health and socially based care in ways that are protective and possibly preventive of chronic stress and depression to effectively support African American mothers exposed to the traumas of discrimination and indifferent treatment."[22] This is a moment when, as a National Public Radio story suggested, Black women can be "taught to embrace breastfeeding" and to forget what one interviewee described as images of a "tribal woman, with elongated breasts, earrings, and tribal jewelry" or what Freeman describes as images of "a bare-breasted African woman. These types of images, prevalent in the popular magazine *National Geographic* and in other 'educational' media make breastfeeding by Black women appear to be a primitive practice."[23] This education in breastfeeding takes the form of generating a new archive of images to visualize the Black breast neither as sexualized nor as "primitive" but instead as a technology of Black gold, as a form of physical and emotional sustenance that shields Black life from the slew of forces that operate to render it vulnerable.

My understanding of compassion's political and affective valences is drawn from Lauren Berlant's work, which argues that in the United States "the word compassion carries the weight of ongoing debates about the ethics of privilege ... and establishes collective norms of obligation and about individual and collective obligations to read a scene of distress not as a judgment against the distressed but as a claim on the spectator to become an ameliorative actor."[24] Compassion, however, is neither necessarily radical nor progressive. Berlant probes the idea of "compassionate conservatism" to reveal that compassion's pulls of obligation can move in myriad political registers and enable an array of political projects. Instead, compassion is a way of thinking about obligation "when we witness the theatrical scene of suffering," a kind of affective and relational response to the "pain of others"—to borrow Susan Sontag's formulation—other than anger, blame, apathy, or pleasure.[25] My analysis of compassion does not neglect the coercive underpinnings of projects "supporting" Black breastfeeding and instead traces how compassion can make coercion and surveillance seem like support and encouragement, like benign interventions.

In treating compassion as *the* singular affective and political response to the gap, I interpret this moment differently than other scholars and popular writers. Both Allers and Freeman, for example, view the state not as a compassionate actor responding to the gap but as a key actor—if not *the* key actor—in producing the gap, particularly because of the state's imagined unrelenting support of formula usage. Yet I argue that the state's rhetorical work around the gap has been focused on ameliorating it, using state-sponsored nutritional programs like WIC to promote—and, at times, compel—breastfeeding and generating a slew of images to endorse breastfeeding's health benefits.[26] Freeman offers her critique of the state's nonsupport of breastfeeding:

> We can look at things like the US government being the biggest purchaser of formula in the US and then giving it out free to people who receive WIC—disproportionately Black women. We can see the welfare state forcing women to leave the home when they have infants and that makes it impossible for them to breastfeed. We have a lack of restrictions on formula marketing in the US whereas every other country has agreed to sign on to the WHO Code, the US has not because of its close relationship with the formula industry. We have marketing that happens through hospitals and pediatricians that doesn't even look like marketing.[27]

Even as Freeman critiques the relationship between WIC and formula, other scholars offer diametrically opposed perceptions of WIC, with Courtney Jung reading it as a governmental site that effectively mandates poor women to breastfeed by tethering improved nutritional packages to exclusive breastfeeding, and with Reaching Our Sisters Everywhere, a Georgia-based women of color breastfeeding organization, celebrating WIC as the place where "a large majority of the breastfeeding education in the African American community" unfolds.[28] My own analysis aligns with a reading of WIC as one of the crucial sites through which the state imagines itself as enacting compassion through a de facto requirement of breastfeeding, through rewarding breastfeeding by offering a qualitatively better nutritional program for breastfeeding mothers and their children.

To illustrate how compassion can enable a wide array of political projects—and yet still move and feel quite different from anger, blame, or apathy—I describe two forms that compassionate reactions to the gap have taken. In calling these compassionate, I emphasize that both were undertaken out of a rhetorical concern for racial breastfeeding gaps, with a purported investment in safeguarding Black maternal health, even as the rationales for that investment vary. I find both of these efforts troubling politically and ethically, and so in describing them as "compassionate," I do not seek to rehabilitate or excuse them. Instead, I endeavor to read them as operating in a mode that aspires to move away from the retributive and the punitive, to offer a different kind of response to the gap.

The first effort occurred in 2012, when New York City mayor Michael Bloomberg launched Latch On, a follow-up to his advocacy for city hospitals to earn Baby-Friendly designations. Latch On—which twenty-nine of New York's forty hospitals voluntarily joined—was hailed as a public health innovation designed to boost citywide breastfeeding rates and to rid maternity wards of "aggressive" formula marketing, tactics that were imagined to be particularly geared toward poor mothers. Bloomberg's antiformula initiative, one that has been taken up by advocates operating under the banner of "ban the bag," was already in place in Rhode Island and Massachusetts, both of which eliminated the free bags of formula samples offered to new parents.[29] In this case, the state was imagined to confront powerful corporate interests to support "natural" feeding practices. Latch On "encouraged" hospitals to stop formula giveaways, to restrict access to formula by keeping it in locked cabinets (much as other medicine is kept, effectively enabling hospitals to track formula distribution), to offer formula only to mothers who required it for medical reasons, and to eliminate any promotional material for formula in hospitals. Patients could access formula by request, but only after a mandatory reminder about the health benefits of breastfeeding. Latch On also included a public relations campaign with advertisements reminding the public that "nothing compares with breast milk" and "breast milk is best for your baby."[30] Undergirding Latch On was the sense that the presence of formula in maternity wards could be interpreted as a medical endorsement of formula feeding and that the elimination of formula would align hospitals with their purported view: breast is best.

Compassion was also argued to be at the heart of Medolac Laboratories' controversial attempts to solicit Black women to work as paid breast-milk "donors." As Laura Harrison describes, Medolac collaborated with the Clinton Global Initiative to recruit Detroit-based Black women to "donate" breast milk. The donors would be paid at the rate of $1 for an ounce of milk, and Medolac would then sell the milk at a 600 percent markup, making starkly visible the extraction of Black gold—veiled in the language of Black women's benevolent donation—for corporate profits. Medolac argued that Black women would be encouraged to breastfeed, and to breastfeed longer, if they could earn money from their "donations," and thus it described the initiative as specifically geared toward improving Black breastfeeding rates. Medolac's efforts were met with immediate criticism by the Detroit-based Black Mothers' Breastfeeding Association and by Allers who, in an editorial in the *New York Times*, asked, "What is a for-profit company with no African-American employees, no African-American board members and no meaningful connections to African-American mothers doing starting a campaign targeting low-income African-American mothers in Detroit to sell their breast milk under the promise of economic empowerment? That's a question that deserves an answer, particularly since the company promoting this 'pull yourself up by your own nursing bra straps' approach intends to sell that milk at a profit."[31] Critics emphasized that the "donation" program did not actually respond to the structural issues undergirding lower Black breastfeeding rates, nor did it adequately attend to the histories of Black women laboring as wet nurses. Ten days after the Black Mothers' Breastfeeding Association published an open letter to Medolac (which was accompanied by a social media campaign unfolding under #StopMedolac), the corporation abandoned its Detroit pilot program. I flag both of these examples to emphasize that the rhetoric that surrounded the efforts was about the lack of support for Black breastfeeders and the need for infrastructure—whether in the form of hospital information or payment—to compassionately encourage Black women to breastfeed.

I interpret these initiatives to support Black breastfeeding as unfolding at a moment in which some have viewed breastfeeding as de facto obligatory and where the "obligation" that compassion unleashes is to enable Black mothers access to a now-normative infant-feeding practice.[32] In other words, this form of compassion can be read as, at least in part, ensuring that Black mothers comply with a dominant, affluent white mothering norm, one that is as connected to ideas of nutrition as it is to ideas of breastfeeding as a crucial form of early mother-infant bonding, of attachment. As Hanna Rosin wrote in her polemic against breastfeeding, "in certain overachieving circles, breastfeeding is no longer a choice—it's a no-exceptions requirement, the ultimate badge of responsible parenting."[33] Jung also describes how "the breastfeeding imperative has elevated the parenting habits of that relatively privileged minority to a universal standard of good parenting.... If breastfeeding is the measure of our moral worth, it isn't long before the idea of a mother not breastfeeding her child summons the familiar tropes of bad parenting and irresponsible citizenship that we have long deployed against poor women and minorities."[34] The "evangelism" and "lactivism" that these authors collectively bemoan are often described as most pernicious in the policing of poor women and women of color and the insistence that these women align their parenting practices—including their infant-feeding methods—with what many perceive as an affluent and whitened norm.[35]

If the gap is a space that is itself constitutive of violence, a barren and lifeless terrain that Black women and children inhabit that has been made newly visible in the temporality of crisis, the remainder of this chapter sits with what has become imagined as the singular compassionate response to that space: the recruitment of Black breasts to produce life-affirming Black gold. While this compassionate response has been amplified by different sites—the state, public health campaigns, Baby-Friendly hospitals, Black feminist activists, Black mothers, and lactation consultants—in distinct ways, these sites collectively project a sense of the life-saving capacities of Black gold, of its singular importance in an era newly attentive to the precarity of Black life.

*Crisis Objects*

The current "crisis"—which is described by various scholars as rooted in enslavement, in histories of wet nursing, in ongoing practices of aggressive corporate marketing of formula to Black mothers, in state collaborations with formula companies—has only recently been cast as one that warrants compassionate intervention in the form of education and support.[36] In the not-distant past, the Black breastfeeding gap was thought to be intimately related to another imagined crisis: the obesity epidemic. Black feminist scholars including Sabrina Strings and Margaret Bass argue that this epidemic obsessively represented Black women's bodies as sites of pathological corporeal excess, as a ground zero of nutritional and fiscal irresponsibility. In that earlier iteration of crisis, Black women's imagined corpulent bodies were thought to refuse the risk-mitigating practice of breastfeeding—precisely the practice of infant feeding that could inoculate children against obesity—and Black maternal flesh was thought (yet again) to be a site of deviance and refusal. In this section, I trace how Black breasts have gone from imagined sites of pathological refusal emblematic of what Patricia J. Williams has called "Black anti-will" to sites worthy of compassion through the collaborations of Black feminists, public health, and the state.[37]

THE RACELESS RHETORIC OF "BREAST IS BEST":
NOTES ON NUTRITION

In 2012, the American Academy of Pediatrics (AAP) updated its "Breastfeeding and the Use of Human Milk" policy to declare that "breastfeeding and human milk are the reference normative standards for infant feeding and nutrition."[38]

The statement affirmed the AAP's recommendation of exclusive breastfeeding for an infant's first six months of life and of continued breastfeeding as foods are introduced, for a year or longer, "as long as mutually desired by mother and child."[39] The recommendations hailed myriad health benefits for breastfed babies, including a lowered risk of hospitalization for respiratory tract infections and lowered risk for gastrointestinal infections, SIDS, asthma, eczema, diabetes, leukemia, celiac disease, and obesity.[40] Other research suggests that breastfeeding benefits not only infants but also mothers by reducing maternal risks of breast cancer, ovarian cancer, type 2 diabetes, and rheumatoid arthritis.[41] Some researchers have emphasized that breastfeeding is a "natural" part of the breasts' development, allowing them to serve their biological purpose, to, as Marisa Weiss notes, "finally grow up and get a job, and make milk, and show up for work every day and every night, and stop fooling around."[42] Breast milk, then, is liquid gold not simply for infants but also for mothers, who are thought to immunize themselves against a variety of illnesses—physical and social—through lactation.

The current public health emphasis on breastfeeding as a necessary form of infant nutrition is, however, a departure from earlier medical engagement with breastfeeding. While the AAP has always encouraged breastfeeding, their 1982 statement that "inherent" differences between mothers who provide formula or breastfeed made it impossible to determine which method was preferable, revealing a refusal to disavow formula entirely. Yet fifteen years later, the AAP decisively proclaimed that breastfeeding was fundamentally better than formula feeding, and public health initiatives, including the US Department of Health and Human Services' National Breastfeeding Awareness Campaign (NBAC), represented *not* breastfeeding as a risky form of child "endangerment."[43] NBAC ran a two-year campaign, including TV advertisements, posters, and billboards, that was met with great consternation by the formula industry, which particularly protested an advertisement featuring an image of a rubber nipple atop an insulin bottle. Ultimately, that advertisement, which linked formula feeding to diabetes, was removed from the NBAC campaign, but others emphasizing the health risks of formula usage remained.[44] For example, in a 2005 public health TV advertisement titled "Ladies Night," a pregnant Black woman is riding a mechanical bull. She is tossed in the air but muscles her way back onto the bull. Eventually she is thrown off completely. The text on the screen reminds viewers, "You wouldn't take risks before your baby's born. Why start after." The campaign echoes Joan Wolf's sense that by the mid-1990s the governmental logics of breastfeeding insisted that "no risk is too small and no cost too great when it comes to mother's obligation to optimize children's

FIGURE 1.2. National Breastfeeding Awareness Campaign advertisement by the US Department of Health and Human Services (2005).

health."⁴⁵ Black women, who have long been imagined as the quintessentially risk-prone subjects, became visual fodder for a campaign invested in tethering formula feeding to danger.

The celebration of breastfeeding's health benefits and its imagined alignment with risk mitigation are not separate from breastfeeding's status as a practice linked to raced and classed performances of motherhood in the United States. Breastfeeding remains largely associated with economically privileged Americans, at least in part because those parents are likely to have lengthier leaves from work that enable breastfeeding, pumping breaks at work, and the ability to hire lactation consultants who facilitate the demanding labor of breastfeeding. Corinne Purtill and Dan Kopf note that "breast milk has become a luxury good," and Wolf emphasizes that breastfeeding "is not even an option for many poor and low-income women, at least some of whom might prefer it to purchasing formula. Educated and middle-class women are more likely to breastfeed, to be able to purchase a breast pump, and to work in environments in which breastfeeding is possible."⁴⁶

Breastfeeding is regularly described as a practice congruent with what Sharon Hays terms "intensive mothering"—a "child-centered, expert-guided, emotionally-absorbing, labor-intensive, and financially expensive" form of parenting—and what Wolf calls "total mothering," a maternal "devotion" to "reducing risks to . . . children."⁴⁷ These immersive mothering logics are financially demanding and thus accessible only to particular subjects whose parenting practices are increasingly hailed as dominant, normative, and desirable.⁴⁸ Underpinning these varied conceptions of encompassing mothering are, as Wolf notes, ideas about risk management and the notion that women "must be vigilant about their bodies even before conception in anticipation of pregnancy and motherhood; and that it is every woman's individual responsibility to continuously monitor her babies and children in order to maximize their mental, emotional, and physical health."⁴⁹ Thus, "intensive mothering" is not only about a relationship to attachment and bonding, but also a way to insert risk mitigation as a central maternal ethic.⁵⁰

While breastfeeding's value is often described in public health literature as uncontested, academic and popular scholarship continues to challenge that finding, with some suggesting that breastfeeding's benefits have been "oversold."⁵¹ Wolf, for example, argues that when scholars control for "parenting practices," including "promoting hygiene, avoiding crowded places when babies are young, reading to and otherwise engaging with older children, and exercising," breastfeeding's benefits seem to matter less and less.⁵² As Wolf notes, "For every piece of research linking it [breastfeeding] to better health, another finds it to be irrelevant, weakly significant, or inextricably tied to factors that are difficult to measure with the standard tools of science."[53] Others suggest that the preoccupation with breastfeeding has led physicians and hospitals to overlook crucial aspects of infant health. Organizations like Fed Is Best have emphasized that a focus on exclusive breastfeeding, especially during the first few days of life, can lead to severe and even deathly consequences for infants. Christie del Castillo-Hegyi writes, "My child fell victim to newborn jaundice, hypoglycemia and severe dehydration due to insufficient milk intake from exclusive breastfeeding in the first days of life. . . . I believe we may be inducing hypoglycemic brain injury to many newborns by asking mothers who may not be producing sufficient milk for their newborn's physiologic need to exclusively breastfeed."[54] Fed Is Best argues that exclusively breastfed babies should be carefully monitored—particularly during the first week of life—for jaundice and dehydration, because of their belief that the medical focus on exclusive breastfeeding downplays other risks, including the risk of a lack of sufficient newborn nutrition.

If breastfeeding has been generally hailed for its health benefits, in an earlier statement on breastfeeding the AAP celebrated breastfeeding's "economic benefits to the nation," its capacity to offer the nation fiscal nutrition.[55] The AAP noted that breastfeeding's value includes "reduced health care costs and reduced employee absenteeism for care attributable to child illness. The significantly lower incidence of illness in the breastfed infant allows the parents more time for attention to siblings and other family duties and reduces parental absence from work and lost income."[56] In this figuration, breastfeeding is economically desirable because it maintains parents' capacities to participate in the paid workforce. The AAP has also emphasized the economic cost of formula feeding for parents. In a 1993 statement, it noted that the cost of infant formula for the first year after birth was $855, and in a 2012 statement, it concluded that if US mothers "would comply" with the recommendation to breastfeed for six months "there would be a savings of $13 billion per year."[57] The rhetoric of breastfeeding as having an economic value often unfolds alongside the rhetoric of breastfeeding as outside of the market entirely, as intrinsically good because it is "free." Indeed, breastfeeding is often hailed as a noncapitalist and environmentally progressive form of infant feeding, a form of providing nutrition that is parent controlled and thus outside the market.[58] Martucci notes: "A mother who can feed her baby entirely from her own body, for example, has the ability to reduce her participation in a capitalist consumer-based culture by limiting her reliance on commercial formulas and other infant feeding techniques. Mothers who can breastfeed also have the option to claim knowledge of their infants' care and nutrition for their own, removing it partially from the direct oversight of the medical system."[59] Breastfeeding is imagined as a form of maternal bodily autonomy, one that might be particularly profound for Black women seeking to claim freedom from medical surveillance and corporate strongholds.[60]

While some feminists have championed breastfeeding as a form of anticapitalist freedom, others have challenged this conception, emphasizing that this romanticization of breastfeeding ignores both the intense physical and emotional labor of breastfeeding and the devaluation of women's time that is a hallmark of patriarchal power. In her anti-breastfeeding polemic, Rosin writes: "It [breastfeeding] is a serious time commitment that pretty much guarantees that you will not work in any meaningful way. Let's say a baby feeds seven times a day and then a couple more times at night. That's nine times for about a half hour each, which adds up to more than half of a working day, every day, for at least six months."[61] Rosin's piece—which generated tremendous popular conversation—emphatically argued that breastfeeding should never be considered "free," precisely because of the costs it places on women's bodies, including sleep deprivation, labor extraction, and oftentimes removal from the paid marketplace. Other feminist critiques of the rhetoric of breastfeeding as anticapitalist emphasize that breastfeeding is imbricated with expensive products, costly visits to lactation consultants and other experts, and breast pumps. In Anna Momigliano's detailed accounting of the cost of reproductive labor, she writes:

> We have paid about $690 in breastfeeding-related products and services. Almost $250 went into the purchase of an electric pump; at first I tried to stick to a cheap model ($45), but it was noisy to the point that I soon realized that, if I wanted to keep both pumping *and* my sanity, I needed a better one (found it on sale for $200). About $140 went to a lactation consultant, because Baby and I had a rocky start. . . . Then there were the vitamins ($132), the nursing pillow ($38), the bras (I bought three for $60), the pads (both disposable and reusable: $23 in total), the nipple cream ($13), the bottles (two for $22) and the freezing bags (50 for $16).[62]

Both Rosin and Momigliano stress that breastfeeding is costly—both because of the time it requires and because of the sheer volume of products required to breastfeed. Momigliano's accounting also makes visible the challenges of breastfeeding, underscoring that it often necessitates products and expert intervention to be "successful."

If breastfeeding is celebrated for its nutritional and economic benefits, some also hail it as the linchpin of what is called "attachment parenting," as a practice of transmitting emotional sustenance intergenerationally. In 2012, *Time* magazine's cover featured Jamie Lynne Grumet breastfeeding her three-year-old son. The cover asked "Are You Mom Enough?" and depicted Grumet's son standing on a chair while sucking from his mother's breast. The image was offered as a visual representation of what Bill and Martha Sears have termed "attachment parenting," a child-rearing ideology that celebrates a deep and intuitive knowledge of one's child. As the Searses note, "When you're attached to your baby, you see her as a little person with distinct needs and preferences.... When you're attached to your baby, you become an expert on your baby. This knowledge of her behavior will help you know when she is not feeling well, when she needs reassurance, and when she needs to work out something on her own."[63] Attachment is performed through a set of practices, including breastfeeding (beyond the AAP-recommended six months), cosleeping, and "baby wearing." These practices, which Shannon K. Carter describes as "proximity-based," also encourage "minimal medical and technological interventions into pregnancy and childbirth."[64] Because attachment parenting celebrates "baby reading," a tactic of learning to intuit a baby's needs, breastfeeding is hailed as a primary mode of attachment. As the Searses note, "The maternal hormones associated with lactation—prolactin and oxytocin—give intuitive mothering a boost, since they help women feel more relaxed and calm around their babies."[65] While attachment parenting is often rhetorically aligned with other "intensive mothering" strategies, for the Searses, physical proximity—whether through breastfeeding or cosleeping—"immunizes" children from "social and emotional disease."[66] It is thus not merely a deep form of relationality and a "natural" practice; it is also a form of psychic nutrition that offers the important benefit of physical and emotional attachment. Breast milk, then, is about far more than physical satiety; it promises psychic wholeness.

Ultimately, this body of work suggests that breast milk's status as liquid gold has depended on varied conceptions of what comprises nutrition. For some, it is breast milk's imagined immunization against asthma and eczema among other ailments that marks its nutritional value. For others, what makes it particularly nutritious is the fluid's capacity to contribute to the financial health of a household and the nation's workers, to the emotional bond between mothers and children, or to the health of the environment. What is clear is that breast milk's imagined nutritional capacities are multiple and varied, but at the center is the maternal capacity to unleash "health" for other bodies, including infants, workplaces, national economies, and the environment. As I rehearse the lengthy debates about breastfeeding and varied conceptions of nutrition, it is also worth noting how Black women are largely absent from conversations about the relative health benefits (or lack thereof) of breastfeeding, except to haunt those conversations as the residents of the gap, the bodies that are always distant from nutrition, from health, and even from risk mitigation. In the next section, I describe how Black women have often appeared in public health literature—as proximate to obesity because of an unwillingness to breastfeed—and now, in the time of crisis, as in need of support because of the urgency of valuing Black life.

## THE BLACKNESS OF BREAST IS BEST

In 2010, in a speech at the Congressional Black Caucus promoting her Let's Move campaign, Michelle Obama announced, "Because it's important to prevent obesity early, we're also working to promote breastfeeding, especially in the Black community where 40 percent of our babies never get breast-fed at all, even in the first weeks of life, and we know that babies that are breast-fed are less likely to be obese as children."[67] Black women's breastfeeding—or imagined nonbreastfeeding—entered the public health consciousness, at least in the 1990s and early 2000s, through a connection to obesity, one that Obama amplified in her speech and in her efforts leading Let's Move, a nationwide anti-obesity effort. Black nonbreastfeeding was constructed as a particular kind of crisis because its lack was thought to make Black women and children particularly susceptible to obesity, a public health crisis often represented as a costly failure of self-control. In emphasizing how Black nonbreastfeeding was cast as a root cause of an obesity crisis, and how state initiatives to boost Black breastfeeding were figured as efforts to quite literally ward off "excess flesh," this section underscores how Black nonbreastfeeding was treated as a form of Black women's noncompliance with public health mandates. Put differently, Black mothers were thought to refuse the anti-obesity, lifesaving practice of breastfeeding. This section ends by arguing that Black breasts enter the public health conversation differently in the midst of BLM, as life-preserving sites precisely because of their capacity to manage the fragility of Black life. In tracing this shift, my impulse is to reveal how crisis—as an aesthetic, a sense of temporality, and a physical location—manifests itself and performs its labor by literally remaking the meaning of Black breasts from a site of noncompliance to distinctively capable of producing Black gold.

In her analysis of "slow death," Berlant investigates the construction and representation of obesity as an "epidemic," noting that obesity "became an epidemic and a problem when it interfered with reigning notions of what labor should cost; the disease is now too expensive, which is why privatized health care and business-oriented programs of education are the usual means of diminishing the cost of the symptom."[68] Berlant reveals that obesity is cast as a lack of personal responsibility, as an irresponsible willingness to bear weighty and expensive risk. If we think of Blackness as constructed around "anti-will," it is also imagined as refusing risk mitigation; as drawn toward risky entanglements with sex, desire, food, corporeality, and sensuality; or as an appetite without ends. Thus, Blackness aligns neatly with how Susan Bordo has described the construction of obesity: "an extreme capacity to capitulate to desire."[69] For Berlant, the story of the US obesity "epidemic" is one of its racialization. She notes: "For the large part of this century the defaulted image of the obese was of white people—the aged and the southern.... [I]n the 1970s ... poverty became associated with debates over the welfare state and representations of the poor become disproportionately African American. To the extent that emaciation in the US remains coded as white and weight excess coded as Black, the so-called crisis of obesity continues to juggle the symbolic burden of class signified through the elision of whiteness from the racial markings of poverty."[70] Part of the task of Berlant's analysis of "slow death" is to trace the codification of obesity as a category that adheres to Black flesh—and Black female flesh particularly—which is thought to be "compelled by appetites rather than by strategies of sovereign agency toward class mobility."[71]

Strings's pathbreaking work suggests that fat phobia emerges not from public health and medicine but from racial science and from the nineteenth century's enduring connection between savagery and Blackness, between imagined excess and Black women's bodies. In Strings's analysis, the construction of obesity—and later of the obesity epidemic—is rooted in a "familiar medical trope of the unrestrained Black woman as deadly" and by ideas of "Black female sensualism" and conceptions of Black women as "uninhibited and risk-prone."[72] Her notion of "social dead weight" reveals the framing of Black women as risk-prone bodies whose "sensualism" constitutes a social weight, a drain on the state, a "long-term oppressive burden on public health."[73] Like Berlant's work, Strings's endeavor is to think historically about the racialization of obesity, yet Strings's analysis is rooted in a careful engagement with the racialization of scientific categories. She shows that the connection of Black women to obesity actually depends on a willful misreading of scientific evidence. She notes that "healthy" body mass index (BMI) actually differs by race and that Black women tend to be healthier than white women at heavier weights. Despite the variation in "healthy" BMIs, the WHO, which in the late 1990s defined obesity around BMI—a designation later adopted by the National Institutes of Health in 1998, effectively classifying thirty million Americans as obese—came to quickly racialize and gender obesity, finding that Black women have a "higher prevalence of both overweight and obesity."[74] The public health literature, Strings finds, began to cast Black women as eating more caloric foods and as adopting a mindset about bodies that pathologically accepts larger body sizes.[75] In short, public health became increasingly preoccupied with adopting the mindset of racial science and casting Black women as pathologically situated in relationship to appetite.

If Blackness stands for "morbidly obese," for both an epidemic and a failure to appropriately mitigate risk, for excess appetite and for the quintessential symbol of aversion, the "unwillingness" of Black women to breastfeed has symbolized both Black women's unbearable tolerance for risk and a space where the state could intervene in a strategy of population management and fiscal responsibility. Indeed, the 1990s and early 2000s were marked by public health conversations about state management of obese populations and by a new anxiety about obesity in children, which was often traced to a set of children who were thought to be raised with new relationships to food—particularly "junk food"—to technology (and thus to sedentariness) and to a disconnection from satiety.[76] Obesity is imagined as a fundamental lack of body knowledge, an out-of-syncness between desire and need, and food is figured as something that should be consumed only for corporeal need and not for desire.

In 2005, for example, New York State's report on obesity, "New York State Strategic Plan for Overweight and Obesity Prevention," declared that "the epidemic of overweight and obesity has become one of the most critical public health threats for New Yorkers and Americans."[77] As the report noted, "obesity is expensive" and medical care costs for obesity "add up to $10,000 for an obese person," with obesity "account[ing] for 540 million workdays of lost productivity, 63 million doctors' office visits, 239 million restricted activity days, and 90 million days confined to bed per year." The report underscores that obesity is bad for the state: it produces unproductive workers and unhealthy citizens, and it generates excessive healthcare costs. And, as the report suggests, the risk-prone expensive bodies that were most troublingly "obese" were Black, particularly those of Black women.[78] Black women get tethered to risk and cost; they are not merely "social dead weight" but costly "social dead weight" whose refusal to appropriately mitigate risk produces a fiscal threat for the collective.

In considering how to manage the threat of Black women's imagined corporeal excess, New York turned its attention to a concerted effort to increasing breastfeeding rates. The report indicated that "evidence is accumulating that breastfeeding ... reduces the infant's risk of childhood and adult obesity."[79] Breastfeeding advocacy was celebrated for its capacity to produce a different kind of citizen—one immunized against obesity—and for its ability to yield a fiscally solvent state. As the report noted, plans to "increase initiation, exclusivity and duration of breastfeeding during infancy" would *require* reducing racial and ethnic disparities in breastfeeding rates, a deep attention to the Black breastfeeding gap. New York focused these efforts on its WIC programs, which were already mandated to have breastfeeding coordinators, to offer enhanced breastfeeding packages for exclusively breastfeeding mothers (a program started in 1994), to create "breastfeeding friendly environments," and to require certified lactation consultant training for WIC agency staff. New York was not alone in its concern with breastfeeding as the solution to obesity. Illinois's "Obesity Prevention Initiative Report" also found that low rates of breastfeeding contributed to the obesity epidemic, and it concluded that "children who are breastfed are less likely to be overweight.... A child never breastfed has almost three times greater risk of obesity than a child breastfed for nine months."[80] Illinois, like New York, called for a state-led campaign to increase breastfeeding rates in the population—particularly its Black population—to save the fiscal and physical health of the state.[81]

While state efforts focused on obesity as a public health and fiscal crisis, they were not the only institutional actors marking obesity as an "epidemic" and Black women's bodies as ground zero of that epidemic. In 2012, the Association of Black Psychologists held a Summit on Obesity in African American Women and Girls that convened academics, public health professionals, and members of religious organizations in the service of helping Black women and girls imagine "healthier, productive, and happier lives."[82] While the summit report emphasized an investment in structural rather than individual reasons for Black women's obesity, it emphasized that Black women had developed pathological strategies, including overeating, for "coping" with stress, microaggressions, and structural inequity. Among the host of recommendations that the Association of Black Psychologists offered were a set directed at healthcare professionals, including encouraging breastfeeding, providing adequate support for breastfeeding, and urging community members to create a culture supportive of Black women's breastfeeding efforts. They concluded that breastfeeding support was a crucial cure for low Black breastfeeding rates, for high Black obesity rates, and for the lack of Black happiness and well-being.

The notion of Black breasts as central to ending the state's war on obesity is figured in a few ways: first, some public health studies argue that, for Black women, pregnancy functions as a particularly powerful gateway into obesity.[83] Childbearing has long been found to increase BMI, and some researchers have found that "earlier childbearing, greater weights at the beginning of the childbearing years, and greater childbearing-associated weight gain among African-American women contribute to the higher prevalence of obesity in African-American women than in white women. . . . Because higher educational attainment is associated with more exercise and lower weight, it is possible that the present results underestimate the contribution of childbearing to weight gain in the less educated African-American women."[84] In this figuration, breastfeeding is described as a tactic of postpartum body management that yields healthier outcomes for Black mothers, who are thought to come to pregnancy with riskier relationships to food, appetite, and weight.

Other scholars emphasize that breastfeeding produces less obese future generations, that breastfeeding is a powerful inoculation against obesity, and that its primary labor is oriented toward futurity, even as scientific literature continues to debate the role breastfeeding plays in shaping the size of infants. Some public health literature suggests that breastfeeding helps infants develop a "healthy" relationship to satiety. For example, the *New York Times* reported that, among breastfed infants, the timing of solid food had no correlation to obesity, but formula-fed babies who were given solid foods before four months were more likely to be obese by age three.[85] Here, the introduction of "first foods" early—often imagined to be correlated with nonbreastfeeding, with race, and with poverty—is thought to shape relationships to food, nutrition, and satiety for the life course. Other public health research finds that infants who are bottle-fed are trained to "empty the milk in the bottle" whereas infants who are breastfed are taught a healthier conception of fullness.[86] At times, scholars argue that the "empty the milk in the bottle" logic comes from parents who are "more likely to push them to finish the bottle; feeding becomes a bit less about appetite and more about volume and schedule."[87] Some scholars assert that there is something intrinsic to breastfeeding that encourages babies to understand their fullness because "when they are full, they stop sucking, or switch to a 'comfort' kind of sucking that doesn't produce milk."[88] Indeed, the AAP encourages parents to use a practice of "responsive feeding," one marked by a motto of "you provide, your child decides." This is encouragement to use breastfeeding as a kind of bodily pedagogy, teaching infants "healthy" attitudes toward appetite, hunger, and satiety. In this formulation, the liquid gold of breast milk comes from its capacity to offer life-saving lessons on recognizing fullness.

Other work suggests that the healthiness of the breastfed child extends to the entire family, changing families' food-consumption habits. Dylan B. Jackson and Kecia R. Johnson find that "a negative relationship between breastfeeding and offspring junk food consumption, particularly among low-SES Blacks. To be precise, a longer duration of breastfeeding was associated with lower levels of junk food consumption among low-SES Blacks across the four measured domains: fast-food, soda, salty snacks and sweets consumption."[89] In this figuration, breastfeeding is quite literally an inoculation against "social dead weight," against the intergenerational spread of obesity, a way of preventing the cost—psychic, social, public health, material—of the linkage between weighty Black maternal flesh and weighty Black children. Breastfeeding then is hailed as a form of first food that teaches infants how to manage hunger, how to refuse the sensual pleasures of overeating. It is a crucial training on how to develop and manage a healthy form of appetite—and thus something that Black women and their children are thought to particularly need—not merely about infant nutrition but about an entirely different relationship to consumption, where food is not for comfort, soothing, or pleasure, but for a strictly biological need.

Nine years after Michelle Obama's remarks linking Black breastfeeding to a national crusade against obesity, the AAP offered their first-ever statement on the effects of racism on children's health. In "The Impact of Racism on Child and Adolescent Health," they note, "The impact of racism has been linked to birth disparities and mental health problems in children and adolescents. . . . It is important to recognize that children raised in African American, Hispanic, and American Indian populations continue to face higher risks of parental unemployment and to reside in families with significantly lower household net worth relative to white children in the United States, posing barriers to equal opportunities and services that optimize health and vocational outcomes."[90] The statement called on pediatricians to "be prepared to discuss and counsel families of all races on the effects of exposure to racism as victims, bystanders, and perpetrators" and to "implement systems in their practices that ensure that all patients and families know that they are welcome, that they will be treated with mutual respect, and that high-quality care will be delivered regardless of background using the tenets of family—and patient-centered care."[91] The statement was a plea for pediatricians both to claim their key role in promoting or preventing medical racism and to recognize the medical effects of racism on Black children and Black families. The AAP's statement on medical racism placed compassion and a different kind of medical infrastructure—one attentive to the fragility of Black life—on the public health agenda. In this context, the idea of Black infant precarity and of the necessity of Black maternal nurturance to counteract its vulnerability attaches to breast milk as well. Allers has secured the conception of the precarity of Black infant life through her oft-repeated refrain that Black infants are more likely to be "born too small, too sick, or too soon."[92] This image of "too small" babies, of physical fragility as the hallmark of Black life, is a dramatic departure from the representation of Black life as marked by excess and corpulence. And it suggests that Black breast milk is a kind of shield against the vulnerability that marks "too small," "too sick," "too soon" Black infant life.

At the same time, there has been an increased attention to the medical outcomes of the stress of Black mothering or to what some scholars have termed "weathering," the physical outcomes of racism on Black maternal flesh. Allers, for example, notes, "I hope that in the tragedy of Trayvon Martin, there lies proof of exactly the kind of unique stressors Black mothers contend with. I hope the people who have questioned how stress could be connected with pre-term labor or low birth weight babies or challenged me as to why Black mothers face issues so unique that they are deserving of their own online community, can see exactly what researchers mean. These are not the worries you can Calgon-bath or Yankee-candle away."[93] Of course, this new attention to the embodied effects of quotidian violence—work I refer to in the introduction—productively makes visible the corporeal and even cellular woundings of what Williams terms "spirit murder."[94] This reframing of racism as productive of trauma at even the molecular level, as foundational to Black infant and maternal mortality, has worked to transform Black mothers from pathological and noncompliant patients willing to bear the risk of obesity to being positioned at the front line of securing Black life, with Black breasts becoming a key technology—*the* key technology—to immunize Black children from physical and psychic violence.

*Black Women Do Breastfeed: Self-Representation and the Politics of Attachment*

In 2017, Chocolate Milk Mommies, a Birmingham, Alabama–based group of Black women organized around Black breastfeeding advocacy, used social media to circulate a series of images that received national attention. The images, photographed by Birmingham-based artist Lakisha Cohill, are part of what has become a genre: pictures often circulated under the hashtag #NormalizeBreastfeeding linking Black breastfeeding to Black empowerment, Black care, and the preservation of Black life. In these images, Black gold is figured not simply as infant nutrition but as a crucial act of Black affirmation and as indicative of Black women's intrinsic and often uncelebrated power. Some of these visual campaigns have oriented themselves around the gap by raising the visibility of Black breastfeeding practices and offering encouragement to Black women who seek to breastfeed. Others have insisted that Black women have long histories of breastfeeding that are wholly ignored in the presentation of Black maternal bodies as the site of crisis. The political work of the visual archive is to make evident what is rendered invisible in the ongoing rehearsal of the statistical truth of the gap: Black women *do* breastfeed. These images reject the language of crisis entirely by reading the medical inability to *see* Black lactating bodies as constitutive of the obstetric violence that reproductive justice advocates describe. Other images celebrate particular providers—women of color doulas, midwives, or lactation consultants—who are thought distinctly able to support Black breastfeeders. What these images share is a sense that the gap is largely a representational problem that can be solved through the construction of a radical counter-archive marked by its own visual grammar. In this section of the chapter, I look at two bodies of work that are part of this large counter-archive: professionally taken Black breastfeeding photographs, largely centered on the work of Cohill; and self-produced images that circulate on Twitter, Instagram, and Facebook often under the hashtags #NormalizeBreastfeeding, #BlackMamasMatter, and #LoveOnTop. My focus is on how these images work to represent Black breastfeeding as a radical act of Black empowerment and to refigure Black breasts not as sites of deviance or pathology but as distinctly capable of responding to antiBlack violence with tenderness, nurturance, and care.

REMAKING THE FAMILY PORTRAIT

Cohill's photograph of the Chocolate Milk Mommies (see figure 1.3) aspires to show the communal, regal, and natural underpinnings of Black women's breastfeeding practices. Unlike the Gap advertisement that begins this chapter, which focuses on the mother/child dyad, Cohill offers a vision of breastfeeding as a collective practice that powerfully unites communities of Black women and children. Her description of the picture underscores its emphasis on the majestic and collective nature of Black breastfeeding, noting, "The women were represented as queens, because they all had crowns. And it was just beautiful. Even when I was doing the photoshoot, I was just in awe. Tears were coming down my eyes just to see, just because it was more than just the breastfeeding. It was about Black women coming together in unity. And I knew the bond that these ladies had, and the friendship that we had created. So it

FIGURE 1.3. Lakisha Cohill's *Black Women Breastfeed (Chocolate Milk Mommies—Birmingham, AL)*. Courtesy of Lakisha Cohill.

was just something that was just magical at that moment."[95] For Cohill, Black breastfeeding is an act where Black women "come together," one that is as much about the power of Black gold to immunize Black infants as it is about the power of Black gold to forge deep friendships among Black women and to generate powerful and even spiritually rooted communities.

What does it mean to imagine US Black breastfeeding women as "African queens," and what does it mean to stage a representation of the possibility and pleasures of Black breastfeeding in Alabama, a state that has among the lowest breastfeeding rates in the country? As Cohill notes, "Alabama is so slow. We are one of the most racist states. We lack so much as Black people. I mean Alabama's just crazy. If they could make rules against Black people, they definitely would."[96] Cohill's carefully constructed images remake the family portrait into a site of visual advocacy—one emphatically staged in the context of the US South—that treats Black women's communion with each other, with their infants, and with the natural world as constitutive of family. In Cohill's visual grammar, Black gold becomes the material and psychic glue that bonds infant and child, connects Black women with each other, and unites Black women with the natural world. Black gold is what makes possible the kind of family Cohill both represents and celebrates, one that places Black mothers at its center.

Thy Phu and Elspeth H. Brown describe the family photograph as "the most conventional of genres, often attesting to lofty aspirations and seldom lingering in the depths of disappointment."[97] These images—of weddings, births, graduations, birthday parties, religious ceremonies—are repositories of the quotidian. They are scripted and even predictable, featuring smiling faces, togetherness, and "positive themes of unity, mobility, prosperity, and futurity," often, as Phu and Brown argue, masking the "mixed feelings" that can reside at the heart of family life.[98] Yet even as Phu and Brown sit with the aspirational pulls at the center of the family photograph, they also attend to what it means to be part of these images for those whom the genre never anticipated, for those who were not imagined to even have the will to project themselves into an unknown future. Similarly, Tina M. Campt writes, "Photography offers individuals . . . a medium through which to create a vision of themselves that does not always square with how they are popularly perceived or with what we associate with those contexts in the present. Time and again, our conversations returned to the same point: that images matter to Black folks."[99] Collectively, these authors ask us to consider questions like the following: What are the political and intimate desires that attend to Black people posing for a photographer, projecting an image for posterity? What might it mean to read the family photograph as making a stake at political legibility, or even at normativity?

My understanding of Cohill's photographs is informed by the critical queries Phu, Brown, and Campt pose and by Black feminist engagement with visuality, including work by Nicole R. Fleetwood on prison photography and carceral intimacy and by Deb Willis on visual representations of Black beauty. I explore what happens when the family portrait is a genre that is remade, where family is reconfigured not as a heterosexual nuclear formation but as a community of women collectively breastfeeding, and when nutrition—the emotional, political, and physical nutrition that breast milk is imagined to provide—makes itself visible in the portrait. The Black breast enters the visual field not as evidence of "excess flesh" or of Black pathology but as evidence of a Black woman's commitment to use her body—put it to work—in the service of holding Black life tenderly.

Cohill's staged portraits—many of which feature women she met or "scouted" in Birmingham—emphasize the communal elements of breastfeeding. In a widely circulated image, the conventional family portrait of mother and child is remade, with the act of breastfeeding transforming the very conception of family into a community of women and children. While each woman is entirely focused on her child, tenderly holding her child as she nurses, the women collectively form a whole, bound together by their practice of breastfeeding, which is presented here as regal because all of the women wear crowns. Cohill's image insists not only that breastfeeding is natural—that *Black* breastfeeding is natural—but also that Black women have a historical and even spiritual connection to the natural world, one they can particularly tap into by participating in "ancient" practices like breastfeeding. While Cohill describes these images as "unapologetically Black," I emphasize that they are unapologetically part of reconstituting a narrative of Black family. In Cohill's hands, the Black family is about the community of mothers and children, here cast not as the imagined pathological absence of Black fathers but as a celebratory emphasis on Black women's distinctive capacity to nurture, protect, and connect Black infants. The image shows that Black women—Black mothers—are the barriers between Black life and Black death, the only figures who can protect Black life and only with the materiality of their bodies. While the celebration of Black maternal strength offers a crucial rejoinder to the patriarchal notion that the presence of male bodies is required to forge heteronormative family, it also suggests the particular physically demanding labor that breastfeeding demands from women's bodies.

In Cohill's more recent work, Black women's "natural" capacity to breastfeed as an extension of their communion with the natural world is deepened. In an untitled photograph (figure 1.4), Cohill's maternal models wear only body paint and flower crowns, conjuring images of majestic and indigenous traditions, and the children they feed seem to be older than infants. We might think of how this Black feminist aesthetic response to crisis runs deeply against what Freeman described as the problematic representations of imagined "tribal" African women from *National Geographic*. For Cohill, a fictionalized Africa, an imagined natural past, becomes a source of strength and empowerment. In this image, Black mothers are queens, but they also seem to be warriors, protecting their children—even their older children—and perhaps even the natural world they stand in front of and represent. Their direct and fearless gazes suggest that they understand Black maternal life as marked by the labor of acting as bodyguards to protect Black life. Black mothers seem to hold the fate not only of the Black child, the precious territory they make and nurture, but also of the natural environment itself, which requires their care and protection.

While most of Cohill's portraits feature Black mothers and their children, suggesting that the family that Black gold produces is one of mothers and

FIGURE 1.4. Lakisha Cohill's portrait of Black mothers as queens. Courtesy of Lakisha Cohill.

children, her work also includes more conventional family portraits featuring fathers, mothers, and children. Yet in these images, the Black breast is also present, an emphatic visual reminder of the role of Black gold in forging Black intimate life. In one image, a Black man, a Black breastfeeding woman, and another child sit together, united by white outfits that visually mark them as a family. Cohill posted the image on Instagram with the caption "The father of a breastfed baby will reap the benefits of a healthier partner and healthier infant. Traditionally, fathers view themselves as providers and protectors of their families. . . . His support, encouragement, and direct help can be the decisive factor in a woman's breastfeeding success."[100] Cohill's caption suggests that the image is meant to celebrate Black fathers who "support" Black breastfeeding. The presence of the Black breast in the family portrait becomes evidence of both maternal tenderness and the family's collective commitment toward a physically and emotionally labor-intensive form of infant nutrition. Indeed, the image shows that Black gold requires not only family "support" but also a rewriting of normative heterosexual gender scripts to recognize the key role that breastfeeding mothers play in acting as "providers." The family portrait then shows what Cohill terms "parenting done right." The bared Black breast becomes a performance of a kind of Black respectability that refigures Black flesh not as a sign of sexual pathology but as a sign of familial health.

Cohill's images are seductive in their saturated colors, in their stunning beauty, and in their aesthetic commitment to representing Black maternal heroism in the form of the Black breast. They are also powerful in their desire to make visible and legible alliances among Black women, to act as a visual archive of the labor of organizations like Chocolate Milk Mommies that respond to the continued conditions that make breastfeeding generally, and Black breastfeeding specifically, unbelievably demanding. The images hail the Black breast as itself able to mitigate violence, to engage in risk reduction, to remake Black babies, families, and communities. They suggest that Black gold might be powerful enough to alter the conditions of the present or at least to forge space for Black life. They affirm that it is Black tenderness and care—a willingness to engage in the time-consuming act of breastfeeding—that can tend to Black life. They also, though, reveal the political and ideological pressure on Black breasts to save Black children, Black communities, Black ecosystems, and even the natural world. The Black breast is represented here as a powerful force that can undo the trauma of institutionalized medicine, Black precarity, and vulnerability. Of course, the notion of heroic Black breasts—like the notion of heroic Black motherhood—can be deeply seductive. This iconography also places a tremendous amount of political weight on Black breasts, recruiting Black mothers to quite literally extract labor from their bodies for the collective good of the community and for future generations.

ORDINARY (BLACK) BREASTS

In 2007, Vanessa Simmons was four months pregnant and had lost thirty pounds. When her doctor insisted that the weight loss was "totally normal," Simmons concluded that institutionalized medicine was marked by a "lack of support" for Black women, a "lack" that allowed her severe hyperemesis gravidarum (persistent vomiting and nausea that causes weight loss) to be dismissed as something "normal." Though #NormalizeBreastfeeding—Simmons's digital revolution—would not take shape for another seven years, she narrates these early experiences with obstetricians as foundational to the genesis of what would become a social media movement. While the means of this revolution—social media—are relatively new, Simmons emphasizes that her commitment to the radical potential of breast milk is rooted in African traditions. Like Cohill, she reads breastfeeding generally, and Black breastfeeding specifically, as an act of reclaiming a heritage that has been taken from Black women. In describing her own commitment to breastfeeding, she notes, "Mama Dokua is my great, great, great grandmother, and I'm actually named after her. . . . She was actually a very, very well-known queen mother who helped to bring a lot of peace to the area at that time. Now, I don't know too much about her maternal health situations, but I would assume in Africa that if she had children and all of that, that she had a very natural situation. So I really just pulled from my roots."[101] For Simmons, pulling "from her roots" is an act of empowerment and an imagined connection to a past—one of royalty, of natural wisdom. Pulling from her roots also became a reservoir of strength as she refused the noncare of institutionalized medicine and insisted on trusting her own knowledge of her body.

In 2014, Simmons launched the campaign #NormalizeBreastfeeding. It responded to highly publicized stories of breastfeeding mothers excluded from public spaces or harassed for refusing to conceal their feeding children and their breasts. Simmons wanted to demonstrate the normalcy of breastfeeding by saturating the digital visual field with images of breastfeeding bodies. Even as her investment was to publicize breastfeeding, Simmons always held a particular commitment to constructing a rich archive of Black breastfeeding, insisting on its presence, political importance, and possibility. She rooted her commitment to rendering breastfeeding ordinary in her identity as a Ghanaian

American woman who "refused to just be another statistic" and who sought to make an "online village for Black moms. All the stuff we go through. Oh my gosh. It has been such a great resource for us to be able to connect and rebuild those villages that we no longer have and find people who will support us on our journey."[102] For Simmons, Black women have a particularly urgent need for images of Black breastfeeders, images that can connect Black women, "normalize" Black breastfeeding, and build a visually rooted "online village." While #NormalizeBreastfeeding intends to saturate the visual field with representations of breastfeeding, it emphasizes that an abundance of images will ultimately despectacularize breastfeeding entirely. The more representations of breastfeeding that circulate, the less breastfeeding will be remarkable. The more we see lactating breasts—particularly lactating Black breasts—the less exceptional they will be. While Simmons created a digital space for these images and offered a conceptualization of how to bring them together, #NormalizeBreastfeeding continues to be shaped by both Simmons and those drawn to share their own photographs. It is a shifting, ephemeral, organic archive constituted by those who choose to upload selfies and more formally staged photographs.

Simmons emphasizes the necessary visual nature of the response to crisis, even as her conception of the crisis is expansive, including medical racism, institutionalized noncare, and the policing of women's bodies in public spaces. If the proliferation of images that Simmons champions centers breasts in public view, Simmons underscores that the work she has gravitated toward—and her own visual work (she now works as a professional photographer)—rejects staged photographs entirely. She notes, "She's [a photographer who staged images] got that wonderful picture in the field, and the wind's blowing her hair, and it's like, this is not real. This is not real. This was totally staged for an image. And if you notice any of my images, I don't do that with my work!"[103] For Simmons, the call for normalization is to one that is undergirded by making apparent the quotidian nature of breastfeeding. She says, "I want people to see what it really looks like. Whether that's the middle-of-the-night experience where you're half awake and trying to breastfeed, or if that's that middle of the day, I've got to get to this work meeting, I'm pumping for my baby, storing my milk, and then we've got to go. You know what I mean?"[104] This archive of the ordinary upends the logic of Black breast spectacularity and thus wholly resignifies Black breasts.

The tens of thousands of images that have appeared under #NormalizeBreastfeeding feature women breastfeeding in their cars, while eating breakfast,

FIGURE 1.5. An image from Vanessa Simmons's #NormalizeBreastfeeding campaign. Courtesy of Vanessa Simmons, CLEC, founder of Normalize Breastfeeding.

during meetings, and in sterile offices. (At times, though, Simmons's work is staged—including Simmons's photograph of military women breastfeeding while in uniform.) The backdrops contain unmade beds, kitchen tables littered with dirty dishes, a bedroom with a small pile of dirty laundry. The overriding message of the campaign is that Black tenderness is an ordinary practice, an unglamorous one, staged in the midst of the demands and even banalities of life. It is this willingness to engage in breastfeeding in the midst of life that actually indexes a Black maternal commitment to Black life. More than that, these images of Black tenderness present a different face to "crisis"—instead of violence, trauma, or pain, Black breastfeeding is presented as serene, as a calming practice of devotion that rewrites Black maternal and child affect. Yet in their insistence on Black tenderness as staged through the Black breast as the "answer" to the problems of the present, and in their emphasis that the saturation of the visual field with images of Black breastfeeders is a crucial political tactic, the "solution" to the problems of the present comes to rest on Black

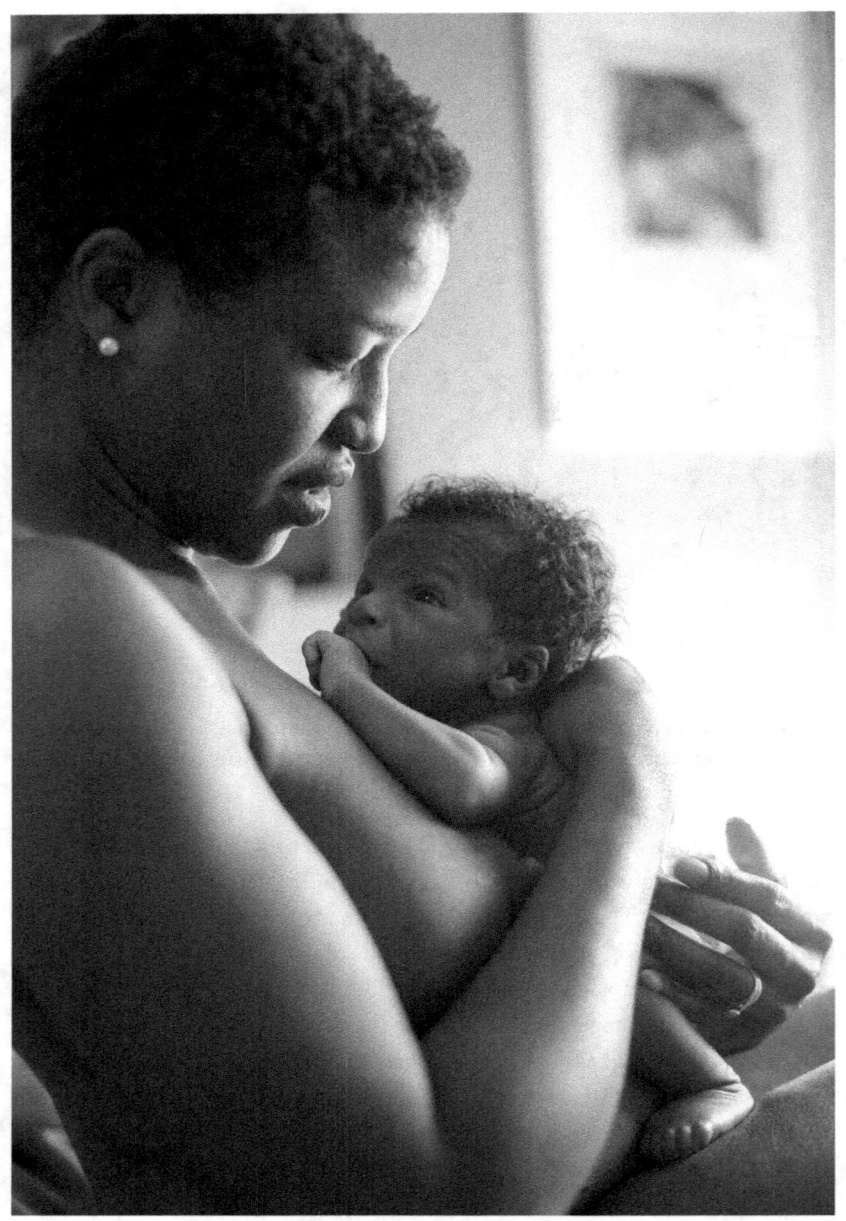

FIGURE 1.6. An image from Vanessa Simmons's #NormalizeBreastfeeding campaign. Courtesy of Vanessa Simmons, CLEC, founder of Normalize Breastfeeding.

maternal flesh, perhaps even producing a new category of Black deviance: the Black mother who simply chooses not to breastfeed, who "refuses" to offer her child and her community the inoculation of Black gold.

Even as Simmons argues for the power of normalization to transform Black maternal life, in our conversation she noted the challenges she faces as a photographer: pregnant and postpartum Black women simply do not want to be photographed. She says, "Why did they not want to be photographed? Why do they not want to be documented? Is there a shame? Do they feel like this is going to inhibit them in some way? Because I've had serious issues trying to get Black women in front of my camera for the things that I'm documenting. I still to this day have not photographed a Black woman giving birth, and I've been doing births since 2010."[105] While #NormalizeBreastfeeding reveals the potential political power of the ordinary to resignify Black breasts as neither erotic nor spectacular but instead laboring in the service of Black life, Simmons's reflections on the challenges in finding Black women willing to be photographed reveal the potential costs of representations. Some Black mothers are wary of what Black women know all too well—the complicated and taxing burden of representation. Indeed, the quest to represent breastfeeding as an ordinary practice often means that some bodies bear a great deal of vulnerability in allowing their flesh to serve as the medium for a political message. Similarly, having the camera turned on the "Black interior"—whether the vagina (as in the case of Simmons's ongoing attempt to photograph Black births) or Black domestic spaces where Black women breastfeed—can feel both like liberation and surveillance, and that always bears the threat of being taken up as evidence of myriad forms of Black pathology.[106]

*Eye of the Storm*

In a 2013 article introducing the launch of Black Breastfeeding Week, Allers reminds her readers, "We have to save ourselves. We have to change our conversation. . . . We have to ask ourselves why we find it quite okay to use breasts to sell chicken wings and beer or to backdrop our music videos, but we are 'uncomfortable' to see a mother feeding her child. We need to shout from the rooftops in our own neighborhoods the importance of reclaiming our community responsibility for the health of our infants."[107] Allers's call for "saving ourselves" underscores that this salvation must take a decidedly different visual form: we must replace a comfort with "using breasts to sell chicken wings" with images of Black breastfeeding. Her comment suggests that the crisis has both a visual underpinning—the inability to imagine the productive labor of

Black breasts—and a visual solution. This chapter has wrestled with ongoing debates about the Black breastfeeding gap, arguing that an array of efforts by Black women, corporations, and the state have fundamentally transformed the very meaning of Black breasts from pathological sites of sexual alterity to life-affirming spaces of Black gold that possess the capacity—and perhaps even the responsibility—to inoculate Black life from vulnerability and fragility. The visual field has become crucial terrain for making visible Black gold's transformative capacity and for recruiting Black breasts to labor for Black children and Black communities.

Of course, these campaigns have reimagined Black breasts by showing how breasts can be put to work in the service of saving Black life, eradicating Black infant mortality, and protecting the fragility of new Black life. In this configuration, Black breasts stand for emotional, physical, and psychic nutrition, offering an immunization that only Black mothers can provide. The labors of Black feminism and public health—even as both are motivated by different politics, different commitments, and different conceptions of the work of "Black woman"—cohere around producing the Black child as the symbol of life and the Black mother as the symbol of the protection of that life. Indeed, crisis rhetoric often performs its work by treating Black children as the site of crisis and by positioning Black mothers as the agents who must mitigate and resolve that crisis, who must "save" Black children.

What might a different kind of Black feminism add to this ongoing cultural conversation, including a Black feminist reproductive justice commitment to nonbreastfeeding, not, as Allers suggests, in the problematic register of choice but in the name of noncoercion or even in the name of bodily and sexual autonomy? My exploration of the complex politics of Black breastfeeding suggests that the rhetoric of Black gold continues to relegate some Black women to the category of bad mothers, because of their failures to tap into their gold, their imagined capacity to sustain life, to prevent fragility. What might happen if Black feminism figured the responsibility for preserving Black life—again, imagined only as Black children—as not exclusively in the hands of Black women and if it reamplified a critique of the gendered costs of reproductive labor? What I suggest here is a Black feminist praxis that thinks differently about the phrase "Black life," untethering it from its exclusive attachment to Black children and instead thinking about Black mothers as bodies with aspirations, desires, appetites, needs, wishes, and dreams that might include and exceed being solely responsible for the lives of Black infants.

We ended the doula training with pneumatics gunshot wound training. I remember having a deep conversation with my husband and one of my friends about how knowing how to potentially save someone from a gunshot wound was related to birth. People are understanding the connections between how we come into this world and the rest of our lives.
—LAUREN

I'm on the front lines.
—LYNDA

TWO. **IN THE ROOM**

*Birthwork by Women of Color in a State of Emergency*

It is easy to spot Lauren in the crowded grocery store in Chicago's Loop. She is wearing a bright yellow shirt that says, "Mama. Midwife. Fierce." She pushes a shopping cart through the store's produce section while her four-year-old daughter exclaims, "Bananas and kiwis and apples!" Nestled inside the cart is Lauren's three-month-old son, who has just fallen asleep, thanks to the wagon's steady motion. We move to the store's family room, a small space adjacent to the loading docks that has ample baskets of wooden fruits and vegetables, small utensils, and a miniature kitchen. Lauren's daughter pretends to make us breakfast, and every few minutes, she runs to our table and asks, "Do you want syrup with your pancakes?" My conversation with Lauren is fractured. We are both, in an unspoken way, deeply aware that the presence of her children means that we can talk only in short spurts. Because we expect to be interrupted, Lauren talks with a sense of urgency, and she often bangs her palms against the table to emphasize an important point. She leans in and says,

> The birth world is focused on birth justice. This means: How do we parent? How do we parent when parents are incarcerated? I have a doula friend who is starting a farm and her handle is the Farm Doula because, you know, pregnant women need to eat. We *need* to eat. I think it's just becoming so different than even five years ago. And I think that's really important to people in Chicago where you know, our right to parent, to have babies, and to not get killed by the police are really, really things that are emergent. I always felt like me becoming a midwife and being a doula was an emergency.

For Lauren, a Black midwife, lactation consultant, and doula working on Chicago's South Side, birthwork is lifework, and the process of "catching a baby" is as much about caring for birthing Black bodies as it is about ensuring pregnant Black women have access to healthy food and saving community members from gunshot wounds.[1] Working as a birth doula is both laboring *in* an emergency and responding *to* an emergency.

The year after my conversation with Lauren, *Chicago* magazine, the city's "lifestyle" magazine, celebrated women of color (WOC) doulas for their collective work on the city's "front lines."[2] WOC doulas, because of their capacity to move inside and outside of conventionally medicalized spaces, were hailed as the necessary—and perhaps only—stopgap preventing Black mothers and children from dying from obstetric violence. Qiddist Ashé, one of the doulas profiled in the article, describes her practice as focused on "bringing the power of birthing back into the community and collaborating with providers as needed and when they're wanted, but [it's especially about] placing the birthing person at the center of any experience."[3] Ashé's community-centered conception of birthwork positions doulas' labor as caring for Black life on multiple levels: there is a baby to be "caught," a birther whose physical and psychic labor needs to be supported, and a wider Black community desperately in need of care that respects their collective bodily autonomy and fundamental personhood.

In the wake of a new public attention to the Black maternal mortality crisis, birthworkers—particularly birth doulas—have become increasingly visible agents of birth justice. Doula-assisted pregnancies have been described as successful not only in transforming some birthers' perinatal experiences, but also, some argue, in improving the health of mothers and infants, even as there remains debate about what precisely it is that makes doulas' presence in the birthing room transformative.[4] Doulas, particularly WOC doulas, are imagined to play their most politically and ethically significant role in the birthing experiences of Black mothers who birth in a milieu marked by stark racial disparities and often deathly outcomes. Dána-Ain Davis describes WOC doulas as "radical birth workers" who "seek to ensure that birthing parents are treated respectfully and understand the consequences of the procedures to which they might be subjected. Along with working toward facilitating informed decisions, they actively engage in advocacy, care, and medical practices that seek to shift adverse birth outcomes."[5] In this chapter, I turn sustained attention to WOC doulas, but I read them quite differently than Davis, examining them as actors who have become foot soldiers in a birth justice movement that is rooted in Black feminist praxis and increasingly supported by both state actors and nonprofit organizations invested in eradicating—or at least downplaying— the crisis. This movement recognizes the endless threats against Black life as beginning in utero, and it draws connections among state violence, environmental racism, nutrition, quality schools, and access to transportation to craft a broad conception of the conditions necessary for Black life to thrive. Thus, the movement thinks capaciously about the radical interventions and reparative political work that doulas can stage simply by being "in the room."

Under the auspices of reproductive justice, WOC doulas are recruited by community-based doula programs and by state-financed doula initiatives to transform the birthing experiences of women of color and to disproportionately fill the ranks of pro bono doula programs that provide low-cost or free doula services to vulnerable communities. These pro bono programs have been celebrated by the state in the face of crisis, even as that celebration unfolds with little financial backing for the programs and with little or no compensation for the doulas whose labor is imagined as integral to preserving Black life.[6] New York City and Baltimore, for example, have begun training doulas to mitigate the Black maternal health crisis. New York's doula program—which was designed as a state response to staggering Black maternal mortality rates— expands Medicaid coverage to include doulas, while Baltimore's program trains doulas to become both "independent contractors" committed to ending racial disparities in infant mortality and maternal health and key symbols of a state investment in Black maternal health, even as the state reminds doulas that they are performing a community service and will be unlikely to earn a living as a doula.[7] WOC doulas have debated the meaning and effects of these efforts, with many arguing that the limited state remuneration continues to make birthwork unlivable; others suggest that the entry of the state "into the room" can quickly complicate the question of who a doula serves: her birthing client, or the state that reimburses her for her services. WOC doulas are increasingly imagined as medical missionaries whose antimedical ethics are precisely what is required to save the lives of Black women laboring in medicalized spaces. As Davis suggests, "Doulas provide care that can shift the terms of the medical commodification of birthing by offering an alternative to the systems that may perpetuate racism."[8] Yet WOC doulas are more than medical missionaries, more than bodies who, by simply being "in the room," tend to birthing Black mothers. Being "in the room" is imagined to be a practice of intramural care that remakes Black social life, making "the room" a metaphor for the transformative possibilities of Black collectivity more generally.

For some scholars, birth doulas are best understood in the context of feminist efforts rooted in the "women's health movement of the 1970s, which criticized the medicalization of birth in the hospital setting as patriarchal and disempowering to women. As such, many of the goals of doula care run parallel to feminist principles: expanding the range of reproductive choices for women, centralizing embodied knowledge, and promoting self-help and solidarity among mothers."[9] In this framing, doulas are a critical part of feminist efforts to demedicalize birth, to decenter patriarchal medical authority, and to place empowerment and autonomy at the heart of women's birthing experiences. They are thought to perform their radical work by responding to the physical challenges of birth not with epidurals, inductions, and other medical interventions but with, as one doula noted, "comfort measures, things like acupressure, aromatherapy, deep breathing, meditation, relaxation, light massages," and with "things that stimulate the senses: visualization, sound, music, smell, different oils, touch, soft things that feel comfortable.... And lots of affirmations." Yet contemporary representations of doulas often treat the profession as part of a "growing demand for personal service (the doorman, the yoga teacher, Amazon Prime)."[10] Here, doulas are conceptualized as part of a larger shift toward customization and privatization, one where "boutique experiences" are increasingly the demand in all aspects of life.[11]

Both of these representations, however, obscure the particular labor of WOC doulas at a moment when they are situated in the eye of a political storm, called on to eradicate racial birth inequities through their very presence "in the room"—a phrase many doulas use to describe both the location and the urgency of their practice. Being in the room describes the physical, emotional, and even political presence of WOC doulas who labor as "bodyguards" protecting Black mothers and their children and who see this work as protecting Black life more broadly. In this chapter, I treat WOC doulas as actors who have, by being in the room, put into practice—and brought into institutional visibility—a set of Black feminist frameworks, including allegiances to reproductive justice, a commitment to Black life, and an investment in care and love as radical world-making forms of being-together.[12] Moreover, I treat WOC doulas as instrumental in recasting the pregnant Black body not as a medical or embodied category, but as a political one. For WOC doulas, the pregnant Black body is vulnerable and precarious, subjected or potentially subjected to myriad forms of antiBlack violence. The role of the doula is to protect the fragility of Black maternal life and to ensure the safe arrival of Black infant life. More than that, the doula's willingness to carefully "catch" the baby is thought to act as an early psychic immunization against other forms of violence inflicted on Black bodies.

Yet the rhetoric of the utter urgency of being in the room can produce the temporality of crisis that doulas attempt to ameliorate. This chapter traces three tensions that undergird contemporary doula practice: questions about training and professionalization, questions about the meanings of medicalization, and questions about the exceptionality of birthing. In all three cases, while doulas are called on—by the state, nongovernmental organizations (NGOs), and birth justice advocates laboring in the name of Black feminism—to be agents of crisis mitigation, these tensions complicate efforts to "resolve" the crisis Black mothers face and at times further suture Black maternal bodies to crisis, placing these bodies as sites in need of remediation, repair, and transformation.

My analysis draws on twenty-three interviews I conducted in 2018 with birth doulas—most of whom identified as women of color—working in the Chicago metropolitan area. These doulas performed their work at a moment when Illinois was increasingly attentive to maternal and infant mortality rates, particularly in light of the state's 2018 Maternal Morbidity and Mortality Report, which found that, since 2008, more than 650 women had died of pregnancy-associated deaths in the state and that Black mothers were six times more likely than their white counterparts in the state to die from pregnancy-related complications.[13] In 2018, a collective of state representatives and senators introduced the Mothers and Offspring Mortality and Morbidity Awareness Act (MOMMA Act) to collect data on infant and maternal mortality and to establish statewide protocols for obstetric emergencies. That same year, the state recommended expanded state engagement with perinatal women, including universal home visits to all mothers within three weeks of birth, home-visiting programs for "high-risk" mothers, and state-funded doula programs for "high-risk" mothers. Bruce Rauner, the governor at the time, applauded the efforts of the Illinois Maternal Mortality Review Committee, saying: "The work of [this committee] is essential for reducing maternal deaths and improving the health of all women. I am proud that Illinois has prioritized this issue and, along with [the Centers for Disease Control (CDC)], is setting national standards for reviewing and ultimately preventing these deaths."[14] Illinois continues to invest in an array of efforts to ameliorate the maternal mortality crisis, including Illinois's Maternal Infant and Early Childhood Home Visiting Program, which supports doula programs in Illinois, and the Chicago Doula Project (run by the Illinois Bureau of Maternal and Infant Health and focused on providing doulas to pregnant adolescents). The state also supports nonprofit efforts like Health Connect One's community-based doula program (which has been replicated nationwide) and the Ounce of Prevention Fund's doula training program. Illinois, like a number of other states including Oregon and New York, has also recently proposed legislation for Medicaid to cover doula services.

Chicago is home to a vibrant institutionalized WOC birthworker landscape. Its established Chicago Volunteer Doulas (CVD) program—a birth justice initiative that includes an on-call pro bono doula program to provide doula care to birthers delivering at eight of metro Chicago's hospitals—has become a training ground for many of the city's doulas. In fact, most of my interlocutors secured the practice hours that are a prerequisite for some—but not all—doula certifications through CVD. CVD's commitment to serving vulnerable populations, and its new doula training program for incarcerated women at Logan Correctional Facility, makes it an organization that largely serves WOC clients and that includes a number of WOC doulas, even in its leadership. The city is also home to the Chicago Birthworks Collective, an agency founded in 2018 by a WOC mother and daughter committed to providing birth care to families of color, and to Healthy Moms and Babies—a program run by the Cook County Sheriff's Justice Institute—which offers doula services to incarcerated women in Chicago.[15] The WOC birthwork community, then, contains a sizable group of doulas, herbalists, childbirth educators, peer lactation consultants, certified lactation consultants, and reiki practitioners who collaborate—and, at times, compete—to safeguard Black life *even as* these practitioners have different relationships to credentialization and certification, to professionalization and training.

For the doulas whom I interviewed, the specificity of practicing birthwork in Chicago, a city described as "basically inventing modern segregation" and as marked by equally intense segregated patterns of gun violence, was paramount to how they described the urgency of their work.[16] Lauren explicitly described birthwork as a form of Black life-giving staged in the face of Chicago's gun epidemic. As she described her training, she noted, "We ended the doula training with pneumatics gunshot wound training. And I remember having a deep conversation with my husband and one of my friends about how knowing how to potentially save someone from a gunshot wound was related to birth. It's, like, it's just so many things." For Lauren, being a Black doula practicing birthwork in Chicago required both delivering babies and treating gunshot wounds as practices of caring for Black life.[17] To provide context, 530 people were murdered in Chicago in 2018, and while those numbers had fallen from 781 murders in 2016,[18] Chicago was represented in national media (including by Donald Trump who, in 2017, threatened to "send in the feds" to the city to end the "carnage") as marred by urban violence.[19] So, care for the Black maternal body was imagined as a kind of synecdoche for care of the Black community, precisely because the birthing Black body was seen, in and of itself, as making Black social life possible.

My interviews also unfolded against a landscape where Jackson Park Hospital— one of the South Side's community hospitals that often used the motto "here to stay and to serve"—was threatening to shut down its obstetrics unit. While the rumors about Jackson Park's closure started intensifying in 2018—the same year the hospital advocated that women in the South Shore neighborhood "would benefit from increased access to maternal care"—it was not until 2019 that the hospital's board unanimously voted to shut the maternity ward because of low birth numbers (only 180 babies were delivered at the hospital each year, compared to 2,615 deliveries at University of Chicago Medical Center).[20] Some Jackson Park nurses protested the decision to close the unit, arguing that because 99 percent of deliveries at the hospital were by Black mothers, the shuttering of the maternity ward would "only exacerbate the maternal health crisis between 57th and 93rd Streets."[21] The closure of the maternity ward at Jackson Park was part of a larger trend in Chicago where smaller obstetrics units at community hospitals were closing because of falling birth rates throughout the state and because of affluent patients' preferences for deliveries at women's centers and research hospitals (Northwestern Medicine Women's Hospital, a research hospital in the city center, attracts women from across the metropolitan area and has boasted annual increases in its delivery rates).[22] Christie Lawrence emphasizes that the closure of obstetric units is never race-blind and asserts, "The closure of these hospitals/obstetric units will cause a greater disparity for Black mothers and their babies and further complicate access to care issues. The health of a mother and child need not be predetermined by their zip code. Yet, many of these facilities are in communities disproportionately affecting the care to African American patients."[23] The closure of Jackson Park's maternity ward—because of the relatively low number of babies actually delivered there—was seen as a symbol of precisely the paradox that marked the present: an ongoing rhetorical attention to Black maternal health and the simultaneous systemic divestment from institutions that serve Black mothers. In this context—one marked by the materiality of gun violence and the disappearance of community-based hospitals serving Black mothers—WOC doulas described their work in the room as a necessary response to a state of emergency.

*In the Room*

If the first chapter examined the Black breastfeeding gap as one of the crises swirling around Black maternal health, this chapter attends to another: Black infant and maternal mortality. The United States is known for its poor maternal health outcomes. As nations around the world have seen vast improvements in maternal health, US maternal mortality rates have actually increased. A study by the Commonwealth Fund compared high-income countries, including the United States, Canada, France, Germany, the United Kingdom, and Australia, and found that US women had the highest rate of maternal mortality, dying at a rate of 14 deaths per 100,000 births (the CDC reports the rate to be even higher: 18 deaths per 100,000).[24] US Black women die at a much higher rate, 40 per 100,000, and the CDC's analysis of pregnancy-related deaths found that Black women were 3.3 times more likely than white women to die from a pregnancy-related death.[25] Much of the attention to the maternal mortality crisis has focused on mapping disparity at local and state levels, often even with a granular attention to the sites—cities and hospitals—that have become death-worlds for Black mothers and infants. In this sense, the materiality of crisis is described through data collection and metrics that enable public health scholars and activists to map the topography of Black maternal death.

But the crisis is also described through a taxonomy of violence that calls attention to the space of the room as a primal site of antiBlack misogynistic violence that WOC doulas mitigate. WOC doulas and birthworkers have been instrumental in developing and circulating terms that describe the violence of the room, and of institutionalized medicine, and thus make clear the necessity of their intervention, the life-saving work of doulas. In other words, the taxonomy of violence that birthworkers mobilize also stands as an argument for the urgency of the work itself. In this section, I sit with the variety of terms that circulate to map and describe violence and to advocate for the essential labor of doulas. I see this taxonomy as a way of both establishing the particular violence of institutionalized medical spaces (and thus, at times, arguing for divesting from institutional medical spaces for perinatal bodies) and arguing for the urgency of the presence of a bodyguard in the room. When I ask Lynda to tell me about the space of the room and how she positions herself in it, she tells me the following story:

> I had a birth with a teen mom. This was at a hospital I had never been to, and it was the nurse's first shift. This was a new nurse. It was her first day. This was a younger mom, she had her mom, grandma, and her boyfriend with her.... The nurse was telling her, "Okay, you can start pushing," and she [the nurse] left the room. She *left*. It was me, the mom in the bed, the boyfriend, the grandma who was sitting behind me, and then a student nurse standing over there in the corner.
>
> And she told her to start pushing, I was, like, "Well, why did she just leave?" And then I was, like, from what I know, first-time moms do take a long time so maybe we're okay here. Well, the mom kept pushing, she didn't stop, and then I looked, and she was bearing down, the baby was coming. I looked at the student nurse, and I looked down at the mom. You could see the hair and I was, like, "Go get somebody, go get anybody." The way that the mom was positioned, I knew if she delivered her baby, the baby would've been probably paralyzed or something. The student just looked shocked, I was, like, "I don't care you need to go, get somebody else." And so the baby was delivered in another couple of minutes, and I was, like, had I not been there or told this mom to lay back because I'm kind of worried about your position, that baby would've come out and most likely have been paralyzed or fallen on the floor.

Lynda's account of the room is of institutionalized neglect, which can manifest itself with deathly consequences. She described how younger moms, particularly younger Black mothers—often designated as "teen moms"—are treated with a particularly dangerous form of disregard that makes the work of a doula even more urgent and even more high stakes. This is also, of course, an account of Lynda's necessary work—"had I not been there," she reminded me, to guard her client, the hospital could have left the mother and her child for dead. This is birthwork in a time of emergency.

The temporality of crisis has been bolstered by the detailed taxonomy of birth violence that birthworkers have generated and proliferated, a vocabulary for describing the forms of trauma that have unfolded around seemingly normative birthing experiences and the particular and intensified forms of harm that Black mothers experience. As Lauren Berlant suggests, the production of a taxonomy of violence is unfolding in myriad intellectual and political spaces.[26] She notes, "We are fighting for new ways to care about, redress, and refuse the reproduction of the ordinary of violence."[27] While I think desires for care and recognition partially underpin the elasticity of the term *violence*—at least in "identity knowledge" fields like Black studies and women's studies—mapping violence's expansive territory, at least in the context of birth, has worked both to secure the rhetoric of crisis, endlessly yoking Black women's bodies to trauma and pain, and to make clear the necessary "foot soldier" work of doulas.[28] Charting the routinization of violence—how it is intrinsic to medicalized birthing experiences—has made Black women's birthing experiences the paradigmatic example of obstetric violence.

While birthworkers have developed various terms to describe particular forms of birth violence, including *trauma, medical apartheid, medical racism, birth rape,* and *birth injustice,* in recent years, the term *obstetric violence* has circulated among birthworkers, birth justice advocates, and scholars working on race and reproduction as a tool to capture myriad forms of birthing trauma.[29] As a term, *obstetric violence* describes and aggregates the "phenomenon of mistreatment during childbirth" from "less dramatic forms of subtle humiliation to coercion, unconsented clinical care, and more extreme instances of verbal and physical abuse."[30] Elizabeth Kukura suggests that obstetric violence is sufficiently capacious to describe and contest forms of physical, mental, and spiritual abuse; discrimination; practices of coercion; and experiences of disrespect. Importantly, the feminist deployment of obstetric violence highlights violence as the condition of the ordinary where, as Emily Varnam notes, "You pretty much one percent of the time see women getting the care that is appropriate for them. Whether that's from lack of evidence-based care or lack of compassion, or lack of respect for the human race, you pretty much just never see care that feels appropriate. Either it's how they're spoken to, or nonconsensual vaginal exams. It's nonconsensual episiotomy or coercion, or bullying, or scare tactics."[31]

While the term *obstetric violence* currently circulates in US feminist birthing circles and among WOC birthworkers to describe the trauma Black women's bodies bear in the room, it has a particular juridical history outside of the United States. In 2004, Argentina granted women the right to a "humanized" birthing experience and offered a legal guarantee of the right to be treated "respectfully" throughout pregnancy and childbirth.[32] Three years later, Venezuela recognized obstetric violence as a form of violence that law could redress. The Organic Law on the Right of Women to a Life Free of Violence defined obstetric violence as "the appropriation of the body and reproductive processes of women by health personnel, which is expressed as dehumanized treatment, an abuse of medication, and to convert the natural processes into pathological ones, bringing with it loss of autonomy and the ability to decide freely about their bodies and sexuality, negatively impacting the quality of life of women."[33] The law criminalizes nonconsensual C-sections and inductions performed without informed and voluntary consent, and it roots itself not in tort law but in human rights law, thus casting injuries as forms of gender-based violence. This juridical conception of obstetric violence, which offers both a recognition of harm and a form of redress, has been expanded by activist groups. In Spain, for example, the Left group La Revolución de las Rosas defines obstetric violence broadly to include "the act of disregarding the spontaneity, the positions, the rhythms and the time labor requires in order to progress normally when there is no need for intervention."[34] Even as the term *obstetric violence* has provided a framework for activists to describe normalized violence and for the state to, at the least, offer a gesture toward remedying that violence, the term has also become a site of anxiety for physicians in Latin America, with the Federal Council on Medicine in Brazil describing the term as "an assault on the medicine and specialty of gynecology and obstetrics, contrary to established scientific knowledge, reducing the safety and efficiency of good care and ethical practice."[35]

In recent years, obstetric violence has become a rhetorical and political touchstone for WOC doulas who use it to describe the field in which they seek to intervene, one where obstetric medicine, as practiced, is itself constitutive of the field of violence.[36] Davis develops the term *obstetric racism*—a fusion of obstetric violence and medical racism—which she argues constitutes "a form of gender-based violence experienced by people giving birth who are subjected to acts of violence that result in their being subordinated *because* they are obstetric patients.... Obstetric violence includes dehumanizing treatment and medical abuse such as birth rape, or violations experienced during childbearing."[37] Racial disparities in birthing experiences, outcomes, mortality, and postpartum health suggest that Black women's perinatal experiences are the quintessential case of obstetric violence, most deeply and explicitly indicative of the violence of birth. The presence of a doula's body in the delivery room is intended to shield Black women's bodies from the violence that is routinely inflicted on them. One Washington, DC–based doula, Ravae Sinclair, noted that her Black clients increasingly view the labor of a doula to be managing medical racism. She describes her clients' concerns as "I want one day—me bringing my innocent child into the world—to not be infused with racism, with me having the burden of being Black. I don't want to have to manage anybody else's baggage, because what I am managing is labor, which is big."[38] WOC doulas, then, increasingly position themselves as actively protecting Black life from discrimination and death, and Black birthing mothers are increasingly positioned as requiring a birth advocate to ensure that they leave hospitals alive.[39]

Obstetric violence can take the form of controlling information or rushing mothers into medical decisions, and some doulas underscored that the hurried temporality of obstetric care should itself be understood as a form of violence. Many doulas emphasized that medicalized spaces traffic in fear and often compel mothers to opt for increased medical intervention out of a sense of impending danger or threat. Imani described a birthing experience marked by the temporality of rushing:

> The nurse tried to boss my client around. Just like "You need to do this," "You're not advancing, you need Pitocin, you need this, you need this." And basically telling her things like, "If you don't do this, are you willing to risk you baby's life?" And these type of things were causing the blood pressure to go up—which then made the baby's heartbeat go up. So then it was the proof that something needed to happen. So it was, like, "Oh, my gosh, well, I won't let anything happen to my baby." I had to say, "Hey, take fifteen minutes, your baby's fine, take fifteen minutes." I teach her how to read the chart, these are when you're having contractions, this is the baby's heartbeat, this is what's normal, this is when you need to be alarmed. Because clearly anyone can tell you anything. I just remember thinking this is the reason why so many births end up the way that they do.

Doulas emphasized that the combination of wielding medical authority and rushing mothers into decisions is precisely why so many birth outcomes "end up the way that they do." As PJ noted, "All I see in the hospital is obstetric violence—intrusive providers, supposedly medical decisions made out of fear or wanting profits or just being rushed. Nobody is listening to the mom. You come out of there feeling bruised." The work of the doula, then, is to offer a different kind of temporality—one that not only sits with the nonlinearity of birth with patience but also refuses the rushed timeframe of medical capitalism, which often wields fear and a threat of illness or death to compel mothers to further medicalize their experiences of labor and delivery.

The term *birth rape* has also circulated among some birth activists—particularly in popular writing—to foreground, much as feminist labor around sexual violence has, the pervasiveness of misogynistic abuse and medicine's toleration of this violence. Scott Dunlop defines birth rape as "happening when a medical professional uses forced or unnecessary procedures in order to facilitate a birth, without the mother's consent (or even in direct contradiction of her wishes). It could be the insertion of forceps into the woman's birth canal, or, as shocking as it sounds—as bad as the experience of a mom who was drugged with general anesthetic and given a C-Section without even being aware that it was being done."[40] For Dunlop, nonconsent marks experiences of birth rape. For other writers, like Zion Lights, birth rape describes experiences of disrespect and disempowerment. Lights writes, "The term 'birth rape,' [is] used by women whose bodies are treated like machines when they are most vulnerable to other people's wills. Labouring women whose minds and wishes are not respected or consulted. The power is taken from mum's hands to gloved hands the second you enter the ward, and you cannot take it back."[41] The mobilization of the term *birth rape* has generated significant debate in popular feminist writing about the elasticity of the term *rape* and the potential harm that might inflict on sexual assault survivors.[42] What *birth rape*—and the debates that have swirled around it—has aspired to do is to help people view birthing violence as a form of gendered terror, both ordinary and ubiquitous, as both prevalent and wholly escaping legal redress or response because of the power dynamics involved.

For some doulas, birth violence often unfolds as institutionalized medicine's willful blindness to women's experiences of sexual assault and trauma and as a prioritization of protocols over patients' needs. Institutionalized medicine's inability to reckon with the realities of sexual trauma for many women, and with how that trauma might be triggered or reactivated by medical personnel, reveals the cruelty of medical bureaucracy. Lynda described the end of a young mother's delivery, when the placenta was delivered:

> The resident was like, we have to check you because of the bleeding. . . . I'm standing with her [the patient] and obviously trying to keep my face on, and finally they were checking her and she was saying, "No, stop, no, stop, no, stop!" They didn't, so I immediately was, like, what am I going to do in this situation, I know she is a survivor, so she's had previous trauma, what can I do? They stopped checking her and said, okay, we have to check again, and I immediately, before they could touch her again, I stepped in and I said, "Okay, are you ready for them to check you again?" I kind of watched them look at me, and I was, like, I don't really care what you think right now, she's telling you, "No, stop, no."

For Lynda, and many other doulas, explicitly talking to clients about experiences of sexual violence and how those histories might shape labor and delivery is a crucial part of doulas' radical work. Standing between patient-survivors and medical staff to advocate for the bodily integrity of patients—even when it contradicts medical protocol—is the life-affirming work of doulas. Many WOC doulas told me that it is precisely their willingness to challenge protocol that can make them unwelcome in the room. Many reported tensions with doctors, and even with nurses and midwives, because of a sense that they will disruptively name violence that unfolds under the banner of medical practice. Imani described one midwife who saw her enter the room and said, simply, "I hope you're not gonna be burning sage in here," casting doulas as mystical practitioners rather than trained professionals.

In many ways, the elaborate taxonomy of violence is part of a larger feminist critique of routine violence and describes how, in the context of medicalized birthing, gendered and racialized violence can be "business as usual." These taxonomies make critical linkages between various normalized practices, suggesting that they are all undergirded by structural inequity. Davis describes some of these forms of noncare, including "neglect, lack of information, dismissiveness, disrespect, and interventions without explanation."[43] This effort also attempts to think about a wide range of practices—including trauma, nonconsent, noncare, and feelings of being unseen—as rightfully falling under the auspices of the violent. Yet it is crucial to note that the taxonomy of violence that feminist birthworkers have mapped—and constructed institutional remedies around—takes Black women's bodies and experiences as a rhetorical and discursive starting point, seeing the birthing traumas that Black women experience as emblematic of the very worst kind of birth violence that must be ameliorated. Arguments for the necessity of doulas (which often take the form of the increasingly popular slogan "everyone deserves a doula") are often rhetorically rooted in the particular urgency of doulas for Black women, where the doula's necessity is made visible precisely because of the threat of Black maternal mortality.[44]

As feminists labor to imagine and pursue forms of birthing justice, this complex taxonomy of violence is underpinned by multiple desires, including longings for juridical recognition (and redress) for birthing injuries, shifting conceptions of medicine that make birthing a space for more compassionate and humane forms of being-together, and by a cultural recognition of birth as a profound site of psychic pain and institutional injury. Here we see the paradoxes of feminist institutional practices: the labor of naming trauma is both descriptive (e.g., an attempt to do justice to birthing experiences) and normative (e.g., an attempt to seek a specific juridical remedy); it is both critical of the language of rights because of a commitment to reproductive justice frameworks that refuse the atomizing labor of rights discourse, and it also desperately clings to the language of rights to secure some modicum of legal protection for birth freedom. This taxonomy of violence—one which has been perfected by describing the particular experiences of Black mothers—has also worked to prove indispensable the labor of doulas. In tethering birth and trauma, and in centering the necessary maternal labor of actively crafting a nontraumatic birth, doulas have made the case for their own urgency, for their necessity in creating a birthing space marked by (counter)ethics of togetherness, intimacy, and deep patience with the temporality and spiritual components of birth. Doulas, thus, construct themselves as one of the antidotes to birth violence, as precisely the bodies required to envision a different kind of birthing experience that does justice to birth's imagined transformative capacity and that centers bodily autonomy and racial justice at the heart of birthing experiences.

The feminist birthing industry has performed its work, at least in part, by offering a rich vocabulary for describing a set of injurious practices, and it has made *violence* an elastic term that captures a variety of ordinary birthing experiences and practices. At times, this mapping has taken the form of a desire for a certain form of redress—the Latin American obstetric violence movement has organized as a radical demand for law to penalize medical staff that disregard birthing mothers' bodily autonomy and sexual integrity. At times, this mapping is rhetorical work, with terms like *birth rape* making visible the violence of the normative birthing experience, the prevalence of a culture of birth trauma and violence. Ultimately, this feminist attempt to map the crisis has made visible the conditions of the ordinary as constitutive of crisis by shoring up visions of Black women as the quintessentially violated bodies and of WOC doulas as performing indispensable life-affirming labor. This vision of vulnerable Black maternal flesh has become institutionalized in birthwork and is increasingly installed in state efforts to partially support doulas as the solution to Black maternal and infant mortality.

*Paraprofessional Foot Soldiers*

"We began," Samantha told me when I asked her about her doula training, "by talking about how we were called to the work. Sometimes the calling comes in your dreams." Her training ended with newly minted doulas washing each other's feet, a profound symbol of birthwork as a commitment to service. She described how her trainer also required each "sister" to offer "words of praise" for another at the completion of the two-day course. For Samantha, the training focused on an ethos of service that posited birthwork as a commitment to life was an urgent introduction to the practice of being in the room. What should the training be for those who are charged with the responsibility of saving Black mothers' lives? What preparation is required to be a foot soldier? And if the state enlists—or even recruits—these foot soldiers, how involved should it be in their training?

Though my interlocutors all identified as birth doulas, they labored under vastly different conditions: one works full-time as a doula in an agency she runs with two business partners; two work full-time through a combination of solo practice and agency work; and all of the other doulas are engaged in part-time birthwork and other full-time work, generally in feminized fields like childcare.[45] Moreover, the number of births they each had attended and the amount of training they each had completed varied significantly, and the nature of their trainings was quite different, with some extensively knowledgeable about the physiology of birth and others describing training rooted in the spiritual aspects of birth. I take this variation in training, certification, and experience as evidence of the paraprofessionalism of doula work, and I argue that the paraprofessionalism of the work—its capacity to evade standardization—is precisely what enables many doulas to describe their labor as radical, fugitive, and politically transformative. Indeed, I want to sit both with how doulas' labor is hailed as urgent, necessary, and life-saving *and* with how it is unregulated, with doulas' training experiences vastly differing. In highlighting the paraprofessionalism of the field, I am interested *both* in how WOC doulas flag this as a deeply political and even fugitive component of their work *and* in what it means for the state to rhetorically invest in Black mothers' health by encouraging care administered by largely unregulated actors.

When I use the term *paraprofessional*, I do not mean it as a valuation (or devaluation) of the tremendous physical, emotional, and spiritual work that doulas perform as advocates, healers, guides, witnesses, and travelers (to use a few of the terms doulas deployed to describe their labor). Instead, I mean it to describe the lack of regulation and organization of a birthing profession that is increasingly hailed as the touchstone of reproductive justice and as precisely the birthing innovation that will save Black women and children's lives. *Paraprofessionalism* describes the "low-tech" nature of doulas' work (indeed, one doula described her approach as "low tech, high touch"), which emphasizes being-together as a radical birth practice.[46] I also capture the fact that while doulas emphasize that they are not medical practitioners and often define themselves against conventional medical institutions, they remain actors who perform the majority of their labor in medicalized spaces (namely, hospitals) and alongside workers whose professions are not at all paraprofessional, including midwives, lactation consultants, nurses, and doctors. Doulas' capacities to reside in medical spaces while maintaining minimal (if any) medical training can make murky the relationship between birthwork and medical care, a murkiness that is perhaps most profound—and potentially most dangerous—for birthing mothers who are at once reminded that doulas are not medical professionals, and yet they primarily encounter doulas in medical settings. While the "low-tech" nature of doula work is often celebrated as what allows it to be a fugitive form of birth justice, it also makes getting an account of the profession challenging. With at least four major training organizations offering doula certifications in the United States, and hundreds of community-based programs nationwide, it is virtually impossible to get a complete account of the number of people laboring as doulas or to have a systematic accounting of the training that those laborers have. Again, for some doulas it is this refusal to be counted that constitutes the kind of fugitive birth labor that doulas perform, that makes the profession powerful, transgressive, and ultimately radical.

All of the doulas I interviewed had participated in a two- or three-day intensive training, though the content of that training varied tremendously. Some classes are led by formal organizations like Doulas of North America (DONA), Childbirth and Postpartum Professional Association (CAPPA), ToLabor, or ProDoula; others are facilitated by community organizations or even by campus initiatives specifically designed to train WOC doulas. Most of the doulas I interviewed identified strongly with their training institution, particularly those who had elected community-based doula trainings, which were often imagined to index a commitment to WOC birthing bodies. For most doulas, the training was an experience of self-transformation, community building, and solidarity more than an orientation to the physiology of labor or the physical experience of birth. Faith, for example, described her training as organized around "spiritual and emotional connection," and she noted that it transformed a group of strangers into "doula sisters," women she still texts every day to discuss challenging births, to share "doula stories," and to exchange "affirming messages." Faith described her "doula sisters" as her most attentive and committed friends, an "army of Black women" who talk about birth but who also send each other daily affirmations as a form of mutual support. She noted, "You can read every book but it's really just learning about compassion. I think you have to have it in you. You can read anything on doula work you want but it's about having compassion." In many ways, Faith suggested that a robust doula training should not focus on "book-learning," but should instead center ethics of witnessing and empathy, even as she paradoxically noted that a doula's most important trait—compassion—cannot be learned. Morgan described her training as "centered in traditional Black practices, from the Black midwives." She noted,

> It was just very centered in Blackness, it was very centered in traditional Black practices that have gotten lost throughout time, from when the granny midwives would come from Africa and bring a lot of those practices here. We are the women who have birthed an entire country. We have raised white babies, we birthed white babies. We birthed our own babies. So really centered in that practice, a lot of the herbal remedies that are used, the rituals that are done. We started every day with rituals to chant, we ended in a ceremony, it was very intentional. Everything about it was intentional, it was very centered in tradition and Blackness and that's what I wanted to learn. That's where I found traditional Black practices.

For Morgan, doula training was a return to a kind of native practice and a recognition of Black women's long and powerful birthing history.

Perhaps most controversial was the question of how much training should focus on the business of birthwork. A number of doulas mentioned that one of the profession's main organizations—the for-profit ProDoula—had become far too focused on encouraging doulas to organize efficient and viable businesses and had lost sight of the compassionate ethics at the heart of birthwork (paradoxically, this concern was often voiced by doulas who reported that they had not found a way to make birthwork a viable full-time profession).[47] Indeed, one doula who described a sense of "competition" in the Chicago doula community noted that business-focused trainings were the main source of divisiveness among birthworkers. ProDoula's mission to help doulas become "entrepreneurs" and to "turn passion into a paycheck" was regularly mentioned by doulas as a source of anxiety and confusion. ProDoula, with its insistence that it "wants you to be fulfilled, emotionally and financially by this rewarding career," distinguishes itself from other doula certification programs by its heavy emphasis on professionalization and its member benefits, which include discounted printing, discounted liability insurance, and access to networking events. In its investment in making birthwork a viable full-time profession for its members and its commitment to transforming doulas into entrepreneurs, the organization is often cast as making birthwork a neoliberal business endeavor. Moreover, the organization's emphasis on doulas as workers often led its founder, Randy Patterson, to critique volunteer doula initiatives—the pro bono initiatives most closely associated with birth justice, and most often staffed by WOC—as undermining the economic viability of the profession by discounting birthworkers' labor. Indeed, the WOC doulas I spoke to all participated in the city's volunteer doula program, and they found it to be both a valuable form of service that enabled them to serve precisely the communities with whom they identified and an important training ground that allowed them to attend the number of births required to earn formal accreditation if they were seeking it.[48]

Despite WOC doulas' critiques of corporate logics entering birthwork, some doulas noted the importance of professionalization to make possible the birthing togetherness that doulas promise. Jasmine described DONA's certification as a "bit of a process" but felt it was ultimately appealing because "I want to be accessible to multiple moms and partners. The credentials look nice, you put the abbreviation next to your name." For Jasmine, the "abbreviations" were imagined as something that would appeal to a wider clientele and might even enable her to make birthwork a viable profession. Similarly, Joanne noted that "DONA is anytime you look anywhere, attached to hospitals, even agencies. Everyone tells you they have DONA." The notion of DONA as the gold standard for birthworkers made the credentializing process appealing for some doulas, and it was imagined to offer more professional opportunities. Finally, Jasmine also insisted that the DONA certification made her easier to find. While doulas often advertise on websites like doulamatch.com, professional organizations, including DONA and ProDoula, maintain searchable databases of their members that allow clients to find local credentialized doulas with ease. My WOC doula interlocutors almost all found clients through word of mouth or through active solicitation, and Jasmine insisted that her completion of the DONA training allowed her to attract a "steadier stream" of clients.

Community-based doula trainers often set their "community" orientation against the imagined corporate logics of organizations like ProDoula. Miriam, who works at a nationally recognized community-based program, described their trainings as powerful because they "come from the people who will benefit from the learning" and because they tailor the curriculum to the needs of the community. While community-based programs are often cast as more radical than their "corporate" counterparts, it is worth noting that this particular community-based program actually demanded far more doula training than national organizations like DONA and ProDoula. There, twenty three-hour sessions covered topics including the physiology of pregnancy, stages of labor, birth processes, breastfeeding, C-sections, and infant death, as opposed to the fourteen to sixteen hours of training provided by many of the professional organizations. The community-based program emphasized its desire to train doulas to work in their own communities, yet they emphasized—in much the same vein as the bemoaned corporate models, including ProDoula—that doulas are not volunteers. Miriam said,

> From a woman-centered point of view, women are generally undervalued. And in the US, we are capitalists. The way we determine value is with money. It's not enough that you're an elder, or that you're an esteemed and talented person. If you don't get paid for that, it doesn't count. One of our central components is that the community-based doulas are employed, and preferably they are employed with a salaried living wage, not an hourly wage, not a per-contact or a per-birth wage, but with an ongoing, dependable, every two weeks or every month, the same amount you can depend on to live with, wage. So in that way we're not looking for people to be entrepreneurs or volunteers.

For Miriam, community-based doula programs must empower their trainees to become employees and must enable them to receive regular salaries. The training, then, aspires to make doula work livable for its trainees, in much the same way oftentimes-disavowed corporate programs do, even as community-based programs are often celebrated as the radical counterpart to professional organizations' trainings. Ultimately, the fight over professionalization was imagined as an index of a birthworker's politics: is birthwork simply a job, or is it an opportunity to be a guide on a mother's spiritual journey? If, as many doulas—particularly WOC doulas—indicated, one is "called" to birthwork, then what is the place of a doula's desire for a livable wage in relationship to this "calling"? And how does a doula reconcile a desire to serve vulnerable populations who might not be able to afford birthwork with her own need to survive?

If professionalization debates constituted a battle over the ethics of the work itself, doulas also debated the lack of standardization in the field. Doulas are outliers in the larger field of birthwork. Midwives and lactation consultants, the birth professions often associated with doulas, require substantial training, certification, and licensure, and many doulas note that the costs associated with meeting credentializing mandates have made those professions unavailable to WOC. Miriam, who began her career as a lactation consultant, noted the "impossibility" of finding a Black lactation consultant in Illinois because of the cost of certification and the demands that she felt had been imposed only to the benefit of the field's credentializing bodies. She noted, "Peer counseling is nonclinical, and doulas used to be like that and there was no money in it. There's still no money in breastfeeding peer counseling and there's no competition. The competition is around licensure and credentials, and now lactation consultants have a monopoly to the exclusion of other lactation support. Even so, it's peer counselors who are more effective. We actually got better outcomes with less credentials." Miriam reveals that, despite the efficacy of peer counseling, lactation consultants are privileged in the breastfeeding consultant sphere because of their elaborate and expensive credentializing. Indeed, for some doulas (including Miriam), the growing visibility of the field led to anxieties around possibilities for standardization, for uniform certification requirements that could exclude WOC, unleash further competitiveness, and make impossible what many WOC doulas I spoke to had been doing long before their training—practicing doula work. Miriam suggested that any push toward standardization would simply serve the field's professional organizations, not birthing mothers and especially not birthing Black mothers. She noted: "What happens with standardization is the one who can make the most money is the one who ends up on top. The one who has the highest credentials ends up on top. DONA was started by a group of specialists in neonatology and their friends, and DONA is still not a member-run organization, it is a certifying body that with your membership you get to maintain your certification. CAPPA is similar. . . . Making everybody ascribe to one standard is oftentimes the enemy of true equity." The threat of standardization—and even professionalization—is its erosion of "equity" and its exclusivity. Standardization undermines the field's paraprofessionalism, which, for the doulas I described, constitutes the radical promise of the field, its capacity to labor in medical spaces and subvert those logics, its capacity to bring intimacy into institutional spaces, and its insistence that physical pain can be responded to with pressure points, rebozos, and breathing together.

For those doulas who view birthwork as a calling, the field's "radical" paraprofessionalism affords them the opportunity to select clients who match their ethics, namely those who are imagined as most vulnerable to forms of birth violence. A number of WOC doulas articulated a preference for working with WOC clients or described their "pro-Black" orientation—a term Brianna used—as part of how they imagine their practice. Samantha, for example, noted that she had not worked with a white female client, and she emphatically stated, "I don't feel safe with white women." Sydney suggested that WOC and white clients come to birthwork with different agendas and aspirations and that her practice aligned with the priorities of her WOC clients. She noted, "Women of color and queer birthers need a doula for birth justice. White birthers use doulas because they want boutique birthing experiences." And Imani—who splits her work between her solo practice and laboring for an agency—described her dislike of the agency's primarily affluent white clients even as she appreciated the steadiness of the work and the consistency of the paycheck. She noted:

> She [the owner] has completely catered to people in Brownsville [a suburb]. She has catered to that demographic, that socioeconomic status. Those are the clients. Those are the attitudes about who I am, and what I am there to do. It's especially for postpartum clients. It tends to be, like, I am there for servitude. Sometimes I get lucky enough and there's a connection and people value me for my unique gifts, but mostly it's "Hey, my baby is crying. Can you do the work so I can go to sleep?" . . . With my own clients, I have only one client where we have not become friends.

One of the benefits of solo WOC doula practice, then, is the ability to eschew professional (and medical) norms of distance and to embrace the possibility of friendship and intimacy with clients. All of the WOC doulas I talked to described birthing together as the beginning of a long-lasting friendship. For many the friendships born through birth constitute the radical possibility of doula work to transform both Black mothers and Black communities more generally. Imani noted, "I see it as building that community. You have more and more people, a doula becomes your friend, your midwife becomes your friend, then you have this vast network of people who are constantly looking out and supporting you. Especially when it comes to the health disparity, because if you can have a sister come with you every time you go to the doctor . . . things are very different just having another person there." For Imani, the capacity to select Black clients allows her to nurture precisely the transformations she imagines birthing together to make possible: granting Black mothers access to a nurturing and caring "community." What the paraprofessional nature of doula work makes possible—even if not economically viable—is a racial selectivity about clients, a selectivity that allows WOC doulas to work with birthing mothers in the service of community-building and radical carework.

At the heart of the complex politics of doulas' paraprofessionalism is the elevation of doulas to medical missionaries in the face of "crisis." The state has increasingly latched on to doulas—birthworkers who labor in a largely unregulated and antistandardized field—as the solution to the problem of Black maternal and infant death. Yet the outsourcing of care to nonmedical staff (and to those who explicitly reject medicalization, as I describe in the next section) can seem a troubling solution to a problem that unfolds in medicalized spaces and that implicates institutionalized medicine. Put differently, if doulas are the bodies mobilized by the state to save Black women's lives, what does it mean that they are not required to be licensed or credentialed, that many are minimally trained? And what does it mean that the state has outsourced Black maternal and infant health to workers who are governed by their own caste system: highly paid doulas laboring in white agencies are often able to sustain full-time doula work, and Black solo practitioners generally must seek other employment to do the work they want? In posing these questions, I am not at all critical of doulas who engage in demanding physical and affective labor out of a genuine belief in the possibility of care, togetherness, and witnessing as transformative, particularly for Black mothers and children. Rather, as feminists continue to map our institutional entanglements, it is worth us rigorously interrogating what it means for the solution to what has been deemed a "crisis" in Black women's healthcare to be an increased state reliance on a politically committed group of laborers who are organized, at least at times, around a rejection of formal certifications and professionalism staged in the name of feminism and Left politics. We might, then, ask how the state's embrace of doulas' fugitive and paraprofessional practices might actually stand as evidence of the state's deep divestment in Black maternal health.

*The Political Aesthetics of Birth: Ruminations on Medication*

Imani described an unmedicated birth as presenting Black mothers with an unparalleled opportunity. She told me, "I'll say spiritually, if you have an unmedicated birth or a birth without a lot of intervention, you get to see, probably for the first time for a lot of people, how your body kind of can come through for you." If doulas' collective labor can produce a healthy birth that makes possible Black life, doulas often share a sense that *how* birth unfolds—with (or without) medication, with (or without) other forms of medical intervention—indexes something about the birth's capacity to produce social and political meaning for Black mothers, Black families, and Black communities. In this section, I move from the paraprofessionalization of the field and its relationship to doulas' social justice projects to the rhetoric surrounding the birthing event itself and its relationship to doulas' collective conceptions and productions of "good" birthing experiences. While I focus here on doulas' particular preoccupation with unmedicated births, I should note that the feminist birthing industry has produced an elaborate taxonomy of good (and bad) births, and "good" births include the highly celebrated VBAC (vaginal birth after cesarean), unmedicated births, and long births (which I call "slow birthing" in other work), and the C-section is cast as the paradigmatic "bad" birthing experience, often because C-sections are presumed to be unwanted. Unmedicated births are often imagined as the touchstone of doula-led birthing, even if not all doula-facilitated births are unmedicated. While most doulas used the terms *medicated* and *unmedicated* to describe birthing experiences, a few still used the term *natural* interchangeably with *unmedicated*, capturing a collectively held perception that unmedicated births are the hallmark of the body's "natural" state. Indeed, all doulas emphasized a desire to treat pregnancy not as a time of unwellness that warrants medical intervention but as a "natural" part of a birther's life, one that should be treated with minimal medical intervention and with a deep respect for the body's inherent birthing process. As Davis suggests, "We might also consider reframing pregnancy so that is viewed not only as a risk but as a life event—unless, of course there is an actual risk."[49] The idea that aligning pregnancy with risk makes it dangerously enmeshed with medicalization leads to the concept of an unmedicated birth as an imagined site of safety.

While an unmedicated birth was the preference of every doula I interviewed, the rationale undergirding this preference was disputed. For some, an antimedicalization politic unfolded as a critique of medical capitalism that grounds itself in an insistence on granting birthers complete autonomy over the birthing process. The violence of medical temporality inflicts itself on maternal flesh in the forms of epidurals and compulsory C-sections and by a refusal to simply let birthing bodies birth in their own time. At other times, the preference for unmedicated birth was rooted in a desire for the spiritual transformation of Black mothers, and thus Black communities, a transformation that was imagined to be made possible only through "natural" birthing methods. In these cases, the preference for unmedicated births couched as a political commitment to togetherness—to a radical patience with the time required to let maternal bodies labor without intervention—actually contained an aesthetic preference as well. "Natural" birthing was thought to produce more authentic and more "natural" forms of Black motherhood.

WOC doulas often cast the medicalization of pregnancy and labor as a particular kind of obstetric violence inflicted on Black women that seeks to regulate and discipline Black women's reproductivity. Brianna described how her doula practice is shaped by her own traumatic birthing experiences. She said, "I went with the midwives and they were a good experience, but the midwife kept asking the same question. I got to wondering do you ask all of them that, about birth control, about a hysterectomy, about permanent birth control. I told you no and you keep asking me. I told her I'm getting offended because you keep asking me and I keep telling you no. Do you ask white women that all the time? I'm only on baby #2." For Brianna, it is the medicalization of pregnancy and labor, the institutionalization of medical authority, that allows medical staff to encourage women of color to seek "permanent" birth control and that permits doctors to police what she called her "plus size, Black woman body." This labor unfolds as simply offering medical advice. Her "pro-Black" stance requires an antimedicalization stance since it is medicine that is the site of antiBlack misogynist violence, the space that seeks to curtail Black women's reproductive freedom.

For other WOC doulas, critiques of medicalized births are also criticisms of the violence inherent within medicalized spaces. Imani noted that she encouraged all of her WOC clients to "seriously consider" birthing at home, and she described how her decision to deliver at home was shaped by experiences of medical racism:

> I just started to play back every experience besides when I was a child—as an independent person—every experience I've had at a doctor's office. It was never good. And I think they made assumptions about me, maybe because I look so young. They made assumptions. You don't know anything. Also you're Black. I was just, like, with all of that plus everything I had researched about infant and maternal mortality in the Black population, I thought I don't want to chance it. I feel like my chances are higher if—people thought it was risky to be just, like, I'm having my baby at home. . . . What's risky is for me to go in a place where I know I won't be respected.

For Imani, home is cast as a site of Black women's safety and control, a place of autonomy and respect, and the hospital as a space of risk, of racial and gendered violence, a death-world where a Black mother has to guard her unborn child and her own body's health. In this formulation, the myriad ways that home itself can also be a space of violence are effaced, and histories of Black women—and women generally—dying at home during birth are also erased in the service of making clear the ubiquity and trauma of institutional medical violence. Put differently, home birthing is imagined as a strategy of risk mitigation for Black women, one that suggests that the possibility of Black survival hinges on the physical space in which birthing unfolds.

For other WOC doulas, an antimedicalization stance constitutes a critique of medical temporality and medical capitalism. Sydney described conventional medicine as undergirded by an attempt to place all births on a normative timeline that birthing bodies simply refuse. She noted, "Doctors and nurses—with the exception of midwives—just think of all the things that can go wrong, and they preemptively treat it versus letting things happen naturally in their own time.... Physicians have time limits, they are taught that birth has to happen this particular way in a particular time frame. If you are past your due date, you have to have an induction." Here, medical time is imagined as a structure of discipline, a normalizing device that seeks to align birthing bodies with constructed conceptions of time. Moreover, some doulas suggested that the hypermedicalization of birth allows doctors (and insurance companies) to earn money. Epidurals, painkillers, and other drugs are additional items billed to patients that enable doctors and hospitals to additionally profit from births. Brianna noted that her own birthing experience taught her to see "dollar signs everywhere," with each pill, procedure, and expert opinion wearing a price tag that she would ultimately bear. That many doulas also charge money for their labor is, of course, another tension undergirding birthwork's antimedicalization and anticapitalist worldview. Doulas never cast their own needs—or desires—for an income to sustain a livable life as part of "medical capitalism."

This same critique of medicalization often unfolded as a spiritual one, an analysis of unmedicated birth as a rich opportunity for Black mothers' self-discovery. For some doulas, medicated pregnancies rob mothers of an experience to recognize unknown strength, grace, or endurance. Imani said, "If you have an unmedicated birth, or a birth without a lot of interventions, you get to see probably for the first time how your body can come through for you. Sometimes people compare it to running a marathon.... Without medications, you can experience that and when you're showing up against a challenge, when your body shows up, and it's completely without your thought, it builds this level of trust in something that's unseen and something you can't touch."

Medicalization forecloses an important opportunity for mothers to recognize their body's inherent strength, to develop a kind of faith in "something that's unseen." For Imani, this potential for transformation through pain is even more important for Black mothers, since, as she notes, "If you can birth your baby, and you feel like everything this baby needs, I got. I can do it. That changes the way you parent, it changes your family structure, it changes the way people's children grow up. It's for the mom, it's for the baby, it's for the community to be fully empowered." Unmedicated births, then, empower Black mothers to mother differently, with a fundamental sense of their own capacity and with a deep regard for their embodied strength and wisdom. For Imani, the revelation of internal strength that unmedicated births afford Black mothers engenders "empowered" Black communities. Thus, unmedicated births serve not simply Black mothers (and their infants) but Black communities more generally, acting as a larger catalyst for urgent forms of togetherness waged in the face of myriad forms of violence that threaten Black life.

Unmedicated births serve various kinds of aesthetic and political work for WOC doulas. The preference for unmedicated births is often articulated as saving Black women from the "violence" of medical intervention and even from the "violence" of the hospital—the scene of risk. Yet unmedicated births are often hailed because of their transformative capacity for Black mothers and for Black communities and thus are seen as a gateway into a different kind of sociality and into maternal practices rooted in strength, endurance, and internal reserve. For some doulas, the experience of enduring pain and coming through it stands as a metaphor for the kinds of emotional and psychic reserves required of Black mothers generally, and thus unmedicated birth is a kind of metaphor and training ground for the faith in what "can't be seen," precisely the kind of faith that mothering in the midst of crisis requires. In this regard, unmedicated birth is cast as a crucial preparation for Black motherhood and as a central metaphor for Black mothering in crisis.

## A Birth Like No Other Birth

While WOC doulas often described their labor in the room as essential, much of their capacity to shape the room and its outcomes emerges from relationships that doulas form with clients before delivery. It has become standard practice among doulas to meet clients at least once, and usually twice, before labor, to develop a rapport before delivery and to discuss what birthers desire from their birthing experiences. Here, desires are about far more than a completed birth but include wishes about how birth unfolds (with or without medication) and how babies and mothers are treated in the postpartum period. For some WOC doulas, the investment in lengthy and often intimate conversations *before* being in the room together suggests the importance of honoring the distinctiveness and exceptionality of each birth, while others emphasize that birthing is an experience that confounds discourses of exceptionality and that produces Black communion.

If birth is a moment of intense self-discovery, many doulas advocate that their clients prepare for birth by imagining what they want for their "birthing experiences." They noted that these desires vary—sometimes they are explicitly medical decisions (e.g., decisions about pain medication, when to cut the umbilical cord, if the baby should receive antibiotic eye treatment) and sometimes they are preferences that seem aesthetic (e.g., birthing music, preferred lighting).[50] The increasing expectation that mothers enter labor with a detailed "birth plan," an expectation that is particularly advocated for mothers planning to have unmedicated births in medicalized settings, underscores just how much birth has been reconstituted as a space where mothers articulate their individuality. Even as doulas emphasize that a birth plan is merely a statement of wishes and not a binding medical contract, the increasing elaborateness of the template birth plans that doulas often provide clients suggests the detailed ways in which mothers are encouraged to visualize the birth they want. Crucially, then, doulas are instrumental in treating birth as a space that mothers design and in making explicit birth as a site of dense meaning-making onto which mothers should project—and hopefully realize—their aesthetic, physical, and political desires.

The feminist birthing industry is, of course, a crucial part of the production of birth as "transformative," "intimate," "sacred," and deeply personal (and, thus, customizable). This conception of birth means that doulas often emphasize how every birth is distinctive and unique, even as this exceptionality is described differently. For example, Camille noted, "Every birth is different. I learn something from every birth. We're never just going to the same hospital and dealing with the same care team. The care looks different depending on where you give birth. It looks so different depending on where you go." For Camille, the distinctiveness of each birth is rooted both in how all births present their own challenges (and thus something that can be learned from) and in the variety of forms institutionalized care can take. Camille uses extensive prepartum meetings to offer strategies for birth customization, for navigating birth's medicalization through a practice of personalization that does justice to the particularities of each birther's experience, and for attempting to mediate the many ways in which labor unfolds in unexpected ways. She described how her birthwork practice was shaped by her first pregnancy: "We were living in Oaktown and found out we were pregnant; we had no support and didn't have any family around. I was going in to my appointment with my provider feeling like why doesn't anyone want to know anything about me? This is the most intimate experience of my life and no one seems to care what I want." The notion of her birth as "the most intimate experience" of her life shaped her commitment to asking prepartum clients "intimate questions," including "if they have planned their pregnancy, how they met their partner, and then getting into the birth stuff, . . . especially if they experienced something in their past that might impact their birth experience." For Camille, the intimacy of birth requires an intimate relationship between doula and mother, a deep willingness to "care [about] what clients want" and about the personal histories that shape their relationship to birthing. These specific and distinct personal histories create the wishes that birthers bring to labor and thus are crucial for doulas to understand as they assist mothers in fashioning a transformative birth.

In this light, a pervasive critique of the medicalization that I described in the previous section is, in part, the unwillingness of medical staff to recognize individualization in all of its valences, including that bodies labor differently and according to timelines that often resist neoliberal medicine, and that the medical experience eliminates the spiritual, psychic, and intimate dimensions of birthing by presuming that all births can—or should—look the same. The work of the doula, then, becomes to ensure the particularity of every labor, insisting that medicalization of the birthing process has stripped the personal, the distinctive, the "transformative" from the work. The doula's task is to personalize labor, to help craft a particular experience (in fact, Jasmine described her key role in "producing good memories of birth, happy personal memories a mom can look back on"). The "boutique experience" that Sydney attributed to white mothers is transformed into a form of feminist, antiracist justice that ensures that all birthers—particularly Black mothers—are seen and recognized as wholly complex birthing subjects.

For other doulas, the mantra "every birth is different" and "I learn something from every birth"—phrases that multiple doulas repeated—underscored the unpredictability of birth. Despite doulas' emphasis on birth planning as a prepartum strategy, doulas underscored the importance of remembering that birth rarely unfolds according to plans and that their primary emotional work often involves helping mothers recover from disappointment when birth does not proceed according to what was desired, to what was wished for in birth plans. These "surprises" unfold in various ways, including births that proceed faster or slower than anticipated, unexpected C-sections, desired VBACs that did not happen, and sometimes death. Indeed, loss haunted my conversations with every doula, as each noted that the possibility of death that attends to every birth is precisely what makes the job hard. Imani noted:

> Last fall, I had two births—one was a premature birth. The baby was born at twenty-three weeks, she ended up passing a month later, but her mom had an emergency C-section and it was my first experience with loss. It was really hard for me, it prompted me to get more training in loss, and abortion. I wasn't prepared and I felt even though I know—and I tell people your doula isn't responsible for the outcome, she can enhance it—something in me felt responsible. . . . A month later, [a client] asked me to be her doula, and she was six months at this point and we were scheduling our first prenatal—it was around Thanksgiving—and

she was like, okay, after the holidays. And since it was the holiday, I don't celebrate, but I sent her a message and she said you must have felt me, I am in the hospital right now, I went into preterm labor and they checked the heartbeat and there's no heartbeat. The baby is gone. She had to have a stillborn.

For Imani, the unpredictability of labor includes the always-present possibility of loss that haunts each birthing experience, one that she cannot prevent and that her body's presence in the birthing room is supposed to mitigate. The notion of birth's unpredictability reveals how deeply crisis shapes doulas' work: they are the very bodies that are supposed to mitigate crisis—particularly for Black women. Death, loss, and crisis are precisely what doulas' bodily presence—the togetherness they engender—is supposed to guard against, even as they emphasize that they cannot promise any particular birth outcome.

While many doulas emphasized the particularity of each birth, for many WOC doulas, birthwork underscores the deep togetherness of all birthing bodies, interrupting a narrative of the exceptionality of birthing experiences. Imani noted, "The way that I see birth . . . is very spiritual. When I'm working with mothers I try my best to remind them that, yes, every birth is unique, but we are a part of this larger universe just like the plants, the other mammals, we are just doing our job in the chain of life. Being able to complicate the unique experience can be great." For Imani, birthing's power comes from its capacity to upset narratives of our exceptionalism, to situate mothers in a larger "chain of life." The power of the birth experience comes, then, from its capacity to remind us of our deep embeddedness in the "larger universe," our place among all living things. Imani also emphasized that birth powerfully ushers Black women into the collective experience of motherhood, one that she described as marked by the "seriousness" of dedicating one's emotional, affective, spiritual, and financial resources toward someone else. In this account, it is the ordinariness of birth that produces its radical capacity, and the labor of doulas is to urge birthing mothers to recognize birth as a moment when they are ushered into deep communion with other birthing bodies.

Doulas' prevailing notion of birth as a time of wellness is a demand to see birth as ordinary, as part of healthy bodies' functioning, even as doulas have been instrumental in recasting birth as exceptional and as particular to each birthing body. Here, the investment in birth's spiritual and self-making capacities insists that each birth is exceptional, and a doula's primary task becomes honoring maternal desires for a birth that reflects her wishes. This notion of birth as both ordinary and exceptional is a tension that WOC doulas are always navigating as they labor on behalf of Black mothers, insisting on demedicalizing and de-exceptionalizing Black women's birthing experiences while also arguing for the fundamentally revolutionary nature of birth for Black women and Black communities. It is this notion of birth as a space of wishing, as a site of projecting personal and political fantasies, as a practice that is self-consciously shaped and tailored that doulas have successfully championed as a Black feminist practice.

*Saving Yourself*

Audrey, who is trained as a social worker, told me, "I incorporate a lot of mental health services in my doula work. My first prenatal visit is usually around anxieties, a lot of concerns. Because I feel like whatever mental blockage you have, it's gonna come out in your birth, and I've seen it. If you have fears around giving birth, if you have some kind of trauma you've experienced, it really blocks you from having not a successful birth, but it makes it more difficult, it makes it more uncomfortable, you stop yourself from having that full agency to do what your body does." She emphasized, as all of my interlocutors did, that the labor of WOC doulas far exceeds "catching a baby." It includes thinking about how to hold space for Black life, considering Black tenderness and Black love as necessary preconditions for ushering life into the world, and it involves understanding connections between the gun violence epidemic, mental health services, environmental justice, and parenting.

For some doulas, encouraging Black mothers to financially invest in hiring a doula is a way of encouraging them to invest in Black life. Imani said, "Historically, we haven't really valued ourselves, much less our experience with reproduction and fertility. I really want to find ways to bring a different awareness and try to communicate to Black women, 'Hey, this is valuable and, yes, you're paying $1,000 for a doula but . . . research will show you. This is the difference in your, not only your birthing experience, but your postpartum experience and your life, when you make this small investment beforehand.'" Here, the willingness to pay a doula—though many of the WOC doulas I spoke to provide pro bono or highly discounted services to Black clients—is a way of learning to "value" oneself and one's community. And the very act of hiring a doula becomes imagined as a profound act of intergenerational care that can transform infant and maternal health outcomes.

This chapter argues that the rhetoric doulas mobilize to make visible the importance of being in the room participates in remaking the category of "Black mother," changing birthing Black women's bodies into deeply political sites. At once, WOC doulas' labor interrupts the "crisis" facing Black maternal bodies, and it uses togetherness—the proximity of maternal bodies and doula bodies in the space of labor—as a strategy of solidarity and advocacy that both exposes and remedies obstetric violence. And yet WOC doulas' work on behalf of Black mothers often reproduces the ongoing cultural tendency to endlessly yoke Black women's bodies to trauma, injury, and suffering in the service of uplifting, transforming, and aiding them, shoring up the notion of Black maternal bodies as the scene of the crisis. "Black mother" risks becoming a symbol that stands in for trauma, violence, and woundedness. WOC doulas' important carework, then, can secure the idea of Black women's bodies as in need of reform rather than radically rejecting the myriad ways Black women's bodies are called on to symbolize and make meaning, including at this moment when Black maternal bodies are rhetorically gestured to as evidence of the un-mattering of Black life.

My interest in theorizing WOC doulas' collective labor in remaking both birth and the category "Black mother" emphasizes the centrality of WOC doulas' work in feminist birthing projects and in shaping a new political birth agenda. I see the feminist birthing industry and state engagement with Black maternal bodies as fundamentally remade by Black feminist tenets of reproductive justice, birth autonomy, and freedom from obstetric violence. My efforts to track the institutional life of Black feminist practice are a refusal of the ongoing feminist romanticization of Black feminism as an anti-institutional practice and of Black women as quintessential (and always radical) outsiders. Instead, my interest is in understanding how WOC doulas' investment in antimedical logics is increasingly taken up by the state as these very doulas are called on by the state to be underresourced "foot soldiers" and as these doulas claim the resources of the state to buttress their labor. I am equally invested in understanding a moment when more and more agencies, NGOs, and state-funded projects mobilize the Black feminist language of "birth justice" and "reproductive justice" to describe work that may or may not center on eradicating birth inequities.

As doulas, particularly WOC doulas, are increasingly hailed by the state and by nonprofits as agents of birth justice as evidence of the state's commitment to eradicating maternal and infant health disparities, feminists must contend with the complexities of our ongoing institutional practice. Black feminists must struggle with this moment in which the state has invested in paraprofessional WOC birthworker labor, rather than in a wholesale reimagination of institutionalized medical practice, as the solution to Black maternal and infant mortality. I am equally invested in having Black feminists struggle with this moment in which our own tools, analytics, and investments in love, care, and spirituality have been harnessed by the state and other institutions in the creation of a low-wage carework industry populated by WOC who are often juggling other (low-wage, feminized) jobs as they engage in the "community service" of affirming Black life. This is a moment where the struggle for Black children and mothers quite literally to live is still exclusively and entirely in our own (underpaid or unpaid, largely untrained) hands. I want Black feminists to grapple with this moment in which, despite the discursive explosion of crisis rhetoric, the only bodies mobilized to care for Black women's lives are other women of color and that care is increasingly described as a "community service." This is, of course, an older (Black feminist) lesson: in 1974, the Combahee River Collective noted—or, perhaps, warned—that "the only people who care enough about us to work consistently for our liberation are us."[51] Yet my chapter probes this moment when it is institutionalized Black feminist efforts that have led to the conditions where the only bodies mobilized to care for Black women and their children are other women of color. Ultimately, despite the discursive explosion of the rhetoric of crisis, despite politicians' gesturing to the need to eradicate maternal health disparities, despite sustained popular attention to medical apartheid, it remains the case—thanks largely to efforts by WOC birthworkers to make visible the benefits of doulas for Black mothers—that the only people laboring for Black mothers' health are Black women.

She [Beyoncé Knowles] has transformed from a booty-shaking single lady to a ring-flashing wife to a belly-rubbing fertility goddess, bringing joy and waves of confidence to countless fans.
—ALICIA WALLACE, "A Critical View of Beyoncé's 'Formation'"

THREE. **BLACK MATERNAL AESTHETICS**

*The Making of a Noncrisis Style*

In 2017, two images of Black pregnant women generated media frenzies. In June, Serena Williams graced the cover of *Vanity Fair*. In many ways, the Williams photograph—taken by celebrated photographer Annie Leibovitz—was a continuation of *Vanity Fair*'s tradition of spectacular photographs of female bodies, including Leibovitz's 1991 photograph of nude, pregnant Demi Moore. But this photograph of Williams—who had been hailed by Claudia Rankine as the paradigmatic example of "Black excellence" and who had been subjected to endless racist and sexist critiques of her body, her clothing, her hair, and her unprecedented dominance of women's tennis—was new representational territory.[1] Williams was eight months pregnant and appeared nude, with one hand covering her breasts, the other resting on the small of her back, a simple jeweled band around her waist. A single word was at the bottom of the image: "Serena."

A few months earlier, Beyoncé Knowles shared an announcement on Instagram: "We would like to share our love and happiness. We have been blessed two times over."[2] The image of Knowles wearing a burgundy bra and pastel blue underwear, clutching her pregnant belly, and kneeling on an altar of flowers generated eleven million "likes" by the end of the year. Two weeks later, wearing a gold shimmering gown much like Oshun—the Yoruba fertility deity— and a giant golden headpiece that gave her the appearance of a Virgin Mary, Knowles performed songs from *Lemonade* at the Grammys. Knowles decided to have her performance introduced by her mother, Tina Knowles, and when Knowles accepted her award for best urban contemporary album, she said, "It's important to me to show images to my children that reflect their beauty so they can grow up in a world where they look in the mirror, first through their own families, as well as the news, the Super Bowl, the Olympics, the White House and the Grammys, and see themselves. And have no doubt that they're beautiful, intelligent, and capable."[3] The *New York Times* described this "new" aesthetic as the birth of "Beyoncé 3.0, the reimagining of Mrs. Knowles-Carter not just as the Queen of Sound, or as a Black Lives Matter activist who uses her celebrity to speak up, but as the Mother of Us All: the avatar of female fecundity, her creative muscles stretching beyond making music to making life itself."[4]

Eleven years before Williams's and Knowles's respective pregnant bodies entered the national spotlight, becoming part of what Vanessa Friedman described as "the public pregnancy route," another Black woman leveraged motherhood as part of her celebrity persona.[5] Michelle Obama labeled herself "mom-in-chief," a descriptor she would invoke repeatedly over her eight years as First Lady, reminding audiences that "at the end of the day, my most important title is still 'mom-in-chief.' My daughters are still the heart of my heart and the center of my world."[6] She even suggested that her primary policy initiative, Let's Move, which focused on curbing obesity, stemmed from her experiences as a mother concerned about her children's weight. As Jodi Kantor notes, "She took on issues that were vital but hard to disagree with: She was pro-veteran, anti–childhood obesity. The approach worked brilliantly, protecting and elevating her, putting her as far above reproach as anyone in the mosh pit of American politics can hope to be. The less explicitly political she sounded, the more political influence she accrued, in convention speeches and other key moments."[7] Obama wielded the seemingly apolitical category of mother to garner tremendous political currency, even as she faced critique—often waged in the name of feminism—that her "mom-in-chief" moniker "did not capture [her] true depth, originality and directness."[8]

In this chapter, I follow these three contemporary performances of Black celebrity maternity, all of which unfold alongside an intense attention to Black motherhood as the site of crisis and as the only space through which Black life can be rescued and preserved. My investigation of these three figures and their performances of Black motherhood, focuses on self-conscious Black maternal aesthetics that both understand crisis's constitutive role in the shaping of Black maternal subjectivity and also refuse crisis as the entirety of the Black maternal identity. In this chapter, I make three claims about these Black maternal performances: first, I argue that motherhood's seemingly apolitical nature enables them to leverage maternity to publicly renarrate their investments. In so doing, they marshal motherhood to create a new platform that allows them to speak, perhaps for the first time, in the register of the universal—not as Black mothers, but simply as mothers. Even in moments when these figures discussed issues particular to Black maternal health or to Black children, they were imagined to speak about *motherhood*, about *children*, about the non-racially marked collective. I aspire to sit with the complex choreography that enables celebrity Black mothers to inhabit the universal position, neither romantically celebrating nor bemoaning this rhetorical strategy.

Second, I trace how these Black maternal celebrity performances center Black female friendship as a Black maternal ethic, as a distinct form of relationality that Black motherhood renders possible. Knowles, Williams, and Obama have appeared in each other's work, championed each other, and performed their celebrity, at least in part, through their proximity to each other. Obama, for example, celebrated the release of Beyoncé's 2019 *Homecoming* documentary film, noting, "Hey queen! Girl, you have done it again, constantly raising the bar for us all and doing it flawlessly. I'd say I'm surprised, but I know who you are. I've seen it up close and personal."[9] Obama also joined other celebrities who observed Knowles's birthday by dressing in the iconic black hat and silver choker that Knowles wore in the "Formation" music video. Serena Williams, who danced alongside Knowles in the music video for "Sorry," simply noted, "Beyoncé is a powerful individual. She motivates me."[10] The affection among these women was also apparent when Knowles said of Obama, "Loving Michelle Obama wasn't much of a choice. It was something that came naturally, because of how she carried herself. Because she resembled us and was moving in spaces where, as Black Americans, we weren't exactly meant to be, she seemed so powerful."[11] This friendship has also been forged through their shared commitment to reshaping narratives about maternal affect, postpartum bodies, and the sheer demands of mothering, as when Knowles noted simply, "Right now, my little FUPA and I feel like we are meant to be," or when

Williams shared her postpartum feelings on Instagram, writing, "Not only was I accepting some tough personal stuff, but I just was in a funk. Mostly, I felt like I was not a good mom."[12] This is a kind of Black female friendship cemented through a commitment to sisterhood—and how these women celebrate each other—and through a carefully constructed vulnerability about the physical and affective challenges of postpartum life.

Finally, I argue that this conception of Black maternal friendship is staged quite differently than another contemporary, hypervisible public performance in the same genre: Mothers of the Movement. Described by Valerie Castile as the "fucked-up mothers club," the group—including Sybrina Fulton, Lezley McSpadden, Lucy McBath, Gwen Carr, and Geneva Reed-Veal—is a political affiliation forged through shared trauma.[13] Their shared losses might be understood as born both from the death—or murder—of a child and from the state inaction that marked many of these cases, such as slews of nonindictments and not-guilty verdicts. In the second section of this chapter, I argue that Knowles, Obama, and Williams offer a markedly different performance of Black maternal friendship, one rooted not in shared loss but in Black maternal pleasure, glamour, and playfulness, even as the collective—particularly Knowles—often operates in solidarity with Mothers of the Movement.

In this chapter, I treat Knowles, Obama, and Williams as "masters of self-fashioning"—or masters of maternal self-fashioning—who circumvent the prevailing constraints of the Black maternal political role.[14] As Samantha Pinto and I argue elsewhere, Black maternal political visibility continues to be possible only through proximity to dead Black male flesh, a proximity that is imagined to make both legible and respectable Black female political desires.[15] Yet the Black maternal aesthetics I study here quietly place pressure on the conception of crisis by foregrounding other Black maternal ethics and by asking what happens when the fragility of Black life becomes centrally about the Black pregnant and mothering body, not the Black (male) child. This trio refashions Black motherhood, figuring it not as a position of urgency but instead as a complex and self-authored aesthetic.

In considering these three Black female celebrities as inaugurating a distinct and highly visible Black maternal aesthetic, I am deeply aware of how each figure is carefully constructed, often by a slew of actors who consciously craft celebrity personas. Indeed, my analysis here is informed by Pinto's conception of "Black female celebrity" as a crucial way through which Black women are ushered into the category of the political and thus into visibility.[16] In my analysis, I emphasize how each celebrity constructs her performance and her brand without assuming this artifice as politically suspect. In "Marketing Michelle," for example, Caroline Brown describes the First Lady as deploying "twinned narratives of motherhood and corporeal perfectability" in her crafted persona, one that was the result of the collective labor of a team committed to building a compelling brand for the United States' first Black First Lady.[17] Brown writes, "By combining God and motherhood, national pride and a devotion to the military, Michelle struck a chord that has resonated with the American public. Her carefully calibrated words and commitments to particular social causes have shaped an identity at once socially engaged and maternal."[18] Brown's analysis emphasizes the self-conscious task of brand management at the heart of Obama's persona, a task made more complex and more delicate by negotiating the hyperpoliced intersection of race and gender. Knowles and Williams are also regularly referred to as brands, at least in part because of their tremendous wealth and because of their collaborations with commercial brands including Ivy Park (an activewear company Knowles cofounded), Adidas, and Tidal for Knowles, and endorsements by Nike, Delta, and Gatorade for Williams. Indeed, Alicia Wallace reflects on how Knowles in particular has managed to self-consciously perfect a performance of *seeming* to be open to the public, of offering the Beyhive a glimpse into her intimate life, while also insisting on her privacy. Wallace writes, "She is able to enjoy a private life while giving the illusion that she shares it, if only in part, with the people who closely identify—or want to identify—with her."[19] My analysis of Black maternal aesthetics considers the place of motherhood in these figures' respective brand-management projects. Ultimately, this chapter treats Black motherhood as an aesthetic that can be playful, sensual, and fabulous, even as it sits with loss and grief and in solidarity with more recognizable Black maternal political efforts like Mothers of the Movement.

*(Black) Motherhood as Rebranding*

In 2008, while she campaigned for her husband in Milwaukee, Wisconsin, Michelle Obama said, "For the first time in my adult life, I am really proud of my country. Not just because Barack is doing well, but I think people are hungry for change. And I have been desperate to see our country moving in that direction and just not feeling so alone in my frustration and disappointment. I've seen people who are hungry to be unified around some basic common issues, and it's made me proud."[20] Her comments were quickly taken up as a clear indication of her lack of "patriotism" and as confirmation of her husband's imagined non-Americanness—a rumor that Donald Trump spread through his insistent demand to see Barack Obama's birth certificate, to have visual proof of Obama's Americanness. More than anything, her remarks were thought to reveal a lack of preparation for the demands of the campaign trail where any utterance could cost the Democrats the election. A few months after her widely critiqued statement, the *New Yorker*'s cover cartoon, "The Politics of Fear," represented Barack Obama as a Muslim and Michelle Obama as a militant Black radical. While the magazine insisted that the image was a satire, intended to problematize the rumors about the Obamas as insufficiently American and secretly Muslim (with Muslim and American always imagined to be antithetical), the cartoonist was accused of trafficking in precisely the racial-sexual stereotypes that would galvanize the white supremacist "Make America Great Again" movement for Donald Trump's 2016 presidential campaign.

In the wake of Michelle Obama's representation as an anti-American Black militant, her strategically adopted "mom-in-chief" title allowed her to make potent political jabs. During the 2016 election cycle, when the Obamas campaigned for Hillary Clinton, Michelle Obama offered motherly wisdom that became the Democrats' central refrain. She said: "That is what Barack and I think about every day as we try to guide and protect our girls through the challenges of this unusual life in the spotlight. . . . How we explain that when someone is cruel, or acts like a bully, you don't stoop to their level—no, our motto is, when they go low, we go high. With every word we utter, with every action we take, we know our kids are watching us."[21] The call to "go high" even in the face of violence, a direct response to candidate Trump's platform of institutionalized cruelty, was cloaked in wise advice passed down from mother to daughters and thus never named itself as a critique of Trump's racism and misogyny. Indeed, Obama's statement was able to perform its powerful political work by wearing the guise of mother-wisdom, by cloaking itself in the kinds of labor mothers are thought to perform when they offer their children ethical instruction. That it was delivered in the exact moment that Obama disavowed politics, repeatedly assuring the US public that she had no interest in pursuing political office at the end of her husband's two-term presidency, the very moment when her approval rate skyrocketed to 68 percent, reveals precisely the political power of Black maternal aesthetics. These quietly political jabs were also levied in the moment when Obama was hailed for her sense of aesthetics: her clothing choices were celebrated, and she, in turn, championed relatively affordable brands (at least for wealthy politicians) like J. Crew—announcing "Ladies, we know J. Crew. You can get some good stuff online!"[22] She received substantial attention for her bangs and her "sculpted biceps" and "flawless arms," which prompted endless "Obama Arm Workouts."[23] In her description of Obama in 2013, Elizabeth Warren noted simply, "I love Michelle Obama.

She's a real fighter. Just take a look at those biceps."[24] The preoccupation with her body, her hair, and her clothing solidified a cultural perception of her as apolitical.[25] In other words, her politics were hidden by aesthetics, enabling her to appear to be apolitical, domesticated, maternal.

How might we understand this transformation, from her imaging as a militant Black radical to a beloved "mom-in-chief," a dedicated discount shopper, and an avid gym goer. Obama's strategic deployment of motherhood acts as a kind of rebranding strategy, one that allowed her to powerfully rewrite a past that was constructed as problematically political—her problematically Black past. Of course, the notion of needing to be "redeemed" from either Blackness or its imagined excesses, including its imagined excess politics, is a fantasy animated by antiBlackness, as Joseph Winters argues.[26] Yet I sit with rebranding's complicated political valences to trace what happens when Black female celebrities invest in a redemption narrative's capacities to rewrite their public personas, to rewrite their celebrity. In this section, I study how Black female celebrities have managed to marshal motherhood to modify the narrative about their politics and to fashion a new relationship to a past that was imagined as dangerously proximate to Blackness. I argue that this new platform is one that we might think of as a universal one. This universal platform confers upon Black mothers the capacity to speak *as mothers*, not as Black mothers, a position readily denied to Black subjects who are thought to always only speak in and from a Blackened location.

Perhaps the most emblematic case of the rebranding possibilities of motherhood for Black female celebrities is Serena Williams. Williams's domination of women's tennis—she is the winner of thirty-nine Grand Slam titles—is unprecedented, as is the scrutiny she and her sister, Venus Williams, have received, a scrutiny that is always about their Black/female bodies in the white space of professional tennis. As Nicole R. Fleetwood notes, "From very early in the sisters' careers, journalists and critics made comments on their clothing and hairstyle (especially the signature braids and beads of their teenage years) as much as on their aggressive playing style."[27] The construction of the Williams sisters' clothing and hairstyles as "aggressive" fed into a perception of their playing style as "aggressive," and that revealed—yet again—the racialization of aesthetics. As Delia Douglas notes: "In light of tennis' heritage of race, gender, and class elitism in the United States, the sport remains available to select groups, as evidenced by its enduring association with resorts, country clubs, and tennis academies. Thus the arrival of two talented Black American female teenagers from the unlikely city of Compton, California, a location readily understood as a site of urban decay and gang violence, profoundly disrupted the White racial order ... of the Women's Tennis Association."[28] The notion of the Williams sisters as out of place in professional tennis, as constituting a breach in the established white order of tennis, continues as does their fundamental transformation of the sport.

If Williams "disrupted the White racial order" of professional tennis through her athletic dominance, she was also represented as a problematically reactive and ungracious figure. This image of an impolite and even bad-mannered Williams was perhaps most spectacularly proliferated around the 2018 US Open final match when she faced Naomi Osaka. In the second set, Williams received a code violation when the umpire decided that her coach was making an illegal hand gesture from the stands, instructing Williams where to stand (Williams insisted that she was not coached from the stands). Later in the set, when Williams had an unforced error, she broke her racket in frustration and received another code violation, this one with a point penalty. When Williams realized that the code violation had cost her a point, she approached the umpire and said, "You owe me an apology. I have never cheated in my life. I have a daughter and I stand for what's right for her and I have never cheated. You owe me an apology."[29] Later in the set, she said to the umpire, "You stole a point from me, you're a thief, too."[30] He issued another code violation, this one costing Williams the game. Brian Earley, a tournament referee, and Donna Kelso, the Grand Slam supervisor, entered the court to mediate the dispute, and Williams said, "Do you know how many other men do things that are—that do much worse than that? This is not fair. There's a lot of men out here that have said a lot of things, but if they're men, that doesn't happen to them."[31] When Osaka ultimately prevailed, winning her first US Open, the crowd audibly booed. Osaka pulled a visor over her face and cried. Williams addressed the crowd, and declared, "I just wanted to tell you guys she played well. This is her first Grand Slam. And I know you guys were here rooting and I was rooting too but let's make this the best moment we can, and we'll get through it. Let's give everyone credit where it's due. Let's not boo anymore, we're gonna get through this and let's be positive. Congratulations, Naomi! No more booing."[32] While Williams and Osaka would later make public their friendship—with Osaka describing Williams as her "mom"—the press attacked Williams. Described as having an "outburst" and a "series of epic meltdowns," Williams was represented as a sore loser, as incapable of controlling her emotions.[33] Writing in the *New York Times*, tennis legend Martina Navratilova noted, "There have been many times when I was playing that I wanted to break my racket into a thousand pieces. Then I thought about the kids watching. And I grudgingly held on to that racket."[34] The public scolding that Williams received for her "meltdown"—including a 2018 Australian racist and sexist caricature of Williams jumping on her racket after losing the US Open—and the collective sense that she ruined Osaka's first US Open victory entrenched perceptions of Williams as infantile, difficult, and ungracious.

My endeavor is to understand how motherhood has allowed Williams to rebrand herself, to cast herself as someone other than—or beyond—a disruption in the white subdued landscape of tennis. My claim is not that anything about Williams's political life or commitments has changed—this is, in fact, unknowable to me. Instead, I am invested in how motherhood allowed her to narrate herself, her commitments, her desires, and even her proximity to pasts, often deemed troubling, anew. The labor of rebranding that motherhood made possible for Williams has often unfolded in the terrain of the aesthetic, and it is perhaps most visible around an iconic outfit, which was once condemned and later celebrated. In 2002, Serena Williams wore a black Puma catsuit to the US Open and the "body-clinging, faux leather, black cat suit" was the subject of endless debate.[35] It was deemed "outrageous" and "controversial," a performance of sartorial and corporeal excess that ruptured the white uniform of women's professional tennis and called attention to precisely what was always already discussed: Williams's body.[36] Otis Gibson of the *Australian Sunday Telegraph* noted, "On some women [the catsuit] might look good. Unfortunately, some women aren't wearing it. On Serena, it only serves to accentuate a superstructure that is already bordering on the digitally enhanced and a rear end that I will attempt to sum up as discreetly as possible by simply referring to it as 'formidable.'"[37] In an article in the *Washington Post*, Robin Givhan describes the outfit as "salacious" and "trashy" and noted that it 'did her a disservice."[38] I reproduce these quotes—in all of their antiBlack and misogynistic violence—to foreground how intensely the conversation about the 2002 US Open focused on Williams's attire rather than on her athletic prowess.

In 2018, Williams played at the French Open. It was her first professional match after her maternity leave, and she decided to inaugurate her return by wearing another catsuit. After the match, she dedicated the catsuit to the "moms out there who had a tough recovery from pregnancy. . . . If I can do it, so can you."[39] Later, she noted, "It feels like this suit represents all the women that have been through a lot mentally, physically, with their body to come back and have confidence and to believe in themselves."[40] Yet even as she emphasized its capacity to represent "all the women," she also described it as a "Wakanda-inspired catsuit," referencing the *Black Panther* film that had been released earlier that year. The reference underscored something fundamentally Black—and perhaps even Black utopian—about the suit.[41] In the wake of Williams's unveiling of the catsuit, French Open officials declared that it was imposing rules to regularize its players' outfits—announcing, "You have to respect the game and the place"—and Williams's catsuit was immediately banned.[42] Williams responded by arguing that the catsuit had health benefits for new mothers who, like Williams, had suffered postpartum health complications: her garment, she told the media, prevented blood clots and made possible her return to tennis. The French Open's policy was widely critiqued, including by Billie King who noted, "The policing of women's bodies must end. . . . Criticizing what she wears to work is where the true disrespect lies."[43] The *New York Times* celebrated Williams's fashion as "a political tool: an unabashed statement of female empowerment and independence not just for herself, but for all," and Nike featured Williams in her catsuit in print advertisements that declared, "You can take the superhero out of her costume, but you can never take away her superpowers."[44] Maternity fundamentally transformed the catsuit from a reviled and pornographic garment into an "empowering," celebrated, and even health-affirming postpartum garment.

Understanding the transformation of the catsuit—its rewriting from pornographic object to postpartum empowerment garb—requires engaging with other images of Williams that represent motherhood as a transformation of both her politics and her affect. In 2017, the year before the French Open banned Williams's outfit, she appeared in the news for another story: her marriage and her pregnancy. She was featured on the cover of *Vanity Fair*, and the article enticed readers to discover a "love story." In fact, the article was steeped in the trappings of heterosexual romance: "The marriage? How can it not thrive when the first date was six hours in Paris—with no particular destination—where no matter how crowded the streets and alleyways winding through the city, there was no one else except the two of you."[45] This was an account of how Williams and Alexis Ohanian, a cofounder of Reddit, came to be engaged and then to learn that Williams was pregnant. This was a new image of Williams far removed from a prevailing representation of an "aggressive" athlete. This was an account of heterosexual, interracial, extremely wealthy courtship. The 2017 Leibovitz portrait of Williams that graced the magazine's cover performed its aesthetic work in part by removing what has long been thought to be Williams's signature—and perhaps most controversial—site: her clothing. Instead, as Jessica Diehl, the magazine's style director, noted, the choice to dress Williams in a flowing caftan was meant to be a calculated break from earlier representations of Williams, which had "been about celebrating and showcasing the perfection of the physique of an athlete. . . . [T]his time it felt more appropriate to bring in a bit of softness. Hence the caftan."[46] The photograph forecloses a conversation about how Williams's clothing refuses to hide her "curves" and instead reimagines her "curves" as her rounded pregnant belly. In fact, "curves" are literally refigured from an ongoing preoccupation with Williams's buttocks, so often the sign of Black female sexual excess, into an investment in her round belly. This image of maternal abundance, Williams's rounded stomach exposed and displayed, was widely celebrated as a representation of maternal beauty rather than a political act and as documenting the feminine affect imagined to attach to perinatal life: calm.

Importantly, the photograph of the nude Williams was part of a larger archive of Leibovitz photographs of the Williams sisters. As Leibovitz indicated, she had been photographing Serena since she was sixteen, offering a kind of visual document of her decorated career. A few years earlier, for example, Leibovitz had photographed Williams topless for the 2016 Pirelli calendar. The calendar, which the *New York Times* had characterized as "the arty soft-core ode to pinups," was remade by Leibovitz's photographs, which centered powerful, assertive, and strong women from various avenues of public life.[47] Amy Schumer, who was also photographed nude for the calendar, described her photograph as "beautiful, gross, strong, thin, fat, pretty, ugly, sexy, disgusting, flawless, woman," a tribute to Leibovitz's own investment in capturing a kind of female corporeal authenticity.[48] In Leibovitz's portrait of Williams, it is Williams's body, and not her face, that is the subject of the photograph. We see Williams from the back, and it is her unclothed muscular back and her sculpted legs that constitute the centerpiece of the image. Perhaps this is a visual metaphor for her refusal to engage with the endless critiques of her clothing, her style, her dominance of tennis, and to instead turn the gaze back on the sheer physical strength of her body. The image emphasizes athletic prowess and endurance and unapologetically celebrates Williams's capacity to dominate her opponents.

Yet the *Vanity Fair* image from a year later suggests that to become a mother is to find oneself newly oriented toward what Elizabeth Alexander describes as the Black interior, "a metaphysical space beyond the Black public everyday toward power and wild imagination that Black people ourselves know we possess but need to be reminded of and know: it is a space that Black people ourselves have policed at various historical moments."[49] It is, as the style director suggests, to find the body reimagined from its association with athletic prowess to something quieter, a different visual representation of Black female strength, here fashioned as the physical and psychic power required to hold another, to create breathing room for life. The interior is represented as a space that is wholly different from the "excessive" public life of Williams's prematernal athletic performance, one marked by a relentless pursuit of winning and by a willingness to respond to racism, however it manifests itself, including in umpires' bad calls. The *Vanity Fair* image, by contrast, displayed Williams's body as an icon of fecundity and fertility, of maternal abundance and quiet calm. With her eyes closed, and her face relaxed in serenity, the image suggested that pregnancy had rewritten Williams's affect from ferocious competitor to tranquil, expectant mother.

Inside the magazine is another image focused on Williams's newly transformed body. In this image, she is draped in a sheer fabric that clings to her belly, her protruding belly button, and her nipples. She has one hand raised, her eyes closed, and while her clothing and hair seem to be dramatically in motion, as if Williams is standing in the midst of a storm, her closed eyes and calm face suggest deep composure. If Williams's clothes were the source of endless controversy before her pregnancy because of their refusal to mask her "curves," here the simple drape that covers—and also fails to cover—her pregnant body constitutes a celebration of the serenity that maternity is thought to produce. A body that was an icon of strength and dominance is here an icon of maternity, where maternal abundance has transformed not only the body but also the affect of the photographed subject, engendering a deep, almost sacred calm. Pregnancy transforms not simply the maternal body—now curved anew—but the maternal felt life. In the hands of Leibovitz, then, Williams's public image is fundamentally rewritten, with her body cast not as a site of alterity, deviance, and radical politics but as a calm, serene, and even joyful, fecund body—as maternal affect is constructed to be transformed by the physical and emotional demands of pregnancy, to be quite literally remade. The images reinforce the conventional notion that motherhood, which is represented as an embodied transformation, is actually an affective one that orients the self away from anger, hostility, and defiance.

Leibovitz's photographs of Williams suggest Black motherhood's imagined capacity to rewrite Black female feeling—and perceptions of Black female feeling—in a way that gestures toward the psychic and political redemption of motherhood. Black motherhood is figured to allow access to a deep form of serenity, one that performs its communal work—which is often cast as apolitical—in the name of the collective, under the banner of respectability rather than anger, and in the service of "More Life." If Williams's prematernal life was thought to be oriented toward a politics of excess, her emphatic insistence on her presence in the white space of professional tennis, her postmaternal life was thought to be marked by different attachments: toward futurity. Williams mobilized the cultural perception of motherhood as an affective shift to effectively rewrite her public image.

It is this sense of Black motherhood—as an affective reorientation—that I argue makes it something beyond an embodied experience, as a kind of performance that can be harnessed by Black female celebrities to rewrite their present. If motherhood is imagined as a reorientation of Williams's demeanor, it also allows her to powerfully speak simultaneously in two registers—*as a mother* making claims for the universal category of woman and *as a Black woman* making claims for the dire necessity of attention to Black maternal health. In this capacity, she was able to take a garment denounced as pornographic and recast it as a tool of maternal well-being even as that recasting enabled her to continue to wear the suit, now not as indicative of her excess flesh or her willingness to flaunt the rules and customs of tennis but as indicative of her maternal pride. In other words, motherhood allowed Williams to rebrand both the catsuit and her image as a rule breaker who would daringly wear attire that challenged the conventions of professional tennis.

In the wake of the birth of Williams's child, she became a new kind of icon, one laboring in the name of maternal health. Indeed, the story of Williams's postpartum health challenges has demonstrated the necessity of fundamental changes in institutional medicine. In the hours following her delivery, Williams reported an intense pain that was the start of a postpartum blood clot, pain that was largely ignored by medical staff. Williams's experience with pulmonary embolisms, postpartum clots, and medical neglect of her symptoms became the basis of reminders—even published in mainstream media—that doctors need to "Stop! Look! Listen!" as they respond to women's pregnancy-related medical concerns. Williams's story was, at times, presented as a call for renewed attention to the particular medical crises affecting Black mothers—Williams, for example, encouraged Black women to "get feisty," saying, "I think it's important to speak up loud and clear and say: 'No, this isn't right. Treat me the same way that you're treating . . .' How am I going to explain to my son that he is getting more? How am I going to explain to my daughter that she is getting less than my son? To me it's impossible to explain this."[50] Her willingness to speak publicly about her postpartum complications was imagined as an apolitical and universal plea for a renewed attention to maternal health. Even months later, when Williams joined an investment group to support the Black-owned Mahmee—a technology company designed to mobilize data to respond to the Black maternal health crisis—her postpartum persona was still powerfully constructed around a position of universality (she engaged in advocacy as a mother) rather than from a position of particularity, precisely the space to which Black women are so often relegated.

A few weeks after Williams's return to the French Open sparked endless debates around clothing regulation, Williams ignited another public debate: one focused on maternity leave policies for professional tennis players. Several top women's players had returned to competition after pregnancy and had been penalized for their leave. Victoria Azarenka, for example, who was ranked fifth before having a child in 2016, had an unseeded return to Wimbledon. But when the French Open announced it would not seed Williams for her return, it generated a particular and intense controversy. Following the French Open's decision, the US Open announced that it would revise its seeding policy to avoid punishing players who took maternity leave. Williams was described as experiencing what "so many other moms" encounter when they return to work: discrimination and the "motherhood penalty."[51] Williams partnered with Allstate Foundation's Purple Purse program to advocate for universal expanded leave, noting, "I have my own job and I make my own schedule, but even then I still have commitments, and I can't imagine moms that get two weeks off and have to go back to work."[52] She insisted on the importance of parental leave for all and described herself as a "working mother" navigating the demands of professional life and parenting. Williams's husband, Ohanian, also publicly championed the necessity of parental leave, arguing that paternity leave, in particular, has the capacity to rewrite gender roles. Ohanian asserted: "Getting dads (and in turn, families) off on the right foot begins at birth, and it can't just be up to individual businesses to ensure that happens. We need a federal bill that mandates quality paid family leave for everyone—birth parents, adoptive parents and caregivers alike. Until that happens, dads, let me be your air cover. I took my full 16 weeks and I'm still ambitious and care about my career. Talk to your bosses and tell them I sent you."[53] Williams and her husband became spokespeople for the necessity of equitable parental leave as a fundamental right and as a form of gender equity. Williams's experience of returning to tennis unseeded—of facing harder opponents and financial penalties for childbearing—was mobilized by her to speak generally about mothers' experiences of workplace discrimination and the continued lack of adequate parental leave in the United States. Put differently, the issue of gendered workplace discrimination allowed Williams to speak *as a mother* and *for mothers*, effectively inhabiting an unracially marked category.

While Williams spoke emphatically about the cost of workplace discrimination against mothers, she also raised another employment discrimination issue: drug testing. In 2018, the same year Williams returned to professional tennis from parental leave, *Deadspin* revealed that she had been tested for drugs at a much higher rate than her peers in professional tennis. In July, Williams tweeted, "And it's that time of the day to get 'randomly' drug tested and only test Serena. Out of all the players it's been proven I'm the one getting tested the most. Discrimination? I think so. At least I'll be keeping the sport clean."[54] Her insistence that her subjection to frequent drug testing was the result of "discrimination" raised questions about how race colors ideas of doping and about the ongoing racialized surveillance that Williams's body receives. This story, which was reported as wholly disconnected from Williams's maternal flesh, generated little attention to the ongoing practices of race-based discrimination that mark professional athletics or to the intersections of raced and gendered discrimination that affect Black female athletes particularly. In fact, the story was reported with far less rigor and intensity than her unseeded return, even as both centered issues of inequity. I sit with these two examples to highlight how the maternal allowed Williams a capacity to make a case for the apolitical urgency of policies designed to support families, to make a case for a bipartisan and collective investment in "families," while the drug testing—which Williams clearly marked as related to racial discrimination—never transcended the category of "race."

The transformation of the catsuit from pornographic object to postpartum outfit reveals the capacity of the Black maternal aesthetic to allow Black female celebrities the agency, power, and pleasure to offer different narratives about Black female flesh, including narratives that sound in the register of the universal, which enable Black women to use their bodies to speak broadly about the conditions and experiences of subjects who may not identify as Black women. The capacity to mobilize the grammar of the universal allows Williams to talk about fair wages, about family-friendly workplace policies, and about maternal health in a register that is seemingly apolitical. This ability to transcend a past that was previously deemed by many as too political and too proximate to Blackness is what I treat as rebranding, a form of image-remaking that relies on maternity.

If the catsuit reveals the capacity of redemption to renarrativize Black women's political commitments, Beyoncé Knowles's deep identification with motherhood allowed her to rewrite *Lemonade* from its association as a "political" BLM soundtrack to an introspective, personal rumination on marriage and family. In the case of Knowles, rebranding has a different trajectory: although she was once thought of as a pop goddess whose work was imagined to eschew the "political" in songs like "Bills, Bills, Bills," she was described as "becoming political" in the wake of BLM. Even as *Lemonade* was hailed as Knowles's most personal effort to date, an act of "Black women magic" marked by both a commitment to truth-telling and a vulnerable rumination on allegations of her husband's marital infidelity, it was also both celebrated and decried as Beyoncé's political coming-of-age, with "Formation," one of *Lemonade*'s tracks, described as an urgent performance of Black rage.[55]

On February 6, 2016, "Formation" was released on the streaming platform Tidal and on YouTube, and the following day, she performed the song at the Super Bowl half-time show. The song's video featured Knowles atop a slowly sinking New Orleans police car, reminding its viewers of the iconography of Black death that marked Hurricane Katrina in 2005 and connecting the state's neglect of Black life during Katrina and its aftermath to the state's relentless attack on Black people in the form of police violence. Later in the video, a young boy dances in front of police officers wearing a hoodie—a garment that has become another icon of Black death after Trayvon Martin's murder in 2012—and the video cuts to another image: graffiti sprayed on a wall with the simple slogan "Stop shooting us." At the Super Bowl, Knowles appeared surrounded by "natural"-haired dancers clad in black leather leotards and black berets. The dancers' hair and outfits were read as an homage to the Black Panthers, and Knowles's outfit—a leather jacket and bandolier—was a tribute to Michael Jackson's costume from his 1993 Super Bowl performance. Taken together, the performance was imagined to rewrite the genre conventions of the apolitical half-time show. The day after the performance, the *New York Times* described it as a "high-level, visually striking, Black Lives Matter–era allegory. The halftime show is usually a locus of entertainment, but Beyoncé has just rewritten it—overridden it, to be honest—as a moment of political ascent."[56] In this narrative, the apolitical pop artist, who had celebrated the pleasures of being "dangerously in love," was now grown and political.[57]

And these politics garnered attention in the forms of celebration and anxiety. "Formation" was hailed either as proof of Knowles's status as, in Marquis Bey's words, a "pathogen in the milieu of the normal, codified, of course, through whiteness and maleness," or, as in Piers Morgan's words, "inflammatory" and "agitating."[58] The Miami police union called for a boycott of Knowles's tour and asserted that her performance had attempted "to divide Americans by promoting the Black Panthers."[59] Similarly, Rudolph Giuliani noted that Knowles should use her "platform" to encourage her fans "to respect the uniform, not to make it appear as if they are the enemy."[60] What these varied interpretations of the Super Bowl performance reveal is that "Formation" was evidence of a newly politicized Knowles, who had been transformed by BLM. As Daphne Brooks noted, "Never before have we seen a pop icon, especially an African-American woman, use her platform as a musician, as a celebrity, in order to make some of the boldest, most ferocious, most inspiring political statements about the Black freedom struggle."[61] Importantly, the debate about the politics of "Formation" often hinged on its interpretation as a BLM anthem and about its visual iconography in support of Black self-defense.

If the Super Bowl performance of "Formation" constituted—at least for some—the high watermark of Knowles's Black "radical" politics, her Grammy performance in February 2017 seemed to hail something different, a performance of maternity as a spiritual calling and site of wisdom, a representation of Black motherhood as a space of affective abundance. Knowles reinterpreted the politics of BLM into a call for a recognition of the sacred, urgent, and necessary labor of Black mothers, reimagining Black mothers as themselves vessels of Black life. Knowles was introduced by her mother, Tina Knowles, which situated Knowles in a lineage of powerful mothers who had given of their bodies to produce life. Knowles appeared onstage draped in gold jewelry, with a gold headpiece framing her flowing hair and with her pregnant belly on display. The first words of the performance were spoken in a quiet voice: "Do you remember me? Are you thankful for the hips that cracked? The deep velvet of your mother and her mother and her mother?" The performance was a tribute to maternity—a celebration both of her own pregnant body and of the power of mothers generally, whose "deep velvet" make possible our own lives. It suggested that self-fulfillment and actualization require a reckoning with the figure of the mother whose life-giving capacities must be acknowledged and celebrated. The performance, then, was a call to "remember" our mothers, their corporeal sacrifice, generosity, and power. It called on its viewers to see that memory as life-affirming and sacred. In the final moments of the performance, when she declared, "If we're gonna heal, let it be glorious," the promise of "healing" seemed to be as much about a repair of her "broken" marriage as about the healing potential of mothers to renew and restore, to generate communal wellness. What the Grammy performance allowed the world to see, then, was Knowles's transformation from sex goddess into fecundity goddess (and her insistence that a fecundity goddess was also a sexual subject, which I will discuss later in this chapter). This quick rewriting of Knowles from political subject into seemingly apolitical maternal subject was a powerful rebranding that allowed Knowles to renarrate her relationship to her earlier more overtly political work (and to suggest that the maternal work was not political).

What do we make of this set of events—that unfold in close proximity—where Knowles is cast as a Black radical critiquing state-sanctioned violence, linking Black death in Hurricane Katrina to Black death in the form of police killings, to Knowles recast as a maternal figure who embodies and performs calm and abundance? Knowles's representation as Mother suggests that what was earlier imagined as both overtly sexual and overtly political has been replaced by an ethic of maternity that is communal and humanistic. What was once figured as a militant and angry response to state violence has been replaced by something inward-focused and tranquil. In imagining this as another form of Black celebrity rebranding, I want to underscore not that Knowles distanced herself from the "political" labor of "Formation" or that her investments shifted. Indeed, I probe what constitutes the political and why certain performances are deemed political and others escape this label. In so doing, I analyze the kinds of self-fashioning that motherhood made possible for Knowles, refiguring herself from problematically political to transformatively communal. For both Williams and Knowles, motherhood is not merely an act of rewriting their relationship to a past that was hailed—at least by some—as troublingly political and troublingly proximate to Blackness. It is also a platform for speaking *as a mother* even as both celebrities speak about the particular forms of violence that Black mothers encounter, as well as the complexities of mothering while Black. Both have harnessed motherhood as offering them the capacity to speak in a universal register, perhaps because motherhood is so often figured as apolitical or unpolitical, capacious in its investment in a communal good that is managed to elide political divides entirely. The universal is a powerful grammar that obscures its political work, with motherhood figured as a fundamental commitment to the good of the collective. It is the power of motherhood to offer Black female celebrities the ability to quite literally recast themselves not simply as Black mothers but as the mothers of us all, as precisely the figures we all need for salvation, that makes this universal grammar so powerful.

*Reading Black Maternal Friendship*

In 2016, the *New York Times* reported that Mothers of the Movement had become a "force" for Democratic presidential nominee Hillary Clinton.[62] Clinton flew the collective to Chicago and asked to hear their stories. She urged them to collaborate and said, "You are the mothers of the children who are dying in the streets. You have a lot of power individually. But collectively, you need to come together. The country needs to hear from you."[63] The Clinton campaign paid the collective's travel expenses so its members could come to the Democratic debates, and Clinton introduced them as "a group of mothers who belong to a club no one ever wants to join." If at first they were a force for Clinton, and for the Democratic Party, they have increasingly become their own visible political subjects. "United by death," these women have rewritten themselves as both activists and politicians, with three of them running for office, seeking to transform the national political conversation around gun control, surveillance, and state accountability for police violence.

Mothers of the Movement provide a kind of ur-narrative of the relationship between Black death and Black maternal friendship, where trauma constitutes the foundation of Black maternal relationality. Shared grief is what is imagined to make possible the intimacy of their friendship, and it is what births and authorizes their political activism. Gwen Carr describes the powerful affective bond undergirding the group: "We mothers know what it is to have to bury a child when that child is supposed to have buried us We can embrace each other, we can encourage each other. Sometimes, when we're feeling down, we can call each other—it's nothing when I get a call from one of the other mothers at three or four in the morning. If there's something that's on their mind, or if they're hurting—sometimes you can bring a little light into their life for that moment."[64] Yet the narrative of unconditional, apolitical maternal friendship rooted in trauma obscures tensions and conflicts within the group, perhaps most notably a split between Eric Garner's mother and daughter over whom to endorse for president (Garner's mother supported Clinton while Garner's daughter supported Bernie Sanders). It insists that grief trumps dissent, that loss is a sufficient affective glue to bind the group.

The Black female trio at the center of my story in this chapter offers a different account of the possibilities of Black maternal friendship, suggesting that Black maternal joy, playfulness, and even sensuality, rather than simply shared grief and trauma, can be the basis of Black maternal solidarity. While Mothers of the Movement is often a key reference point for the celebrities I describe—particularly for Knowles, who gave the Mothers a cameo in the music video for "Freedom" in the film *Lemonade* and who brought four of the Mothers to the MTV Video Music Awards—Knowles, Williams, and Obama present us with a different iconography of Black female friendship, one that is forged through the nexus of motherhood and celebrity. Here, I interpret their friendships differently from how Brittney Cooper analyzes the connection between Knowles and Obama as part of a long tradition of Black women's intimacies. Instead, I read them as a counternarrative to stories of Black women's friendship as cemented by trauma and as a kind of relationality that is cemented by motherhood. In this section, I analyze how Knowles, Williams, and Obama perform their intimacy through a process I call *celebrity citation*. In other words, each of these figures builds her celebrity persona through citing the others and through referencing her admiration for the others. This citation takes many forms. At times, it takes the form of publicly championing each other; other times, it takes the form of artistic collaboration. Sometimes it takes the form of simply showing up for each other—sitting in the stands of a tennis match, making a cameo in a music video. This includes Obama's celebration of Knowles's birthday, Williams appearing in Knowles's music video for "Sorry," Knowles's performance at Obama's inauguration, Obama attending the US Open to cheer for Williams, and Williams and Obama dancing together to celebrate Obama's Let's Move initiative.

Motherhood is often at the heart of the intimate act of celebrity citation. For example, in her celebration of Michelle Obama in *Time* magazine, Knowles notes that seeing Obama as a mother was powerful. Knowles writes, "I am so grateful that my daughters and my son live in a world where Michelle Obama shines as a beacon of hope who inspires all of us to do better and to be better."[65] The world that Obama makes possible for future generations of Black children, one marked by "hope" and "inspiration," has crystallized Knowles's appreciation of Obama. The public performance of admiration for each other and friendship, one intensified through their shared identities as Black mothers, offers a different archive of Black maternal relationality, one that is framed through something other than injury. They offer us a grammar of Black maternal friendship oriented not toward trauma or anticipated loss but toward something else that we might think of as joy, pleasure, and play.

At times, the friendships forged among the trio have been the subject of cultural fascination. In 2019, the *Washington Post* described Obama and Knowles's friendship as a "love story" and noted that the two share a "mutual admiration," one that Cooper described as a "mutual girl crush."[66] In a short film documenting their "admiration" for each other, Obama announced that if she could have any occupation, she would want to be, simply, Beyoncé. And in an episode of James Corden's *Carpool Karaoke*, Obama belted out "Single Ladies" and detailed her unabashed love for the Beyhive. Writing in *Time* magazine, Knowles celebrated Obama: "I'm honored to know such a brilliant Black woman who's spoken about the sacrifice it takes to balance her passions while remaining a supportive partner and mother, and now a best-selling author with *Becoming*."[67] The two have developed a rich and dense web of citationality, cheering for each other—as when Knowles released *Homecoming* and Obama noted, "Girl you make me so proud, and I love you. I also love that your new Netflix film 'Homecoming' is informed by the Black leaders, thinkers and poets who've paved the way for folks like us."[68] Cooper notes, "Excepting Oprah and Gayle, we have rarely been treated to seeing unabashed admiration between two sisters at the top of their game. The other exception would be the Williams sisters, but then, they are actual blood kin. Black women know full well that our lives are nothing without the sisters who inspire us, pull our cards, make us laugh uproariously, and show up for every manner of celebration or rescue mission, depending on what is required. We are our sisters' keepers."[69] In other moments, the friendship among the trio has consisted simply of showing up for each other, as when Knowles cheered for Williams at the US Open in 2016. Here, I focus on two moments when members of the trio have appeared to support each other—Williams's appearance in Knowles's visual album *Lemonade* and Obama's appearance in a visual campaign to celebrate Knowles's birthday—and read them as offering us a counternarrative to the dominant conception of Black female friendship forged through the shared connection of motherhood.

The video for "Sorry," one of the tracks from Knowles's highly decorated 2016 *Lemonade*, begins simply with the word "Apathy" and a warning authored by poet Warsan Shire whispered by Knowles: "So what are you gonna say at my funeral now that you've killed me? Here lies the body of the love of my life whose heart I broke without a gun to my hand. Here lies the mother of my children both living and dead. Rest in peace my true love who I took for granted, most bomb pussy. . . . Ashes to ashes, dust to side chicks." We might think of "Sorry" as part of a longer Black feminist tradition of critiquing both the demand of Black women's apologies and how apologies mask violence, much as Ntozake Shange captured in a choreo-poem: "One thing I don't need / is any more apologies."[70] While "Sorry" is a plea for women to put their "middle fingers up, put them hands high, wave it in his face, tell him 'boy bye,'" it builds its representational currency through the presence of Williams in the video. Williams wears a black leotard and a cape, and she twerks in front of Knowles, who reclines in a throne. If Knowles's lyrics were a rebuke to an unfaithful lover—one who was invested in "side chicks," including "Becky with the good hair"—Williams noted that the song spoke to her because "I am not sorry for who I am. . . . I am not sorry about anything. I really connected to those lyrics and felt good about that."[71] In Williams's narrative, "Sorry" is an anthem of confidence and self-assuredness, about a refusal to perform "sorry." Indeed, the inclusion of Williams in "Sorry" reveals the layered genius of *Lemonade*. While *Lemonade* has always (and obsessively) been read as a tell-all response to Jay-Z's real or imagined infidelity, it is also about Black women's communion, their connection to a shared past and their willingness to construct a new kind of future together.

*Lemonade* is also centrally about Black women's collective refusal to perform apology for their needs, desires, bodies, and intimate and political longings, and this is precisely what makes Williams's appearance in the video so compelling. As Sarah Olutola suggests, we can interpret Williams's presence as a response to an earlier political moment when her dancing was deemed too proximate to Blackness. In 2012, after defeating Maria Sharapova in the Olympics, Williams celebrated with a dance—the "crip walk"—and the dance, rather than her achievement, again became the subject of controversy, with one reporter noting, "It was as if Serena just couldn't seem to avoid dipping into waters of controversy even as she'd ascended to the top of her sport."[72] Williams simply noted: "It was just me. I love to dance. I didn't know what else to do. I was so happy, and next thing I know I started dancing and moving."[73] Her collaboration with Knowles allows Williams to use her body, and her desire to move it—to dance, to sway, to twerk—performs an emphatic refusal to be "sorry." We might think, then, of "Sorry" as enabling Williams and Knowles both to stage a critique of a white patriarchal society that demands Black women apologize for their very presence and to perform critiques that emerge from their particular experiences of highly scrutinized and public Black celebrity lives. If "Sorry" enabled both Williams and Knowles to build their celebrity around and through each other, through a practice of citationality, it also emphasized that a position of "not sorry" was made possible through Black motherhood. Knowles's insistence that "the mother of one's children, living and dead" deserves a kind of recognition and compassion suggests that her capacity to assert her "not-sorry" position is intimately related to her identity as a mother. Indeed, it is motherhood that makes possible participation in a communion of Black women who collectively say "I'm not thinking about you," who cheer "middle fingers up," who refuse the logics of mastery and control by being together.

In 2017, in honor of Knowles's thirty-sixth birthday, various celebrities recreated her outfit from the video "Formation." Kelly Rowland, Michelle Williams, Michelle Obama, and Serena Williams all appeared dressed as Knowles, as did Tina Knowles, Hattie White (Beyoncé's grandmother), Gloria Carter (Jay-Z's mother), and Blue Ivy (one of Beyoncé's daughters), making the celebration of Knowles's life tethered to a celebration of Black women's intimacies across generations. The *Washington Post* read Obama's participation as a remaking of the First Lady portrait, noting, "By allowing herself to be photographed alongside other members of Beyoncé's inner circle, Obama reclaimed her image from the annals of stodgy first lady portraits. And, she did it by embodying Beyoncé's."[74] This was a reading of Obama's dress-up that insisted that, in her post–White House life, she had found her "inner Knowles," that this was her final act of moving beyond the First Lady role. Yet I want to think about this collection of celebratory images differently, querying how citational celebrity—here performed quite visibly and literally through a slew of Black women *becoming* Beyoncé, transforming themselves into embodied citations of "Formation"—actually hinges on a narrative of female kinship. In this reading, Obama places her body in a lineage of women who are connected to Knowles as mothers, daughters, and sisters. In my reading, the familiar First Lady portrait is remade into a family portrait that emphasizes the powerful relationships among female kin.

The loved ones who "got in formation" to celebrate Knowles's birthday were not merely an "inner circle," as they were called by the *Washington Post*, but mothers and daughters and friends who might be described as sisters. Indeed, what is most surprising about the visual celebration of Knowles is that while it contains numerous celebrities, it also centers Knowles's maternal kin and her daughter, all of whom take on Knowles's iconic "Formation" outfit. While we can interpret the photo shoot as a celebration of Knowles's celebrity, it is also a tribute to the life-affirming power of female intimacies, the necessary labor of the Black maternal to make possible—in every sense of the word—both Knowles's life and her work. Indeed, the effacement of the individuality of the women in the image suggests that they are unified both by their visual transformation—they have *become* Beyoncé—and by their placement in an image that celebrates Black female collectivity. A year later, as Knowles publicly reflected on her thirty-sixth year, she noted, "At 36, I became a new mother of 3. I breastfed twins. I renewed my vows with my husband of ten years. I came back home to the stage to do Coachella, after pregnancy."[75] Knowles emphasized the importance of motherhood to her year, and she cast her achievements around her parental labor. Read in this light, her birthday image becomes a tribute both to her celebrity and to the power of Black motherhood to unite, connect, and produce communion.

Of course, the Black dead are not apart from the Black maternal friendships that the trio forges. This is perhaps most visible in Knowles's ongoing conversations about the deep trauma of miscarriage—which have importantly called attention to the unspoken realities of Black women's experiences of loss—and in Knowles's inclusion of Mothers of the Movement in *Lemonade*. Various scholars and commentators noted that the participation of these mothers and the ghostly presence of their sons—the mothers held portraits of their slain sons—performed significant and radical political work. Treva B. Lindsey notes, "We know these women because of the unbearable pain they continue to endure. Their inclusion is both a way of bearing witness and of loving out loud the women whose pain bring them into a kinship based in state violence. But they press on and we must press on because their pain is a call to love, a call to fight, a call to never forget, and a call to imagine a world in which Trayvon,

Eric, and Mike could survive, live, and thrive."[76] For Lindsey, the presence of the Mothers is a kind of "love out loud," a public declaration of solidarity with mothers whose very presence signifies unbearable pain and inexplicable loss. Similarly, Cooper writes, "What I love is that Bey took the time to make public space for these Black mothers to grieve. And including them, particularly Sybrina Fulton, a full four years after Trayvon's death, reminds us that though some of us may have moved on, these Black mothers must live with this grief every day."[77] Indeed, Mothers of the Movement become another form of maternal relationality that Knowles cites in her work, revealing that the porous boundary between living and dead is part of her maternal aesthetic and her practice of celebrity citation. Yet Knowles suggests that that there are different affective circuits of maternal friendship, that Black maternal friendship can emerge from trauma and joy, that even when it is rooted in joy and playfulness, it can unfold with a deep understanding of the materiality and proximity of loss.

The Black maternal celebrity citational practices that I trace here are elastic, and they have expanded to include other Black maternal celebrities. For example, Williams and Knowles have both been invested in supporting Meghan Markle, the former Duchess of Sussex, particularly after the birth of her child. Markle gained publicity through the tremendous scrutiny she received as a new mother, and her critiques of the media's intrusive publicity, especially after she said, "I never thought that this would be easy," and then, "But I thought it would be fair."[78] The scrutiny was only enhanced when she and her husband decided to leave the royal family in 2020, a decision that the US media read as animated, at least in part, by a response to British racism. Markle has also become a fixture in US media because of her presence at Williams's tennis matches. In fact, Williams described Markle as "literally the strongest person I know and the nicest, sweetest. She flew all the way with a newborn to see me play in New York and flew all the way back that night, and I probably couldn't have done that. That kind of goes to show you what an amazing person she is. That's just one of the many things that she does for me. I call her, text her anytime crying, upset. She's always there and doesn't matter what she's going through, she just sets time away, and she's just so amazing."[79] Markle's recent presence with the trio reveals how their friendship is rooted, at least partially, in a shared sense of the intense demands placed on Black mothering in public.

What these Black female celebrities give us is another archive of Black maternal friendship, one forged neither out of the political currency of Black women's grief nor out of shared loss. In representing the possibility of Black female intimacy and relationality beyond trauma, they effectively offer us different ways of seeing Black women: coming into view through affection, play, and pleasure. Cooper notes, "When you get right down to it, that kind of Black girl friendship is regular as rain" and yet we can consider how representations of Black women's friendship are so often cemented only through loss and tragedy, not through joy, mutual admiration, or respect.[80] What the trio allows us to see are celebrities who build their "brand" and visibility in and through their proximity to each other, who reject a logic of scarcity and competition and instead insist that their visibility as celebrities is only enhanced through their closeness. They also collectively emphasize that motherhood and its imagined communal politics, its insistence on a "we" that can be protected, is in and of itself a bedrock for friendship. They provide us, then, with another grammar of Black maternal relationality, rooted in joy, pleasure, intimacy, and glamour.

*The Ordinary and the Spectacular*

I conclude by thinking about how the trio claims Black maternal glamour alongside an investment in the Black maternal ordinary as a strategy for balancing an ethic of playfulness alongside an ethic of Black familial privacy. The ordinary—as it is described and championed by the trio—is a strategy for publicly insisting on a private life, while the insistence on Black maternal glamour becomes a public-facing crafted persona that tethers Black maternal life to the fabulous. Ordinariness is, at times, a way of describing a mothering ethic, a practice of shielding children from scrutiny, or desiring a particular kind of "normal" family life, while glamour is a way of styling the body for public attention. The trio navigates the tightrope of privacy and scrutiny, publicity and ordinariness, always in an effort to maintain a semblance of the "Black interior," the sanctity of a private domestic life.

Michelle Obama long emphasized her investment in crafting an ordinary life for her daughters, Malia and Sasha, even as their childhoods were lived under conditions far from ordinary, including intense media attention. In one interview, Obama described the importance of maintaining quotidian domestic practices, even in the White House, noting that her daughters "couldn't do that [order food] at home when we lived in Chicago. They can't pick up the phone and order anything. They're kids. That's the point that I make to them: You live in the White House, but you're a child!"[81] In another interview she noted, "We had to parent by creating this cocoon of normalcy in a pretty crazy, abnormal world. We spent eight years just going, 'It's OK! You'll be fine, this is normal, just go to school. You have men with guns . . . hey, you know, you're safe, don't complain! You have food, so don't complain to me.'"[82] Obama secured the idea of the "cocoon of normalcy" as a maternal ethic. She branded herself as "a girl from Chicago's South Side" whose primary labor was providing a "cocoon," one made largely possible by the presence of her mother, Marian Robinson, in the White House. Robinson steadfastly avoided media and insisted on maintaining autonomy and privacy even in her life inside the White House (in one interview, she described how she did her own laundry). Obama noted her mother's presence as necessary for her daughters' collective sense of normalcy:

> I wanted them [Malia and Sasha] to come home to family. There were just parts of the girls' lives that I knew would be OK because Mom was there. When I traveled internationally, grandma was there. When I wasn't home at the end of the day, grandma was there. When the kids were still little and they needed to have someone be with them in school—think about it, my girls were being driven around in a motorcade of three cars with at least four grown adults with guns in each of those cars. I thought that's a really unnatural way for a little second grader to go to school, well, Mom would ride with the car with her to make it feel like a regular carpool.[83]

Robinson's largely invisible presence in the White House as the safeguard of normalcy, as invested in a life apart from the spectacle, and as there to shelter her granddaughters, only underscored the Obama family's collective investment in ordinariness as an ethical way of structuring their children's domestic life. For Obama, ordinariness becomes a Black maternal aesthetic, even as it was performed by Black celebrity, even as it is often far from the ordinary most of us would count as familiar. It acted as a tactic for shielding her daughters from public scrutiny and as a strategy for insisting on an as-close-to-normal life as possible. Obama regularly walked the tightrope of privacy and disclosure, revealing in her memoir that her children were conceived through IVF and insisting on their privacy, their right to the simplicity, complexity, and even mistakes of ordinary girlhood. Indeed, Obama fashioned a Black maternal aesthetic that allowed her at once to be a "girl from the South Side" and to have daughters who live regular lives, even as they are driven to school by armed guards. In so doing, she reveals how celebrity and selective publicity can be a tactic of insisting on Black maternal privacy and how ordinariness itself can become a Black maternal aesthetic.

Williams and her husband, Ohanian, have also collectively forged a kind of selective privacy and celebrity simultaneously through the creation of an avatar,

Qai Qai. Qai Qai, their daughter's doll, has a digital life of her own, with over 140,000 Instagram followers; the *New York Times* referred to her as "America's most important doll."[84] Qai Qai has even conducted interviews—as she did for *Oprah Magazine*—explaining her regular use of the phrase "boss up" on social media. Williams described Qai Qai's origins as political: she wanted her daughter's first doll to be Black. Yet in the years since Qai Qai's creation, the doll avatar has allowed Williams and Ohanian collectively to craft their own public narrative (they are posited as the doll's grandparents) that allows their hungry fans selective access to their private lives. The ordinary life of Qai Qai constitutes both a practice of openness and a shield, showcasing what appears to be Williams's ordinary life and also shielding it by offering only a carefully cultivated view.

If ordinariness functions as a Black maternal aesthetic, one that permits a modicum of privacy, glamour has acted as a public-facing project that offers limited views of celebrity's imagined lives. Glamour is both a form of revelation that allows a desirous public access to images of celebrity icons and also, importantly, a shield that selectively and carefully offers only partial glimpses into celebrity life. In 2017, Serena Williams posted a selfie on Snapchat. She wore a yellow bathing suit, held her sunglasses by her side, and showcased her small "baby bump." Over the image was a simple caption: "20 weeks." The image was celebrated for the revelations of Williams's pregnancy and that her Australian Open title had been earned during her first trimester. But there was something else—here the pregnant body was represented not as vulnerable or as asexual (as the maternal is often figured as antisexual, or previously sexual) but as elegant, as glamorous, as unabashedly cool, much as Knowles had appeared in her glamorous, sensual, and even vulnerable Instagram pregnancy announcement, her carefully crafted image that married fecundity and eroticism. How might we treat these celebrities as rewriting the relationship between the Black maternal body and the glamorous? What does it mean that Williams and Knowles—even while documenting their postpartum struggles—have become icons of maternal sexiness? How do we understand how Obama's rebranding as "mom-in-chief" included a public celebration of her fashionable clothing and her toned arms? How might we consider this trio's use of glamour as a Black maternal aesthetic that allows strategic access to private lives, with a collective emphasis on fashion, beauty, and fabulousness as not merely Black female aesthetics but also as Black maternal aesthetics, as perhaps made all the more fabulous because of a proximity to motherhood?

madison moore has excavated the "fabulous" as a Black queer aesthetic. As moore notes, "One of the greatest creative gifts of marginalized people and social outcasts is that power of abstraction—the ability to see through the here and now and to live dangerously through radical style, art, music and ideas."[85] He emphasizes that his exegesis of the fabulous circumvents the celebrity because "that's a book that has already been written many times," instead thinking about the fabulous quotidian, and he notes that "fabulousness does not take a lot of money" and that "it's an aesthetic that requires high levels of creativity, imagination, and originality, but there is no blueprint for fabulousness."[86] For moore, the fact of queer of color survival makes style never simply a matter of aesthetics—"it's also a form of protest, a revolt against the normal and systems that oppress and torture us all every day, things like white supremacy, misogyny, transmisogyny, patriarchy, toxic masculinity, gender policing and racism."[87] For moore, the fabulous constitutes practices that index Black life "in the wake," that show "excelling as the best possible revenge."[88]

In the hands of my trio, Black motherhood itself is remade as a site of glamour and fabulousness, a time of fashion, chicness, and even sexiness. While I read this investment in Black maternal glamour as a technology of producing Black domestic privacy, I remain acutely aware, following Erica Edwards's cogent analysis of the "Black normal," of how this Black glamour can get put to work to support violent narratives of nation and empire. For example, Knowles's efforts to trademark her daughter's name, Blue Ivy Carter, insist that Blue Ivy is a "cultural icon" and that corporations should not be able to use her name to generate profits of consumer interest. Here, Black life becomes a Black feminist commodity, one that aspires to be trademarked and protected in the name both of privacy and of safeguarding its own potential profits. Thus, my investment is not in celebrating the Black glamourous—though I remain deeply curious about how motherhood gets rewritten as erotic, sensual, and sexy—but instead in probing how its commitment to publicity coexists with a desire to shield, protect, and insulate Black domestic life, particularly life for Black children.

This chapter has argued that Black maternal celebrity offers a new grammar of the Black maternal that I describe as Black maternal aesthetics. The Black maternal is not merely an identity category, but also a relationship to representation. In the case of the trio I describe here, it is a relationship to representing Black motherhood anew. This is not a counter-aesthetic to grief, as these three women often stage celebrity by reckoning with various forms of maternal trauma and by standing in solidarity with grieving Black mothers. This is, though, an aesthetic of Black motherhood that centers abundance, sensuality, friendship, and the interplay of the ordinary and the glamorous as intrinsic to Black maternal life. The trio members insist on a vision of Black mothers as playful, creative, erotic subjects, and they strategically mobilize motherhood to renarrate their celebrity, to offer themselves new registers through which to speak and to be heard. Perhaps most important, they use motherhood as a form of being together, a profound form of relationality, a common ground for forging celebratory affirmative relationships, for being friends. Finally, this trio remakes the very conception of Black life from its well-worn association with potential life, futurity, and Black children. Instead, the trio powerfully reads Black mothers themselves as a locus of Black life, as precisely what must be held, preserved, and celebrated, not because of its capacity to reproduce, but because of its capacity to speak from a distinct and urgent position. What this trio suggests, then, is that Black motherhood offers Black celebrity the ability to narrate itself anew, to tell its story on its own terms, and to even recraft the platform from which Black mothers can speak and be heard.

Nothing is private. Nothing is sacred. There is nothing I keep to myself. Being your mother has required one act of vulgarity after another, and I am so strung out on you I couldn't care less. I don't know if I can define myself anymore, now that I'm your mother. You've consumed me. Being your mother has cooked me right down to the bone.
—CAMILLE DUNGY, *Guidebook to Relative Strangers*

## FOUR. WRITING BLACK MOTHERHOOD

*Black Maternal Memoirs and Economies of Grief*

Camille Dungy's *Guidebook to Relative Strangers: Journeys into Race, Motherhood, and History* is a memoir about Black motherhood that is also, perhaps surprisingly, a celebration of hiking. She writes, "Outside long enough, I lose the contours of my body and become part of something larger. What I watch for on a good hike are moments of permission, the times my interactions with what is beyond me provide opportunities to know the world in ways different from how I'm used to knowing it."[1] If the natural world can be a site of radical possibility, she reminds readers that it can also be a space of threat. In an essay titled "A Good Hike," Dungy transports readers to a November afternoon when she and a group of friends hike the Adirondack Mountains in New York. As darkness sets in and the group descends the mountain, Dungy feels her ankle snap. The pain is debilitating. She describes herself as "a hurt animal curl[ed] around itself, pained and snarling, needing assistance, but daring anyone to come near."[2] There is an imminent threat, a crisis even. Darkness is coming, she is unable to put any weight on her ankle, and her friends begin to debate how to get Dungy off the mountain. Should they carry her? Should she crawl? How would they take the weight off of her swelling ankle and ensure that they finished the walk before nightfall? "Let go and let gods," she tells herself, and she allows her friends to bear her full weight, to carry her body down the hill as darkness falls.[3] She writes, "The group of people on whom I found myself dependent were relative strangers. And yet, as I was at their mercy in the wild, this was the best group I could imagine falling among."[4] Dungy's foray "into the wild" suggests a host of surprising turns that writing about Black motherhood has taken in recent years. Why, the reader might ask of Dungy's work, does telling the story of Black motherhood jettison the logics of emergency that have come to be expected of the Black maternal, and instead sit with descriptions of the natural world and the collective vulnerability it engenders? Why does Dungy's exploration of "race, motherhood, and history" celebrate her "dependence" on "relative strangers," and what is it about Black motherhood that makes discovering a kind of "mercy" possible?

This chapter studies contemporary Black maternal memoirs with an attention to how Black maternal life-writing conforms to and upends the temporal, political, and aesthetic demands of crisis. I argue that Black maternal memoirs push against the parameters of the crisis framing, at times resisting it entirely by emphasizing ecstatic, spiritual, and "natural" mothering, and at times attending to grief but troubling its expected logics by refusing respectability or by inflecting loss differently through a focus on infertility, miscarriage, or broken mother-daughter bonds. I examine an archive of contemporary Black maternal memoirs because of how profoundly underrepresented this work has been in both Black feminist scholarship and literary studies scholarship, with the exception of interventions by Kimberly Killen, Stephanie Hartzell, Kate Baldwin, Felicia R. Stewart, and an article I coauthored with Samantha Pinto on the "strange intimacies" represented in memoirs by members of Mothers of the Movement.[5] This scholarly absence persists despite an outpouring of popular work that traces the "whiteness" of the maternal memoir genre but largely ignores the substantial body of Black maternal life-writing that the very construction of the maternal memoir—what Nefertiti Austin terms the "white mommy memoir status quo"—often elides.[6] I examine this understudied and popular archive because it has garnered visibility in and through the frame of crisis, yet it often challenges what precisely constitutes the crisis, or, in the case of Dungy, it presents Black motherhood as a space of communion, tranquility, and connection, rather than precarity and trauma.

The last decade has been marked by the publication of myriad maternal memoirs, including Emma Brockes's *An Excellent Choice: Panic and Joy on My Solo Path to Motherhood* (2018), Laura Jean Baker's *The Motherhood Affidavits* (2018), Molly Caro May's *Body Full of Stars* (2017), Laura June's *Now My Heart Is Full* (2018), Jessica Friedmann's *Things That Helped* (2017), Meaghan O'Connell's *And Now We Have Everything* (2018), Rachel Cusk's *A Life's Work* (2002), Maggie Nelson's *The Argonauts* (2015), and Anne Enright's *Making Babies* (2012).[7] In 2018, Parul Sehgal noted that the "girls" that had captivated the publishing industry—as in the novels *Gone Girl* (2012) and *The Girl on the Train* (2015)— "have been replaced, improbably perhaps, by mothers, if this vertiginous pile of memoirs and novels on my desk is any indication. There is a sudden flurry of fascination with my people (full disclosure: a small, surly child thrashes in her sleep just to the right of that pile)."[8] Lauren Elkin treats this proliferation of maternal texts as inaugurating an aesthetic and political claim, in that "they demand that the experience of motherhood in all its viscera be taken seriously as literature. They put the mother and her perspective at the center of their concerns. We have lacked a canon of motherhood, and now, it seems, one is beginning to take shape."[9]

The last decade has also been marked by a pointed critique of the maternal memoir as a "white" genre. In a 2016 polemic, Austin describes "the difficulty of selling my story to the publishing industry that makes millions from books about motherhood—but insists that Black mom narratives are too marginal to sell. I am hardly the first to make this observation."[10] Nancy Reddy echoes this, noting, "Motherhood's in the literary zeitgeist for the moment, and these books—along with the reviewers who discuss them as a group—are shaping the contours of a new genre. And currently it's a genre steeped in largely unexamined whiteness. (I'm using white as a bit of a catchall here for the normative experience of motherhood captured in these books, all written by women who are white, straight, partnered, middle class, college-educated.)"[11]

Even as the maternal memoir is bemoaned as a "white" genre, recent years have seen the growth of Black maternal memoirs as a visible genre alongside the publishing industry's growing rhetorical investment in diversity. In the last decade, Black maternal memoirs have become their own visible genre, one intimately related to the new economy for Black writing, and Black life-writing specifically, that Black Lives Matter (BLM) has produced. This economy includes memoirs like Sybrina Fulton and Tracy Martin's *Rest in Power* (2017) and Lezley McSpadden's *Tell the Truth and Shame the Devil* (2015); novels like Angie Thomas's *The Hate U Give* (2017); and nonfiction like Michael Eric Dyson's

*Tears We Cannot Stop* (2017), Jesmyn Ward's *Men We Reaped* (2013), and Ta-Nehisi Coates's *Between the World and Me* (2015), which was hailed as BLM's "foundational text."[12] This new attention to BLM as a literary market coincides with calls to publish "diverse" children's and young adult books (an attention largely born from the efforts of organizations like We Need Diverse Books and projects like the #1000BlackGirlBooks campaign), critiques of the lack of "diverse" staffs in publishing houses, attention to the limited conception of what constitutes "diverse" books, efforts to tackle "diversity" in genres like romance and mystery, and the publishing industry's increasing use of "sensitivity readers," who, as the *New York Times* noted, "provide feedback on issues like race, religion, gender, sexuality, chronic illness and physical disabilities."[13] If Black women documented a publishing industry that largely ignored their mothering stories even as the maternal memoir rose in prominence, publishing has now recognized Black maternal stories as their own market, one that can be capitalized on.

In what follows, I trace Black women's complex representations of "mothering while Black" and the literary markets that have grown to represent and commodify Black maternal labor, affect, and politics, at times showing that the literary market that presumes Black maternal trauma is at odds with what this archive represents and imagines.[14] In turning attention to the Black maternal memoir, I aspire to understand, study, and locate the place of—and the market for—Black maternal memoirs in the midst of the publishing industry's recent creation of a maternal "boom." If the white maternal memoir is presumed to offer an account of ambivalence yet actually gives us a rich glimpse into the rearrangement of the maternal self, the Black maternal memoir—especially in a BLM era—is imagined (and marketed) to show us something else. Its labor is not about documenting a fraught relationship with the child, where the child becomes an imposition on an otherwise coherent conception of the autonomous self. Nor is its task revealing a surprising pleasure in motherhood. Instead, the Black maternal memoir directs its grief, anxiety, and rage at a deathly world imagined to be *outside* the boundaries of home, of community. These are texts thought to document the feelings of expected loss that attend to Black motherhood, that grapple with the simultaneous life-giving labor of motherhood and the terror of the life-stealing world of antiBlackness. These memoirs make Black grief—whether the grief about a slain child or the anticipated grief of watching a child navigate an antiBlack world—public, and they represent the child not as an object of maternal destruction but as a figure who requires intensive maternal care. As Mychal Denzel Smith notes, this vision of the Black maternal memoir aligns with what "has become an obligation for Black families to mourn in public.... Black grief belongs to the world, and is regulated by the same forces that caused such deep pain in the first place. Black families become advocates, activists, and spokespeople, historians, journalists, and policy experts, while also being the gatekeepers of the legacy and humanity of those they've lost."[15] The Black maternal memoir's imagined investment in making Black pain visible reveals how Black maternal pain is a political commodity, much as Trayvon Martin's hoodie was, much like Jay-Z's decision to produce the documentary *Rest in Power: The Trayvon Martin Story* (2018), or like Beyoncé's inclusion of Mothers of the Movement in her visual album *Lemonade*. Yet, as I argue in this chapter, the Black maternal memoir actually offers myriad grammars of ecstatic, creative, and spiritual mothering, of "natural" mothering, that complicate monolithic visions of "mothering while Black," even as they necessarily contend with a marketplace where Black maternal grief is what gives Black motherhood, and Black maternal writing, legibility. They are texts that are given visibility and urgency by crisis, and yet they sit with crisis—its meanings, valences, and experiences—in ways that unsettle the frame itself.

I consider here how Black maternal memoirs engage with the political commodity of Black maternal grief in a host of ways, offering complex fashionings of Black motherhood in an era of "crisis." This chapter unfolds in four parts. I begin with reading two canonical mothering memoirs: Adrienne Rich's *Of Woman Born* (1976) and Alice Walker's "One Child of One's Own: A Meaningful Digression Within the Work(s)" in *In Search of Our Mothers' Gardens* (1983). In pairing these texts, I upend the pervasive telling of maternal writing that reads the political projects of Black and white maternal writing as in tension. I think reparatively about feminist writing in Black and white, at a moment in which white feminism is described, obsessively and repeatedly, as a form of patriarchal violence, and Black feminism is hailed, again and again, as an anti-institutional and fugitive form of world-making. I then turn to Rebecca Walker's *Baby Love* (2007) and Dani McClain's *We Live for the We* (2019). Even as these texts have different relationships to racial politics, they both fashion the maternal memoir as a space that represents a resistant Black motherhood in the face of relentless forces that threaten the sanctity of Black domestic life—for Rebecca Walker, feminism; for McClain, antiBlackness. For Walker, ecstatic motherhood is an embrace of the "natural" capacity to care deeply, to be intimately bound to another subject, and a refusal of what she imagines to be feminism's violent rejection of children. For McClain, the intense labor of forging a safe, private Black domestic world is an intensely pleasurable act of creativity and spirituality that indexes her love for her daughter. The texts share a sense that resistant Black mothering is forged through ideas of natural mothering, maternal creativity, and spirituality. I then turn to Dungy's *Guidebook to Relative Strangers* (2017) and McSpadden's *Tell the Truth and Shame the Devil* (2016) and argue that each presents Black motherhood as holding a distinct relationship to temporality. For Dungy, Black motherhood is constituted by a kind of ecological time, one that places Black maternal bodies in deep communion with the natural world. For McSpadden, Black motherhood is marked by endurance, by a deep capacity to withstand, to persevere, to respond to relentless demand with stamina. The chapter concludes with a coda that follows Emily Lordi's call to read Michelle Obama's memoir, *Becoming* (2018), as a maternal memoir. I trace how Obama offers us a different way to think about Black maternal grief and loss through miscarriage and infertility.

This chapter's argumentative work hinges, at least in part, on the assembly of its archive: a selection of contemporary Black maternal memoirs that remain underanalyzed and underexamined in scholarly work. I center Black maternal memoirs that received significant media coverage, like Obama's *Becoming* or McClain's *We Live for the We,* alongside texts that have been foundational to the literary archive of BLM, like McSpadden's *Tell the Truth and Shame the Devil*. Yet I also aspire to push at the parameters of what constitutes the BLM canon (and historical moment) both by including earlier texts like Walker's *Baby Love* and by exploring why a text like Dungy's *Guidebook* falls outside the parameters of this canon.

Taken together, my readings of these memoirs explore how Black maternal writing challenges the foundations of a market that hails Black women as tragic agents authorized by grief, even as some of the texts I analyze grapple with various forms of loss and trauma. I sit with the maternal aesthetics and ethics these texts generate and circulate, which move alongside myriad kinds of trauma and pain *and* which complicate the notion of proximity to death—where death takes the form of a slain child—as the condition of Black maternal life. I use this archive to push conceptions of Black motherhood beyond its marketed bounds even as the archive depends on frames of grief and violence for its very visibility and legitimacy.

*Mothering Stories in Black and White*

In challenging the notion that the Black maternal memoir performs its aesthetic work around grief, I necessarily complicate a story about the white maternal memoir as well. I seek to contest the notion that "ambivalence" is the affective heart of the genre, and so I look at how these two kinds of maternal writing are often pitted against each other, with one hailed as apolitical—and perhaps, at times, as trivial—and one celebrated as expansively political. Descriptions of the "white" maternal memoir—a term I deploy even as I seek to unsettle it—have generally been marketed as having a distinctive affective attachment to ambivalence, whereas Black maternal memoirs are often marketed as attached to grief and trauma, to loss and injury.[16] Roberta Garrett writes, "Maternal writers engage with the longstanding feminist fight to write the unspeakable, those abject discourses of (traditionally feminine) experience and emotion that transgress gendered and social norms to the extent that they are forcibly repressed in quotidian interaction and communication."[17] Ruth Quiney similarly describes the maternal memoir as "pursu[ing] the tensions and conflicts and contradictions of mothering rather than trying to resolve them, and thus expos[ing] the conundrums of maternal ambivalence, and of cultural ambivalence about maternity."[18] Quiney argues that the maternal memoir often receives a "hostile critical reception" because it is deemed navel-gazing and narcissistic, committed to exploring maternal "negative emotions."[19] These are memoirs that are thought to expose the erosion of the maternal self the child is imagined to engender, that foreground the confinement to the domestic sphere that can mark maternal life, and that document the experience of inhabiting a newly transformed body in a capitalistic patriarchal moment that presumes maternal bodies should quickly and privately return to their eroticized "before" status.

Yet ambivalence does not fully capture the complex affective registers of the so-called white maternal memoir, a genre that I see as grappling with the unmaking and remaking of the self that maternity can produce and also with how new forms of intimacy and relationality can reorient the self. In naming a genre "white maternal memoirs," I am not using "white" in the same way that it is now regularly used as a prefix to "feminism," to damn its politics or to suggest that it is feminism gone awry. I am instead using it to mark how these memoirs are marketed by the publishing industry and discussed (and, at times, condemned) in popular and scholarly work. For some authors, these are welcome shifts, and for others, they are disorienting, alarming, or, as Rachel Cusk describes, "fundamental, catalytic cris[e]s of selfhood."[20] This "catalytic crisis" is one produced in the juncture between the *before* and *after* that birth engenders. While some memoirs sit with maternal unhappiness or unease, others chart the delight of mothering. In Maggie Nelson's *The Argonauts*, for example, queer motherhood is figured as akin to romance, and she writes, "It isn't like a love affair. It *is* a love affair. Or, rather it is romantic, erotic and consuming—but without tentacles. I have my baby, and my baby has me. It is a buoyant *eros*, an *eros* without teleology. Even if I do feel turned on while I'm breastfeeding or rocking him to sleep."[21] Here, the maternal memoir performs its work not by making visible ambivalence, but through its radical embrace of the transformative self-reconfiguration that babies engender.

The white maternal memoir generally performs its investigation of maternity's remaking of the self through two strategies: accounting and exposure. These texts offer an account of the quotidian—describing breastfeeding, pumping, cleaning bottles, folding laundry, preparing meals—in the service of capturing the imagined banalities of maternal life. As Cusk writes, "After a child is born the lives of its mother and father diverge, so that where before they were living in a state of some equality, now they exist in a sort of feudal relation to each other. A day spent at home caring for a child could not be more different from a day spent working in an office."[22] This description of the deeply gendered nature of reproductive labor is akin to other feminist projects of exposing the "second shift" that women primarily shoulder, and it highlights the intensely private, highly devalued, and deeply isolating nature of infant care.[23] In foregrounding the sheer tedium of infant care, they disrupt the widespread cultural romance around reproduction.[24] As Quiney suggests in her careful engagement with Cusk's work, these are attempts "to articulate new developments in maternal subjectivity, amid the bewildering socio-economic shifts of a globalized world economy, and in the aftermath of twentieth century feminist activism."[25] This accounting is, of course, part of a long-standing feminist practice of making visible the uncompensated, unseen work that is part of the reproduction of life, but it is also a way of flagging the relationship between this invisible labor and the self, signaling that the relentlessness of maternal work can threaten the coherence and even recognizability of the maternal self. To find one's day suddenly organized around the temporality of (someone else's) naps, feedings, and sleep schedules is often a fundamental and troubling reorientation of the self.

Yet accounting can also be a way of naming the corporeal and affective changes that are a source of wonder and even beauty. Nelson writes:

> The *capaciousness* of growing a baby. The way a baby literally *makes space* where there wasn't space before. The cartilage nub where my ribs used to fit together at the sternum. The little slide in my lower rib cage when I twist right or left that didn't used to slide. The rearrangement of internal organs, the upward squeezing of the lungs. The dirt that collects on your belly button when it finally pops inside out, revealing its bottom—finite, after all. The husky feeling in my postpartum perineum, the way my

breasts filling all at once with milk is like an orgasm, but more painful, powerful as a hard rain.²⁶

For Nelson, the detailed accounting of bodily change, of an internal "rearrangement" engendered by pregnancy, is offered with a sense of unbridled surprise: look, Nelson seems to say, at how deeply and magically this body has been reorganized by its task of making space for another body.

If these texts offer a profound accounting of the mundane, the rhetorical promise of this accounting is to "break the silence," to expose the maternal labor that so often is hidden under the rubric of a "labor of love." Garrett uses the term *confession* to capture the tone of these memoirs, and Quiney describes them as *confessional*, explaining how maternal memoirs "explored the spoiled identities of mothers who, by their own admission, had fallen far short of the standards of feeling and behavior required to conform to current standards of good motherhood."²⁷ I argue this exposure is not about managing "spoiled identities" but instead about rehearsing maternal demands and doing so in a repeated and obsessive way, as if each memoir is the first to mine this ground. At times, what is exposed is the unwantedness of the child or the child as a destructive object. Other times, what is revealed is the relentlessness of the labor itself, which, for some authors, is a source of isolation or, for others, is a site of delight. When I describe the obsessively repetitive nature of this genre, I underscore that each book relishes its rupture of the silence around motherhood, each positions itself as providing a distinctive and unadulterated look at the banalities or pleasures of maternal life even as it considers its repetitive nature—and the nature of maternal labor's representation. In its promise to offer a surprising glimpse into the realities of maternal life, each forgets that it is part of a canon of maternal texts that have also sought to break silences, and that the genre itself is constituted by a promise of truth telling.

I begin with two maternal memoirs that complicate the prevailing narrative about maternal memoirs, affect, and race, thus setting the analytical stage for the work that I pursue in this chapter. I treat Rich's *Of Woman Born* and Walker's essay "One Child of One's Own" as foundational texts in the maternal memoir genre that necessarily challenge the dominant conception of the aesthetics and politics of the genre. In reading these texts together—texts that have distinctive relationships to racial politics and even to conceptions of freedom—my desire is to tell a different story about the maternal memoir, one that thinks about the intellectual and creative exchanges between Black and white women that are often written out of the current casting of the maternal memoir as white women's stories about ambivalence or Black women's stories about anticipated loss. Instead, I investigate what these texts share, namely, a preoccupation with motherhood as a felt experience and with mother-daughter intimacies as the cornerstone of maternal feelings, even as they write those feelings in distinct ways.

Rich's *Of Woman Born*, which has been hailed as a feminist classic, was the subject of tremendous criticism when it was published. Susan Sheridan notes, "Reviews of this work, in their extremes of applause and denigration, broke all the rules of polite reviewing. Rage was not too strong a term for some reactions."[28] D. Lynn O'Brien Hallstein argues that part of the reason Rich's text elicited such a strong reaction was because of its form, its willingness to traverse memoir, history, and literary analysis.[29] While Rich's text is only partially a memoir, she makes clear the necessity of the genre conventions of memoir to her larger argumentative project: to reveal and expose the "institution" of motherhood and to imagine what a woman-centered, experientially driven conception of motherhood might resemble. Rich's work describes motherhood as an institution "which aims at ensuring that that potential—and all women—shall remain under male control. This institution has been a keystone of the most diverse social and political systems. It has withheld over one-half the human species from the decisions affecting their lives; it exonerates men from fatherhood in any authentic sense; it creates the dangerous schism between 'private' and 'public' life; it calcifies human choices and potentialities."[30]

Even as Rich maps the violence of compulsory motherhood and the unequal distribution of household and affective labor that undergirds it, she seeks to reclaim the "experience" from the institution, to untangle quotidian pleasures from patriarchal violence. For Rich, the project of recuperating the "experiential"—and even the possibilities of an empowered motherhood—requires the form of memoir. As she notes, "It seemed to me impossible from the first to write a book of this kind without being often autobiographical, without often saying 'I.' . . . This is in some ways a vulnerable book."[31] What Rich suggests, then, is that the labor of exposing motherhood's institutionalized workings, its capacity to conscript women to the private sphere, and the possibility of maternal pleasures and identities is something that can only be theorized through the most personal and "vulnerable" of forms. The work of accounting for the felt experience of motherhood, which includes describing maternal labor and maternal feelings, follows what Rich called for in another of her canonical works, "Notes toward a Politics of Location," where she wrote, "Perhaps we need a moratorium on saying 'the body.' For it's also possible to abstract 'the' body. When I write 'the body,' I see nothing in particular. To write 'my body' plunges me into lived experience, particularly: I see scars, disfigurements, discolorations, damages, losses, as well as what pleases me."³² The requirement that we write from the specific historical and embodied fleshy locations we inhabit is a call for radical particularity as a feminist ethic. This notion of writing from "*my* body," from singular "lived experience," becomes, Rich argues, a requirement for grappling with the feelings and practices that compulsory motherhood generates and for excavating the maternal feelings that Rich argues are left intact but buried underneath prevailing maternal ideologies.

For Rich, life has a singular origin story, one that she rehearses repeatedly: "All human life on the planet is born of woman. The one unifying, incontrovertible experience shared by all women and men is that months-long period we spent unfolding inside a woman's body. . . . [M]ost of us first know both love and disappointment, power and tenderness, in the person of a woman."³³ The task of the memoir is to make visible the process of coming to this realization and the emotional consequences of sitting with our origins rather than rejecting them. Rich's origin story—one where all bodies *come from* woman—is one that haunts her work generally, acting as a touchstone for her theory of "compulsory heterosexuality," which treats heterosexuality as an institution that orients women away from their primary source of love and tenderness: other women.³⁴ "For most of us," Rich writes, "a woman provided the continuity and stability—but also the rejections and refusals—of our early lives, and it is with a woman's hands, eyes, body, voice, that we associate our primal sensations, our earliest social experience."³⁵ Mothers are the bodies that are "primal," our native lands, that constitute the self before we have a firm sense of the self's boundaries.

If mothers are our original territory—our home—the effort of *Woman Born* is to link institutional motherhood to the severing of maternal/daughter intimacy, a severing that Rich suggests is akin not just to "los[ing] your mother," to borrow Saidiya Hartman's term but to losing one's homeland. The effort to write "the great unwritten story," one that is about "this cathexis between mother and daughter—essential, distorted, misused," requires daughters to remember mothers, and necessitates reconfiguring the category "woman" to mean "daughter."³⁶ She writes, "The core of my book, and I enter it as a woman who, born between her mother's legs, has time after time and in different ways tried to return to her mother, to repossess her and be repossessed by her, to find the mutual confirmation from and with another woman that daughters and mothers alike hunger for, pull away from, make possible or impossible for each other."³⁷ Indeed, Rich suggests that "repossessing" mother—coming to know her again and claiming her, remembering that we come to this world from "between [a] mother's legs"—is a strategy for upending the "matrophobia" (the "fear of *becoming one's mother*") that marks patriarchal culture.[38] The task of asserting that motherhood is an experience, and claiming mothers as our origins, is a practice of honoring women's "native lands."

While Rich's critical memoir is often hailed as suturing white maternity—or affluent, heterosexual white maternity—to a performance of restlessness, and at times is described as a kind of urtext of white maternal ambivalence, I emphasize that it actually performed different argumentative work: Rich reveals that the maternal memoir stages its work on behalf of recuperation, suturing mothers to daughters, returning daughters to their "native lands."[39] This is not, then, a story of maternal ambivalence but an account of loss, one that sits with the afterlives of daughters' separations from their mothers. It is a reminder—in the language that Rich uses—that women are daughters and that we forget that identity at our peril. Rather than ambivalence, Rich's memoir is a love letter penned by a daughter in honor of her mother, one waged in the name of women's political freedom that takes the form of finding and reclaiming mothers.

Seven years later, Alice Walker would also study maternal feelings in a Black feminist project focused on reclaiming mothers *and* radically rewriting the political project of Black motherhood. In *In Search of Our Mothers' Gardens*, Walker revealed that Black women's "search" for our mothers' gardens is an attempt to recover histories of Black women's fugitive creativity. Walker asks, "What did it mean for a Black woman to be an artist in our grandmothers' time? In our great-grandmothers' day? It is a question with an answer cruel enough to stop the blood."[40] If the story of "our" mothers is one of antiBlack and patriarchal violence policing their creativity, it is also one of how Black women's creativity continued to flourish. Walker tells the story of her mother, who had five children, worked in the fields beside her father, made her children's clothes, made quilts to cover her children as they slept, and who planted and tended a magnificent garden, one "so brilliant with colors, so original in its design, so magnificent with life and creativity, that to this day people drive by our house in Georgia—perfect strangers and imperfect strangers—and ask to stand or walk among my mother's art."[41] This practice of beauty-making in the midst of violence, of grace in the midst of precarity, of creativity in the face of terror, is what Walker argues is the condition of Black women who have always had "this ability to hold on, even in very simple ways."[42] She tells us that freedom is the act of remembering these mothers, these "artists." Freedom is the act of "fearlessly pull[ing] out of ourselves and look[ing] at and identify[ing] with our lives the living creativity some of our great-grandmothers were not allowed to know."[43] For Walker, Black female identity—and Black womanist identity—becomes aligned with daughters remembering, honoring, and restoring mothers.

Walker makes visible the labor and political possibilities of searching for our mothers as she details her quest to find her metaphorical mother, Zora Neale Hurston. Walker travels through Eatonville, Florida, searching for information about Hurston, who, at the time of her death, was living in obscurity (Hurston's recovery and canonization was an institutional project of remembering spearheaded by Walker).[44] When Walker finds herself in an overgrown cemetery searching for the place where Hurston might be buried, she writes, "There are times—and finding Zora Hurston's grave was one of them—when normal responses of grief, horror, and so on, do not make sense because they bear no real relation to the depth of the emotion one feels. It was impossible for me to cry when I saw the field full of weeds where Zora is."[45] To recognize a mother's "garden"—whether Walker's mother's meticulous and stunning arrangement of flowers or the overgrown field where Hurston's body rests—is a practice of respect for the creative genius of Black women's lives and an act of honoring the self and its histories. As Walker reminds us, "A people do not throw their geniuses away. And if they are thrown away, it is our duty as artists and as witnesses for the future to collect them again for the sake of our children and, if necessary, bone by bone."[46] For Walker, our "geniuses" are our mothers; they are the women whose daily acts—cooking, cleaning, sewing, quilting, gardening—have been written out of history. The task of securing a kind of freedom, Walker tells her readers, is one of investing in collecting these histories "bone by bone," engaging in the demanding corporeal and emotional labor of recovering mothers' gardens.

If Walker celebrates maternal labor and the daughter's urgent work of "searching" for maternal histories, she approaches the materialities of mothering in more complex ways. In her essay "One Child of One's Own," Walker interrogates a form of knowing she terms "women's folly"—including her own mother's "folly"—that urges women to have multiple children, a "folly" that Walker discovers she must reject for her sanity. For Walker, motherhood constitutes a transition "from a woman whose 'womb' had been, in a sense, her head—that is to say, certain small seeds had gone in, and rather different if not larger or better 'creations' had come out—to a woman who . . . had two wombs! No. To a woman who had written books, conceived in her head, and who had also engendered at least one human being in her body."[47] The child is a threat to the garden-making she celebrates, to a creative life, to the possibility of cultivating the womb "in one's head." The birth of a child is the death of the birthwork that Walker celebrates: creativity.

Yet Walker's account of the child as an interruption in an artistic life is challenged in the very same essay when Walker turns her attention to Judy Chicago's mid-1970s art installation "The Dinner Party." Walker focuses on Chicago's representation of Sojourner Truth, the only plate at the dinner table that features a face instead of a representation of a vulva. Walker writes:

> Perhaps it is the Black woman's children, whom the white woman—having more to offer her own children, and certainly not having to offer them slavery or a slave heritage or poverty or hatred, generally speaking: segregated schools, slum neighborhoods, the worst of everything—resents. For they must always make her feel guilty. She fears knowing that Black women want the best for their children just as she does. But she also knows Black children are to have less in this world so that her children, white children, will have more (in some countries, all). Better then to deny that the Black woman has a vagina. Is capable of motherhood. Is a woman.[48]

For Walker, the violence of racism (and racist patriarchy) operates through white women's failure to see Black women *as* women and, more particularly, the failure to imagine Black women *as* mothers. This is a fundamental inability to see Black women as life-giving. But it is this realization—her engagement with representations of Black women that refuse Black maternity—that leads Walker to a reconsideration of her vision of Rebecca, her daughter. Walker writes,

> It is not my child who tells me: I have no femaleness white women must affirm. Not my child who says: I have no rights Black men must respect. It is not my child who has purged my face from history and herstory and left my-story just that, a mystery.... Not my child, who in a way *beyond* all this, but really of a piece with it, destroys the planet daily, and has begun on the universe. We are together, my child and I. Mother and child, yes, but *sisters* really, against whatever denies us all that we are.[49]

What Chicago's work makes possible for Walker—and perhaps what antiBlack misogynistic violence makes visible for Walker—is the realization that Black motherhood engenders a different kind of kinship, one where daughters are sisters, where mothers and daughters are aligned in a "togetherness" against the misogynist and racist forces that seek to "purge their faces" from history. In this account, Black mothering is actually *sister*ing, a recognition of the deep alliance between Black mothers and daughters. It is this realization that leads Walker to her famous (or perhaps infamous) closing poem:

> You have Rebecca—who is
> much more delightful
> and less distracting
> than any of the calamities
> above.[50]

The daughter, while still a "digression" in the creative life, is, then, not a calamity but a "delightful" interruption, a reminder of the transformative possibility of Black female sisterhood and its capacity to act as a form of both survival and creativity. An essay that begins with maternal ambivalence ends with treating Black mothering as a radical remaking of time and relationality, as a recognition of an intergenerational intimacy between women forged against the backdrop of antiBlack and misogynistic violence and secured by love and tenderness.

In her reading of Walker's essay, Marianne Hirsch describes how she initially analyzed it as a performance of maternal ambivalence and even rage directed at Rebecca. Hirsch recounts presenting the paper at a conference and fielding a number of questions from the audience including "why I focused my analysis on only one aspect of Walker's essay, her anger at her mother and her possible anger at her daughter, thereby ignoring 'what the essay was really about,' her anger at white feminists."[51] If Chicago's art installation stands for "white feminists" and their engagement with Black women's bodies, then her work allows Walker to forge a particular Black maternal ethic, one that both eschews "women's folly" and embraces the temporality-bending intimacy that Black mothers and daughters share. Chicago's art installation permits Walker to see—perhaps for the first time—a kind of communion between Black mothers and daughters, bound by the urgent task of navigating antiBlackness and misogyny.

I began with these two "foremothers," Rich and Walker, because both are imagined to stand as foundations for the maternal memoir genre, and to secure the notion of maternal life-writing as having particular and singular ethics and politics: white ambivalence and Black grief. These memoirs—in black and white—offer complex analyses of maternal life, attempts to theorize freedom, creativity, and sexuality. They are also endeavors to think daughters and mothers side by side, to suggest that the reclaiming of history is a radical act of self-knowledge and self-possession for women. Walker's and Rich's works suggest the need for more sustained and rigorous engagements with maternal affect beyond "ambivalence" and "loss," for explorations that help us understand the complex relationalities the maternal memoir seeks to map and chart.

Reading them together also upends the too-firm boundaries between white and Black maternal writing created and entrenched both by the publishing industry, particularly in the decades following publication, and by feminists themselves increasingly interested in thinking Black and white as identity categories, political genres, and ethical positions. Reading them together maps how maternal life-writing tackles freedom, creativity, autonomy, and interiority in ways that surprise and even confound the parameters of the genre itself.

*Un-becoming Daughter: On Ecstatic Mothering*

*Baby Love* (2007), a memoir written in diary form, stages its celebration of pregnancy in the face of Rebecca Walker's fraught relationship with her mother, the novelist, essayist, poet, and activist Alice Walker, discussed above. R. Walker's memoir was published before the birth of an organized BLM moment and before the publishing industry capitalized on that movement as a market that made Black women visible political subjects through their public grief. *Baby Love* was published the same year that then senator Barack Obama announced he was planning to run for president, a declaration that ushered in a particular iteration of an ongoing US postracial fantasy. BLM has its roots not only in the state-sanctioned assassination of Black bodies and the fascist rise of Trump but also, of course, in Obama's election—its rhetorical promises of hope and change—and the violent antiBlack "backlash" it inspired. I turn to R. Walker's memoir, then, to think about what it means to write Black motherhood at a moment when, for example, Michelle Obama was positioning herself as "everywoman, a wife, professional, mother, volunteer" and in the year before Barack Obama gave his "A More Perfect Union" speech in response to the Reverend Jeremiah Wright "scandal," which threatened to end his campaign.[52] During that speech, Obama reminded his supporters, "I can no more disown him than I can disown the Black community. I can no more disown him than I can my white grandmother—a woman who helped raise me, a woman who sacrificed again and again for me, a woman who loves me as much as she loves anything in this world, but a woman who once confessed her fear of Black men who passed by her on the street, and who on more than one occasion has uttered racial or ethnic stereotypes that made me cringe."[53] I begin my analysis of the contemporary Black maternal memoir, then, with R. Walker's text, one that predates the conventional temporalities of BLM but that represents Black motherhood at the dawning of both an Obama presidency and the rise of Michelle Obama to "mom-in-chief."

R. Walker's vision of Black motherhood begins from a refusal to rehearse the precarity of Black life, and instead she claims pleasure, sensuality, corporeal excess, and the logics of consumption as the territory of Black mothering. *Baby Love* maps the terrain of the Black ecstatic maternal, the excessive and unnameable corporeal and psychic pleasures that motherhood opens up, and suggests that maternal pleasure—and perhaps even the practice of Black maternal life-writing—is about staging motherhood apart from daughterhood. For R. Walker, maternal pleasure comes from forging a kind of maternal identity that is fundamentally disconnected from one's biological mother. In R. Walker's hands, telling the story about *becoming-mother* and *un-becoming-daughter* requires sitting with her painful history with her own mother, Alice Walker, in the face of a (feminist) generational logic that she seeks to expose and reject. Here, R. Walker's memoir moves in complete opposition to her mother's essay "One Child." She refuses the position of "daughter" and even reads a daughter identity as a kind of death-world, as the antithesis of maternal freedom.

Alice Walker enters *Baby Love* as a callous and removed figure, as a mother who embodies and performs ambivalence. R. Walker tells us that "the effect of living with my mother's ambivalence about the role of children in a woman's life, the role of *me* in her life, could not bode well for me having my own. Ambivalence itself is rarely positive. Ambivalence about one's offspring is a horrific kind of torture for all involved."[54] R. Walker suggests that her mother's "ambivalence" was corrosive, toxic, long-lasting, that it left her with enduring questions about the nature of her mother's affection. She writes, "But this is the price of ambivalence over a lifetime: it doesn't go away. It seeps into otherwise healthy tissue and tinges it with seeds of pathology. Does my mother love me unconditionally? Will it be possible to love my own child this way?"[55] R. Walker argues that the labor of the mother should be "unconditional" love, and that ambivalence chips away at this promise of constant and unending affection, effectively undermining a daughter's sense of self.

Un-becoming a daughter requires a deep reckoning with the power of mothers, with their place in the formation of the daughter's self. R. Walker writes, "Because mothers make us, because they map our emotional terrain before we even know we are capable of having an emotional terrain, they know just where to stick the dynamite. With a few small power plays—a skeptical comment, the withholding of approval or praise—a mother can devastate a daughter."[56] R. Walker casts her mother as a deeply powerful figure, one who created a daughter's most intimate territories and thus knows exactly "where to stick the dynamite." It is this capacity for destruction that the un-becoming daughter moves away from, forging a conception of motherhood rooted in logics apart from the impulse toward annihilation. This casting of Alice Walker as the brutally and tragically ambivalent mother is made most visible when Rebecca Walker describes her mother's disavowal of the title of "mother" entirely:

> She writes back that she has apologized enough and that children should forgive their parents and move on. She tells me that she and all of her friends think that because I have asked for this apology, I have lost my mind. I write her that asking people, even one's parents, to be accountable for their actions is the epitome of sanity, and that I am sorry that her friends, all of whom I know and love, don't have the courage to stand up to her. When I write that if she can't apologize, I don't want contact because I feel she is too emotionally dangerous to me and my unborn son, she writes that she won't miss what we don't have and that to her, our relationship has been inconsequential for years. She writes that she has been my mother for thirty years and is no longer interested in the job. Instead of signing "your mother" at the end of the letter, she signs her first name.[57]

Alice Walker's decision to sign her name not as "your mother" but as, simply, "Alice" resonates with her conception in her canonical essay that Black mothering undoes temporality and mother-daughter bonds, making them into simply two women, sisters even. Yet for R. Walker, this refusal to perform the role of mother and its imagined unconditional and unyielding affection produces a desire for rupture, for a different kind of relationship to unborn life.

If the un-becoming daughter is about a conscious move away from maternal violence, it also centers a refusal of the logics that prevailed when R. Walker was being raised, a refusal of certain imagined forms of feminism. She writes: "Mine is the first generation of women to grow up thinking of children as optional, a project that might pan out to be one of many worthwhile experiences in life but also might not. We learned that children were not to be pursued at the expense of anything else. A graduate degree in economics, for example, or a life of renunciation, devoted to a Hindu mystic."[58] If an ethic of deferral marked an earlier imagined feminist relationship to children, R. Walker's memoir insistently offers the flip logic, a radical embrace of the idea of children as foundational to a complete self and maternity as an act of radical self-discovery and creativity.

The realization of the power of motherhood—from the vantage point of the forgotten and traumatized daughter—is what prompts a different kind of motherhood for R. Walker, one that relishes in delight, that refuses to "stick the dynamite," and one that interrupts the notion of the child as a "digression" in a creative life. R. Walker treats motherhood as a site of welcome self-transformation, a welcome rearranging of the self, a sense "that your heart is cracked open forever."[59] Motherhood is cast as a welcome reorientation of the self toward vulnerability, connection, and intimacy, because, as R. Walker notes, "The fact is that when you almost die so that someone else can live, you become a much larger human being."[60] For R. Walker, though, the bulk of the experience of becoming a "larger human being" emerges in pregnancy, and most of the memoir unfolds in the anticipatory months of pregnancy, not in the process of childrearing. R. Walker luxuriates in the corporeal changes pregnancy produces, with her physical transformation figured as matching the kind of spiritual and psychic rearrangements she argues motherhood produces, ones that are only possible through biological reproduction (R. Walker controversially wrote, "I don't care how close you are to your adopted son or beloved stepdaughter, the love you have for your non-biological child isn't the same as the love you have for your own flesh and blood."[61] The outcry among adopted parents and advocates for adoption in the wake of the book's publication led R. Walker to double down on her position noting, "The adoptive parents who are so fixated on wanting this sameness, I just think it's unhealthy. As a biological parent, I feel like it's a kind of erasure of the specificity of a biological experience. It's OK for the adoptive experience to be what it is, different, and with its own terrain."[62]) This sense of being "cracked open," of "almost dying" for someone else, means that maternal practices and even perinatal decision making are elevated to the level of the spiritual. To care for another being, or to care in anticipation of another being, is, for R. Walker, a sacred act. When R. Walker describes discussing vaccines with her partner, she notes, "I was practically in tears. The magnitude of the decisions, my God, does it ever stop?"[63] Here, maternal tasks—the relentless tasks that the white maternal memoir had critiqued in its accounting for maternal labor—become sites of spiritual practice and evidence of the immensity of the task of caring for another.

This conception of motherhood as a site of radical openness, of a form of care that alters the self by linking it to an Other, is, for R. Walker, a deeply pleasurable transformation. I think of this as a representation of ecstatic motherhood in precisely the way I describe ecstasy in my earlier work—a site of complex and corporeal pleasures that include the sense of being undone and remade, and feelings that are often thought of as apart from pleasure like worry and anxiety. José Esteban Muñoz suggests that we might think of ecstasy as a desire made "despite the crushing force of the dynasty of the here and now" that constitutes an "invitation to desire differently, to desire more, to desire better."[64] R. Walker's notion of motherhood as a newly vulnerable self—transformed through its capacity to be undone—epitomizes this call. She argues that Black motherhood is about "desiring differently" and "desiring better" precisely because it opens the self toward the precious, fragile, and tender life of someone else. In R. Walker's hands, care—including worrying, anticipating, and imagining—is a practice of disconnecting from the threat of ambivalence and a radical act of un-becoming daughter. To relish the role of mother in all of its demands, to find deep pleasure in those demands, is to claim the capacity of the maternal self to care without limits. It is to fully un-become daughter—a figure who was wounded by a distant mother—and to inhabit a loving, nurturing maternal role that embraces the ecstasies of maternal life.

Writing about R. Walker's book, one reviewer noted, "She sorely tests the reader's patience while settling into a pregnancy of privileged contemplation, achieved with relative ease under the ministrations of a homeopath—just one in a 'small army of healers' she assembles for ailments that often seem more psychic than physical (though when her son is born with meconium in his lungs and sent to the neonatal intensive care unit, it comes as a profound relief that she jettisoned the plan for a home birth with a 'polytheistic fiesta theme')."[65] For this reviewer, R. Walker's ecstatic and anticipatory mothering is its own site of "privileged contemplation," commodification, and consumption, suggesting that the sensual pleasures R. Walker roots in motherhood are related to her own largely untheorized class position. But what might it mean for Black mothers to claim a space of "relative ease," to refuse representations of Black mothering as an experience of precarity, injury, and woundedness? Instead, the trauma that R. Walker imagines as intrinsic to her experience of motherhood is a broken mother-daughter relationship, one that she jettisons through un-becoming daughter, through forging new maternal logics rooted in pleasure. Indeed, R. Walker suggests that recovery from trauma requires the kind of ecstatic motherhood she documents and that sensual, corporeal, and immersed parenting is the remedy to the ambivalence she experienced from her mother.

In the afterlife of the book's publication, R. Walker has become a staunch advocate for early biological reproduction. In one interview, she notes, "I keep telling these women in college, 'You need to plan having a baby like you plan your career if it's something that you want.' Because we haven't been told that, this generation. And they're shocked when I say that. I'm supposed to be like this feminist telling them, 'Go achieve, go achieve.' And I'm sitting there saying, 'For me, having a baby has been the most transformational experience of my life.'"⁶⁶ R. Walker actively repudiates what she imagines to be feminism's disavowal of children and what she has described as her mother's disavowal of children. She also suggests that motherhood can perform its political work through refusing scripts of liberation from children, through embracing reproductivity as a site of self-making and self-transformation. In R. Walker's hands, the idea of crisis is not the precarity of Black life but the wrong-headed or even false promised goals of feminist liberation—with the crisis of interpersonal trauma, the refusal of unconditional love, and the sense that freedom comes from moving away from motherhood that they entail. Mothering is then a response to trauma that sits in vulnerability, in a deep gratitude for the rearranged self that motherhood engenders; it views "unconditional maternal love" as a practice that frees both mothers and daughters to inhabit new kinds of futures.

These new futures are, of course, not uncomplicated as evidenced by the public and ongoing feud between Alice and Rebecca Walker. In 2008, R. Walker published an essay—promoting *Baby Love*—describing her mother as "just plain selfish."⁶⁷ In 2013, Alice Walker responded to R. Walker's accounts, and to a Wikipedia entry that described the women's estrangement, in a blog post centered on "taking care of the truth." Alice Walker writes,

> As years passed, these charges grew in variety and intensity and centered primarily on my deficiencies as a mother. I was not a perfect mother, whatever that means, but I was good enough. The pain of being unfairly and publicly accused of willful harm, by someone I gave birth to, and raised, to the limits of my ability, someone I've deeply loved, has been at times almost unbearable. For the past decade or so I have borne this injustice as well as I could, in silence, for the most part, but now, being on the other side of the trauma to some degree, I begin to see unexpected ways uncontested slander harms us. This is what I wish to share.⁶⁸

The underside of un-becoming the daughter is the materiality of estrangement, which may feel like freedom and may also feel like loss (and perhaps freedom and loss here are mutually constitutive). What the reader learns from the still-unfolding saga between mother and daughter—a mother who once described her daughter as a "sister"—is that there are costs and risks inherent to the maternal ecstasy R. Walker advances that echo both generational conflicts between "waves" of feminism as well as augur the rise of the Black maternal memoir pre- and post-BLM.

R. Walker offers her readers an account of Black motherhood where "crisis" is constituted by the toxicity of maternal ambivalence and where freedom comes from daughters breaking their lineage to forge new relationships with maternity. Instead of maternal unease, R. Walker presents maternal happiness, ecstasy, and anticipation as ethics of connecting mother and child and as ways of embracing the self, which, she argues, is fundamentally rewritten by the act of mothering (particularly, she asserts, biological mothering). R. Walker presents a universe where Black mothering is a welcome period of experiencing an expansive self.

*Wishing: The Pleasures of Black Mothering*

Dani McClain's *We Live for the We: The Political Power of Black Motherhood* (2019), like Rich's *Of Woman Born*, is both a memoir and a larger analytical engagement with quotidian practices of Black motherhood. It follows Rich's call for "vulnerable" writing as a way of revealing both the institutional and embodied experiences of motherhood. McClain places her own experiences as a Black mother in conversation with data collected from interviews with Black mothers. She focuses on the challenges that Black mothers contend with at various moments in their children's lives: birthing, home life, family, education, sex, and spirituality. But it is always fundamentally a memoir, a deep account of McClain's "quest as a new mother to help my daughter understand as early as possible who she is and what she came to do on this beleaguered planet."[69] McClain emphasizes that it is a memoir deeply wedded to the conditions of the present—the Trump administration, the corporatization of healthcare, the destruction of the planet, BLM activism—and as such it is a memoir that is legible in the context of a Black maternal grief economy, where the anticipation of loss frames both Black motherhood and the conditions of legibility of Black maternal writing. In fact, McClain's book navigates the same political terrain as Lezley McSpadden's, asking "how one Black American mother is reimagining what it means to parent during a time of conservative backlash, growing authoritarian tendencies, and a rise in white supremacist and patriarchal violence and rhetoric. This book explores how to raise a Black girl child in the age of #BlackLivesMatter and #MeToo."[70]

McClain frames Black maternal grief differently, here with a deep emphasis on Black maternal resilience, spirituality, and radical utopianism, and she insists that it is not the dead Black son who engenders the birth of Black maternal political subjectivity but innocent Black girlhood that stands as a symbol of what Black mothers must labor to protect and safeguard. Drawing on Black feminist theorists including Carol Stack, Patricia Hill Collins, and Alexis Pauline Gumbs, McClain offers a picture of Black maternal creativity in the face of precarity. Black mothers figure out how to navigate systems, how to procure resources, how to share knowledge, information, and childcare, precisely because of a prevailing logic of "making a way out of no way." Indeed, the very *doing* of Black motherhood—dressing children, preparing lunches, navigating school systems—is always political and radical, even as the actual, material, exhausting, and deeply individualized labor of all of these acts is often hidden behind "the romance of community," behind the notion that childcare is performed as an act of nourishing the Black community more broadly.[71] The labor of forging a Black domestic world is, for McClain, both an intensely pleasurable act of creativity and spirituality that indexes her love for her daughter, Is, and acts of control that barricade Black domesticity from the threats of the outside world.

The abiding argument of the book is that Black motherhood is marked by anticipation, a sense of the pain, grief, and trauma that is to come. It is this living, surviving, and making in the face of anticipated injury that McClain emphasizes is the shared condition of Black maternal life. Describing her pregnancy, she notes: "You might think that I don't need to worry: I eat a healthy diet; I don't have high blood pressure or diabetes. I am not poor; I have private insurance and a master's degree. I started prenatal appointments at 10 weeks and haven't missed one. But I'm under no illusion that my class privilege will save me. Research suggests that it's the stress caused by racial discrimination experienced over a lifetime that leads to Black American women's troubling birth outcomes, not the individual choices those women make or how much money or education they have."[72] It is this conception of Black motherhood as marked by the threat of violence, the need for vigilance, that gives rise to McClain's central thesis: that Black motherhood is a distinctive formation constituted by its political life, its fundamental commitment to a "we." Black motherhood is a collective formation, it is fundamentally invested in the thriving of the totality, because it is born from conditions that are, as others have argued, "life or death." Out of conditions of dire necessity, Black mothers, McClain argues, are collectively oriented and mindful of community. As Black mothers anticipate violence, death, and trauma, they forge a form of being-together that is fundamentally communal.

The flip side of anticipation, and the utopian impulse of the book, is that Black motherhood is marked by a wish, a deep longing, for a different kind of life for the child and a commitment to actively crafting a world within a world, a place of safety. This intense desire is born from and shaped by the presumption of grief and anticipated violence and harm, and it is manifested in myriad ways in McClain's writing, but always undergirded by the quotidian as a site of wish fulfillment. At times, McClain performs her wishing through her advocacy of "cultural congruence," the sense of humanity and recognition she feels when she and her child are in the company of Black caregivers. She describes her desire for a second opinion about the C-section her provider suggested and notes, "It wasn't until I'd gotten a second opinion from a Black woman ob-gyn that I accepted that a C-section was the right choice. I felt more confident that she'd been able to see me as a human being, just like her."[73] If Black doctors are more able to see her humanity, she aspires for her daughter, Is, to only have teachers, caregivers, and other-mothers who can see, embrace, and reflect that humanity. McClain notes, "I hire only Black caregivers or those who I perceive to be on the margins in some way that will predispose them to see our own humanity."[74] Cultural congruence is a nod of recognition, a feeling of having Blackness seen and reflected back, as when Is's babysitter sings Lalah Hathaway's "Angel." This is the feeling of being seen, and it is one that McClain labors to secure for her daughter.

If "cultural congruence" is a desire to have one's "humanity" recognized, it is also about shielding the privacy and sanctity of Black life. As McClain notes, "I feel uncomfortable displaying the imperfections of my domestic life to white people who aren't longtime friends."[75] Here, visibility is not a radical form of exposure that makes apparent feminist ambivalence about mothering; it is instead a form of racial wounding and othering. The benefit of cultural congruence is that it permits space for Black freedom, McClain's abiding wish for her daughter. She writes:

> Yes, of course, I want my daughter to know how to greet people and say goodbye. I want her to use polite words like "please" and "thank you." I want her to recognize the feeling of being welcome so that she can make others feel welcome and understand the value of hospitality and kindness. I don't want her to scratch or bite or hit her classmates. I don't have a problem with most of the values and norms that are being transmitted to Is now, but I know this will change at some point. She'll be taught to stand and recite the Pledge of Allegiance. She'll be subjected to school dress codes that impose retrograde standards of femininity and propriety. As the mother of a Black girl, I want her to be able to quickly recognize when she is being mistreated or manipulated so that she can act accordingly and protect herself.[76]

For McClain, cultural congruence is a longing for recognition and affirmation. It is a wish for a different kind of world and that constitutes the very heart of Black motherhood. This is evident even in how much the book rehearses

McClain's "wants" for Is. She notes, "I . . . want our home to be a microcosm of the world I want to live in, a place where kindness, compassion, and justice are valued and consistently worked toward"; "I want her to be able to find sanity in the midst of chaos. I also want her to feel a connection to the sacred, that which has the power to transform us and which reaches us from somewhere beyond the intellectual"; "I want Is to have a power analysis as early as possible"; and "I want Is to have her Blackness affirmed, but I want something else for her, too: a sense of political or intellectual belonging. For me, this hasn't only come through association with other Black people or even other people of color."[77] The emphatic and constant "wanting" that appears in the book represents desire and imagining as the critical technologies of Black mothering. Anticipation is not merely about trauma and injury but also about the wanting of a different kind of world and about actively crafting a domestic space, a literal Black interior, that can fulfill those wishes.

This investment in the "want" requires McClain to root herself deeply in the domestic, a space that is treated as a sanctuary, a space for making a different kind of life. In other words, McClain's wishes can manifest themselves in a practice of retreating. Following a tradition of Black feminists, including bell hooks and Shoniqua Roach, who seek to claim Black domesticity not as a space of patriarchal tyranny or a site of the pervasive "second shift" but as a site of freedom and radical self-making, McClain also celebrates the private as a sanctuary for Black maternal dreams and for Black children's innocence. McClain writes, "It's true that I've retreated into private life. I've slowed way down, turned inward. I've long been interested in nutrition, but now my research on the topic and the food prep I do as a result feels all-consuming."[78] If the white maternal memoir used to offer an accounting of the banalities of motherhood to foreground the gendered inequalities of reproductive labor, McClain gives a different kind of accounting. Her attention to the banalities of maternal life reveals the political labor of the Black quotidian because even small actions are about Black survival: what is eaten, where one shops, how one accesses information, what music is heard.

The daily acts, then, are infused with political meaning and attention to how the domestic becomes a technology of radical politics. For example, McClain writes, "I start noticing how much I and the other adults in her life are on our phones around Is. I buy an analog clock for the kitchen, so I won't have to touch my phone whenever I need to know the time."[79] Here, the largely unintentional and ubiquitous act of checking one's phone becomes a form of troubling disconnect, an imposition on the domestic sphere that ruptures what the homespace *could* and *should* be—a Black sanctuary. As McClain indicates, it is crucial to guard the "protected space in our home and in the small orbit in which she moves, an oasis where she as a Black girl can feel free and empowered and dignified. That's meant the right books and the decision not to spank and all the organic, whole foods, and on and on."[80] This "no-screens, no-pesticides, no-sexist-books standards" is a practice, an intention that transforms vigilance—often thought to be the hallmark of white affluent "helicopter parenting"—into the heart of Black political mothering.[81] If the pervasive arguments about the tyranny of housework is that it steals time, that time is a proxy for power and freedom, McClain flips this argument, treating the capacity to luxuriate in the time to research recipes, to learn about food, as a radical practice of Black women's freedom. She writes, "I am claiming for myself and my child time that was historically denied Black women and children who wanted and needed to bond. I am taking the time that so many Black women before me could not, because they were caring for someone else's child or cooking someone else's food or toiling away in someone else's field."[82] As with R. Walker's conception of ecstatic mothering, McClain's notion of time is that devoting it to a child is a form of life-giving, a natural and even radical act.

In McClain's hands, the child is represented as a site of collective investment. Yet the paradox is that even as the child is "community property," and even as Black mothers are living for the "we," the acts of Black maternal collective-making that McClain celebrates unfold in the private sphere, in the household, in seemingly atomistic ways that seem far removed from the collective sense of motherhood she describes. McClain's conception of Black mothering as an act of collective wishing—even as it is actually manifested in deeply individualized ways—offers another vision of the Black maternal as oriented toward a particular affect, a longing for a different kind of futurity. For McClain, the fulfillment of this wish requires ordering her world in very particular ways, organizing her domestic space in ways that she thinks will protect and shield Is and produce the safe world she longs for. Finally, we might ask what it means for a Black maternal memoir to valorize and even romanticize the labor—including the quotidian gendered labor—that the maternal memoir is imagined to disrupt, when salvation comes from making sandwiches, bathing a child, cooking dinner. For both R. Walker and McClain, the making of a sanctuary—whether in the form of the pregnant body physically stretched to make space for a growing Other or in the form of a house that is fortified from the violence of the outside world—suggests that the act of wishing as it is staged within Black domestic life is a radical form of self-making and world-making that Black motherhood makes possible. For McClain, crisis generates the anticipation of different valences. While her memoir is haunted by the anticipation of racial violence, it is also marked by the anticipation of world-making, by the labor of forging a world-within-a-world in the Black domestic sphere. What the crisis of antiBlack violence makes possible—and necessary—is Black maternal creativity, which McClain celebrates as an urgent form of Black life giving.

*Natural Time*

In *Guidebook to Relative Strangers*, Camille Dungy describes her newfound identity as a mother: "Since you came to live inside me, much of my sense of propriety is gone. It is as if there were many doors to our apartment. Every door is open, and anyone can walk inside. Strangers talk to me about their own incontinence and I tell them about my weeping breasts. . . . Nothing is private. Nothing is sacred. There is nothing I keep to myself. Being your mother has required one act of vulgarity after another, and I am so strung out on you I couldn't care less."[83] Like R. Walker, Dungy rehearses a rupture in her sense of time: dividing life into a before, and a life lived in the midst of an *after*. This new life is marked by intense feeling, by new forms of demanding labor, by new anxieties and attachments. And like R. Walker, Dungy views this transformation as the birth of a different self. She writes, "It is true, I cannot fully recall who I was before Callie. I *was* someone before Callie was born. . . . But now we are both fundamentally changed."[84] But unlike how R. Walker felt, this new feeling is not about *un-becoming daughter* but about *un-becoming a stranger*. For Dungy, mothering is about the surprising embrace of interconnectedness, about the disappearance of the stranger as a category, about both coming to terms with the portions of one's self that have been rendered strange and unfamiliar and also recognizing ties with others. Un-becoming a stranger is particularly surprising (revelatory, even) since Blackness has, as Dungy and many others have suggested, long been constructed as the quintessential mark of estrangement. Mothering, then, is an embrace of the other, a moment of being ushered into a new form of relationality. In its celebration of interconnectedness as the "natural" state of the world, a realization made possible only through motherhood, Dungy's memoir moves far from ideas of grief and trauma and even far from ideas of the "outside" world as threat. Instead, Dungy suggests that motherhood is about the interconnectedness of people and things, about being vulnerable to others and finding salvation in that vulnerability. The aesthetic and political challenge her book poses is what it means for a Black mother to find the world opened up, rather than violently closed, and to encounter that world as safe and welcoming.

For Dungy, motherhood is centrally about being made visible. But here publicity is not cast as an intrusion, as a kind of surveillance or scrutiny—as Black feminist work has so often understood it—but as a generous and productive form of openness. To be a mother, to mother in public, is not only to be seen but also to find oneself part of a community rather than to find oneself a stranger. The figure of the stranger is a long-standing preoccupation of Black feminist theoretical work. Patricia J. Williams reminds us, "In the Vietnamese language, 'the word 'I' (*toi*) . . . means 'your servant'; there is no 'I' as such. When you talk to someone you establish a relationship.' . . . Very little in our language or culture encourages looking at others as parts of ourselves."[85] As Williams suggests, our culture is oriented toward a separation between self and the other, between the familiar and the stranger. For Williams, the stranger is the quintessentially dispossessed body, and in her analysis, it is the figure of the homeless body—literally shut out of the marketplace of humanity, rendered invisible—that stands for the stranger, the collectively forgotten figure. Yet Williams also highlights the variety of ways in which Black bodies have stood for dispossession, unseen even as obsessively represented, policed out of the category of the human, presumed to be criminal. Dungy suggests that motherhood interrupts the narrative of Black collective dispossession, brings Black women into view, and, perhaps most profoundly, intimately connects Black mothers and Black children with the universe of people and things.

Dungy's collection begins not with a meditation on motherhood but with a rumination on the stranger. She describes a moment when she was "not yet married and was nobody's mother."[86] She was, instead, identified as an artist and was participating in an artists' colony when a tense dinner conversation started about the movie *The Hours*, a film about three women whose stories are connected by Virginia Woolf's *Mrs. Dalloway*. The film, one she had no desire to watch, had nothing to do with her Black female body, a fact she found difficult to explain to her dining companions. The polite tone of the artists' colony was ruptured by the dinner-table disagreement over the film's politics of representation. This was a moment, Dungy reveals, of feeling like the stranger, the outsider. What does it mean to have to explain one's feelings and to presume they will not be understood? How are milieus of politeness and "niceness" ruptured by conversations about race and by Black women's very presence? The same artists who celebrate *The Hours*, Dungy describes, marvel at their comfortable rooms, which are efficiently cleaned each morning by women who labor invisibly around the colony. Dungy writes, "There is something about privilege that can place one in a position to erase the realities of others. Those weren't fairies pushing the vacuum cleaner and cleaning the tub. They were women with lives and flesh and families and histories. My life and flesh and family and history demand that I recognize them where and how I can."[87] The Black or Brown woman is the quintessential stranger—the cleaner of rooms, the maker of beds, the "fairy" whose invisible labor is unnoticed even as her labor is fundamental to the reproduction of society. She is also the figure of unhappiness who is the stranger at the table, the "killjoy" whose view on *The Hours* can spoil the collective mood.[88] She is the figure whom Williams described as "removed" "not just from the market but from the pseudo-spiritual circle of psychic and civic communion."[89]

It is motherhood that dislodges the feeling of the stranger for Dungy, allowing her to discover a deep familiarity with the world around her. She writes:

> There was so much at stake now that the fourth wall had fallen. I was connected to more people—had a bigger family. I was exposed to a much larger network of success and failure. I worried about the safety of those I loved. I worried about tsunamis, debt, car accidents, brown recluse spiders, who would care for my baby, and how we were going to survive. I worried about the 20 percent of children in Alameda County—our home—who experienced food insecurity in 2011. I saw these children around me all the time. I knew some of their names. If I could put a face to suffering I would call that suffering face into my dreams.[90]

At times, motherhood permits a sense of collective ecology, allowing Dungy to recognize her "bigger family" and to cultivate a feeling of worry and regard for the world around her. "Tsunamis, debt, car accidents," and the specter of suffering children are bound together precisely because anyone can face disaster, because of the shared vulnerability of the world to pain, injury, and trauma. And it is motherhood that renders Dungy distinctly open to viewing collective suffering, to feeling a sense of "worry" about the very condition of the shared world. Yet Dungy suggests it is not simply her desire toward others that has changed. The world is suddenly alive with people who are not-strangers, who *receive* her, and it is her "status" as mother, her body's proximity to her daughter's body, that makes possible her new position in the interconnected web of the world.

For Dungy, this is manifested through traveling. If travel is often an experience of estrangement, for Dungy—thanks to her frequent trips with her daughter, Callie—travel becomes a site of deep communion. As the memoir unfolds, Dungy and Callie take planes. They collect their suitcases. They check in to hotels. They rely on the kindness of strangers to navigate airports, train stations, and taxis. In an airport in Maine, Dungy struggles with her suitcases and her toddler, and she asks a stranger to watch her pile of bags as she attends to her daughter. She says to a woman standing nearby, "Folks must really trust each other here," and a woman responds, "Who would want to steal your things?"[91] The pile of bags that a stranger guards while Dungy assembles Callie's toddler paraphernalia is evidence of a world transformed by maternity—or perhaps by the presence of a child—a world where "traveling mercies" are ubiquitous.[92] Indeed, it is mothering that allows Dungy to see her pile of belongings not as something that someone might simply take but as something that someone else will protect for her. Dungy's book flips the conventional narrative of the travel memoir as one that describes estrangement and instead reveals how traveling with her "lap child" allows the universe to claim her, protect her, and honor her humanity.

If travel is a site where Dungy finds there are no strangers, where the world becomes deeply familiar, it is also because it is an in-roads into history, a way of seeking a larger home in a historical narrative. Being a historical subject, Dungy argues, is a profound feeling of rootedness, even if it is a rootedness in a history of dispossession and violence. Here, she echoes Williams's claim: "I, like so many Blacks, have been trying to pin myself down in history, place myself in the steam of time as significant, evolved, present in the past, continuing into the future. To be without documentation is too unsustaining, too spontaneously ahistorical, too dangerously malleable in the hands of those who would rewrite not merely the past but my future as well. So I have been picking through the ruins for my roots."[93] If the stranger is a Blackened position and a location marked by being out-of-time or denied access to history, then claiming one's history, "picking the ruins for roots," is a profound form of self-making and self-invention. Dungy treats motherhood as an act of "picking the ruins for roots," an act of both forging and claiming a history. Nowhere is this more evident than in Dungy's analysis of naming Callie. Dungy writes at length about the process of selecting her name, which is a process of writing a subject into historical existence. A name, Dungy reveals, is not merely an aesthetic choice; it is situating someone in a family, and it is an act of love (and perhaps even ownership) to name someone. She writes, "At some point you will decide what the world should call you. Callie or Callie Violet or some other, as yet undetermined, name. I can't know what the future will name you, but when I call you Sweet Pea or Turtle Dove, Abena or Pumpkin, Callie Violet or my sweet girl, I do it always in the same tone, so you have learned to turn when I speak."[94] Dungy reminds her readers that "one of the easiest ways to strip a person of her power is to take away her right to choose her name."[95] And Dungy reveals that being nameless is a sign of dispossession, that a body in a morgue, for example, is "a body without history," simply "John or Jane Doe."[96] To name Callie, and to imagine Callie's capacity to name herself, is to make her into a body *with* history. This ability to birth a historical subject, to ground a body in time and place, is the radical act of Black motherhood.

The notion of motherhood as the end to estrangement even extends to the natural world. In a chapter titled "Tales from a Black Girl on Fire, or Why I Hate to Walk Outside and See Things Burning," Dungy says simply, "When I lived in Virginia, I associated open fire with historically informed terror."[97] The natural world, then, is a place inflected with historical trauma, that bears the imprint of violence. Yet when she finds herself in an artists' colony in Maine, the natural world feels different, apart from histories of trauma and, as Dungy notes, "I was again, at liberty, in the wild."[98] This feeling of being "at liberty, in the wild" is not merely about the shift from Virginia to Maine but about a change in vantage point that motherhood engenders. Indeed, what makes it possible to feel "at liberty" is not a disavowal of the violence that the natural world makes visible but a deep recognition of how that very world is shaped by the institutionalized cruelty of everyday life. If, as Dungy reminds us, "it's a tinderbox, this country," what the natural world reveals is that "the whole family's in danger. The whole neighborhood. Acres of wild country. All the beasts and all the birds. You had to look. You wouldn't look away. . . . When those sparks found wind you could not quench the flame. And now, this terrifying blaze. You knew. You know. You've been taught not to play with fire."[99] What motherhood makes possible is her sense of her place in the natural world, as embedded in the "beasts and all the birds," as part of a large, capacious, and interconnected "whole family." Dungy's vision of togetherness, her insistence on Black mothers' place in a larger collective family of living things, is amplified in a BLM moment where Black maternal life-writing garners its visibility through its proximity to death. Yet, for Dungy, Black motherhood is marked not by its proximity to death but by its intimacy with various forms of life.

Dungy's refusal to amplify a vision of death-bound Black maternity—or to amplify the possibilities of death otherwise—has made her memoir in some ways "forgotten," with some critics noting surprise that her book did not receive the critical acclaim it warranted.[100] But perhaps it is precisely because Dungy aligns Black mothering with nature, with communion, with being part of what poet Mary Oliver would term the "family of things," that makes the book unfamiliar and ultimately challenging, particularly in a moment when the affective terrain of Black motherhood's grief and anxiety must center on state-sanctioned violence.[101] In an interview, Dungy notes:

I . . . wanted to write about an experience of Blackness in America that is not the normalized view. I'm from a relatively affluent and highly educated family, my daughter had been on forty-six flights before she was three years old. That's not what some people might think about when they picture a Black mother. It was clear from my interactions with people that my daughter and I often came as something of a surprise. I like the idea that we might help expand the possibilities of what people understand a Black woman to be, and of the ways we might connect.[102]

This notion of writing another kind of Black maternal life, of "surprise" as its own Black maternal political project, is the terrain that Dungy's book maps. Dungy's book suggests that Black motherhood is a site of natural communion, a space of finding refuge in the world, a project of seeing the outside world as a space not of insecurity but of safety and welcomeness. The labor of *Guidebook*, then, is to reveal how motherhood opens up possibilities of intimacies with others beyond the child, making the entire world a Black woman's home.

*Endurance*

In August 2018, Lezley McSpadden, Michael Brown's mother, announced that she was running for Ferguson City Council in Missouri. "I know a lot of people may ask what makes me qualified," she said. "But I'll tell you if a mother had to watch her son lay in the street for four and a half hours and watch a community be completely disrespected by elected officials that we elected, what would you do? You would stand up and fight too."[103] McSpadden makes evident the dominant logics of the political life of Black motherhood: political "qualifications" are rooted in grief, in the deeply traumatic experience of seeing a slain child's body lying exposed for four hours in the "unrelenting summer sun," in the long pursuit of justice, and in the deep realization of the state's affirmative noninvestment in redressing racial terror.[104] McSpadden's carefully crafted public persona—as aspiring public official, as a Mother of the Movement, as an endorser of Hillary Clinton (McSpadden appeared onstage at the Democratic National Convention), as a partner of the Thurgood Marshall Civil Rights Center's efforts to pass legislation to provide mental health services for those impacted by police violence—aligns with the "civil rights widow," a Black wife or mother whose suffering, trauma, and grief are respectably put to work in the service of a quest for national racial reconciliation and redemption.[105] McSpadden is a figure whose trauma is made salvific through its connection with grief—rather than rage—and imagined as what the nation needs. This notion of transformative Black maternal or spousal grief is precisely what Smith argues constitutes "an obligation for Black families to mourn in public," whether as civil rights widows or Mothers of the Movement. This is grief that is imagined to be pedagogical for America, as when Mamie Till-Bradley "let the world see" her son's brutalized body, or when Valerie Castile warned listeners that "it never seems to fail us, the system continues to fail Black people and they will continue to fail you all. Because . . . when they get done with us, they are coming for you. . . . You will be standing up here fighting for justice just as well as I am."[106] This is the respectable grief that Myrlie Evers-Williams describes in the foreword to McSpadden's memoir as she recounts transforming her rage into respectable political and personal action: "As a mother, I say to Lezley, sometimes you pick up the pieces slowly; other times your progress seems to come fast, fueled by anger, even a degree of hatred. How do you overcome that? You find something positive. Like Lezley, I had children to take care of. I had to go back to school. I had to work. I had to develop careers. I had to be a community activist, all of which was a little difficult for me."[107] This notion of "finding something positive," of "overcoming" trauma because of maternal responsibilities to biological children and to a larger Black community, constitutes the very same grief economy that makes possible, legible, and marketable McSpadden's book.

Yet McSpadden fits uneasily in the category of the grief-ridden, respectable Black mother, the civil rights icon who, as Brenda Tindal argues, is the "grieving female subject whose public life bears the imprint, or in some instances the burden, of a martyr's legacy."[108] If Trayvon Martin is figured in the national imaginary as "forever seventeen," Brown—and the protests that swelled in Ferguson in the light of a grand jury's decision not to indict Darren Wilson—has come to be imagined as an icon of Black urban unrest, for the underside of BLM's relentless demands for a justice system marked by an "investment in our communities and the resources to ensure Black people not only survive, but thrive."[109] The particularities of Ferguson—including the protests that transformed the landscape of the city—have also rewritten McSpadden (and Brown) as figures tied to rage and not grief, to public outcry and not personal trauma. Even the Amazon.com reviews of McSpadden's memoir are a testament to this imagining. As one reporter indicated:

> Just as the turmoil following Brown's death surfaced the societal divides affecting St. Louisans lives on a daily basis—Black v. white, city v. county, police v. civilians—McSpadden's book is surfacing the polarized emotional

reactions her story continues to evoke. The one-star reviews criticize McSpadden for the way she parented Brown and accuse her of lying about his death. One particularly chilling review says simply, "Loved the ending!" "The 'truth' is that if you had been a better parent your son would probably be alive today," says one review with 69 up-votes from other Amazon users.[110]

The racist cruelty staged around "customer" reviews of the book reveals precisely how uneasily McSpadden sits in frameworks of grief-stricken, respectable Black maternal loss.

McSpadden's memoir, *Tell the Truth and Shame the Devil*, performs a complex choreography, at once standing as an authorized text that claims a place in the respectable civil rights canon and as a text that insists, as Samantha Pinto and I have argued, on telling its story through tracing both Black motherhood and Black daughterhood as always marked by violence, precarity, and trauma. In the face of the brutally racist and misogynistic accusations that McSpadden's failure to adequately "mother" Brown led to her son's murder and the mainstream media describing her son as "no angel," McSpadden's memoir disavows the civil rights widow framework (despite Evers-Williams's foreword to the book, which places Brown's death in a lineage of civil rights deaths and noting "Mike Brown is the Emmett Till of this generation").[111] It is a memoir that insistently "tells the truth" even as McSpadden navigates a world where that "truth"—one marked by violence and poverty—is often spun and wielded by the antiBlack state to justify Brown's murder. As she notes, "What I do know for sure is that I was just a kid when I had Mike Mike. I made a lot of mistakes when I was young, but in raising him I got stronger, wiser. What we endured together, especially in his years as a small child, is a story that only his mother can tell. One that I have held close until now."[112] In "telling the truth," her memoir insists on redeeming both her son and herself outside of the logics of respectability, a way of thinking about Black value and Black humanity otherwise in the name of an ethic of truth telling. And even as she uses the form of the memoir with its premium on disclosure, she mobilizes the genre to shield her son from exposure and to focus instead on her own coming of age. She writes, "You don't know about Mike Mike. You don't know about me. Now, you might know something, some snippet, some half a moment in time, but you don't know my son's life and what it meant, and an eighteen-second video doesn't tell you anything about eighteen years."[113] This insistence that "you don't know" is maintained throughout the book as McSpadden recounts *her* story, not *his*, offering Brown privacy even as she "tells the truth."

Ultimately, McSpadden suggests that endurance is a Black maternal ethic she wants to hold on to, that this endurance is worthy of being told, and that it is endurance—including living through loss—that is constitutive of Black maternal subjectivity.

"Telling the truth" requires offering an account of Black girlhood, Black adolescence, and Black maternity that centers institutionalized cruelty and entrenched poverty and carefully analyzes how violence and love often sit side by side. McSpadden writes: "I never finished high school. It was once one of the most uncomfortable and embarrassing facts about my life. . . . I was raised in a single-parent house and watched my mother work hard on jobs she should have been paid more for doing, make sure my brother, me, and my sister had clothes on our backs and food on the table. I knew what her struggle had been. I've worked for years barely making minimum wage, sometimes at two jobs, to put clothes on my children's backs, and shoes on their feet."[114]

McSpadden documents how economic precarity wears on the body and the soul, revealing the psychic costs of working to earn too little to survive. She also describes how economic strain puts pressure on intimate life, on forms of relationality, and how gendered norms—including compulsory heterosexuality—come to make excusable brutal forms of violence. She painfully describes the abuse her mother endured at the hands of Mister, her mother's boyfriend, and her sense that "Mama made me feel like having Mister with her was more important than me. So I was sent to live with my granny."[115] The pain of realizing the importance of her mother's relationship with Mister—even as her mother suffered physical abuse—was an early lesson about living with violence that wears the guise of love and about the value placed on heterosexual intimacy that made enduring intimate abuse seem bearable to her mother. She also "tells the truth" about discovering she was pregnant, about her mother's violent response to her decision to move in with Big Mike (Michael Brown's father) and his family; about her fraught relationship with Big Mike, one that she ultimately ends when she decides "I was determined he wasn't going to stop my flow. I wasn't married or on anybody's lockdown. I was young and free and working on getting me in order"; and about the violence that marked her subsequent relationship with Andre.[116] Indeed, her memoir describes the ordinariness of abuse, how it touches every aspect of life, how it swirls underneath the surface of daily existence. Every time McSpadden seeks her "flow," her "freedom," there is another form of brutal violence awaiting her. And while much of the abuse she documents unfolds in intimate settings, her memoir relates the sheer ubiquity of violence. Late in the memoir, she recounts learning that Andre, her boyfriend, had been murdered. The police discovered his body in his own car, and McSpadden even lingers with the detail that his killers had used his car, his phone, his credit cards, had gone for a "joy ride" in his car, perhaps even sitting next to Andre's corpse. As the reader sits with the cruelty of this detail, we also learn that, at Andre's funeral, McSpadden finds out, for the first time, that Andre had eight children. To "tell the truth" requires not covering the pain of any of this, not hiding the very logics that the Right often mobilizes to condone or excuse antiBlack state violence. "Telling the truth" demands naming all of the traumatizing forces that mark daily life and arguing that none of them excuse the violence inflicted on her son or justify her loss.

At the end of her memoir, McSpadden reveals how all of this "truth telling" has remade her conception of motherhood entirely. In a portion of the book that she drafts as a letter to Mike Mike, she writes, "There isn't a day that goes by that I don't think about you, Mike Mike. I've accepted that you were God's before you were mine. He just let me borrow you for eighteen years."[117] McSpadden offers a new conception of Black motherhood, rooted in precisely the precarity her memoir describes, of borrowed children and of borrowed maternity. She suggests that Black motherhood is not constituted by ownership—as parents are often figured as owning their children, as children are often figured as property—but by a realization and radical reckoning with what cannot be owned, with what cannot be controlled. Your child is never yours, McSpadden's memoir reveals, and the task of the Black maternal is coming to terms with this fact and enduring it. If Mike Mike *belongs* to God, her memoir also suggests the painful reckoning that the city of Ferguson also tried to lay claim to him, both in the state agent's act of taking his life and in the city's act of leaving his body on a street in the sweltering summer sun. In this radical rewriting of motherhood, one where children are not simply "community property," as Karla FC Holloway suggests, but also borrowed companions for a shared amount of time, the reckoning that Black motherhood produces is a different form of being-together, one that connects a still-living mother and a dead-too-soon son. The specter of loss and the constant intrusions of state surveillance and state violence rewrite Black relationality and offer an understanding of Black maternity that is, of course, suffused with grief but that also underscores the necessity of enduring. In McSpadden's hands, endurance does not perform its work as a form of triumph, as the endpoint of a narrative that transforms trauma into radical acceptance. What is endured is both the ordinary nature of violence *and* the sense that one's child can be taken at any time. What is endured is the fact that there is only so much about the most intimate portions of one's life that can be controlled.

## Coda: Becoming (Black) Mother

In an article published in the *New Yorker* in 2019, Emily Lordi argues for reading Michelle Obama's eagerly awaited *Becoming* as part of the maternal memoir canon. Lordi writes, "It's a canon that has been dominated by the accounts of white, straight writers, but it now includes Michelle Obama's blockbuster memoir, *Becoming*."[118] Lordi underscores that Obama's memoir emphasizes the dynamic creation and innovation at the heart of mothering, an emphasis that places the book squarely within the parameters of the highly popular and visible genre. She argues, "What Obama brings to this genre is, first, a powerful sense of self, which precedes and exceeds her domestic relationships—the book's three sections are titled 'Becoming Me,' 'Becoming Us,' 'Becoming More'—and, second, a conviction that the roles of wife and mother are themselves undefined. She makes and remakes her relationship to both throughout her adult life."[119] While *Becoming* is both a literary and political product, published in the aftermath of President Obama's last days in the White House and during the beginning of the nightmarish Trump regime, it is also, following Lordi's lead, part of a Black maternal memoir canon that takes up themes of Black maternal grief but inflects them differently, as a particular kind of political commodity. As with the other memoirs I describe here, Obama's *Becoming* offers ethics of Black mothering, ones that touch on crisis but inflect it anew.

For Obama, Black maternal grief is described as the pain of *not* being able to conceive a child and the trauma of miscarriage, both of which she reveals in the memoir as she seeks to describe the project of "becoming us." Indeed, one of the most-spectacularized aspects of *Becoming* was Obama's reflection on her struggles to get pregnant. She writes, "It turns out that even two committed go-getters with a deep love and a robust work ethic can't will themselves into being pregnant. Fertility is not something you conquer. Rather maddeningly, there's no straight line between effort and reward. For me and Barack, this was as surprising as it was disappointing. No matter how hard we tried, we couldn't seem to come up with a pregnancy."[120] This revelation—one that details how Barack Obama would race home after work to ensure he "could hit [her] ovulation window"—is a profound act of disclosure that centers the wish for Black reproduction and that refuses the mythology of Black hyperfertility by offering another narrative, one closer to what statistics show: that Black women struggle with infertility at staggering numbers.[121] In the pages that follow, Obama describes the relentless monitoring of her body for signs of pregnancy. As she writes, "After many years of taking careful precautions to avoid pregnancy, I was now singularly dedicated to the opposite endeavor, I treated it like a mission."¹²² What does it mean, her memoir asks, for Black women to be on a "mission" to get pregnant, to organize their lives around a desire for "More Life" in its most reproductive and biological sense? What does it mean to make visible Black nonreproductivity when Black women are figured as hyperreproductive and hyperfertile? What does it mean for Black maternal grief to be tied to absent-life, to not-born life, rather than to life violently taken at the hands of the state?

After a miscarriage, which Obama describes as "lonely, painful, and demoralizing almost on a cellular level," she and Barack Obama pursue IVF.¹²³ She narrates how she felt "the acute burden of being female," of being poked and prodded, of having blood drawn, of intrusive medical tests, physical burdens that she suggests Barack never experienced.¹²⁴ These intrusions, and the gendered loneliness of becoming-patient on the way to becoming-mother, stand as evidence for maternal desires, for the longing to have children. As is typical of a political memoir, Obama's story is also cast as one of triumph as she details how the birth of her daughter Malia fulfilled her desires and reordered herself. Malia's arrival meant "motherhood became my motivator. It dictated my movements, my decisions, the rhythm of every day."¹²⁵ Even in the midst of the new grind of the everyday, Obama details Malia's birth as a kind of deep fulfillment, as the end of a period of grief: "This was the new math in our family: we had two kids, three jobs, two cars, one condo, and what felt like no free time."¹²⁶ As she documents in her memoir, Black motherhood was a key pivot as she went from "becoming me" to "becoming us," and motherhood, which includes a fundamental commitment to maintaining the sanctuary of her home, is cast as deeply apolitical even as the project of the memoir is deeply politicized. In many ways, Obama's reflections on the desire to have children, the emotional toll of miscarriage, the thrill of her daughters, and the stress of juggling work and family perform the role of making celebrity life seem ordinary. Yet I want to examine what it means to see Black maternal life as staging a different kind of mourning, the grief of unfulfilled maternal desires and the trauma of miscarriage. Obama's memoir also suggests that Black maternal grief can have an endpoint, that the arrival of her deeply desired children is an end to the traumatic period of wanting, as well as the beginning of a new "us" marked not by grief but by longed-for demands. Indeed, *Becoming*'s emphasis on triumph over the struggles to conceive inflects Black maternal grief differently, suggesting its finitude rather than its capaciousness, its possibility to end. Her memoir reveals that Black grief can be moved through, that it has parameters and limits. This is a conception of Black loss that sees trauma not as constitutive of Black motherhood even as it has shaped it.

This chapter complicates the prevailing narratives around Black maternal writing and the ways that Black maternal life-writing is presumed to be framed around grief and death and a proximity to loss and trauma. Instead, this chapter argues that Black maternal life-writing pushes against the parameters of the crisis framing, at times resisting it entirely by emphasizing ecstatic and natural mothering, at times sitting with grief but refusing to perform respectability, and at times reiterating grief anew by inflecting it differently, focusing on infertility and on miscarriage. What these texts collectively perform is to take up Dungy's notion that Black motherhood is about being "cooked to the bone" even as that cooking *feels* different and is lived differently across this archive. Is this feeling of being cooked to the bone one of being cannibalized, consumed, dissolved? Is it about a self made into something else, something unbelievably and unbearably tasty? And what does it mean to have one's edges undone, to be quite literally melted and dissolved, by the presence of another? These texts take the Black maternal self and read it not as inherently grief-stricken or proximate to trauma, but as porous, and they suggest that this porousness is an ethic that should be embraced. Whether it is the self remade through un-becoming daughter or un-becoming stranger, the radical "truth telling" of economic precarity and borrowed maternal life, or the wishing for safety for Black children, these texts collectively share a deep awareness of the penetrable self, of being "cooked down to the bone" as about what happens when we lose a commitment to the edges of ourselves as firm and fixed and instead surrender to our capacity to be dissolved.

# CONCLUSION

*The Afterlives of Jazmine Headley*

In December 2018, Jazmine Headley visited a Brooklyn office to find out why the public assistance benefits that helped pay for her son's daycare had been curtailed. She had to miss a day of work to make the trip, and she brought her one-year-old son, Damone, with her. When she arrived at the office, she realized she would have to wait. Waiting, of course, is one of the hallmarks of the lived experiences of the poor, whose time is considered expendable as they navigate the bureaucratic state.[1] When there was no place to sit in the waiting room, she sat on the floor next to her son's stroller. She knew they would be waiting a long time—they spent more than three hours in the office—and she wanted to keep Damone entertained. A security guard (New York City calls them "peace officers") instructed her to move because she was blocking a fire exit (she wasn't), and when she refused, the New York Police Department was called. What happened next was captured by bystanders and circulated quickly on social media: a gut-wrenching video of officers restraining Headley and ripping her child from her arms, and Headley's strong voice again and again: "You're hurting my son. Let me get up, I have my rights." In a last effort to keep her child from the hands of police officers, she clenches his shirt in her teeth. Headley was arrested and charged with resisting arrest, acting in a manner injurious to a child, and trespassing.

If the entire encounter had not been recorded, there is little doubt that Headley's experiences—waiting endlessly, having her child ripped from her arms, spending nights incarcerated on Rikers Island—would never have garnered public attention or even a state apology. "Churning," a term used to describe how public benefits offices close benefits prematurely to force people to reapply, and even call the police regularly, is one of the conditions of ordinary bureaucratic cruelty inflicted on poor people of color, something that is simply to be endured.[2] But in the weeks that followed Headley's arrest, her name circulated in local and national media as a symbol both of the violence inflicted on poor Black women and their children and of the indignities of poverty. The *New York Times* reported, "Ms. Headley has become a cause célèbre for New Yorkers who depend on food stamps and cash public assistance and who say they are often met with hostility and are sometimes threatened with arrest at city benefits offices."[3] The Brooklyn Defender Services noted that "the entire country is talking about her."[4] A few months later, when Headley publicly testified about her treatment to the New York City Council, a council speaker, Corey Johnson, said to Headley, "I am similarly deeply, deeply grateful for your bravery, for you wanting to tell your story, for you wanting to ensure that this doesn't happen to anyone else."[5] Later that year, the city paid Headley $625,000 to settle the federal lawsuit she levied against the city. Her victory was largely celebrated in mainstream media, which hailed it as evidence of a larger state realization of the violence inflicted on poor Black mothers as they navigate bureaucracies that are, by design, primed to humiliate, disempower, and wound.

In many ways, this is the paradigmatic story of the blatant disregard of Black maternal life and its symbolic reentry into the public sphere following tragedy—much like Malaysia Goodson's story, which began this book. These stories are about the disposability of Black maternal life, particularly about poor Black mothers who are so often rendered invisible in public spaces. These mothers, hailed in earlier eras as ground zero of an imagined Black pathology, have been imagined anew in a Black Lives Matter (BLM) era. They are now taken up both as symbols of the persistent crisis of violence against Black mothers and as evidence of Black maternal heroism, as women who literally hold onto their children in the face of death and violence, whether by clenching their teeth around their children's shirts or clutching their children underneath their bodies to keep them safe. Black mothers are now imagined as the ones who do not let go, even if that means bearing assaults on their own flesh or risking their own deaths.

*Birthing Black Mothers* has explored how Black mothers come to be visible not as signs of pathology but as "causes célèbres," visible because they stand for suffering and trauma. Indeed, the synonymousness of "Black mother" with grief (or expected grief), pain, and trauma brings Black women into view as political subjects, and that makes the invocation of Black maternal flesh valuable currency for the US Left. If Black mothers like Headley and Goodson are celebrated for their dedication to their children's lives, I argue that there is also a particular BLM-era investment in the birthing Black mother, the perinatal Black body, that is imagined—in perhaps the most literal way—to be a vessel of Black life. If, as Helena Andrews-Dyer notes, "Black wombs are trending," newly discovered as territories of antiBlack violence, *Birthing Black Mothers* argues that Black wombs are now imagined as the ground zero of crisis, as spaces under siege that require special protection to ensure the viability of Black life.[6] The Black perinatal body has come to be figured as the paradigmatic site of antiBlack violence, of systematic attacks on Black life that begin in utero and continue in hospitals and institutionalized medical spaces that practice noncare and disregard Black mothers and their families. It has become a common refrain that BLM's politics center Black men and boys as the only victims of anti-Black violence, as the dead and anticipated dead—so much so that the Black feminist pleas to "say her name" have highlighted an inattention to violence against Black women and girls. My interest is in how Black maternal flesh has also come to stand as the central symbol of state violence in this era.

If the temporality and affect of crisis are what bring Black mothers—their bodies, political desires, and most pressing physical needs—into view, it is always an obstructed view, one that emphasizes Black maternity as a disordered space in need of intervention, even if the form of that intervention is presumably benign, rooted in support and encouragement rather than pathologization and condemnation. As I argue here, support also often takes the form of discipline and surveillance. Thus, *Birthing Black Mothers* has sought to study the political consequences of crisis discourse for Black mothers, even as it remains attentive to the materiality of Black mothers' lives, including experiences of birthing trauma, medical racism, and institutional noncare, experiences that are proximate to violence. I grapple with the host of ways that crisis has been a genre that operates not just for the state and for corporations rhetorically invoking Black maternal life, but also for Black feminists both in their struggles for "More Life" and in their desires for representations that do justice to their own "complex personhood."[7] In considering how the state and Black feminists at times find themselves surprisingly aligned, this project has asked what it means for Black feminists to be seduced by the rhetoric of crisis, to find the language of Black maternal heroism and the new support and encouragement lavished on Black mothers inspiring, generative, and even potentially transformative.

To inhabit a moment when Black mothers are imagined as heroines rather than pathological *feels* like an important shift, one that can be seductive in much the same way as the rhetoric of "cite Black women" or "Black women did it first." This is a rhetoric that hails Black women's "magic," insists on their genius, and celebrates their perseverance—and thus feels qualitatively different from narratives about Black women that condemn and denigrate. Yet, as I have argued throughout this book, the consequence of these varied forms of marking Black women is to render us symbols and metaphors, to fail to contend with either our fleshy materiality or our complex needs and desires. The political thrust of this book, then, is to imagine a Black feminist project that refuses the lure of making Black women into symbols of any kind, that can be as attentive to the pathologization of Black women as to their romanticization.

This is also, then, a project that thinks seriously about Black feminism's own institutional wills and desires. Black feminist theory is regularly cast as an anti-institutional and even fugitive project marked by radical acts of refusal, one that recognizes the incorporation of difference by various institutions and also stands outside of institutional power. My project tells a different story, thinking about both Black feminism's conscription into state projects *and* its creation of state projects that are presumably designed to save Black women's lives, even as they often hinge on plunging other Black women—doulas, peer lactation counselors, and other birthworkers—into economic precarity, or shore up the idea that Black women have to save ourselves. My impulse in telling this story is not to condemn Black feminism's will to power, but instead to trouble a prevailing "story" in both women's studies and Black feminist studies that posits Black feminism as outside of and against dominant forms of power.

Much as I seek to disrupt a conception of Black women as heroines, I also aspire to trouble the notion of Black feminism as a fugitive tradition, an account that relies on a romance about the tradition. In this romantic narrative, scholars neglect Black feminism's ongoing and profound attachment to institutions, perhaps most notably its attachment to the university, despite an insistence that the university can be a death-world, one that can kill Black women, cannibalize Black feminist thought, and extract diversity labor from Black women. In considering Black feminism's attachments to institutionality,

I have included a robust engagement with Black feminist partnerships with the state to encourage or perhaps compel Black breastfeeding, and Black feminist partnerships with the state to expand coverage for—though not necessarily credentials for—birthworkers. While these forms of advocacy have been pursued in the name of Black women's health and freedom, they have come at the cost of other forms of Black feminist activism that critically interrogate the new representation of Black mothers as in need of supportive reformation.

Finally, because this is a book invested in Black mothers, I close with an account of Black motherhood that neither traffics in nor refuses crisis, but instead sits with its psychic costs. In 2019, Helena Andrews-Dyer wrote an article for the *Washington Post* that reported on the Momference, which she described as "a gathering of millennial mothers of color in its second year that feels as intimate as a family reunion, as celebratory as a 21st birthday and as necessary as a therapy session."[8] Andrews-Dyer's account grappled with Black perinatal life waged in the face of crisis in all of its granular materiality: what does it *feel* like to be a pregnant Black person when the pregnant Black body is constructed (again) as a particular kind of problem, when pregnant Black women hear—again and again—that pregnancy can lead to death, that hospitals are deathworlds, that conventional obstetricians neglect Black women's pain? This is a story about a cohort of pregnant Black women navigating their pregnancies against a discursive milieu that has told them repeatedly that they should be "preparing for battle."[9] Andrews-Dyer writes, "Forget putting your feet up or sticking your head in the sand. That isn't an option for Black women staring down a plus sign. These days your pregnancy must be 'woke,' 10 months filled with research and study and planning. As a Black woman, it's not enough to 'stay hydrated,' make your prenatal appointments and curate the perfect nursery on Pinterest. There are studies to digest, articles forwarded by your best friend on C-section rates to read, summits to attend on combating implicit bias, and doctors to screen for implicit bias. It is exhausting work."[10] What does it feel like to experience Black perinatal life when the experience is overdetermined by "horror stories," "alarming anecdotes," and "gut wrenching quotes"? What might it mean to think about the materiality of living—reproducing—when one's body is presumed to be in crisis, when one is presumed to enter pregnancy in "battle mode"? How do Black mothers navigate pregnancy, labor, delivery, and postpartum life when their bodies and experiences are overdetermined by narratives of trauma? And given our new cultural awareness of the embodied and even molecular consequences of stress, how do we—Black feminists—contend with the material consequences of telling Black mothers again and again that they are close to death?

I offer this not because of a desire to advocate for a model of luxurious pregnancy free from worry or to presume that Black women will ever have—or have ever had—experiences of institutional medicine that are free from violence, trauma, or injury. Instead, I invite Black feminists to theorize, organize, and freedom-dream in ways that imagine Black motherhood apart from anticipated trauma, a vision that has material consequences for Black women as they navigate perinatal life. I encourage Black feminism to be a theoretical and political project that can do justice to the violence that Black mothers experience *and* refuse to reproduce Black motherhood as a trauma category. I ask these questions because of the project's indebtedness to not just thinking about the category of "birthing Black mothers" as a political one but also thinking about the embodied and material experiences of Black mothers who navigate around the now-entrenched meaning of the category itself, a meaning produced as much by institutionalized medicine as by Black feminists working in the name of Black mothers.

# CODA

*"All Mothers Were Summoned
when George Floyd Called Out
for His Mama"*

By the summer of 2020, the world had changed. COVID-19's rapid spread reconfigured our lives, even as it did so in distinct ways, with particular—and particularly deathly—effects on Black people. As the state eschewed responsibility for our collective welfare, prioritized economic stability over public health, and ordered us to become individual risk managers, "essential workers"—overwhelmingly Black and Brown—were ordered to risk their lives, to keep the grocery stores, hospitals, and public transportation running. It was the summer when the murders of George Floyd (by the Minneapolis police), Breonna Taylor (by the Louisville police), and Ahmaud Arbery (by white vigilantes in Glynn County, Georgia) galvanized a broad coalition mobilizing the mantra of Black Lives Matter (BLM) to imagine a rearranged social order. It was the summer when a video of Amy Cooper calling the police on Christian Cooper, a Black man bird-watching in New York's Central Park, sparked a nationwide conversation about the "weaponization" of white women's tears, and when the abolitionist impulse of BLM flirted with a carceral desire to see Amy Cooper arrested (she was ultimately charged with a misdemeanor—filing a false report—while Christian Cooper, the bird-watcher, insisted he would not participate in the prosecution). It was the summer when the *New York Times* bestseller list was dominated by books about antiracism, when institutions released statements signaling solidarity with protesters organizing for Black life, and when corporations including Amazon and Ben & Jerry's pledged their commitment to BLM. All the while, the numbers of people dying from COVID-19 continued to soar, with 142,000 people in the United States confirmed dead by July; Black people accounted for nearly a quarter of those COVID-19 deaths.[1] The year 2020 is the year of crisis, in its most bare, most stark. As I write this coda, embedded in the conditions of the present, I ask about the symbolic trajectory of Black mothers in a world order spectacularly marked by crisis. If Black mothers are crisis currency, how are they understood, represented, and invoked in a moment when crisis is the order of the day?

In July 2020, as the United States was engulfed in pandemic and protest, Woodhull Medical Center in the Bedford-Stuyvesant neighborhood of Brooklyn attracted national attention. On July 2, a few days after her due date, Sha-Asia Washington went to Woodhull for a routine stress test. When doctors discovered her blood pressure was high, they gave her Pitocin to induce her labor and then administered an epidural. (The hospital says it "offered" her an epidural; her boyfriend reports that the epidural was "forced" on her.)[2] Washington's boyfriend told reporters that he saw his girlfriend raced to the operating room where she suffered a cardiac arrest and died. Doctors performed an emergency C-section and saved Khloe, Washington's daughter. The family's independent autopsy determined that the unwanted epidural was the cause of Washington's death.[3] A week later, Woodhull released a statement about Washington's death, situating it in the context of Black maternal mortality in the United States, in New York, and in Bedford-Stuyvesant, which the city's Department of Health concluded has one of the highest rates of maternal complications in the city.[4] The hospital's statement noted, "The persistently high rates of maternal mortality that disproportionately affects people of color is a grave, national crisis. Here in New York City, we will not stand for this status quo, and remain undeterred in our mission to eliminate structural inequities and guarantee comprehensive and quality care for all New Yorkers."[5]

The hospital connected Washington's death to Black maternal mortality rates more generally, mobilizing the language that reproductive justice activists have long deployed to describe the persistence of the Black maternal health crisis; the statement read Washington's death not as singular or exceptional but as part of a pattern of racialized obstetric violence. As activists connected Washington's death to two other cases of Black maternal death that had received considerable local attention in New York in 2020—Amber Rose Isaac and Cordielle Street—Woodhull made the same connections.[6] Indeed, both activists and hospitals had been trained to describe Washington's death as related to the practice of institutional medicine and its fundamental neglect of Black maternal health. A GoFundMe was set up for Washington's family, and it raised nearly $90,000. Amy Schumer shared the GoFundMe link on Instagram and wrote, "This woman died in Brooklyn at Woodhull hospital a few days ago and never met her little girl. #Shaasiawasshington scream her name.... We need to wake up and do better every day."[7] E. J. Dickson reports, "Washington's story has since gone viral as a symbol of the dire need for improved medical care for black mothers," and by mid-July, New York State senator Julia Salazar had released a statement noting, "Sha-Asia's story is devastating, and it is far too familiar.... Ms. Washington's death is for each of us a call to action."[8]

A few days after Washington's death, as New York City had "flattened the curve" and the rest of the country experienced a frightening escalation in COVID-19 rates, protesters gathered in front of Woodhull holding signs like "black births need black doulas," "black womxn die in hospitals 2," and "Woodhull has blood on their hands." Desiree Williams, the mother of Washington's boyfriend, addressed the crowd and declared, "They killed her. They know they killed her. My son is broken down."[9] Images from the protest made painfully visible the intersecting conditions of the present: a protester in a mask and gloves—symbols of the deathly threat of COVID-19—carried a sign connecting BLM's call for racial justice to the urgent needs of Black mothers.

A few weeks after Washington's death, after Woodhull's statement had been released, after the state Senate had weighed in, after the protests had quieted, Washington's name stopped circulating in newspapers and on social media. Like Goodson and Headley—whose stories I shared in this book—Washington's name traveled in death, went "viral" as a symbol of the hospital's deathly disregard for Black maternal life, for the urgent need for a reimagination of the hospital, and for more attention to the "mattering" of Black mamas. Her name was emblematic of what some activists called the "third pandemic," alongside COVID-19 and the persistence of antiBlack state violence—the deaths of Black mothers in hospitals.[10] Indeed, Washington's death coincided with a moment when hospital birthing itself was seen as in crisis. How would pregnant people deliver babies in what one journalist called the "covid hospital"?[11] And how would pregnant Black people, whose laboring experiences are already marked by vulnerability and violence, navigate the now even more deathly landscape of the hospital? Reproductive justice activists reminded us that the health risks that Black mothers face under ordinary conditions are profoundly amplified

FIGURE C.1. A protest outside Woodhull Medical Center in July 2020. Courtesy of Rose Adams and *Brooklyn Paper*.

by COVID-19. One study concluded that Black and Latinx pregnant people in Philadelphia are five times more likely than white pregnant people to have been exposed to COVID-19.[12] As Latham Thomas writes, "A system that was failing to meet our needs is now seriously overburdened."[13]

The rhetoric of the "third pandemic" bridged two crises: the public health crisis of COVID-19 and the juridical crisis of law enforcement murdering Black people with impunity. As A. Rochaun Meadows-Fernandez writes, "As Black mothers, we are living in an especially troublesome time—sandwiched between the current public health threat of Covid-19 and the longtime reality of police brutality. We are trapped in a double-bind of racism."[14] Washington, however briefly, illuminated the central role Black mothers' bodies play in a reconfigured social world, one that recognizes medical racism as state violence, birth justice as ground zero of Black life, and BLM as a plea to support Black mamas. Her death and the brief period of activism around it revealed that Black peri-

FIGURE C.2. A protester outside Woodhull Medical Center in July 2020. Courtesy of Erik McGregor.

natal flesh was thought as critical connective tissue bridging the call for Black life and the call for Black maternal health.

In the "third pandemic," Black mothers are icons, key symbols, whose bodies come to stand for Black life itself. In this iteration of Black mothers' iconicity, they "raise the dead" and "defend the dead."[15] They lovingly hold what Elizabeth Alexander calls the "Trayvon generation" when she describes Black motherhood as a kind of "magical thinking": "A being comes onto this earth and you are charged with keeping it alive. It dies if you do not tend it. It is as simple as that. No matter how intellectual and multicolored motherhood becomes as children grow older, the part that says *My purpose on earth is to keep you alive* has never totally dissipated. Magical thinking on all sides."[16] They are activists whose grief authorizes their political work as when Wanda Cooper-Jones advocated for Georgia to pass hate-crime laws to respond to the murder of her son, Ahmaud Arbery, noting "Ahmaud is just one of the many black lives that has been lost due to hatred. Georgia lawmakers, pass a hate-crime bill."[17] But they are called upon—or perhaps call upon themselves—to be more than all of this. They are increasingly icons of Black life itself, bodies whose health, well-being, and survival are imagined as essential for the literal and metaphorical reproduction of Black life. Their bodies have made visible powerful critiques of the hospital as a carceral space and of institutionalized medicine as a technology of state violence. And thus they are bodies that have been recruited, conscripted, and called upon to live, breathe, and survive in the name of Left politics, with Black wombs increasingly imagined—compassionately, supportively, encouragingly—as the centerpiece of the struggle for Black life and larger social justice causes.

Washington's story suggests both the seductive lure and problematic politics of the symbolic, which is only heightened during the "third pandemic" when Black maternal bodies are invoked with greater currency than ever before, when they stand for the intersections of medical and legal violence. Her name traveled in death—as Malaysia Goodson's did—with tremendous velocity, standing as evidence of myriad failures, and offering Left credentials to the governmental officials who invoked her. This brief publicity was followed by silence, perhaps one of the most troubling aspects of Black maternal currency: it is fleeting. As I argue throughout this book, the symbolic currency afforded to Black maternal flesh is alluring precisely because it moves in the register of support, encouragement, and assistance, rather than earlier discourses that sutured Black maternal bodies to pathology and brokenness. Yet this symbolic currency attaches Black mothers to a different kind of crisis, leaving their bodies vulnerable to endless state recruitment *and* Black feminist recruitment—whether through breastfeeding campaigns designed to "encourage" Black breastfeeding or through state efforts to outsource Black maternal care to paraprofessional birthworkers—which can describe itself as benign intervention but can feel like surveillance and policing of a different sort. In 2020, as Valerie Castile watched the coverage of George Floyd's murder and his final plea for his mother, as protesters took to the streets with signs that said "All Mothers Were Summoned When George Floyd Called Out for His Mama," she told an interviewer, "For years, I've cried for other women's children."[18] Her tragic statement exposes the repetitive and seemingly endless nature of antiBlack violence, and it also reveals how Black mothers have been positioned and have had to position themselves to garner political visibility, as always proximate to tragedy and grief. Black mothers cry "for other women's children" because of the persistence of antiBlack violence, and they have come into political focus and view because of tragedy. This book is animated by a different impulse: what it means for a Black feminist theoretical project and politic to be undergirded by a desire to understand the *variety* of Black mothers' political needs and the multiplicity of their affects ranging from grief to rage, from trauma to ecstasy. In this reconfigured imagination of Black mothers, they could be—perhaps for the first time—more than a political category mobilized to signal either pathology and deviance, or compassion and support, far more than a Left credential conferring political virtue on those who utter their names.

# Notes

**INTRODUCTION**

1. Only about a quarter of the subway system's 472 stations have elevators, and the ones that exist are often out of order. Ameena Walker, in "Here's What the NYC Subway Map Looks Like," shows a map of the NYC subway system that includes only accessible stations to make visible these profound issues.
2. In March, the medical examiner released her cause of death as an irregular heartbeat that was complicated by an enlarged heart and an "overactive thyroid." Reakes, "Cause of Death Determined for Stamford Woman."
3. An example of this callousness occurred when the Metropolitan Transit Authority (MTA) issued an official apology after it was revealed that no one from the MTA had called Goodson's family to offer condolences. Their chief said, "It's generally customary that police officials do that. Let me cut to the chase. Sorry that it didn't happen. That's regrettable. What happened with Ms. Goodson was unbelievably tragic . . . and that's why we're re-doubling our efforts to make our system a lot more accessible." See Siff, "MTA Chair." For the invisibility of poor Black mothers, see, for example, Gold and Fitzsimmons, "A Mother's Fatal Fall"; Rosenberg," A Young Mother"; and Wong, "Cities Aren't Built." Wong writes, "In an email, Amanda Freeman . . . observed that when she was a single mother of a baby, passers-by often offered help to pregnant women, but they were less inclined to support those 'toting crying, wiggling, screaming babies on the subway.'" See also Ettachfini, "NYC's Inaccessible Subway System"; and Chiusano, "What Malaysia Goodson Was Carrying." Chiusano writes, "Goodson had just moved from Connecticut to New York, and she seemed to have been headed from Manhattan to a Queens homeless shelter—maybe she was carrying concern about the future down the stairs with her."
4. Abdur-Rahman, "A Tenuous Hold," 38. A GoFundMe campaign was set up for Rhylee. At the time that I wrote this introduction, $22,000 had been raised.
5. Warren qtd. in Seelinger, "Elizabeth Warren Tackles Maternal Mortality."
6. See Warren, "Sen. Elizabeth Warren on Black Women Maternal Mortality."
7. Gillibrand, "Democratic Debate Transcript."

8   Angela P. Harris, "Race and Essentialism," 596.
9   Chambers-Letson, *After the Party*, xxi.
10  The Villarosa article is titled "Why America's Black Mothers and Babies Are in a Life-or-Death Crisis." See the Illinois public act founding a Task Force on Infant and Maternal Mortality among African Americans Act (Illinois HB1), http://ilga.gov/legislation/BillStatus.asp?GA=101&SessionID=108&DocTypeID=HB&DocNum=1. Danielle Jackson describes an "outpouring of news stories, from multiple national outlets, about infant and maternal mortality over the past twelve months." See Jackson, "Frustrating Year of Reporting." For a sampling of this coverage, see Poole, "Digging Deeper"; Hosseini, "Black Women Are Facing a Childbirth Mortality Crisis"; Bowen, "Black Moms in Illinois"; Martin and Montagne, "Black Mothers Keep Dying after Giving Birth"; and Drum, "How Can We Reduce Black Maternal Mortality?"
11  Roeder, "America Is Failing Its Black Mothers."
12  Roeder, "America Is Failing Its Black Mothers."
13  See this "plan" in Warren, "Protect a Woman's Right to Choose."
14  See Briggs, *How All Politics Became Reproductive Politics*, 2.
15  K. Harris, "Democratic Debate Transcript."
16  See P. Collins, *Black Feminist Thought*.
17  Davis, *Reproductive Injustice*, 202. Khiara Bridges's work examines how the construction of the "wily patient" operates in racialized and classed ways. She writes, "The wily patient's pregnant body is not read as a symbol of infinite possibility, joy, or self-fulfillment—a reading that may only be reserved for the non-poor. Rather, in light of TANF [Temporary Assistance for Needy Families] and the condemnation of welfare mothers in political and popular discourse, the (poor) wily patient's pregnancy is realized as the event that makes the welfare queen possible, the condition that makes the entire welfare apparatus necessary" (Bridges, *Reproducing Race*, 227).
18  Hamlin, *Crossroads at Clarksdale*, 6, 61.
19  Wells qtd. in P. Collins, *Black Feminist Thought*, 193; P. Collins, *Black Feminist Thought*, 194.
20  Lawson, "Bereaved Black Mothers," 716.
21  Feldstein, "'I Wanted the Whole World to See,'" 109.
22  Feldstein, "'I Wanted the Whole World to See,'" 110.
23  Cooper-Jones, "How Was My Son Ahmaud Arbery's Murder Not a Hate Crime?"
24  Burns, "Police Say DeKalb Gunman Used Anti-gay Slur."
25  Capelouto, "Swastikas Found Spray Painted at High School."
26  Rojas, "Georgia Teenager Plotted a Knife Attack."
27  A YouTube video posted by the *Washington Post* on June 16, 2017, shows Castile's mother's speech. See https://www.youtube.com/watch?v=RJsD4c-CpUA.
28  Castile qtd. in Forgrave, "For Mother of Philando Castile."
29  Simmons, "Quiet Crisis among African Americans."
30  Waldman, "How Hospitals Are Failing Black Mothers."
31  Villarosa, "Why America's Black Mothers and Babies Are in a Life-or-Death Crisis."
32  For the text of the Preventing Maternal Deaths Act, see https://www.congress.gov/bill/115th-congress/house-bill/1318/text. See also Kaplan, "Reducing Maternal

Mortality." The Black Maternal Health Caucus "explore[s] and advocate[s] for effective, evidence-based, culturally-competent policies and best practices for improving Black maternal health." See Underwood, "Let's Vow That No Mom Should Die Giving Life." For information about the MOMMA Act, see Kelley, "How the MOMMA Act Will Help."

33   Turman, "Cory Booker and Ayanna Pressley Introduce Bill."
34   Sadurni, "New York to Expand Use of Doulas."
35   Kwon, "San Francisco Doula Program Tackles Birth Equity."
36   McDaniels, "Baltimore Enlists Doulas."
37   Dr. Barbara Levy qtd. in Kubota, Burkett-Hall, and Bernstein, "DC 'Most Dangerous Place to Give Birth.'" New York Times Editorial Board. "Easing the Dangers of Childbirth for Black Women." See also Kubota, Burkett-Hall, and Bernstein, "DC 'Most Dangerous Place to Give Birth,'" on the lack of maternity wards east of the Anacostia River in Washington, DC, leading Dr. Barbara Levy from the American College of Obstetricians and Gynecologists to note, "Washington DC is the most dangerous place to give birth in the United States if you are African American. If you are a white woman, you'll do very well in the nation's capital. We have a major disparity problem here in D.C."
38   Rabin, "Huge Racial Disparities."
39   Jackson, "Frustrating Year of Reporting."
40   Cole, "Reproduction on Display," 93.
41   Villarosa, "Why America's Black Mothers and Babies Are in a Life-or-Death Crisis."
42   Roeder, "America Is Failing Its Black Mothers."
43   This is Saidiya Hartman's formulation.
44   Villarosa, "Why America's Black Mothers and Babies Are in a Life-or-Death Crisis."
45   Blair, "Presidential Candidate Beto O'Rourke."
46   For rehearsal of the 1850 statistic, see Owens and Fett, "Black Maternal and Infant Health"; PBS News Hour, "Why Are Black Mothers and Infants Far More Likely to Die?"; and Lakhani, "America Has an Infant Mortality Crisis."
47   Berlant, *Cruel Optimism*, 102.
48   Berlant, *Cruel Optimism*, 101.
49   Roitman, *Anti-crisis*, 3.
50   Roitman, *Anti-crisis*, 8.
51   See Mahone, "State Legislators," for a full round-up of legislative efforts at the state level.
52   Wanzo, *Suffering Will Not Be Televised*, 3.
53   Wanzo, *Suffering Will Not Be Televised*, 10.
54   Wanzo, *Suffering Will Not Be Televised*, 6.
55   My formulation of motherhood as institution and experience is an intentional citation of Adrienne Rich's pathbreaking work in *Of Woman Born*.
56   For "unmothering," see Freeman, "Unmothering Black Women." "Afterlives of slavery" is from Hartman, *Lose Your Mother*, 6.
57   Morgan, *Laboring Women*, 115.
58   Morgan, *Laboring Women*, 115.

59  Morgan, "Partus Sequitur Ventrem," 1.
60  Weinbaum, *Afterlife of Reproductive Slavery*, 8.
61  Weinbaum theorizes the "surrogacy/slavery nexus." See Weinbaum, *Afterlife of Reproductive Slavery*, 8.
62  Roberts, *Killing the Black Body*, 6.
63  Ross and Solinger, *Reproductive Justice*, 9.
64  Ross and Solinger, *Reproductive Justice*, 169.
65  Ross and Solinger, *Reproductive Justice*, 169.
66  See Bridges, *Reproducing Race*.
67  Turner, "Nameless and the Forgotten," 245.
68  R. Williams, "Toward a Theorization of Black Maternal Grief as Analytic."
69  Davis, "'Bone Collectors' Comments," 9.
70  Jenkins, "Black Women and the Meaning of Motherhood," 206.
71  "Other mothers" is from P. Collins, *Black Feminist Thought*, 235. "All our kin" is from Stack, *All Our Kin*. The Holloway quotation is from Holloway, *Passed On*, 8.
72  See Gumbs, "'We Can Learn to Mother Ourselves.'"
73  P. Collins, *Black Feminist Thought*, 119, 180.
74  Bichell, "Scientists."
75  American Academy of Pediatrics, "Impact of Racism."
76  Quotes are from Heard-Garris et al., "Transmitting Trauma," 2. See also Heard-Garris, "Commentary," in which Heard-Garris likens vicarious racism to secondhand smoke, noting, "Vicarious racism can be experienced by individuals not directly involved with the racist event, but who can still be affected by it, similarly to how non-smokers can develop illnesses due to inhaling secondhand smoke—cigarette smoke exhaled by others."
77  Garvey, Woode, and Austin, "Reclaiming the White Coat for Black Lives." See also https://whitecoats4Blacklives.org/.
78  See Geronimus, "The Weathering Hypothesis."
79  Geronimus, Hicken, Keene, and Bound, "'Weathering,'" 828. See also J. Collins, "Disparate Black and White Neonatal Mortality Rates."
80  Geronimus, "On Teenage Childbearing."
81  Geronimus, Hicken, Pearson, et al., "Do US Black Women Experience Stress-Related Accelerated Biological Aging?"
82  Geronimus, Hicken, Pearson, et al., "Do US Black Women Experience Stress-Related Accelerated Biological Aging?," 23.
83  For popular coverage of weathering, see Braithwaite, "Biological Weathering"; Campbell, "Lifelong Health Toll of Schoolyard Racism"; Thayer, "Racism Hurts Your Health"; and Ryan, "Racism Got You Stressed?" See also Heard-Garris et al., "Transmitting Trauma."
84  Geronimus qtd. in Demby, "Making the Case That Discrimination Is Bad for Your Health."
85  Roeder, "America Is Failing Its Black Mothers."
86  Taylor, *From #BlackLivesMatter to Black Liberation*, 153.
87  Both quotations are from Sharpe, *In the Wake*, 10.

88   See Winston, "Eric Garner Death." Lt. Christopher Bannon's texts were read at a police disciplinary hearing for the officer who killed Garner (a grand jury had decided not to indict the officer). Upon learning of Garner's murder, Bannon replied, "Not a big deal. We were effecting a lawful arrest."
89   Garza, "Herstory of the #BlackLivesMatter Movement."
90   I analyze the details of the Zimmerman case in my article "Unwidowing."
91   The "no angel" description is in Eligon, "Michael Brown." Eligon writes, "Michael Brown, 18, due to be buried on Monday, was no angel, with public records and interviews with friends and family revealing both problems and promise in his young life."

   For the militarized response, see, for example, Beavers and Shank, "Get the Military Off of Main Street," which notes that "Ferguson, MO has become a virtual war zone. In the wake of the shooting of an unarmed Black teenager, Michael Brown, outsize armored vehicles have lined streets and tear gas has filled the air. Officers dressed in camouflage uniforms from Ferguson's 53-person police force have pointed M-16s at the very citizens they are sworn to protect and serve." See also Li, "Evolution of Police Militarization in Ferguson and Beyond," which describes the 1033 Department of Defense Program that sends surplus military equipment to state and local police.

   Brown's body is described in Bosman and Goldstein, "Timeline for a Body." They write, "For about four hours, in the unrelenting summer sun, [Brown's] body remained where he fell. Neighbors were horrified by the gruesome scene."
92   As I was writing this book, Attorney General William Barr dropped pending federal civil rights charges against Officer Daniel Pantaleo.
93   See German, "Testimony before the Congressional Black Caucus." There has also been increasing attention to what Jim Salter calls the "culture of fear that persists in Ferguson 4½ years after Brown's death." Salter describes how the deaths of six men who were active in Ferguson protests "drew attention on social media and speculation in the activist community that something sinister was at play." One activist described to Salter her experiences of "harassment, intimidation, death threats, and death attempts." See Salter, "Puzzling Number of Men"; and Dickson, "Mysterious Deaths."
94   Reed-Veal qtd. in Gamino and Beckett, "Mothers of the Movement."
95   McBath qtd. in Kaleen, "Black Lives Matter!"
96   McBath qtd. in Herndon, "Lucy McBath"; Coates, "'I Am Still Called by the God I Serve to Walk This Out.'"
97   Fulton, *Rest in Power*, 328.
98   We might also consider the rhetorical power of this missionary language, which secured McBath's victory in a Georgia congressional race in 2018. It was also deployed by both Lezley McSpadden in her City Council race in Ferguson, Missouri, in 2019 (McSpadden lost that election) and Sybrina Fulton in her run for a seat on the Miami-Dade County Commission in 2019 (she also did not win her election).
99   The "group of mothers who belong to a club no one ever wants to join" is how Hillary Clinton has repeatedly described the collective.

100  Arissa Hall qtd. in Chisholm, "Activists Organize to Bail Out Black Mamas for Mother's Day"
101  See Christian, "Diminishing Returns," 214.
102  See Jung, *Lactivism*.
103  Bliss, "Black Feminism out of Place," 727.
104  Bliss, "Black Feminism out of Place," 747. I borrow the idea of "stories we tell" from Hemmings's *Why Stories Matter*.

### CHAPTER ONE: BLACK GOLD

1  Meadows-Fernandez, "That Viral Gap Ad."
2  See Bowen, "Model for Gap Paused to Breast-Feed Her Toddler."
3  The "dismal" description is from Maheshwari, "Gap Plans to Spin Off Old Navy." The "kind of win" quote is from Fumo, "Gap Applauded by Moms." The quote about supporting Black breastfeeding mothers is from Moroney, "Whoa! Gap Just Released an Ad with a Woman Breastfeeding."
4  If my project seeks to denaturalize the links among "Black woman," Black breasts, Black women's birthing capacities, and ethical Left politics, I necessarily sit with how cisgendered Black women remain the centerpiece of conversations about the Black breastfeeding gap. Of course, I recognize that breastfeeding is not exclusively performed by cisgendered women or by subjects who identify as women. In 2018, for example, *Transgender Health* reported on trans women breastfeeding after a regimen of estradiol, progesterone, domperidone, and breast pumping, and the article concluded that "modest but functional lactation can be induced in transgender women" (Reisman and Goldstein, "Case Report," 24). Scholarly and popular attention to breastfeeding by nonbinary and trans parents has urged the use of inclusive terms like *chestfeeding* and *nursing parent* to describe infant-feeding practices, and breastfeeding organizations like La Leche League (LLL) have developed statements of support for trans and nonbinary parents, emphasizing that the singular goal of the organization is ensuring that infants access human milk. For example, one of their statements notes that "LLL supports everyone who wants to breast-feed or chestfeed. . . . Trans men, trans women, and non-binary individuals may choose to breast-feed or chestfeed their babies. You do not need to have given birth to breast-feed or chestfeed, as we can also see in the experiences of those nursing adopted babies" (see La Leche League International, "Support for Transgender and Non-binary Parents"). However, it remains the case that the responsibilities and demands of infant feeding remain largely on the shoulders of cisgendered women and that the national imaginary of infant feeding is tied to cisgendered women's breasts. See Lee, "Breastfeeding and Sexual Difference"; Reisman and Goldstein, "Case Report"; MacDonald et al., "Transmasculine Individuals' Experiences"; de la Cretaz, "Troubling Erasure of Trans Parents Who Breast-Feed"; and de la Cretaz, "What It's Like to Chestfeed."
5  McKinney et al., "Racial and Ethnic Differences in Breastfeeding." McKinney's research was publicized in the *New York Times*. See S. Miller, "Working to Close the Breast-Feeding Gap."

6   McKinney et al., "Racial and Ethnic Differences in Breastfeeding," 9.
7   See, for example, Ellis-Petersen, "How Formula Milk Firms Target Mothers." See also Santhanam, "Racial Disparities Persist."
8   Martucci, *Back to the Breast*, 23.
9   Freeman, "Unmothering Black Women," 1549.
10  A. Johnson, Kirk, Rosenblum, and Muzik, "Enhancing Breastfeeding Rates," 45.
11  It is the case that the majority of breastfeeding is actually breast pumping, something that requires further feminist inquiry. In her critique of breastfeeding, Courtney Jung notes, "Faced with the gap between the standard recommendation to breast-feed exclusively for six months and the absence of federally mandated paid maternity leave, women are expected to pump on the job so that someone else can feed their baby breast milk from a bottle" (Jung, "Overselling"). Similarly, Martucci notes that the dominance of pumping has fundamentally transformed the role of the lactation consultant, who has "become[,] whether she wanted to or not, an expert on breast pumping" (Martucci, *Back to the Breast*, 202).

    While pumping is beyond the scope of this project, I conducted one interview with Devon, the CEO of a "feminist breast-pump" company. She described the need for her product—one that billed itself as "discreet": "I went back to work with my breast pump, and was like, 'This is terrible. This is just terrible.' And for me specifically it was the mode-switching, going from leaving a meeting and being confident and feeling like a professional woman to thirty seconds later, bra is off, nipples are out, hunched over feeling like a patient. . . . The act of taking off my bra and my shirt at work, it's just one thin wall away from my colleagues to have to see me in a different way, or even that moment where either you say, 'I have to go pump now,' or people just realize that's what you got to do, and you can't help that everybody is thinking about your breasts. That's weird." Devon also described the particular niche her product sought to fill—for working "millennial moms." She made visible the fundamental connection between the pump and paid employment, as it is the pump that allows mothers to both satisfy desires and/or demands to breastfeed and desires and/or demands to maintain paid work. She said, "You're still that educated, health-conscious consumer with taste that you were *before* you had a baby, and now we're going to help you integrate the baby and see how you work. Our branding is primarily focused on the woman. Not a mom, but a woman. And then we know that modern moms are working at all-time high rates. That's kind of just the definition of this woman. But I think our brand distinction is we're designing for women, not for moms."
12  The term *Black gold* circulates on Twitter. See, for example, @shynes23, "Breastmilk is Black gold. Black women breast-feeding our babies is a radical act!," Twitter, October 26, 2017, https://twitter.com/shynes23/status/923749655485210625; and by local chapters of Black breastfeeding organizations that also urge participants to "make Black gold!" For more about how Black infants suffer trauma in utero, see Davis, *Reproductive Injustice*.
13  Allers, "Racial Divide of Breastfeeding."
14  "Excess flesh" is from Fleetwood, *Troubling Vision*.

15 McKittrick, "Mathematics Black Life," 18.
16 Allers, "Breastfeeding While Black."
17 Johnson, "'Baby-Friendly' Hospitals." See also Arnold, "Do 'Baby-Friendly' Hospitals Work for All Moms?"
18 For more on geographies of breastfeeding, see Lind et al., "Racial Disparities in Access to Maternity Care Practices." They write, "The results of that analysis indicated that facilities in zip code areas where the percentage of Black residents was >12.2% (the national average during 2007–2011) were less likely than facilities in zip code areas where the percentage was ≤12.2% to meet five of 10 mPINC indicators for recommended practices supportive of breast-feeding. . . . These findings suggest there are racial disparities in access to maternity care practices known to support breast-feeding" (726). For more on breastfeeding as a practice of class stratification, see Purtill and Kopf, "Class Dynamics of Breastfeeding": "Well-off parents have access to the infrastructure that supports breastfeeding: longer maternity leaves, jobs that allow for pumping breaks, the ability to hire outside help to support a new mother, and—perhaps most importantly—immersion in a culture that unconsciously views breastfeeding as a desirable status symbol and pressures them to continue to that hallowed six-month mark and well beyond."
19 Freeman, "'First Food' Justice," 3061.
20 Freeman, "'First Food' Justice," 3086.
21 See, for example, Feldman, "To Promote Breast-Feeding"; and Dornfeld, "Breast-feeding Is 'Life or Death.'"
22 A. Johnson, Kirk, Rosenblum, and Muzik, "Enhancing Breastfeeding Rates," 58.
23 Kathi Barber qtd. in Ludden, "Teaching Black Women to Embrace Breast-Feeding"; Freeman, "Unmothering Black Women," 1574.
24 Berlant, *Compassion*, 1.
25 See Sontag, *Regarding the Pain of Others*; Berlant, *Compassion*, 6.
26 The 2018 Philly Loves Breast-Feeding campaign in Philadelphia, designed to encourage Black breastfeeding, is one such example. As part of the campaign, the Department of Public Health supported billboards with images of Black breastfeeding mothers.
27 Freeman and Allers, "Racial Divide of Breastfeeding."
28 See Jung, *Lactivism*, 5–6; Reaching Our Sisters Everywhere, "Saving Tomorrow Today," 5.
29 For more on this, see J. Nelson, Li, and Perrine, "Trends of US Hospitals"; and Morain and Barnhill, "Do Infant Formula Giveaways Undermine or Support Women's Choices?"; and Allers, *Big Letdown*, 65–66.
30 Even after the end of Bloomberg's tenure as mayor, the city continues to advocate for breastfeeding. Its breastfeeding resources are accessible at https://www1.nyc.gov/site/doh/health/health-topics/breastfeeding.page. For more on racial disparities in infant-feeding practices in New York City, see "Epi Data Brief," no. 57 (August 2015), https://www1.nyc.gov/assets/doh/downloads/pdf/epi/databrief57.pdf.
31 The open letter from the Black Mothers' Breastfeeding Association to Medolac is accessible at http://Blackmothersbreastfeeding.org/2015/01/open-letter-to-medolac

-laboratories-from-detroit-mothers/. See also Allers, "Inviting African-American Mothers"; and Harrison, "Milk Money," 282.

32  While Rosin and Jung suggest the hegemony of breastfeeding, others suggest that breastfeeding remains scrutinized, policed, and pathologized, especially for mothers breastfeeding beyond six months. The ongoing battle over public breastfeeding suggests that even if this form of infant feeding is celebrated, it is still relegated to the private sphere. As with everything about breastfeeding, there remains no consensus about statistics. Some suggest that US women breastfeed at the same rates as women globally. Jung, for example, notes, "American mothers breast-feed just as much, and often for much longer, than women in many other Western countries. Seventy-nine percent of American mothers initiate breast-feeding, and 49 percent are still breast-feeding at six months. We come close to Canada, where just over half of women are still breast-feeding at six months, and we are way ahead of Britain, at 34 percent" (Jung, "Overselling"). Others suggest the United States is staggeringly behind other nations on breastfeeding rates (see, for example, Joan Wolf, *Is Breast Best?*, arguing that our current statistics measure breastfeeding initiation, which means only that a child is breastfed once before leaving the hospital).

33  Rosin, "Case against Breast-Feeding."
34  Jung, "Overselling."
35  Martucci, *Back to the Breast*, 216; Jung, *Lactivism*.
36  Corporations are also, at times, hailed as saviors, particularly in the case of Kellogg, which has invested in "first food" initiatives. Kimberly Seals Allers, for example, received a grant from Kellogg's First Food Friendly Community Initiative. Allers notes, "In my work on the ground, . . . particularly in matriarchal societies, this idea that breastfeeding is something we did for other people, something we were forced to do, something that reminds us of a time we are trying to forget, has been passed on generationally often without a word. . . . Because of that disconnect, it has created a cultural disconnect. . . . I was a first generation breastfeeder, you are a pioneer in your family trying to break down walls and barriers. It's a lot." Allers, "Racial Divide of Breastfeeding."
37  P. Williams, *Alchemy of Race and Rights*, 219.
38  American Academy of Pediatrics (AAP), "Breastfeeding and the Use of Human Milk."
39  AAP, "Breastfeeding and the Use of Human Milk."
40  AAP, "Breastfeeding and the Use of Human Milk."
41  See, for example, Collaborative Group on Hormonal Factors in Breast Cancer, "Breast Cancer and Breast-Feeding"; and Rabin, "Breast-Feeding Is Good for the Mother."
42  Weiss qtd. in Rabin, "Breast-Feeding Is Good for Mothers, Not Just Babies."
43  Wolf, *Is Breast Best?* 113. The archive of advertisements for the campaign is available online at https://webarchive.library.unt.edu/eot2008/20081104210737/http:/www.womenshealth.gov/breastfeeding/index.cfm?page=Campaign.
44  See Wolf, "Is Breast Really Best?" The journal published a response to Wolf's article. See Heinig, "Burden of Proof."

45 Wolf, *Is Breast Best?* 148.
46 See Purtill and Kopf, "Class Dynamics of Breastfeeding"; Wolf, *Is Breast Best?* 149.
47 Hays, *Cultural Contradictions of Motherhood*, 8; Wolf, *Is Breast Best?* xv.
48 See C. Miller, "Relentlessness of Modern Parenting."
49 Wolf, *Is Breast Best?* 75.
50 Intensive mothering is also discussed in Waggoner, *Zero Trimester*.
51 Jung, "Overselling."
52 Wolf, "Breastfeeding Isn't Always Best."
53 Wolf, *Is Breast Best?* xi.
54 Castillo-Hegyi, "Letters to Doctors and Parents."
55 AAP, "Breastfeeding and the Use of Human Milk: Work Group."
56 AAP, "Breastfeeding and the Use of Human Milk: Work Group."
57 AAP, "Breastfeeding and the Use of Human Milk."
58 See Crawford, "Breastfeeding Is Better for Infants."
59 Martucci, *Back to the Breast*, 219.
60 The appeal of breastfeeding's imagined anticorporatism was only enhanced by Donald Trump's anti-breastfeeding stance at the World Health Assembly in 2018.
61 Rosin's "Case against Breast-Feeding" was met with tremendous response, including by scholarly literature. See Hausman, "Motherhood and Inequality."
62 Momigliano, "Breast-Feeding Isn't Free."
63 Sears and Sears, *Attachment Parenting Book*, 9.
64 Carter, "Body-Led Mothering," 17.
65 Sears and Sears, *Attachment Parenting Book*, 5. The Searses do note that it is possible to practice attachment fathering, which includes thinking about kids while at work and carrying their pictures.
66 Searses qtd. in Moore and Abetz, "Uh Oh. Cue the [New] Mommy Wars," 51.
67 For coverage of Obama's speech, see Malcolm, "Michelle Obama Talks Black Obesity, Breast-Feeding and $31 Million."
68 Berlant, *Cruel Optimism*, 201.
69 Bordo, *Unbearable Weight*, 201; Berlant, *Cruel Optimism*, 201. By 2016, there was a new insistence that obesity is genetic and not about "willpower." See Kolata, "Americans Blame Obesity on Willpower."
70 Berlant, *Cruel Optimism*, 203.
71 Berlant, *Cruel Optimism*, 112–13. Margaret Bass's analysis is groundbreaking. She writes, "My fat signifies the perpetuation of a stereotype. Intellectually, I have the right stuff; grammatically I have the right stuff. I drink espresso and latte (still hate wine and beer though), and I know which forks and spoons to use at a formal dinner. But I look like 'mammy' without her bandanna. Self-loathing? Of course it is. If I hated my racial self, I would be the subject of all kinds of studies—pitied by Blacks and whites alike. But this is different; I *should* hate my fat" (Bass, "On Being a Fat Black Girl in a Fat-Hating Culture," 230).
72 Strings, "Obese Black Women as 'Social Dead Weight,'" 108.
73 Strings, "Obese Black Women as 'Social Dead Weight,'" 108.
74 Strings, "Obese Black Women as 'Social Dead Weight,'" 119

75  An example of this public health literature is Ashley Harris et al., "Obesity Related Dietary Behaviors."
76  Holohan, "Epidemic of Obesity."
77  See New York Department of Health, "New York State Strategic Plan."
78  New York Department of Health, "New York State Strategic Plan." Yet, as the report concluded, it was clear that it was not simply the body of color that was proximate to obesity, but the Black body, as the state emphasized that 67.4 percent of non-Hispanic Black adults in the state were overweight, with Black women "at particularly high risk with an obesity rate of 32.9% compared to 25.6% for Hispanic females and 18.1% for non-Hispanic Whites."
79  See New York Department of Health, "New York State Strategic Plan."
80  Illinois Department of Public Health, "Obesity Prevention Initiative Report."
81  Illinois Department of Public Health, "Obesity Prevention Initiative Report."
82  American Psychological Association, "Summit on Obesity."
83  More research on pregnancy and obesity is available through Boston University's Black Women's Health Study. See https://www.bu.edu/bwhs/.
84  L. Rosenberg et al., "Prospective Study."
85  Parker-Pope, "Timing of Baby Food Tied to Obesity Risk."
86  McCarthy, "Real Link."
87  McCarthy, "Real Link."
88  McCarthy, "Real Link."
89  Jackson and Johnson, "Does Breast-Feeding Reduce Offspring Junk Food Consumption during Childhood?"
90  AAP, "Breastfeeding and the Use of Human Milk."
91  AAP, "Breastfeeding and the Use of Human Milk."
92  Freeman and Allers, "Racial Divide of Breastfeeding."
93  Allers, "Why Trayvon Martin."
94  See P. Williams, "Spirit-Murdering the Messenger."
95  Personal communication. August 9, 2019.
96  Personal communication.
97  Phu and Brown, "Cultural Politics of Aspiration," 154.
98  Phu and Brown, "Cultural Politics of Aspiration," 154.
99  Campt, *Image Matters*, 5.
100 These words are from one of Cohill's Instagram posts. Lakisha Cohill (@hc_incorported), "The father of a breastfed baby . . . ," Instagram. August 29, 2018, https://www.instagram.com/p/BnEvHeBD6I_/?utm_source=ig_twitter_share&igshid=1p4pd84c1ave7.
101 Personal communication.
102 Personal communication.
103 Personal communication.
104 Personal communication.
105 Personal communication.
106 Alexander, *Black Interior*.
107 Allers, "Black Moms and Breastfeeding."

## CHAPTER TWO: IN THE ROOM

1. Dána-Ain Davis, in *Reproductive Injustice*, notes, "Catching babies is what midwives call what they do when a baby is birthed. The craft or art of birthing is one that midwives prepare for, and one of the most prized attributes they possess is that they 'do not rush births, they do not rush women in to cesarean sections when laboring goes slowly'" (186).
2. Olsen, "Birthworkers Are on the Front Lines."
3. Olsen, "Birthworkers Are on the Front Lines."
4. See, for example, Gruber, Cupito, and Dobson, "Impact of Doulas on Healthy Birth Outcomes."
5. Davis, *Reproductive Injustice*, 170.
6. A number of metropolitan areas house pro bono doula projects, including the Chicago Volunteer Doulas, New York's Doula Project, the Baltimore Doula Project, the Bay Area Doula Project, and the Minnesota Prison Doula Project.
7. There has been tremendous criticism of Medicaid programs that provide unlivable wages to doulas. For example, Collier Meyerson writes, "The reimbursement fee set for doulas in the pilot program [in New York] is $600, according to an administration official for the governor's office, and will include four prenatal visits at $30 each, plus labor and delivery at $360, and then four postpartum visits each at $30. The official says that comes out to $23 an hour, $7 above the state's minimum wage. Doulas, who are unlicensed, the official says, are expected to make 54 percent of the total Medicaid fee that would be paid to doctors, who are licensed. New York's reimbursement rates are in line with precedent. Minnesota's program, which started in 2014, offers parents on Medicaid up to six doula visits, plus assistance at the birth—all told a doula is entitled to about $400 per client, a paltry amount when you think about how much money it takes a person to live comfortably in a state where the median annual income is about $65,000. Oregon's rate is $350 for only four home visits and assistance during the birth, according to its website. But in New York City, where the average rent for a two-bedroom apartment in Brooklyn is $3,200 some doulas argue that it's nearly impossible to take part in the program and pay their bills" (Meyerson, "Every Black Woman Deserves a Doula").

   Two states, Minnesota and Oregon, include birth doula services under Medicaid coverage. In the spring of 2018, Governor Andrew Cuomo piloted a program to expand Medicaid coverage for doulas in New York. In his public statement, Cuomo noted, "Maternal mortality should not be a fear anyone in New York should have to face in the 21st century. We are taking aggressive action to break down barriers that prevent women from getting the prenatal care and information they need." As of the writing of this chapter, the New York State Department of Health still has not begun its doula program. It is also worth noting that Medicaid coverage—often celebrated by the state as a hallmark of its commitment to birthing Black mothers—has been marked by low reimbursement rates that often make it impossible for doulas to take on Medicaid clients. For more on this, see Dhara Patel, "The Doula Difference: State and Federal Bills Aim at Reducing Maternal Health Disparities through Doula Services," National Health Law Program, March 26, 2019, https://healthlaw.org/the-doula-difference-state-and-federal-bills-aim-at-reducing-maternal-health-disparities-through-doula-services/.

8   Davis, *Reproductive Injustice*, 197.
9   Basile, "Reproductive Justice and Childbirth Reform Doulas," 7.
10  See Hartocollis, "Doulas."
11  Recent popular coverage of doulas—including the *New York Times* article "If Only Everyone Had a Postpartum Doula" —still often relegates conversations about birth doulas to Styles sections, even as the writers of these articles advocate the psychological and physiological benefits of doulas, effectively shoring up the idea that doulas are indulgences that allow birthers to align their experiences with contemporary trends.
12  For foundational Black feminist work on reproductive justice, see Roberts, *Killing the Black Body*; Ross and Solinger, *Reproductive Justice*; and Oparah and Bonaparte, *Birthing Justice*.

    It is worth considering how WOC conceptions of doula work align with what Christina Sharpe terms *wake work*. Sharpe asks, "How can we think (and rethink and rethink) care laterally, in the register of the intramural, in a different relation than that of the violence of the state? In what ways do we remember the dead, those lost in the Middle Passage, those who arrived reluctantly, and those still arriving?" See Sharpe, *In the Wake*, 6.

    See, for example, my earlier work on love-politics as a hallmark of Black feminist thought in Nash, "Practicing Love."
13  See Bowen, "Too Many New Moms Are Dying"; and Bowen, "Black Moms in Illinois."
14  Illinois Public Health Association, "Illinois Releases First Maternal Morbidity and Mortality Report."
15  Conway, "Chicago Is Making the Case."
16  See Moser, "Chicago Isn't Just Segregated."
17  See Oppel and Harmon, "In Chicago, One Weekend."
18  Charles, "Chicago's 2018 Murder."
19  See Wagner and Berman, "Trump Threatens to 'Send In the Feds.'"
20  See Posner, "As Black Women Face Maternal Health Crisis."
21  See Tucker, "South Side OB/GYN Unit."
22  Schencker, "Labor and Delivery Units."
23  Lawrence, "Time to Deliver."
24  Gunja et al., "What Is the Status of Women's Health"; CDC, "First Data Released on Maternal Mortality."
25  CDC, "First Data Released on Maternal Mortality"; Gunja, Tikkanenn, Seervai, and Collins, "What Is the Status of Women's Health?"
26  For signature scholars, see work by Hortense Spillers, Saidiya Hartman, Alexander Weheliye, Calvin Warren, Fred Moten, Katherine McKittrick, Dionne Brand, and Claudia Rankine, many of whom have asked how we might conceptualize "violence," especially when it is inflicted on bodies considered not fully human or not human at all.
27  Berlant, "Without Exception."
28  Wiegman, *Object Lessons*, 1. Wiegman notes, "I use the phrase 'identity knowledges' to reference the many projects of academic study that were institutionalized in the US university in the twentieth century for the study of identity."

29 For foundational texts, see Owens, *Medical Bondage* (developing the term *medical superbodies* to describe Black women); Washington, *Medical Apartheid*; Beck, Driscoll, and Watson, *Traumatic Childbirth*; and Schwartz, *Birthing a Slave*. For popular work on birth rape, see Carmon, "What Is 'Birth Rape'?"
30 Kukura, "Obstetric Violence," 728.
31 Varnam qtd. in S. Tucker, "There Is a Hidden Epidemic." See Belluz, "Shocking Number of Women." See also Vedam et al., "Giving Voice to Mothers Study." Their study concludes: "Of the 2700 women who filled out the survey, one in six (17.3%) reported mistreatment. Among all participants, being shouted at or scolded by a health care provider was the most commonly reported type of mistreatment (8.5%), followed by 'health care providers ignoring women, refusing their request for help, or failing to respond to requests for help in a reasonable amount of time' (7.8%). Some women reported violations of physical privacy (5.5%), and health care providers threatening to withhold treatment or forcing them to accept treatment they did not want (4.5%). Women of colour, women who gave birth in hospitals, and those who face social, economic, or health challenges reported higher rates of mistreatment."
32 For coverage of Argentina, see Vacaflor, "Obstetric Violence."
33 See Borges, "Violent Birth." For more on obstetric violence in the context of Mexico, see Dixon, "Obstetrics in a Time of Violence."
34 Borges, "Violent Birth," 849.
35 The Federal Council on Medicine qtd. in Dias and Machado, "Obstetric Violence in Brazil," 118. See also Barbara, "Latin America Claims to Love Its Mothers."
36 Indeed, popular feminist forums have been marked by a call that obstetrics needs its own #MeToo movement. See, for example, Valeii, "Birth Needs a #MeToo Reckoning."
37 Davis, "Obstetric Racism," 565.
38 Sinclair qtd. in S. Tucker, "Hidden Epidemic."
39 See S. Tucker, "Hidden Epidemic."
40 Dunlop, "Dirty Secrets of Birth Rape."
41 Lights, "It's Time to Start Recognising Birth Rape."
42 See, for example, Montgomery, "The Phrase 'Birth Rape.'"
43 Davis, "Obstetric Racism," 570.
44 See, for example, Fitch, "For Black Women." The article urges the importance of doulas by suggesting that doulas are crucial agents in remediating the skyrocketing Black maternal mortality rate in New York City.
45 Some identified as other kinds of doulas as well, including postpartum doulas, abortion doulas, and death doulas.
46 See the DONA description that describes the doulas' work as "low tech" in Sharon Munza, "New York State Enlists Birth Doulas to Reduce Maternal Mortality in People of Color," DONA International, April 24, 2018.
47 For more on ProDoula, see K. Baker, "This Controversial Company."
48 It is worth interrogating the ethics of both casting birthwork for underserved populations as "training" for doulas and also the role of pro bono programs in enabling doulas to secure the requisite number of trainee hours before receiving credentials that most doulas imagined as crucial for securing more money.

49 Davis, *Reproductive Injustice*, 205.
50 See Counter, "There's No Planning for Childbirth."
51 See Combahee River Collective, "The Combahee River Collective Statement."

### CHAPTER THREE: BLACK MATERNAL AESTHETICS

1 See Rankine, "Meaning of Serena Williams."
2 See beyonce [Knowles-Carter] (@beyonce), "We would like to share . . . ," Instagram, February 1, 2017, https://www.instagram.com/p/BP-rXUGBPJa/?hl=en.
3 Knowles, "Beyoncé's Grammy Speech."
4 V. Friedman, "Beyoncé 3.0."
5 V. Friedman, "Beyoncé 3.0."
6 Obama qtd. in Doll, "Michelle Obama and the Power of Mom."
7 Kantor, "Which Michelle Obama Will We Get?"
8 Kantor, "Which Michelle Obama Will We Get?"
9 Obama qtd. in Borge, "Michelle Obama Just Praised Beyoncé's *Homecoming* Documentary."
10 Williams qtd. in Rosseinsky, "Beyoncé Got Hilariously Confused at Wimbledon."
11 Knowles-Carter, "Michelle Obama."
12 Knowles-Carter, "Beyoncé in Her Own Words"; Williams qtd. in Beiler, "Serena Williams."
13 Castile qtd. in Butler, "On the Vital and Audacious Rage of Valerie Castile."
14 Fleetwood, *On Racial Icons*, 74.
15 Nash and Pinto, "Strange Intimacies."
16 Pinto, *Infamous Bodies*.
17 Brown, "Marketing Michelle," 242.
18 Brown, "Marketing Michelle," 242.
19 Wallace, "Critical View of Beyoncé's Formation," 192.
20 Obama qtd. in Wheaton, "More from Michelle Obama on 'Pride.'"
21 Obama qtd. in Little, "Ain't She a First Lady?," 42.
22 See V. Friedman, "What Michelle Obama Wore"; Gaffney, "The Obamas and J. Crew."
23 Kim, "Farewell to Michelle Obama's Flawless Arms"; McClellan, "How to Get Michelle Obama Arms."
24 Warren qtd. in Camia, "Sen. Warren Praises Michelle Obama's Biceps."
25 La Ferla, "At State Dinner."
26 Winters, "Rescue US."
27 Fleetwood, *On Racial Icons*, 99.
28 Douglas, "Venus."
29 Williams qtd. in Hodgkinson, *Serena*, 118.
30 Williams qtd. in Hodgkinson, *Serena*, 218.
31 Williams qtd. in Hodgkinson, *Serena*, 218.
32 Williams qtd. in Perrotta, "Naomi Osaka Defeats Serena Williams."
33 Callahan, "It's Shameful."
34 Navratilova, "What Serena Got Wrong."
35 Schultz, "Reading the Catsuit," 338.

36  Schultz, "Reading the Catsuit," 338.
37  Gibson qtd. in Peterson, *Too Fat, Too Slutty, Too Loud*, 9.
38  Givhan, "Tight Squeeze at the US Open."
39  Serena Williams (@serenawilliams), "Catsuit anyone?," Twitter, May 29, 2018, Twitter, https://twitter.com/serenawilliams/status/1001540241558261760.
40  Williams qtd. in Greene, "'Catsuit' Controversy."
41  Williams qtd. in M. Friedman, "French Open."
42  French Tennis Federation qtd. in Hodgkinson, *Serena*, 211.
43  Billie Jean King (@BillieJeanKing), "The policing of women's bodies must end," Twitter, August 25, 2018, https://twitter.com/BillieJeanKing/status/1033377436694728704.
44  V. Friedman, "Serena Williams Won't Be Silenced."
45  Bissinger, "Serena Williams' Love Match."
46  Diehl qtd. in Aylmer, "Behind the Scenes."
47  V. Friedman, "2016 Pirelli Calendar."
48  Schumer qtd. in Whittle, "2016 Pirelli Calendar."
49  Alexander, *Black Interior*, 2.
50  Williams qtd. in Fuller, "Serena Williams."
51  Marcoux, "Serena Williams Is Being Penalized."
52  Juneau and Kimble, "Serena Williams."
53  Ohanian, "Paternity Leave Was Crucial."
54  Serena Williams (@serenawilliams), ". . . and it's that time of the day," Twitter, July 24, 2018, https://twitter.com/serenawilliams/status/1021925651815845888?lang=en.
55  See Tinsley, "Beyoncé's *Lemonade* Is Black Women Magic."
56  Caramanica, Morris, and Wortham, "Beyoncé in Formation."
57  Here, my work is informed by Samantha Pinto's analysis of Beyoncé's "disco aesthetics" in "'I Love to Love You Baby'" and by Roach, "Paradox of Black Freedom."
58  Morgan qtd. in Bey, "Beyoncé's Black (Ab)normal," 165.
59  Miami chapter of the Fraternal Order of Police qtd. in Hansen, "Response to Beyoncé."
60  Giuliani qtd. in Hassan, "Police Union."
61  Brooks qtd. in CBS *This Morning*, "Beyoncé Gets Political."
62  Chozick, "Mothers of Black Victims."
63  Clinton qtd. in Chozick, "Mothers of Black Victims."
64  Qtd. in Latif and Latif, "'We Know What It Is to Bury a Child.'"
65  Knowles-Carter, "Michelle Obama."
66  Thompson, "Michelle Obama and Beyoncé"; Brittney Cooper, "Lady O and King Bey," in Chambers, *Meaning of Michelle*, 57.
67  Knowles-Carter, "Michelle Obama."
68  Obama, "Open Letter to Beyoncé."
69  Cooper, "Lady O and King Bey," 65.
70  Shange, *For Colored Girls*.
71  Williams qtd. in Olutola, "I Ain't Sorry," 110.
72  Reid Forgrave qtd. in Adjepong and Carrington, "Black Female Athletes as Space Invaders," 171.

73 Williams qtd. in Vixen, "Serena's Crip Walk Dance."
74 Thompson and Andrews-Dyer, "Michelle Obama Just Ripped Up the Playbook."
75 beyonce [Knowles-Carter] (@beyonce), "At 36, I became a new mother of 3," Instagram, September 6, 2018, https://www.instagram.com/p/BnY7IFDFj_2/?hl=en.
76 Lindsey qtd. in Harris-Perry, "Call and Response with Melissa Harris-Perry."
77 Brittney Cooper qtd. in Harris-Perry, "Call and Response with Melissa Harris-Perry."
78 Markle qtd. in Horswill, "Meghan Markle."
79 Williams qtd. in Bains, "Serena Williams."
80 Cooper, "Lady O and King Bey," 68.
81 Obama qtd. in Bedard, "Michelle's Campaign Book."
82 Obama qtd. in Kasana, "Michelle Obama."
83 See CBS This Morning, "Michelle Obama and Her Mother."
84 Weaver, "Wait—Is Qai Qai America's Most Important Doll?"
85 moore, *Fabulous*, xiii.
86 moore, *Fabulous*, xvi.
87 moore, *Fabulous*, xvi.
88 moore, *Fabulous*, xvi.

### CHAPTER FOUR: WRITING BLACK MOTHERHOOD

1 Dungy, *Guidebook to Relative Strangers*, 178.
2 Dungy, *Guidebook to Relative Strangers*, 178.
3 Dungy, *Guidebook to Relative Strangers*, 194.
4 Dungy, *Guidebook to Relative Strangers*, 194.
5 Nash and Pinto, "Strange Intimacies."
6 See Austin, "#ParentingSoWhite." See also Philyaw, "Ain't I a Mommy"; and Garbes, "Why Are We Only Talking about 'Mom Books' by White Women."
7 While I focus on the maternal memoir, there is also a growing body of fiction devoted to motherhood like Sheila Heti's *Motherhood*, Rumaan Alam's *That Kind of Mother*, and Brit Bennett's *The Mothers*.
8 Sehgal, "In a Raft of New Books."
9 Elkin, "Why All the Books about Motherhood?"
10 Austin, "#ParentingSoWhite."
11 See Reddy, "We Need to Talk about Whiteness."
12 See Clemmons, "Ta-Nehisi Coates."
13 See, for example, Swan, "New YA Books Rewrite Old Cultural Scripts." Swan notes, "Now, more than anytime in recent history, we're hearing the triumphant roar of women of color as they break down longstanding barriers in art, film and literature. In young adult literature in particular, inventive, international stories told in newly empowered women's voices are claiming their rightful place at the table." For diversity issues in publishing, see Lee and Low Books, "Where Is the Diversity in Publishing?" For diverse books, see Miller, "Black Kids." Miller notes, "The typical children's picture books featuring Black characters focus on the degradation and endurance of our people. You can fill nearly half the bookshelves in the Schomburg with children's books about the civil rights movement, slavery, basketball players and

musicians, and various 'firsts.' These stories consistently paint African-Americans as the aggrieved and the conquerors, the agitators and the superheroes who fought for their right to be recognized as full human beings." For diversity in genres, see Alter, "Changing Face of Romance Novels"; and Rosman, "In Love with Romance Novels." For sensitivity readers, see Alter, "In an Era of Online Outrage"; and Shapiro, "What the Job of a Sensitivity Reader Is Really Like."

14  David, *Mama's Gun*, ix.
15  Smith, "Grief Observed."
16  Quiney writes, "Women who might have adopted the anonymous mask of affluent hegemonic motherhood have chosen to reveal the ambivalence of the paradigm itself: to worry at and interrogate the Good Mother, and thus to confront both her hegemony and her disciplinary functions" (Quiney, "Confessions of the New Capitalist Mother," 23). She also notes, "Ambivalence is the dominant emotion that maternal confessional writers express with regard to their children; this in itself renders their work an expression of the culturally unrepresentable" (34).
17  Garrett, "Cavorting in the Ruins?" 227.
18  Quiney, "Confessions of the New Capitalist Mother," 23.
19  Quiney, "Confessions of the New Capitalist Mother," 23.
20  Cusk, *A Life's Work*, 21.
21  M. Nelson, *Argonauts*, 44.
22  Cusk, *A Life's Work*, 5.
23  See Arlie Hochschild's foundational work on the "second shift."
24  This work unfolds alongside ongoing popular and scholarly work on what Sharon Hays termed *intensive parenting*. In 2018, for example, the *New York Times* reported on the "relentlessness" of parenting. Claire Cain Miller, in "Relentlessness of Modern Parenting," writes, "The new trappings of intensive parenting are largely fixtures of white, upper-middle-class American culture, but researchers say the expectations have permeated all corners of society, whether or not parents can achieve them. It starts in utero, when mothers are told to avoid cold cuts and coffee, lest they harm the baby. Then: video baby monitors. Homemade baby food. Sugar-free birthday cake. Toddler music classes. Breast-feeding exclusively. Spraying children's hands with sanitizer and covering them in 'natural' sunscreen. Throwing Pinterest-perfect birthday parties."
25  Quiney, "Confessions of the New Capitalist Mother," 20.
26  M. Nelson, *Argonauts*, 103.
27  Quiney, "Confessions of the New Capitalist Mother," 25.
28  Sheridan qtd. in Hallstein, "Intriguing History," 19.
29  Hallstein, "The Intriguing History."
30  Rich, *Of Woman Born*, 13.
31  Rich, *Of Woman Born*, 16.
32  Rich, "Notes toward a Politics of Location," 449.
33  Rich, *Of Woman Born*, 11.
34  See Rich, "Compulsory Heterosexuality."

35  Rich, *Of Woman Born*, 12.
36  Rich, *Of Woman Born*, 225.
37  Rich, *Of Woman Born*, 218.
38  Rich, *Of Woman Born*, 235.
39  Kara Van Cleaf, for example, in "'Of Woman Born' to Mommy Blogged, "describes Rich's memoir as a rumination "surrounding the ambivalence of mothering" (251).
40  A. Walker, *In Search of Our Mothers' Gardens*, 402.
41  A. Walker, *In Search of Our Mothers' Gardens*, 408.
42  A. Walker, *In Search of Our Mothers' Gardens*, 408.
43  A. Walker, *In Search of Our Mothers' Gardens*, 405.
44  See A. Walker, "In Search of Zora Neale Hurston." For more on Hurston's legacy, see Carpio and Sollors, "Newly Complicated Zora Neale Hurston."
45  A. Walker, *I Love Myself When I Am Laughing*, 313.
46  A. Walker, *In Search of Our Mothers' Gardens*, 92.
47  A. Walker, *In Search of Our Mothers' Gardens*, 368. This is reminiscent of Adrienne Rich's assertation that "for me, poetry was where I lived as no-one's mother, where I existed as myself" (*Of Woman Born*, 31).
48  A. Walker, *In Search of Our Mothers' Gardens*, 374.
49  A. Walker, *In Search of Our Mothers' Gardens*, 382.
50  R. Walker takes this up extensively in "Rebecca Walker Explains Rift with Mother, Alice."
51  Hirsch, *Mother/Daughter Plot*, 192.
52  For coverage of Michelle Obama's description, see Kantor and Zeleny, "Michelle Obama Adds New Role."
53  The full text of Obama's speech is available here: BarackObamadotcom, "Barack Obama: 'A More Perfect Union' (Full Speech)," given March 18, 2008, Philadelphia, https://www.youtube.com/watch?v=zrp-v2tHaDo.
54  R. Walker, *Baby Love*, 46.
55  R. Walker, *Baby Love*, 46.
56  R. Walker, *Baby Love*, 6.
57  R. Walker, *Baby Love*, 167.
58  R. Walker, *Baby Love*, 45.
59  R. Walker, *Baby Love*, 208.
60  R. Walker, *Baby Love*, 50.
61  R. Walker qtd. in Hilpern, "Different Kind of Love."
62  R. Walker qtd. in Hilpern, "Different Kind of Love."
63  R. Walker, *Baby Love*, 117.
64  Muñoz, *Cruising Utopia*, 189.
65  Jacobs, "Hope Springs Maternal."
66  R. Walker qtd. in Hoening, "Feminist's Transformation."
67  R. Walker, "How My Mother's Fanatical Views Tore Us Apart."
68  A. Walker, "Taking Care of the Truth."
69  McClain, *We Live for the We*, 2.
70  McClain, *We Live for the We*, 5.

71 I borrow the phrase "romance of community" from Miranda Joseph's work, *Against the Romance of Community*.
72 McClain, "What It's Like to Be Black and Pregnant."
73 McClain, *We Live for the We*, 16.
74 McClain, *We Live for the We*, 87.
75 McClain, *We Live for the We*, 88.
76 McClain, *We Live for the We*, 101.
77 McClain, *We Live for the We*, 32, 195, 103, 119.
78 McClain, *We Live for the We*, 29–30.
79 McClain, *We Live for the We*, 30.
80 McClain, *We Live for the We*, 160.
81 McClain, *We Live for the We*, 30.
82 McClain, *We Live for the We*, 31.
83 Dungy, *Guidebook to Relative Strangers*, 23.
84 Dungy, *Guidebook to Relative Strangers*, 157.
85 P. Williams, *Alchemy of Race and Rights*, 62.
86 Dungy, *Guidebook to Relative Strangers*, 1.
87 Dungy, *Guidebook to Relative Strangers*, 11.
88 See Sara Ahmed's work on the figure of the feminist "killjoy" developed across multiple books and in her blog, *feministkilljoys*, https://feministkilljoys.com/.
89 P. Williams, *Alchemy of Race and Rights*, 71.
90 Dungy, *Guidebook to Relative Strangers*, 93.
91 Dungy, *Guidebook to Relative Strangers*, 107.
92 Dungy, *Guidebook to Relative Strangers*, 109.
93 P. Williams, "On Being the Object of Property," 5. We might think of this idea of "picking through the ruins" as a kind of Black feminist ethic, as Alice Walker suggests in her quote about how Black feminists engage genius.
94 Dungy, *Guidebook to Relative Strangers*, 18–19.
95 Dungy, *Guidebook to Relative Strangers*, 17.
96 Dungy, *Guidebook to Relative Strangers*, 17.
97 Dungy, *Guidebook to Relative Strangers*, 172.
98 Dungy, *Guidebook to Relative Strangers*, 173.
99 Dungy, *Guidebook to Relative Strangers*, 175, 176.
100 Dungy's book did win the National Book Critics Circle Award in Criticism.
101 See Mary Oliver's poem "Wild Geese."
102 Dungy qtd. in Chakrapani, "More Than Just a Single Identity."
103 Three months later, Lucy McBath, Jordan Davis's mother, won a Georgia congressional race.
104 Bosman and Goldstein, "Timeline for a Body." Bosman and Goldstein note, "But local officials say that the image of Mr. Brown's corpse in the open set the scene for what would become a combustible worldwide story of police tactics and race in America, and left some of the officials asking why."
105 I take this up further in Nash, "Unwidowing."
106 Castile qtd. in Chapman, "Castile Family Reacts to Not Guilty Verdict."

107  McSpadden, *Tell the Truth and Shame the Devil*, x.
108  Tindal, "'Its Own Special Attraction,'" 259.
109  Black Lives Matter, "Defund the Police."
110  Provenzano, "Michael Brown's Mother." See also Toler, "Debate over Ferguson Shooting."
111  McSpadden, *Tell the Truth and Shame the Devil*, xv.
112  McSpadden, *Tell the Truth and Shame the Devil*, 5.
113  McSpadden, *Tell the Truth and Shame the Devil*, 3.
114  McSpadden, *Tell the Truth and Shame the Devil*, 5.
115  McSpadden, *Tell the Truth and Shame the Devil*, 25.
116  McSpadden, *Tell the Truth and Shame the Devil*, 113.
117  McSpadden, *Tell the Truth and Shame the Devil*, 253.
118  Lordi, "Reading Michelle Obama's *Becoming*."
119  Lordi, "Reading Michelle Obama's *Becoming*."
120  Obama, *Becoming*, 187.
121  Obama, *Becoming*, 187; Vega, "Infertility."
122  Obama, *Becoming*, 187.
123  Obama, *Becoming*, 188.
124  Obama, *Becoming*, 189.
125  Obama, *Becoming*, 191.
126  Obama, *Becoming*, 202.

## CONCLUSION

1  Jeffrey, *Time Pass*.
2  See, for example, Broughton, "Bringing the Organization Back In."
3  Southall and Stewart, "They Grabbed Her Baby and Arrested Her."
4  Lisa Schreibersdorf qtd. in Gold and Southall, "Charges Dropped against Brooklyn Mother."
5  Johnson qtd. in Stewart, "Jazmine Headley."
6  Andrews-Dyer, "This Isn't Another Horror Story."
7  "Complex personhood" is Avery Gordon's term. Gordon, *Ghostly Matters*.
8  Andrews-Dyer, "This Isn't Another Horror Story."
9  Andrews-Dyer, "This Isn't Another Horror Story."
10  Andrews-Dyer, "This Isn't Another Horror Story."

## CODA

1  See Dogantekin, "Black Plague"; and Brookings Institute, "Race Gaps in COVID-19."
2  E. J. Dickson reports that "the hospital ended up giving her pitocin, a medication that causes uterine contractions, to induce labor, asking Sha-Asia if she wanted an epidural. After some hesitation, she assented." See Dickson, "Death of Sha-Asia Washington." Rose Adams reports, "On July 2, Washington and her boyfriend visited Woodhull Medical Center, a city-run hospital on Flushing Avenue. Washington went into labor the following day, and shortly before midnight on July 3, doctors escorted Washington's boyfriend out of the room and gave Washington

an epidural despite her protests, her boyfriend's family said. 'They were giving her too much medication. She said she didn't want [the epidural], and they forced it on her,' said Jasmin López, a close friend of Washington's and the sister of her boyfriend." See Adams, "Protesters Slam Bed-Stuy Hospital."

3 Adams, "Protesters Slam Bed-Stuy Hospital."
4 New York City Department of Health, "Severe Maternal Morbidity, 2008–2012."
5 Woodhull statement qtd. in Marcoux, "This Pregnant Mother's Death."
6 Two weeks before her death, Isaac had tweeted, "Can't wait to write a tell all about my experience during my last two trimesters dealing with incompetent doctors at Montefiore [Hospital]." See Carmon, "When Your Zip Code Determines Whether You Live or Die."
7 Amy Schumer (@amyschumer), "Women of color are 12 times more likely to die," Instagram, July 7, 2020, https://www.instagram.com/p/CCXKjıtplBH/?hl=en.
8 Dickson, "Death of Sha-Asia Washington"; Salazar, "Statement on Sha-Asia Washington's Passing."
9 Williams qtd. in Adams, "Protesters Slam Bed-Stuy Hospital."
10 Aponte, "Brooklyn Woman's Death."
11 See de Freytas-Tamura, "Pregnant and Scared of 'Covid Hospitals.'"
12 Wu, "Study of Coronavirus in Pregnant Women."
13 Thomas, "America Was Already Failing Black Mothers."
14 Meadows-Fernandez, "Unbearable Grief of Black Mothers."
15 Holland, *Raising the Dead*; Sharpe, *In the Wake*.
16 Alexander, "Trayvon Generation."
17 Cooper-Jones, "How Was My Son Ahmaud Arbery's Murder Not a Hate Crime?"
18 Castile qtd. in Forgrave, "For Mother of Philando Castile."

# Bibliography

Abdur-Rahman, Aliyyah. "On Ferguson, the Fragility of Black Boys, and Feminist Futures." *Feminist Wire*, October 2, 2014. https://thefeministwire.com/2014/10/ferguson-fragility-black-boys-feminist-futures/.

Abdur-Rahman, Aliyyah I. "A Tenuous Hold." *Black Scholar* 49, no. 2 (2019): 38–43.

Adams, Rose. "Protesters Slam Bed-Stuy Hospital after Black Woman Dies during Childbirth." *Brooklyn Paper*, July 9, 2020. https://www.brooklynpaper.com/they-killed-her-protesters-slam-bed-stuy-hospital-after-black-woman-dies-during-childbirth/.

Adjepong, L. Anima, and Ben Carrington. "Black Female Athletes as Space Invaders." In *Routledge Handbook of Sport, Gender and Sexuality*, edited by Jennifer Hargreaves and Eric Anderson, 169–78. New York: Routledge, 2014.

Alam, Rumaan. *That Kind of Mother: A Novel*. New York: Ecco, 2018.

Alexander, Elizabeth. *The Black Interior*. Minneapolis: Graywolf, 2004.

Alexander, Elizabeth. "The Trayvon Generation." *New Yorker*, June 15, 2020. https://www.newyorker.com/magazine/2020/06/22/the-trayvon-generation.

Allers, Kimberly Seals. *The Big Letdown: How Medicine, Big Business, and Feminism Undermine Breastfeeding*. New York: St. Martin's, 2017.

Allers, Kimberly Seals. "Black Moms and Breastfeeding: Why We Should Care about World Breastfeeding Week." *My Brown Baby*, August 8, 2013. http://mybrownbaby.com/2013/08/Black-moms-breastfeeding-why-we-should-care-about-world-breastfeeding-week/.

Allers, Kimberly Seals. "Breastfeeding While Black Can Be an Isolating Experience." *Forbes*, August 3, 2012. https://www.forbes.com/sites/womensenews/2012/08/03/breastfeeding-while-black-can-be-an-isolating-experience/#393333e143ef.

Allers, Kimberly Seals. "Inviting African-American Mothers to Sell Their Breast Milk, and Profiting." *New York Times*, December 3, 2014. https://parenting.blogs.nytimes.com/2014/12/03/inviting-african-american-mothers-to-sell-their-breast-milk-and-profiting/.

Allers, Kimberly Seals. "Why Trayvon Martin Has Everything to Do with Black Women's Birth Outcomes." *Mocha Manual*, July 19, 2013. http://mochamanual.com/2013/07/19/why-trayvon-martin-has-everything-to-do-with-Black-womens-birth-outcomes/.

Alter, Alexandra. "The Changing Face of Romance Novels." *New York Times*, July 7, 2018. https://www.nytimes.com/2018/07/07/books/romance-novels-diversity.html.

Alter, Alexandra. "In an Era of Online Outrage, Do Sensitivity Readers Result in Better Books, or Censorship?" *New York Times*, December 24, 2017. https://www.nytimes.com/2017/12/24/books/in-an-era-of-online-outrage-do-sensitivity-readers-result-in-better-books-or-censorship.html.

American Academy of Pediatrics (AAP). "Breastfeeding and the Use of Human Milk." *Pediatrics* 129, no. 3 (2012): e827–41. https://pediatrics.aappublications.org/content/129/3/e827.

American Academy of Pediatrics (AAP). "Breast-feeding and the Use of Human Milk: Work Group on Breast-feeding." *Pediatrics* 100, no. 6 (1997): 1035–39. https://pediatrics.aappublications.org/content/100/6/1035.

American Academy of Pediatrics (AAP). "The Impact of Racism on Child and Adolescent Health: Policy Statement." *Pediatrics* 144, no. 2 (2019). https://pediatrics.aappublications.org/content/144/2/e20191765.

American Psychological Association. "Summit on Obesity in African-American Women and Girls." 2014. https://www.apa.org/pi/oema/resources/ethnicity-health/african-american/obesity.

Andrews-Dyer, Helena. "This Isn't Another Horror Story about Black Motherhood." *Washington Post*, September 4, 2019. https://www.washingtonpost.com/graphics/2019/lifestyle/black-motherhood/.

Aponte, Claudia Irizarry. "Brooklyn Woman's Death during Childbirth Spurs Renewed Outcry over Treatment Disparities." *The City*, July 9, 2020. https://www.thecity.nyc/health/2020/7/9/21319623/brooklyn-womans-childbirth-death-maternal-racial-disparities.

Arnold, Carrie. "Do 'Baby-Friendly' Hospitals Work for All Moms?" *New York Times*, January 6, 2020. https://parenting.nytimes.com/feeding/baby-friendly-hospital.

Austin, Nefertiti. "#ParentingSoWhite: Where Are the Black Parenting Memoirs?" *Mutha Magazine*, December 12, 2016. https://www.matermea.com/blog/parentingsowhite-where-are-the-Black-parenting-memoirs.

Aylmer, Olivia. "Behind the Scenes of the Serena Williams Cover Shoot." *Vanity Fair*, June 27, 2017. https://www.vanityfair.com/style/2017/06/serena-williams-cover-behind-the-scenes.

Bains, Pahull. "Serena Williams Says Meghan Markle Is 'Literally the Strongest Person I Know.'" *Fashion*, November 12, 2019. https://fashionmagazine.com/culture/serena-williams-meghan-markle-friendship/.

Baker, Katie J. M. "This Controversial Company Wants to Disrupt the Birth World." *BuzzFeed*, January 4, 2017. https://www.buzzfeednews.com/article/katiejmbaker/doula-drama.

Baker, Laura Jean. *The Motherhood Affidavits: A Memoir*. New York: The Experiment, 2018.

Barbara, Vanessa. "Latin America Claims to Love Its Mothers: Why Does It Abuse Them?" *New York Times*, March 11, 2019. https://www.nytimes.com/2019/03/11/opinion/latin-america-obstetric-violence.html.

Basile, Monica Reese. "Reproductive Justice and Childbirth Reform: Doulas as Agents of Social Change." PhD diss., University of Iowa, 2012.

Bass, Margaret. "On Being a Fat Black Girl in a Fat-Hating Culture." In *Recovering the Black Female Body: Self-Representations by African American Women*, edited by Michael Bennett and Vanessa Dickerson, 219–30. New Brunswick, NJ: Rutgers University Press, 2001.

Beavers, Elizabeth R., and Michael Shank. "Get the Military Off of Main Street." *New York Times*, August 14, 2014. https://www.nytimes.com/2014/08/15/opinion/ferguson-shows-the-risks-of-militarized-policing.html.

Beck, Cheryl Tatano, Jeanne Watson Driscoll, and Sue Watson, eds. *Traumatic Childbirth*. New York: Routledge, 2013.

Bedard, Paul. "Michelle's Campaign Book: American Grown." *Washington Examiner*, May 7, 2012. https://www.washingtonexaminer.com/michelles-campaign-book-american-grown?_amp=true.

Beiler, Des. "Serena Williams Says Feeling That She Was 'Not a Good Mom' Led to Recent 'Funk.'" *Washington Post*, August 6, 2018. https://www.washingtonpost.com/news/early-lead/wp/2018/08/06/serena-williams-says-feeling-that-she-was-not-a-good-mom-led-to-recent-funk/.

Belluz, Julia. "A Shocking Number of Women Are Harassed, Ignored, or Mistreated during Childbirth." *Vox*, June 20, 2019. https://www.vox.com/2019/6/10/18628073/maternal-mistreatment-women-of-color.

Bennett, Brit. *The Mothers*. New York: Random House, 2016.

Berlant, Lauren. *Compassion: The Culture and Politics of an Emotion*. New York: Routledge, 2014.

Berlant, Lauren. *Cruel Optimism*. Durham, NC: Duke University Press, 2011.

Berlant, Lauren. "Without Exception: On the Ordinariness of Violence." *Los Angeles Review of Books*, July 30, 2018. https://lareviewofbooks.org/article/without-exception-on-the-ordinariness-of-violence/.

Bey, Marquis. "Beyoncé's Black (Ab)normal: Baaad Insurgency and the Queerness of Slaying." *Black Camera* 9, no. 1 (2017): 164–78.

Bichell, Rae Ellen. "Scientists Start to Tease Out the Subtler Ways Racism Hurts Health." *National Public Radio*, November 11, 2017. https://www.npr.org/sections/health-shots/2017/11/11/562623815/scientists-start-to-tease-out-the-subtler-ways-racism-hurts-health.

Bissinger, Buzz. "Serena Williams' Love Match." *Vanity Fair*, August 2017. https://www.vanityfair.com/style/2017/06/serena-williams-cover-story.

Black Lives Matter. "Defund the Police." May 30, 2020. https://Blacklivesmatter.com/defundthepolice/.

Blair, Leonardo. "Presidential Candidate Beto O'Rourke Tells Voters Systemic Racism Is Killing Black Mothers and Babies." *Christian Post*, April 6, 2019. https://www.christianpost.com/news/presidential-candidate-beto-orourke-tells-voters-systemic-racism-is-killing-Black-mothers-and-babies.html.

Bliss, James. "Black Feminism out of Place." *Signs* 41, no. 4 (2016): 727–49.

Borge, Jonathan. "Michelle Obama Just Praised Beyoncé's *Homecoming* Documentary." *Oprah Magazine*, April 18, 2019. https://www.oprahmag.com/entertainment/tv-movies/a27196338/michelle-obama-beyonce-homecoming-documentary-reaction/.

Borges, Maria T. R. "A Violent Birth: Reframing Coerced Procedures during Childbirth as Obstetric Violence." *Duke Law Journal* 67, no. 4 (2019): 827–62.

Bosman, Julie, and Joseph Goldstein. "Timeline for a Body: 4 Hours in the Middle of a Ferguson Street." *New York Times*, August 23, 2014. https://www.nytimes.com/2014/08/24/us/michael-brown-a-bodys-timeline-4-hours-on-a-ferguson-street.html.

Bowen, Alison. "Black Moms in Illinois 6 Times More Likely to Die from Pregnancy Related Conditions." *Chicago Tribune*, October 19, 2018. https://www.chicagotribune.com/lifestyles/ct-life-Black-women-mortality-childbirth-20181018-story.html.

Bowen, Alison. "Model for Gap Paused to Breastfeed Her Toddler during a Shoot. The Moment Became the Campaign." *Chicago Tribune*, February 26, 2018. https://www.chicagotribune.com/lifestyles/ct-life-gap-ad-model-breastfeedingbreast-feeding-baby-0226-story.html.

Bowen, Alison. "Too Many New Moms Are Dying. Illinois Health Officials Are Trying to Understand Why." *Chicago Tribune*, August 7, 2018.

Braithwaite, Patia. "Biological Weathering and Its Deadly Effect on Black Mothers." *Self*, September 30, 2019. https://www.self.com/story/weathering-and-its-deadly-effect-on-Black-mothers.

Bridges, Khiara M. *Reproducing Race: An Ethnography of Pregnancy as a Site of Racialization*. Berkeley: University of California Press, 2011.

Briggs, Laura. *How All Politics Became Reproductive Politics: From Welfare Reform to Foreclosure to Trump*. Berkeley: University of California Press, 2018.

Brockes, Emma. *An Excellent Choice: Panic and Joy on My Solo Path to Motherhood*. New York: Penguin, 2018.

Brookings Institute. "Race Gaps in COVID-19 Are Even Bigger Than They Appear." *Up Front* (blog), June 16, 2020. https://www.brookings.edu/blog/up-front/2020/06/16/race-gaps-in-covid-19-deaths-are-even-bigger-than-they-appear/.

Broughton, Chad. "Bringing the Organization Back In: The Role of Bureaucratic Churning in Early TANF Caseload Declines in Illinois." *Journal of Sociology and Social Welfare* 37, no. 3 (2010): n.p.

Brown, Caroline. "Marketing Michelle: Mommy Politics and Post-Feminism in the Age of Obama." *Comparative American Studies* 10, nos. 2–3 (2012): 239–54.

Burns, Asia Smith. "Police Say DeKalb Gunman Used Anti-gay Slur before Shooting Man." *Atlanta Journal Constitution*, June 9, 2019. https://www.ajc.com/news/crime--law/breaking-police-say-dekalb-gunman-used-homophobic-slur-before-shooting-gay-man/fUU1oEt2ZhJg87XlkrrZXP/.

Butler, Danielle. "On the Vital and Audacious Rage of Valerie Castile, the Newest Member of the 'Fucked Up Mother's Club.'" *Root*, June 19, 2017. https://verysmartbrothas.theroot.com/on-the-vital-and-audacious-rage-of-valerie-castile-the-1822521673.

Callahan, Maureen. "It's Shameful What US Open Did to Naomi Osaka." *New York Post*, September 8, 2018. https://nypost.com/2018/09/08/its-shameful-what-us-open-did-to-naomi-osaka/.

Camia, Catallina. "Sen. Warren Praises Michelle Obama's Biceps." *USA Today*, May 29, 2013. https://www.usatoday.com/story/onpolitics/2013/05/29/michelle-obama-biceps-elizabeth-warren/2370019/.

Campbell, Olivia. "The Lifelong Health Toll of Schoolyard Racism." *Pacific Standard*, June 14, 2017. https://psmag.com/social-justice/racism-is-real-and-it-is-making-Black-americans-less-healthy.

Campt, Tina. *Image Matters: Archive, Photography, and the African Diaspora in Europe*. Durham, NC: Duke University Press, 2012.

Capelouto, J. D. "Swastikas Found Spray-Painted at High School in North Fulton." *Atlanta Journal Constitution*, February 4, 2019. https://www.ajc.com/news/crime--law/swastikas-found-spray-painted-high-school-north-fulton/V9vkBlAhhiwV59FxsGehyL/.

Caramanica, Jon, Wesley Morris, and Jenna Wortham. "Beyoncé in Formation: Entertainer, Activist, Both." *New York Times*, February 6, 2016. https://www.nytimes.com/2016/02/07/arts/music/Beyoncé-formation-super-bowl-video.html.

Carmon, Irin. "What Is 'Birth Rape'?" *Jezebel*, September 8, 2010. https://jezebel.com/5632689/what-is-birth-rape.

Carmon, Irin. "When Your Zip Code Determines Whether You Live or Die." *New York Magazine*, May 5, 2020. https://nymag.com/intelligencer/2020/05/when-your-zip-code-determines-whether-you-live-or-die.html.

Carpio, Glenda, and Werner Sollors. "The Newly Complicated Zora Neale Hurston." *Chronicle of Higher Education*, January 2, 2011. https://www.chronicle.com/article/The-Newly-Complicated-Zora/125753.

Carter, Shannon K. "Body-Led Mothering: Constructions of the Breast in Attachment Parenting Literature." *Women's Studies International Forum* 62 (2017): 17–24.

Castillo-Hegyi, Christie del. "Letters to Doctors and Parents about the Dangers of Insufficient Exclusive Breast-Feeding." Fed Is Best, April 18, 2015. https://fedisbest.org/2015/04/letter-to-doctors-and-parents-about-the-dangers-of-insufficient-exclusive-breastfeeding/.

CBS This Morning. "Beyoncé Gets Political with Super Bowl Halftime Performance." February 8, 2016. https://www.cbsnews.com/news/super-bowl-50-beyonce-single-formation-police-brutality-Black-lives-matter-coldplay-bruno-mars/.

CBS This Morning. "Michelle Obama and Her Mother on Adjusting to Life at White House." November 14, 2018. https://www.youtube.com/watch?v=o7vZD9XJiNQ.

Centers for Disease Control and Prevention. "First Data Released on Maternal Mortailty in Over a Decade." January 30, 2020. https://www.cdc.gov/nchs/pressroom/nchs_press_releases/2020/202001_MMR.htm.

Chakrapani, Raj. "More Than Just a Single Identity: A Conversation with Camille T. Dungy." *Rumpus*, November 3, 2017. https://therumpus.net/2017/11/the-rumpus-interview-with-camille-t-dungy/.

Chambers, Veronica, ed. *The Meaning of Michelle*. New York: St. Martin's, 2017.

Chambers-Letson, Joshua. *After the Party: A Manifesto for Queer of Color Life*. New York: NYU Press, 2019.

Chapman, Reg. "Castile Family Reacts to Not Guilty Verdict." CBS *Minnesota*, June 16, 2017. https://minnesota.cbslocal.com/2017/06/16/castile-family-verdict-reaction/.

Charles, Sam. "Chicago's 2018 Murder Total Falls for Second Straight Year but Still Tops 530." *Chicago Sun Times*, December 30, 2018. https://chicago.suntimes.com/2018/12/30/18314619/chicago-s-2018-murder-total-falls-for-second-straight-year-but-still-tops-530

Chisholm, N. Jamiyla. "Activists Organize to Bail Out Black Mamas for Mother's Day." *Colorlines*, May 10, 2019. https://www.colorlines.com/articles/activists-organize-bail-out-black-mamas-mothers-day.

Chiusano, Mark. "What Malaysia Goodson Was Carrying." *AM New York*, January 29, 2019. https://www.amny.com/opinion/columnists/mark-chiusano/malaysia-goodson-stroller-stairs-mta-1.26577324.

Chozick, Amy. "Mothers of Black Victims Emerge as a Force for Hillary Clinton." *New York Times*, April 13, 2016. https://www.nytimes.com/2016/04/14/us/politics/hillary-clinton-mothers.html.

Christian, Barbara. "Diminishing Returns: Can Black Feminism(s) Survive the Academy?" In *New Black Feminist Criticism, 1985–2000*, edited by Gloria Bowles, M. Giulia Fabi, and Arlene Keizer, 204–15. Champaign: University of Illinois Press, 2007.

Clemmons, Zinzi. "Ta-Nehisi Coates Has Given #Black Lives Matter Its Foundational Text." *LitHub*, October 8, 2015. https://lithub.com/ta-nehisi-coates-has-given-Black-lives-matter-its-foundational-text/.

Coates, Ta-Nehisi. *Between the World and Me*. New York: Random House, 2015.

Coates, Ta-Nehisi. "'I Am Still Called by the God I Serve to Walk This Out.'" *Atlantic*, February 25, 2014. https://www.theatlantic.com/politics/archive/2014/02/i-am-still-called-by-the-god-i-serve-to-walk-this-out/284064/.

Cole, Haile Eshe. "Reproduction on Display: Black Maternal Mortality and the Newest Case for National Action." *Journal of the Motherhood Initiative for Research and Community Involvement* 9, no. 2 (2018): 89–101.

Collaborative Group on Hormonal Factors in Breast Cancer. "Breast Cancer and Breastfeeding: Collaborative Reanalysis of Individual Data from 47 Epidemiological Studies in 30 Countries, including 50,302 Women with Breast Cancer and 96,973 Women without the Disease." *Lancet* 360, no. 9328 (2002): 187–95.

Collins, James W., Jr. "Disparate Black and White Neonatal Mortality Rates among Infants of Normal Birth Weight in Chicago: A Population Study." *Journal of Pediatrics* 120, no. 6 (1992): 954–60.

Collins, Patricia Hill. *Black Feminist Thought*. New York: Routledge, 1990.

Combahee River Collective. "The Combahee River Collective Statement." In *How We Get Free: Black Feminism and the Combahee River Collective*, edited by Keeanga-Yamahtta Taylor, 1–15. Boston: Haymarket Books, 2012.

Conway, Sarah. "Chicago Is Making the Case for Releasing Pregnant Inmates." *Atlantic*, December 20, 2019. https://www.theatlantic.com/health/archive/2019/12/doulas-county-jail/603730/.

Cooper-Jones, Wanda. "How Was My Son Ahmaud Arbery's Murder Not a Hate Crime?" *New York Times*, June 9, 2020. https://www.nytimes.com/2020/06/09/opinion/hate-crime-bill-ahmaud-arbery.html.

Counter, Rosemary. "There's No Planning for Childbirth." *New York Times*, March 7, 2020. https://www.nytimes.com/2020/03/07/opinion/childbirth-birth-plan-story.html.

Crawford, Elizabeth. "Breastfeeding Is Better for Infants, But Is It Also Better for the Environment? Yes, Researchers Argue." *Food Navigator*, October 3, 2019. https://www.foodnavigator-usa.com/Article/2019/10/03/Breastfeeding-is-better-for-infants-and

-the-environment?fbclid=IwAR3PROg9StdTqe2EW7TV4x0armE4ogsyiF4uESfp-j3xZANiiB0inRBT2Ac.

Cusk, Rachel. *A Life's Work: On Becoming a Mother*. New York: Picador, 2003.

David, Marlo. *Mama's Gun: Black Maternal Figures and the Politics of Transgression*. Columbus: Ohio State University Press, 2016.

Davis, Dána-Ain. "The Bone Collectors' Comments for Sorrow as Artifact: Black Radical Mothering in Times of Terror." *Transforming Anthropology* 24, no. 1 (2016): 8–16.

Davis, Dána-Ain. "Obstetric Racism: The Racial Politics of Pregnancy, Labor, and Birthing." *Medical Anthropology* 38, no. 7 (2018): 560–73.

Davis, Dána-Ain. *Reproductive Injustice: Racism, Pregnancy, and Premature Birth*. New York: NYU Press, 2019.

de Freytas-Tamura, Kimiko. "Pregnant and Scared of 'Covid Hospitals,' They're Giving Birth at Home." *New York Times*, April 24, 2020. https://www.nytimes.com/2020/04/21/nyregion/coronavirus-home-births.html.

de la Cretaz, Britni. "The Troubling Erasure of Trans Parents Who Breast-Feed." *Huffington Post*, November 30, 2016. https://www.huffpost.com/entry/the-troubling-erasure-of_b_8673664.

de la Cretaz, Britni. "What It's Like to Chestfeed." *Atlantic*, August 23, 2016. https://www.theatlantic.com/health/archive/2016/08/chestfeeding/497015/.

Delgado, Jennifer. "Hospitals Push Breast-Feeding in Hopes of Getting 'Baby-Friendly' Label." *Chicago Tribune*, January 10, 2013.

Demby, Gene. "Making the Case That Discrimination Is Bad for Your Health." *Code Switch*, January 14, 2018. https://www.npr.org/sections/codeswitch/2018/01/14/577664626/making-the-case-that-discrimination-is-bad-for-your-health.

Dias, Murillo, and Valeria Eunice Mori Machado. "Obstetric Violence in Brazil: An Integrated Multiple Case Study." *Humanities and Social Sciences Review* 8, no. 2 (2018): 118–38.

Dickson, E. J. "Death of Sha-Asia Washington, Pregnant 26-Year-Old Black Woman, Highlights Devastating Trend." *Rolling Stone*, July 9, 2020. https://www.rollingstone.com/culture/culture-features/shaasia-washington-death-woodhull-hospital-black-maternal-mortality-rate-1026069/.

Dickson, E. J. "Mysterious Deaths Leave Ferguson Activists 'on Pins and Needles.'" *Rolling Stone*, March 18, 2019. https://www.rollingstone.com/culture/culture-news/ferguson-death-mystery-Black-lives-matter-michael-brown-809407/.

Dixon, Lydia Zacher. "Obstetrics in a Time of Violence; Mexican Midwives Critique Routine Hospital Practices." *Medical Anthropology Quarterly* 29, no. 4 (2014): 437–54. https://anthrosource.onlinelibrary.wiley.com/doi/abs/10.1111/maq.12174.

Dogantekin, Vakkas. "Black Plague: COVID-19 Hits African Americans Hard." *Anadolu Agency*, June 17, 2020. https://www.aa.com.tr/en/americas/black-plague-covid-19-hits-african-americans-hard/1880097.

Doll, Jen. "Michelle Obama and the Power of Mom." *Atlantic*, September 5, 2012. https://www.theatlantic.com/politics/archive/2012/09/michelle-obama-and-power-mom/323963/.

Dornfeld, Ann. "Breastfeeding Is 'Life or Death for Communities of Color.'" KUOW, May 3, 2017. https://www.kuow.org/stories/breastfeeding-life-or-death-communities-color/.

Douglas, Delia D. "Venus, Serena, and the Inconspicuous Consumption of Blackness." *Journal of Black Studies* 43, no. 2 (2012): 127–45.

Drum, Kevin. "How Can We Reduce Black Maternal Mortality?" *Mother Jones*, May 6, 2019. https://www.motherjones.com/kevin-drum/2019/05/maternal-mortality/.

Dungy, Camille. *Guidebook to Relative Strangers: Journeys into Race, Motherhood, and History*. New York: Norton, 2017.

Dunlop, Scott. "The Dirty Secrets of Birth Rape." *Parent 24*, May 18, 2012. https://www.parent24.com/Pregnant/Birth/The-dirty-secrets-of-birth-rape-20120518.

Dyson, Michael Eric. *Tears We Cannot Stop: A Sermon to White America*. New York: St. Martin's, 2017.

Eligon, John. "Michael Brown Spent Last Weeks Grappling with Problems and Promise." *New York Times*, August 24, 2014. https://www.nytimes.com/2014/08/25/us/michael-brown-spent-last-weeks-grappling-with-lifes-mysteries.html?ref=us.

Elkin, Lauren. "Why All the Books about Motherhood?" *Paris Review*, July 17, 2018. https://www.theparisreview.org/blog/2018/07/17/why-all-the-books-about-motherhood/.

Ellis-Petersen, Hannah. "How Formula Milk Firms Target Mothers Who Can Least Afford It." *Guardian*, February 26, 2018. https://www.theguardian.com/lifeandstyle/2018/feb/27/formula-milk-companies-target-poor-mothers-breast-feeding.

Enright, Anne. *Making Babies*. New York: Norton, 2013.

Ettachfini, Leila. "NYC's Inaccessible Subway System Is a Reproductive Rights Issue." *Vice*, January 30, 2019. https://broadly.vice.com/en_us/article/59xbqd/nyc-subway-mta-reproductive-rights?fbclid=IwAR0wm8f_KROx1oydKPcyjTScLuSqZY023NeXjA_t1gVX20_rDmBS4VxwWWI.

Fed Is Best. "Nurses Are Speaking Out about the Dangers of the Baby-Friendly Health Initiative." October 21, 2018. https://fedisbest.org/2018/10/nurses-are-speaking-out-about-the-dangers-of-the-baby-friendly-health-initiative/.

Feldman, Nina. "To Promote Breast-Feeding among Women of Color, Philly Campaign Features Black Moms." *WHYY*, August 29, 2018. https://whyy.org/articles/to-promote-breast-feeding-among-women-of-color-philly-campaign-features-Black-moms/.

Feldstein, Ruth. "'I Wanted the Whole World to See': Race, Gender, and Constructions of Motherhood in the Death of Emmett Till." In *Mothers and Motherhood: Readings in American History*, edited by Rima D. Apple and Janet Golden, 270–301. Columbus: Ohio State University Press, 1997.

Ferré-Sadurní, Luis. "New York to Expand Use of Doulas to Reduce Childbirth Deaths." *New York Times*, April 22, 2018. https://www.nytimes.com/2018/04/22/nyregion/childbirth-death-doula-medicaid.html.

Fitch, Elizabeth Campos. "For Black Women, a Doula Can Make for a Better Pregnancy." *New York Times*, May 31, 2018. http://nyc18.nytimes-institute.com/2018/05/31/doulas-pregnancy/.

Fleetwood, Nicole R. *On Racial Icons: Blackness and the Public Imagination*. New Brunswick, NJ: Rutgers University Press, 2015.

Fleetwood, Nicole R. "Posing in Prison: Family Photographs, Emotional Labor, and Carceral Intimacy." *Public Culture* 27, no. 3 (2015): 487–511.

Fleetwood, Nicole R. *Troubling Vision: Performance, Visuality, and Blackness*. Chicago: University of Chicago Press, 2011.

Forgrave, Reid. "For Mother of Philando Castile, George Floyd's Death a Nightmare Revisited." *Star Tribune* (Minneapolis), June 4, 2020. https://www.startribune.com/for-mother-of-philando-castile-george-floyd-s-death-a-nightmare-revisited/570997652/.
Freeman, Andrea. "'First Food' Justice: Racial Disparities in Infant Feeding as Food Oppression." *Fordham Law Review* 83, no. 6 (2015): 3053–87.
Freeman, Andrea. *Skimmed: Breastfeeding, Race, and Injustice*. Stanford, CA: Stanford University Press, 2019.
Freeman, Andrea. "Unmothering Black Women: Formula Feeding as an Incident of Slavery." *Hastings Law Journal* 69 (2018): 1545–1606.
Freeman, Andrea, and Kimberly Seals Allers. "The Racial Divide of Breastfeeding in the US." *The Takeaway*, August 12, 2019. https://www.wnycstudios.org/podcasts/takeaway/segments/breastfeeding-race-disparity-experience.
Friedman, Megan. "French Open Bans Serena Williams from Wearing Her Life-Saving Catsuit." *Elle*, August 24, 2018. https://www.elle.com/culture/celebrities/a22826732/serena-williams-catsuit-french-open-dress-code/.
Friedman, Vanessa. "Beyoncé 3.0: The Maternal Ideal." *New York Times*, April 27, 2017. https://www.nytimes.com/2017/04/27/fashion/Beyoncé-serena-williams-pregnancy-goals.html.
Friedman, Vanessa. "Serena Williams Won't Be Silenced. Her Clothes Are Doing the Talking." *New York Times*, May 28, 2019. https://www.nytimes.com/2019/05/28/fashion/serena-williams-french-open-fashion-statement.html.
Friedman, Vanessa. "The 2016 Pirelli Calendar May Signal a Cultural Shift." *New York Times*, November 30, 2015. https://www.nytimes.com/2015/12/03/fashion/the-2016-pirelli-calendar-may-signal-a-cultural-shift.html.
Friedman, Vanessa. "What Michelle Obama Wore and Why It Mattered." *New York Times*, January 14, 2017. https://www.nytimes.com/2017/01/14/fashion/michelle-obama-first-lady-fashion.html.
Friedmann, Jessica. *Things That Helped: On Postpartum Depression*. New York: Scribe, 2017.
Fuller, Russell. "Serena Williams: Statistics on Deaths in Pregnancy or Childbirth 'Heartbreaking.'" BBC, March 6, 2018. https://www.bbc.com/sport/tennis/43299147.
Fulton, Sybrina, and Tracy Martin. *Rest in Power: The Enduring Life of Trayvon Martin*. New York: Random House, 2017.
Fumo, Nicola. "Gap Applauded by Moms for Breastfeeding Post." *Forbes*, February 26, 2018. https://www.forbes.com/sites/nicolafumo/2018/02/26/gap-breastfeeding-instagram-ad/#5f38769862c8.
Gaffney, Adrienne. "The Obamas and J. Crew: A Match Made in Publicity Heaven." *Vanity Fair*, January 2009. https://www.vanityfair.com/news/2009/01/the-obamas-and-jcrew-a-match-made-in-publicity-heaven.
Gamino, Lauren, and Lois Beckett. "Mothers of the Movement Channel Black Lives Lost into Support for Clinton." *Guardian*, July 26, 2016. https://www.theguardian.com/us-news/2016/jul/26/Black-lives-matter-mothers-democratic-convention-hillary-clinton.
Garbes, Angela. "Why Are We Only Talking about 'Mom Books' by White Women." *The Cut*, November 1, 2018. https://www.thecut.com/2018/11/why-are-we-only-talking-about-mom-books-by-white-women.html.

Garrett, Roberta. "Cavorting in the Ruins? Truth, Myth and Resistance in Contemporary Memoirs." In *We Need to Talk about Family: Essays on Neoliberalism, the Family and Popular Culture*, edited by Roberta Garrett, Tracey Jensen, and Angie Voela, 224–45. Cambridge: Cambridge Scholars Publishing, 2016.

Garvey, Amy, Denzel R. Woode, and Charlotte S. Austin. "Reclaiming the White Coat for Black Lives." *American Journal of Public Health* 106, no. 10 (2016): 1749–51.

Garza, Alicia. "A Herstory of the #BlackLivesMatter Movement." *Feminist Wire*, October 7, 2014. https://thefeministwire.com/2014/10/Blacklivesmatter-2/.

German, Michael. "Testimony before the Congressional Black Caucus on the FBI's 'Black Identity Extremism' Report." *Brennan Center for Justice*, March 30, 2018. https://www.brennancenter.org/analysis/testimony-congressional-Black-caucus-fbis-report-Black-identity-extremism.

Geronimus, Arline T. "On Teenage Childbearing and Neonatal Mortality in the United States." *Population and Development Review* 13, no. 2 (1987): 245–79.

Geronimus, Arline T. "The Weathering Hypothesis and the Health of African-American Women and Infants: Evidence and Speculations." *Ethnicity and Disease* 2, no. 3 (1992): 207–21.

Geronimus, Arline T., Margaret Hicken, Danya Keene, and John Bound. "'Weathering' and Age Patterns of Allostatic Load Scores among Blacks and Whites in the United States." *American Journal of Public Health* 96, no. 5 (2006): 826–33.

Geronimus, Arline T., Margaret T. Hicken, Jay A. Pearson, Sarah J. Seashols, Kelly L. Brown, and Tracey Dawson Cruz. "Do US Black Women Experience Stress-Related Accelerated Biological Aging?" *Human Nature* 21, no. 1 (2010): 19–38. https://www.ncbi.nlm.nih.gov/pmc/articles/PMC2861506/.

Gillibrand, Kirsten. "Democratic Debate Transcript: July 31, 2019." *NBC News*, July 31, 2019. https://www.nbcnews.com/politics/2020-election/democratic-debate-transcript-july-31-2019-n1038016.

Givhan, Robin. "A Tight Squeeze at the US Open." *Washington Post*, August 30, 2002. https://www.washingtonpost.com/archive/lifestyle/2002/08/30/a-tight-squeeze-at-the-us-open/791ff3f9-9fe2-4dc6-8f47-e34c03d52aa3/.

Gold, Michael, and Emma G. Fitzsimmons. "A Mother's Fatal Fall on Subway Stairs Rouses New Yorkers to Demand Accessibility." *New York Times*, January 29, 2019.

Gold, Michael, and Ashley Southall. "Charges Dropped against Brooklyn Mother Who Had Baby Ripped from Her Arms by Police." *New York Times*, December 11, 2018. https://www.nytimes.com/2018/12/11/nyregion/jazmine-headley-baby-video-nypd.html.

Gordon, Avery. *Ghostly Matters: Haunting and the Sociological Imagination*. Minneapolis: University of Minnesota Press, 1997.

Greene, Nick. "'Catsuit' Controversy, Describes 'Wonderful Relationship' with French Tennis Federation President." *Slate*, August 25, 2018. https://slate.com/culture/2018/08/serena-williams-catsuit-controversy-tennis-star-describes-wonderful-relationship-with-french-tennis-federation-president-bernard-giudicelli.html.

Gruber, Kenneth J., Susan H. Cupito, and Christina F. Dobson. "Impact of Doulas on Healthy Birth Outcomes." *Journal of Perinatal Education* 22, no. 1 (2013): 49–58.

Gumbs, Alexis Pauline, "'We Can Learn to Mother Ourselves': The Queer Survival of Black Feminism, 1968–1996." PhD diss., Duke University, 2010.

Gunja, Munira Z., Roosa Tikkanenn, Shanoor Seervai, and Sara R. Collins. "What Is the Status of Women's Health and Health Care in the U.S. Compared to Ten Other Countries?" Commonwealth Fund, December 19, 2018. https://www.commonwealthfund.org/publications/issue-briefs/2018/dec/womens-health-us-compared-ten-other-countries.

Hallstein, D. Lynn O'Brien. "The Intriguing History and Silences of *Of Woman Born*: Rereading Adrienne Rich Rhetorically to Better Understand the Contemporary Context." *Feminist Formations* 22, no. 2 (2010): 18–41.

Hamlin, Françoise. *Crossroads at Clarksdale: The Black Freedom Struggle in the Mississippi Delta after World War II*. Chapel Hill: University of North Carolina Press, 2014.

Hansen, Dale. "Response to Beyoncé Shows How Far We Still Have to Go." *Huffington Post*, February 23, 2017. https://www.huffingtonpost.com/dale-hansen/response-to-Beyoncé-shows_b_9300448.html.

Harris, Angela P. "Race and Essentialism in Feminist Legal Theory." *Stanford Law Review* 42 (1989): 581–616.

Harris, Ashley, Nymisha Chilukuril, Meredith West, Janice Henderson, Shari Lawson, Sarah Polk, David Levine, and Wendy L. Bennett. "Obesity-Related Dietary Behaviors among Racially and Ethnically Diverse Pregnant and Postpartum Women." *Journal of Pregnancy* (2016). http://dx.doi.org/10.1155/2016/9832167.

Harris, Kamala. "Democratic Debate Transcript: July 31, 2019." *NBC News*, July 31, 2019. https://www.nbcnews.com/politics/2020-election/democratic-debate-transcript-july-31-2019-n1038016.

Harrison, Laura. "Milk Money: Race, Gender, and Breast Milk 'Donation.'" *Signs* 44, no. 2 (2019): 281–306.

Harris-Perry, Melissa. "A Call and Response with Melissa Harris-Perry: The Pain and the Power of 'Lemonade.'" *Elle*, April 26, 2016. https://www.elle.com/culture/music/a35903/lemonade-call-and-response/.

Hartman, Saidiya. *Lose Your Mother: A Journey along the Atlantic Slave Route*. New York: Farrar, Straus and Giroux, 2007.

Hartocollis, Anemona. "Doulas, a Growing Force in Maternity Culture, Seek Greater Acceptance." *New York Times*, February 10, 2015. https://www.nytimes.com/2015/02/11/nyregion/doulas-the-latest-wave-in-maternity-culture-are-organizing-for-more-recognition.html.

Hartzell, Stephanie. "An (In)visible Universe of Grief: Performative Disidentifications with White Motherhood in the We Are Not Trayvon Martin Blog." *Journal of International and Intercultural Communication* 10, no. 1 (2017): 62–79.

Hassan, Carma. "Police Union Calls for Law Enforcement Labor to Boycott Beyoncé's World Tour." *CNN*, February 20, 2016. https://www.cnn.com/2016/02/19/us/beyonce-police-boycott/index.html.

Hausman, Bernice L. "Motherhood and Inequality: A Commentary on Hanna Rosin's 'The Case against Breast-Feeding." *Journal of Human Lactation* 25, no. 3 (2009). https://journals.sagepub.com/doi/abs/10.1177/0890334409341180?journalCode=jhla.

Hays, Sharon. *The Cultural Contradictions of Motherhood*. New Haven, CT: Yale University Press, 1998.
Heard-Garris, Nia. "Commentary: The Long, Harmful Reach of Vicarious Racism and Violence." *US News and World Report*, April 5, 2019. https://www.usnews.com/news/healthiest-communities/articles/2019-04-05/commentary-how-vicarious-racism-and-violence-lingers-and-harms.
Heard-Garris, N. J., M. Cale, L. Camaj, M. C. Hamati, and T. P. Dominguez. "Transmitting Trauma: A Systematic Review of Vicarious Racism and Child Health." *Social Science and Medicine* 199 (2018): 230–40.
Heinig, M. Jane. "The Burden of Proof: A Commentary on 'Is Breast Really Best.'" *Journal of Human Lactation* 23, no. 4 (2007): 374–76.
Hemmings, Claire. *Why Stories Matter: The Political Grammar of Feminist Theory*. Durham, NC: Duke University Press, 2011.
Herndon, Astead W. "Lucy McBath Wins Georgia Congressional Race against Karen Handel." *New York Times*, November 8, 2018. https://www.nytimes.com/2018/11/08/us/politics/lucy-mcbath-georgia.html.
Heti, Sheila. *Motherhood: A Novel*. New York: Henry Holt, 2018.
Hilpern, Kate. "A Different Kind of Love." *Guardian*, December 15, 2007. https://www.theguardian.com/lifeandstyle/2007/dec/15/familyandrelationships.family.
Hirsch, Marianne. *The Mother/Daughter Plot: Narrative, Psychoanalysis, Feminism*. Bloomington: Indiana University Press, 1989.
Hochschild, Arlie Russell. *The Second Shift*. New York: Penguin, 2003.
Hodgkinson, Mark. *Serena: A Graphic Biography of the Greatest Tennis Champion*. London: White Lion, 2019.
Hoening, Carol. "A Feminist's Transformation." *Huffington Post*, November 17, 2011. https://www.huffpost.com/entry/a-feminists-transformatio_b_43697.
Holland, Sharon. *Raising the Dead: Readings of Death and (Black) Subjectivity*. Durham, NC: Duke University Press, 2000.
Holloway, Karla FC. *Passed On: African American Mourning Stories*. Durham, NC: Duke University Press, 2003.
Holohan, Ellin. "Epidemic of Obesity in US Kids Began in Late 90s." *Health Day*, July 21, 2011. https://consumer.healthday.com/mental-health-information-25/behavior-health-news-56/epidemic-of-obesity-in-u-s-kids-began-in-late-90s-654893.html.
Horswill, Ian. "Meghan Markle: 'Never Thought This Would Be Easy . . . Thought It Would Be Fair.'" *CEO Magazine*, October 21, 2019. https://news.theceomagazine.com/world-news/meghan-markle-itv/.
Hosseini, Sarah. "Black Women Are Facing a Childbirth Mortality Crisis." *Washington Post*, February 28, 2019. https://www.washingtonpost.com/lifestyle/2019/02/27/Black-women-are-facing-childbirth-mortality-crisis-these-doulas-are-trying-help/.
Howe-Heyman, Abigail, and Melanie Lutenbacher. "The Baby-Friendly Hospital Initiative as an Intervention to Improve Breastfeeding Rates: A Review of the Literature." *Journal of Midwifery and Women's Health* 61, no. 1 (January 2016). https://onlinelibrary.wiley.com/doi/abs/10.1111/jmwh.12376.
Illinois Department of Public Health. "Obesity Prevention Initiative Report." 2010. http://www.idph.il.us/pdf/Obesity_Report.pdf.

Illinois Public Health Association. "Illinois Releases First Maternal Morbidity and Mortality Report." 2018. https://www.ipha.com/news/post/3474/illinois-releases-first-maternal-morbidity-and-mortality-report#gsc.tab=0 Oct 18 2018.

Jackson, Danielle. "A Frustrating Year of Reporting on Black Maternal Health." *LongReads*, June 13, 2018. https://longreads.com/2018/06/13/a-frustrating-year-of-reporting-on-Black-maternal-health/.

Jacobs, Alexandra. "Hope Springs Maternal." *New York Times*, March 18, 2007. https://www.nytimes.com/2007/03/18/books/Jacobs.t.html.

Jeffrey, Craig. *Time Pass: Youth, Class, and the Politics of Waiting in India*. Stanford, CA: Stanford University Press, 2010.

Jenkins, Nina Lyon. "Black Women and the Meaning of Motherhood." In *Redefining Motherhood: Changing Identities and Patterns*, edited by Sharon Abbey and Andrea O'Reilly, 201–13. Toronto: Second Story Press, 1998.

Johnson, Angela, Rosalind Kirk, Katherine Lisa Rosenblum, and Maria Muzik. "Enhancing Breastfeeding Rates among African American Women: A Systematic Review of Current Psychosocial Interventions." *Breastfeeding Medicine* 10, no. 1 (2015): 45–62. https://www.ncbi.nlm.nih.gov/pmc/articles/PMC4307211/.

Johnson, Rita Henley. "'Baby-Friendly' Hospitals Bypass Black Communities." *Women's E-News*, August 29, 2013. https://womensenews.org/2013/08/baby-friendly-hospitals-bypass-Black-communities/.

Joseph, Miranda. *Against the Romance of Community*. Minneapolis: University of Minnesota Press, 2002.

June, Laura. *Now My Heart Is Full*. New York: Penguin, 2018.

Juneau, Jen, and Lindsay Kimble. "Serena Williams 'Can't Imagine' Taking Just Two Weeks of Maternity Leave: 'It's Impossible.'" *People*, August 26, 2019. https://people.com/parents/serena-williams-maternity-leave-two-weeks-impossible-exclusive/.

Jung, Courtney. *Lactivism*. New York: Basic Books, 2015.

Jung, Courtney. "Overselling Breast-Feeding." *New York Times*, October 16, 2015. https://www.nytimes.com/2015/10/18/opinion/sunday/overselling-breast-feeding.html?login=email&auth=login-email.

Kaleen, Jaweed. "Black Lives Matter! Chant Erupts as Mothers of the Movement Take the Stage at the DNC." *Los Angeles Times*, July 26, 2016. https://www.latimes.com/politics/la-na-dnc-mothers-of-the-movement-20160726-snap-story.html.

Kantor, Jodi. "Which Michelle Obama Will We Get When She Leaves the White House?" *New York Times*, January 3, 2017. https://www.nytimes.com/2017/01/06/opinion/sunday/michelle-obama-can-now-speak-her-mind-will-she.html.

Kantor, Jodi, and Jeff Zeleny. "Michelle Obama Adds New Role to Balancing Act." *New York Times*, May 18, 2007. https://www.nytimes.com/2007/05/18/us/politics/18michelle.html.

Kaplan, Emily Kumler. "Reducing Maternal Mortality." *New York Times*, March 5, 2019. https://www.nytimes.com/2019/03/05/well/family/reducing-maternal-mortality.html.

Kasana, Mehreen. "Michelle Obama Says Raising Her Daughters in the White House Wasn't Easy for Her—or Them." *Bustle*, March 19, 2019. https://www.bustle.com/p/michelle-obama-says-raising-her-daughters-in-the-white-house-wasnt-easy-for-her-them-16968378.

Kelley, Robin. "How the MOMMA Act Will Help to Reverse America's Rising Maternal Mortality Rate." June 5, 2018. https://robinkelly.house.gov/media-center/in-the-news/how-the-momma-act-will-help-to-reverse-america-s-rising-maternal-mortality.

Killen, Kimberly. "'Can You Hear Me Now?' Race, Motherhood, and the Politics of Being Heard." *Politics and Gender* 15, no. 4 (2019): 623–44.

Kim, Monica. "A Farewell to Michelle Obama's Flawless Arms." *Vogue*, January 11, 2017. https://www.vogue.com/article/michelle-obama-best-arms-biceps-moments.

Knowles-Carter, Beyoncé. "Beyoncé's Grammy Speech: Transcript." *New York Times*, February 12, 2017. https://www.nytimes.com/2017/02/12/arts/music/Beyoncé-speech-grammys-trump.html.

Knowles-Carter, Beyoncé. "Beyoncé in Her Own Words: Her Life, Her Body, Her Heritage." *Vogue*, September 2018. https://www.vogue.com/article/beyonce-september-issue-2018.

Knowles-Carter, Beyoncé. "Michelle Obama." *Time*, 100 *Most Influential People 2019* issue. https://time.com/collection/100-most-influential-people-2019/5567670/michelle-obama/.

Kolata, Gina. "Americans Blame Obesity on Willpower, Despite Evidence It's Genetic." *New York Times*, November 1, 2016. https://www.nytimes.com/2016/11/01/health/americans-obesity-willpower-genetics-study.html.

Kubota, Samantha, Jesse Burkett-Hall, and Josh Bernstein. "DC 'Most Dangerous Place to Give Birth in the US' for Black Women." *USA DC*, October 17, 2018. https://www.wusa9.com/article/news/investigations/mothers-matter/dc-most-dangerous-place-to-give-birth-in-the-us-for-Black-women/65-605243922.

Kukura, Elizabeth. "Obstetric Violence." *Georgetown Law Journal* 106 (2018): 721–801.

Kwon, Susan. "San Francisco Doula Program Tackles Birth Equity and Economic Justice in One Fell Swoop." *Next City*, October 14, 2020. https://nextcity.org/daily/entry/san-francisco-doula-program-tackles-birth-equity-and-economic-justice.

La Ferla, Ruth. "At State Dinner, Michelle Obama Grabs Back the Spotlight." *New York Times*, September 28, 2015. https://www.nytimes.com/2015/09/28/fashion/michelle-obama-turns-it-out.html.

Lakhani, Nina. "America Has an Infant Mortality Crisis. Meet the Black Doulas Trying to Change That." *Guardian*, November 25, 2019. https://www.theguardian.com/us-news/2019/nov/25/african-american-doula-collective-mothers-toxic-stress-racism-cleveland-infant-mortality-childbirth.

La Leche League International. "Support for Transgender and Non-binary Parents." 2016. https://www.llli.org/breast-feeding-info/transgender-non-binary-parents/.

Latif, Nadia, and Leila Latif. "'We Know What It Is to Bury a Child': The Black Mothers Turning Mourning into a Movement." *Guardian*, November 22, 2016. https://www.theguardian.com/world/2016/nov/22/mothers-of-the-movement-trayvon-martin-sandra-bland-eric-garner-amadou-diallo-sean-bell.

Lawrence, Christie. "Time to Deliver: Putting an End to Black Women Dying in Childbirth Is Easier Than You Think." *The Grio*, November 18, 2019. https://thegrio.com/2019/11/18/putting-an-end-to-Black-women-dying-in-childbirth/.

Lawson, Erica S. "Bereaved Black Mothers and Maternal Activism in the Racial State." *Feminist Studies* 44, no. 3 (2018): 713–35.

Lee, Robyn. "Breastfeeding and Sexual Difference: Queering Irigaray." *Feminist Theory* 19, no. 1 (2018): 77–94.

Lee and Low Books. "Where Is the Diversity in Publishing? The 2015 Diversity Baseline Survey Result." *Open Book Blog*, January 26, 2016. https://blog.leeandlow.com/2016/01/26/where-is-the-diversity-in-publishing-the-2015-diversity-baseline-survey-results/.

Li, Shirley. "The Evolution of Police Militarization in Ferguson and Beyond." *Atlantic*, August 15, 2014. https://www.theatlantic.com/national/archive/2014/08/the-evolution-of-police-militarization-in-ferguson-and-beyond/376107/.

Lights, Zion. "It's Time to Start Recognising Birth Rape." *Huffington Post UK*, January 19, 2013. https://bit.ly/2TP8D3s.

Lind, Jennifer N., Cria G. Perrine, Ruowei Li, Kelley S. Sanlon, and Laurence M. Grummer-Strawn. "Racial Disparities in Access to Maternity Care Practices That Support Breastfeeding—United States 2011." *Morbidity and Mortality Weekly Report* 63, no. 33 (2014): 725–28. https://www.cdc.gov/mmwr/preview/mmwrhtml/mm6333a2.htm.

Little, Sharoni Denise. "Ain't She a First Lady? Michelle Obama, Black Women's Narratives, and the Rhetoric of Identification." In *Michelle Obama and the FLOTUS Effect: Platform, Presence, and Agency*, edited by Heather E. Harris and Kimberly R. Moffitt, 31–56. Lanham, MD: Lexington Books, 2020.

Lordi, Emily. "Reading Michelle Obama's *Becoming* as a Motherhood Memoir." *New Yorker*, February 5, 2019. https://www.newyorker.com/culture/cultural-comment/reading-michelle-obamas-becoming-as-a-motherhood-memoir.

Ludden, Jennifer. "Teaching Black Women to Embrace Breast-Feeding." *National Public Radio*, December 23, 2009. https://www.npr.org/templates/story/story.php?storyId=121755349.

MacDonald, Trevor, Joy Noel-Weiss, Diana West, Michelle Walks, MaryLynne Biener, Alanna Kibbe, and Elizabeth Myler. "Transmasculine Individuals' Experiences with Lactation, Chestfeeding, and Gender Identity: A Qualitative Study." *BMC Pregnancy and Childbirth* 16 (2016). https://doi.org/10.1186/s12884-016-0907-y.

Maheshwari, Sapna. "Gap Plans to Spin Off Old Navy after a Dismal Year." *New York Times*, February 28, 2019. https://www.nytimes.com/2019/02/28/business/gap-old-navy-spinoff.html.

Mahone, Regina. "State Legislators Are Finally Doing Something about the Black Maternal Health Crisis." *Rewire.News*, April 12, 2019. https://rewire.news/article/2019/04/12/Black-maternal-health-is-still-in-crisis-legislators-are-finally-taking-notice/.

Malcolm, Andrew. "Michelle Obama Talks Black Obesity, Breast-Feeding and $31 Million." *Los Angeles Times*, September 16, 2010. https://latimesblogs.latimes.com/washington/2010/09/michelle-obama-obesity-Black-caucus.html.

Marcoux, Heather. "Serena Williams Is Being Penalized for Taking Maternity Leave—Just Like So Many Other Moms Returning to Work." *Motherly*, May 23, 2018. https://www.mother.ly/news/serena-williams-maternity-leave-is-being-used-against-her-but-she-could-change-things-for-other-working-mamas.

Marcoux, Heather. "This Pregnant Mother's Death Highlights Racial Disparities in Maternal Care." *Motherly*, July 13, 2020. https://www.mother.ly/news/sha-asia-washington-death-maternal-care.

Martin, Nina, and Renee Montagne. "Black Mothers Keep Dying after Giving Birth: Shalon Irving's Story Explains Why." *National Public Radio*, December 7, 2017. https://www.npr.org/2017/12/07/568948782/Black-mothers-keep-dying-after-giving-birth-shalon-irvings-story-explains-why.

Martucci, Jessica. *Back to the Breast: Natural Motherhood and Breastfeeding in America*. Chicago: University of Chicago Press, 2015.

May, Molly Caro. *Body Full of Stars: Female Rage and My Passage into Motherhood*. New York: Counterpoint, 2018.

McCarthy, Claire. "The Real Link Between Breast-Feeding and Preventing Obesity." *Harvard Health Blog*, October 16, 2018. https://www.health.harvard.edu/blog/the-real-link-between-breastfeedingbreast-feeding-and-preventing-obesity-2018101614998.

McClain, Dani. *We Live for the We: The Political Power of Black Motherhood*. New York: Bold Type, 2019.

McClain, Dani. "What It's Like to Be Black and Pregnant When You Know How Dangerous That Can Be." *Nation*, March 6, 2017. https://www.thenation.com/article/what-its-like-to-be-Black-and-pregnant-when-you-know-how-dangerous-that-can-be/.

McClellan, Cornell. "How to Get Michelle Obama Arms." *O: The Oprah Magazine*, May 22, 2019. http://www.oprah.com/health_wellness/michelle-obamas-arm-workout.

McDaniels, Andrea K. "Baltimore Enlists Doulas to Help Bring Infant Mortality Rate Down." *Baltimore Sun*, August 1, 2017. https://www.baltimoresun.com/health/bs-hs-doula-infant-mortality-20170725-story.html.

McKinney, Chelsea O., Jennifer Hahn-Holbrook, Lindsay Chase-Lansdale, Sharon L. Ramey, Julie Krohn, Maxine Reed-Vance, Tonse N. K. Raju, and Madeleine U. Shalowitz. "Racial and Ethnic Differences in Breastfeeding." *Pediatrics* 138, no. 2 (2016). https://pediatrics.aappublications.org/content/138/2/e20152388.

McKittrick, Katherine. "Mathematics Black Life." *Black Scholar* 44, no. 2 (2014): 16–28.

McSpadden, Lezley. "Michael Brown's Mom, on Alton Sterling and Philando Castile." *New York Times*, July 7, 2016. https://www.nytimes.com/2016/07/08/opinion/michael-browns-mom-on-alton-sterling-and-philando-castile.html.

McSpadden, Lezley. *Tell the Truth and Shame the Devil: The Life, Legacy, and Love of My Son Michael Brown*. New York: Regan Arts, 2016.

Meadows-Fernandez, A. Rochaun. "The Unbearable Grief of Black Mothers." *Vox*, May 28, 2020. https://www.vox.com/first-person/2020/5/28/21272380/black-mothers-grief-sadness-covid-19.

Meadows-Fernandez, A. Rochaun. "That Viral Gap Ad Sends a Powerful Message about Breast-Feeding and Black Motherhood." *Washington Post*, March 1, 2018. https://www.washingtonpost.com/news/parenting/wp/2018/03/01/that-viral-gap-ad-sends-a-powerful-message-about-breast-feeding-and-Black-motherhood/?utm_term=.f1d432856d75.

Meyerson, Collier. "Every Black Woman Deserves a Doula." *New York Magazine*, March 5, 2019. https://nymag.com/intelligencer/2019/03/new-yorks-medicaid-reimbursement-plan-for-doulas.html.

Miller, Claire Cain. "The Relentlessness of Modern Parenting." *New York Times*, December 25, 2018. https://www.nytimes.com/2018/12/25/upshot/the-relentlessness-of-modern-parenting.html.

Miller, Denene. "Black Kids Don't Want to Read about Harriet Tubman All the Time." *New York Times*, March 10, 2018. https://www.nytimes.com/2018/03/10/opinion/sunday/children-literature-books-Blacks.html.

Miller, Shannon Shelton. "Working to Close the Breast-Feeding Gap." *New York Times*, August 17, 2017. https://www.nytimes.com/2017/08/17/well/family/working-to-close-the-breast-feeding-gap.html.

Momigliano, Anna. "Breast-Feeding Isn't Free. This Is How Much It Really Costs." *Washington Post*, May 21, 2019. https://www.washingtonpost.com/lifestyle/2019/05/28/breast-feeding-isnt-free-this-is-how-much-it-really-costs/.

Montgomery, Steph. "The Phrase 'Birth Rape' Is Hurting Sexual Assault Survivors Like Me." *Romper*, November 2, 2018. https://www.romper.com/p/the-phrase-birth-rape-is-hurting-sexual-assault-survivors-like-me-13025720.

Moore, Julia, and Jenna Abetz. "'Uh Oh. Cue the [New] Mommy Wars': The Ideology of Combative Mothering in Popular U.S. Newspaper Articles about Attachment Parenting." *Southern Communication Journal* 81, no. 1 (2016): 49–62.

moore, madison. *Fabulous: The Rise of the Beautiful Eccentric*. New Haven, CT: Yale University Press, 2018.

Morain, Stephanie, and Anne Barnhill. "Do Infant Formula Giveaways Undermine or Support Women's Choices?" *AMA Journal of Ethics* (October 2018). https://journalofethics.ama-assn.org/article/do-infant-formula-giveaways-undermine-or-support-womens-choices/2018-10.

Morgan, Jennifer L. *Laboring Women: Reproduction and Gender in New World Slavery*. Philadelphia: University of Pennsylvania Press, 2004.

Morgan, Jennifer L. "*Partus Sequitur Ventrem*: Law, Race, and Reproduction in Colonial Slavery." *Small Axe* 55 (2018): 1–17.

Moroney, Murphy. "Whoa! Gap Just Released an Ad with a Woman Breastfeeding, and Moms Are Seriously Rejoicing." *PopSugar*, March 3, 2018. https://www.popsugar.com/family/Gap-Ad-Woman-Breast-feeding-44616273.

Moser, Whet. "Chicago Isn't Just Segregated, It Basically Invented Modern Segregation." *Chicago Magazine*, March 2017. https://www.chicagomag.com/city-life/March-2017/Why-Is-Chicago-So-Segregated/.

Munn, Allison C., Susan D. Newman, Martina Mueller, Shannon M. Phillips, and Sarah N. Taylor. "The Impact in the United States of the Baby-Friendly Hospital Initiative on Early Infant Health and Breastfeeding Outcomes." *Breastfeeding Medicine* 11, no. 5 (2016): 222–30.

Muñoz, José Esteban. *Cruising Utopia: The Then and There of Queer Futurity*. New York: NYU Press, 2009.

Nash, Jennifer C. *Black Feminism Reimagined: After Intersectionality*. Durham, NC: Duke University Press, 2019.

Nash, Jennifer C. "Practicing Love: Black Feminism, Love Politics, and Post-Intersectionality." *Meridians: Feminism, Race, Transnationalism* 11, no. 2 (2013): 1–24.

Nash, Jennifer C. "Unwidowing: Rachel Jeantel, Black Death, and the 'Problem' of Black Intimacy." *Signs* 41, no. 4 (2016): 751–74.

Nash, Jennifer C., and Samantha Pinto. "Strange Intimacies: Reading Black Mothering Memoirs." *Public Culture* 32, no. 3 (2020): 491–512.

Navratilova, Martina. "What Serena Got Wrong." *New York Times*, September 10, 2018. https://www.nytimes.com/2018/09/10/opinion/martina-navratilova-serena-williams-us-open.html.

Nelson, Jennifer M., Ruowei Li, and Cria G. Perrine. "Trends of US Hospitals Distributing Infant Formula Packs to Breastfeeding Mothers, 2007 to 2013." *Pediatrics* 135, no. 6 (2015): 1051–56.

Nelson, Maggie. *The Argonauts*. Minneapolis: Graywolf, 2015.

New York City Department of Health and Mental Hygiene Bureau of Maternal, Infant, and Reproductive Health. "Severe Maternal Morbidity, 2008–2012." 2016. https://www1.nyc.gov/assets/doh/downloads/pdf/data/severe-maternal-morbidity-data.pdf.

New York Department of Health. "New York State Strategic Plan for Overweight and Obesity Prevention." 2005. https://www.health.ny.gov/prevention/obesity/strategic_plan.htm.

New York Times Editorial Board. "Easing the Dangers of Childbirth for Black Women." *New York Times*, April 20, 2018. https://www.nytimes.com/2018/04/20/opinion/childbirth-Black-women-mortality.html.

*NPR News and Notes*. "Rebecca Walker Explains Rift with Mother, Alice." July 9, 2008. https://www.npr.org/templates/transcript/transcript.php?storyId=92373475.

Obama, Michelle. *Becoming*. New York: Crown, 2018.

Obama, Michelle. "Open Letter to Beyoncé." Facebook, April 18, 2019. https://www.facebook.com/michelleobama/videos/open-letter-to-beyonce-homecoming/454828318392956/.

O'Connell, Meaghan. *And Now We Have Everything: On Motherhood before I Was Ready*. New York: Little, Brown, 2018.

Ohanian, Alexis. "Paternity Leave Was Crucial after the Birth of My Child, and Every Father Deserves It." *New York Times*, August 12, 2019. https://parenting.nytimes.com/work-money/alexis-ohanian-paternity-leave.

Olsen, Caroline. "Birthworkers Are on the Front Lines of Chicago's Maternal Health Crisis." *Chicago Magazine*, July 2019. http://www.chicagomag.com/city-life/July-2019/Chicagos-Maternal-Health-Crisis/.

Olutola, Sarah. "I Ain't Sorry: Beyoncé, Serena, and Hegemonic Hierarchies in *Lemonade*." *Popular Music and Society* 42, no. 1 (2019): 99–117.

Oparah, Julia Chinyere, and Alicia Bonaparte, eds. *Birthing Justice: Black Women, Pregnancy, and Childbirth*. New York: Routledge, 2015.

Oppel, Richard A., Jr., and Amy Harmon. "In Chicago, One Weekend, 66 Shooting Victims, and Zero Arrests." *New York Times*, August 6, 2018. https://www.nytimes.com/2018/08/06/us/chicago-weekend-shootings.html.

Owens, Deirdre Cooper. *Medical Bondage: Race, Gender, and the Origins of American Gynecology*. Athens: University of Georgia Press, 2018.

Owens, Deirdre Cooper, and Sharla M. Fett. "Black Maternal and Infant Health: Historical Legacies of Slavery." *American Journal of Public Health* 109, no. 10 (2019): 1342–45.

Parker-Pope, Tara. "Timing of Baby Food Tied to Obesity Risk." *New York Times*, February 8, 2011. https://well.blogs.nytimes.com/2011/02/08/timing-of-baby-food-tied-to-obesity-risk/?module=ArrowsNav&contentCollection=Health&action=keypress&region=FixedLeft&pgtype=Blogs.

PBS *News Hour*. "Why Are Black Mothers and Infants Far More Likely to Die in US from Pregnancy-Related Causes?" April 18, 2018. https://www.pbs.org/newshour/show/why-are-Black-mothers-and-infants-far-more-likely-to-die-in-u-s-from-pregnancy-related-causes.

Perrotta, Tom. "Naomi Osaka Defeats Serena Williams for US Open Title." *Wall Street Journal*, September 8, 2018. https://www.wsj.com/articles/naomi-osaka-defeats-serena-williams-for-u-s-open-title-1536443162.

Peterson, Anne Helen. *Too Fat, Too Slutty, Too Loud: The Rise and Reign of the Unruly Woman*. New York: Plume, 2007.

Philyaw, Deesha. "Ain't I a Mommy: Why Are So Few Motherhood Memoirs Penned by Women of Color?" *Bitch Magazine*, February 23, 2016.

Phu, Thy, and Elspeth H. Brown. "The Cultural Politics of Aspiration: Family Photography's Mixed Feelings." *Journal of Visual Culture* 17, no. 2 (2018): 152–65.

Pinto, Samantha. "'I Love to Love You Baby': Beyoncé, Disco Aesthetics, and Black Feminist Politics." *Theory and Event* 23, no. 3 (2020): 512–34.

Pinto, Samantha. *Infamous Bodies: Early Black Women's Celebrity and the Afterlives of Rights*. Durham, NC: Duke University Press, 2020.

Poole, Shelia M. "Digging Deeper: Fighting the Lopsided Likelihood of Black Women Dying in Childbirth." *Atlanta Journal Constitution*, April 25, 2019. https://www.ajc.com/news/local/fighting-the-lopsided-likelihood-Black-women-dying-childbirth/yjmHqNDxVkJbnIScOUr86J/.

Posner, Emeline. "As Black Women Face Maternal Health Crisis, Jackson Park Hospital Plans to Shut Down OB/GYN Unit—and Nurses Are Fighting Back." *Block Club Chicago*, June 24, 2019. https://blockclubchicago.org/2019/06/24/as-Black-women-face-maternal-health-crisis-jackson-park-hospital-plans-to-shut-down-its-ob-gyn-unit-and-nurses-are-fighting-back/.

Provenzano, Brianna. "Michael Brown's Mother Wrote a Book and Was Immediately Piled on by Racist Trolls." *Mic*, May 13, 2016. https://www.mic.com/articles/143454/michael-brown-s-mother-wrote-a-book-and-was-immediately-piled-on-by-racist-trolls.

Purtill, Corinne, and Dan Kopf. "The Class Dynamics of Breastfeeding in the United States of America." *Quartz*, July 23, 2017. https://qz.com/1034016/the-class-dynamics-of-breast-feeding-in-the-united-states-of-america/.

Quiney, Ruth. "Confessions of the New Capitalist Mother: 21st Century Writing on Motherhood as Trauma." *Women: A Cultural Review* 1 (2007): 19–40.

Rabin, Roni Caryn. "Breast-Feeding Is Good for Mothers, Not Just Babies, Studies Suggest." *New York Times*, November 23, 2015. https://well.blogs.nytimes.com/2015/11/23/breast-feeding-is-good-for-mothers-not-just-babies/.

Rabin, Roni Caryn. "Breast-Feeding Is Good for the Mother, and Not Just the Baby." *New York Times*, October 26, 2018. https://www.nytimes.com/2018/10/26/well/family/breast-feeding-is-good-for-the-mother-and-not-just-the-baby.html.

Rabin, Roni Caryn. "Huge Racial Disparities Found in Deaths Linked to Pregnancy." *New York Times*, May 7, 2019. https://www.nytimes.com/2019/05/07/health/pregnancy-deaths-.html?action=click&module=Top%20Stories&pgtype=Homepage.

Rankine, Claudia. "The Meaning of Serena Williams." *New York Times*, August 30, 2015. https://www.nytimes.com/2015/08/30/magazine/the-meaning-of-serena-williams.html.

Reakes, Kathy. "Cause of Death Determined for Stamford Woman Who Died in Subway." *Stamford Daily Voice*, June 12, 2019. https://dailyvoice.com/connecticut/stamford/news/cause-of-death-determined-for-stamford-woman-who-died-in-subway/770062/.

Red, Christian. "Years before Black Lives Matter, 41 Shots Killed Him." *New York Times*, July 19, 2019. https://www.nytimes.com/2019/07/19/nyregion/amadou-diallo-mother-eric-garner.html?action=click&module=News&pgtype=Homepage.

Reddy, Nancy. "We Need to Talk about Whiteness in Motherhood Memoirs." *Electric Lit*, December 4, 2018. https://electricliterature.com/we-need-to-talk-about-whiteness-in-motherhood-memoirs-751eaaae4095.

Reisman, Tamar, and Zil Goldstein. "Case Report: Induced Lactation in a Transgender Woman." *Transgender Health* 3, no. 1 (2018): 24–26.

Rich, Adrienne. "Compulsory Heterosexuality and Lesbian Existence." *Signs* 5, no. 4 (1980): 631–60.

Rich, Adrienne. "Notes toward a Politics of Location." In *Feminist Theory Reader: Local and Global Perspectives*, edited by Carole Ruth McCann and Seung-Kyung Kim, 177–81. New York: Routledge, 2003.

Rich, Adrienne. *Of Woman Born: Motherhood as Experience and Institution*. New York: Norton, 1976.

Roach, Shoniqua Danee. "The Paradox of Black Freedom: Black Female Sexuality in Contemporary Performance, 1965–2000." PhD diss., Northwestern University, 2017.

Roberts, Dorothy. *Killing the Black Body: Race, Reproduction, and the Meaning of Liberty*. New York: Vintage, 1998.

Roeder, Amy. "America Is Failing Its Black Mothers." *Harvard Public Health Magazine*, Winter 2019. https://www.hsph.harvard.edu/magazine/magazine_article/america-is-failing-its-Black-mothers/.

Roitman, Janet. *Anti-crisis*. Durham, NC: Duke University Press, 2013.

Rojas, Rick. "Georgia Teenager Plotted a Knife Attack on a Black Church, Police Say." *New York Times*, November 19, 2019. https://www.nytimes.com/2019/11/19/us/Black-church-attack-gainesville-georgia.html.

ROSE: Reaching Our Sisters Everywhere. "Saving Tomorrow Today: An African American Breast-Feeding Blueprint." 2019. http://www.breastfeedingrose.org/aablueprint/.

Rosenberg, Eli. "A Young Mother Carrying Her Baby and Stroller Died after Falling Down Stairs in New York Subway." *Washington Post*, January 29, 2019.

Rosenberg, Lynn, Julie R. Palmer, Lauren A. Wise, Nicholas J. Hortin, Shiriki K. Kumanyika, and Lucile L. Adams-Campbell. "A Prospective Study of the Effect of Childbearing on Weight Gain in African-American Women." *Obesity* 11, no. 12 (2003): 1526–35.

Rosin, Hanna. "The Case against Breast-Feeding." *Atlantic*, April 2009. https://www.theatlantic.com/magazine/archive/2009/04/the-case-against-breast-feeding/307311/.

Rosman, Katherine. "In Love with Romance Novels, but Not Their Lack of Diversity." *New York Times*, October 10, 2017. https://www.nytimes.com/2017/10/10/style/romance-novels-diversity.html.

Ross, Loretta J., and Rickie Solinger. *Reproductive Justice: An Introduction*. Berkeley: University of California Press, 2017.

Rosseinsky, Katie. "Beyoncé Got Hilariously Confused at Wimbledon." *Grazia*, July 11, 2016. https://graziadaily.co.uk/celebrity/news/beyonce-wimbledon-reaction-confused/.

Ryan, Benjamin. "Racism Got You Stressed? That May Be Holding Kids Back at School, Too." *Nation*, October 4, 2016. https://www.thenation.com/article/racism-got-you-stressed-that-may-be-holding-kids-back-at-school-too/.

Salazar, Julia. "Statement on Sha-Asia Washington's Passing and Maternal Morbidity." New York Senate, July 15, 2020. https://www.nysenate.gov/newsroom/press-releases/julia-salazar/july-15-update-statement-sha-asia-washingtons-passing-and.

Salter, Jim. "A Puzzling Number of Men Tied to the Ferguson Protests Have Since Died." *Chicago Tribune*, March 18, 2019. https://www.chicagotribune.com/nation-world/ct-ferguson-activist-deaths-Black-lives-matter-20190317-story.html.

Santhanam, Laura. "Racial Disparities Persist for Breastfeeding Moms. Here's Why." *PBS News Hour*, August 29, 2019. https://www.pbs.org/newshour/health/racial-disparities-persist-for-breast-feeding-moms-heres-why.

Schencker, Lisa. "Labor and Delivery Units Are Closing at Chicago-Area Hospitals. Here's Why." *Chicago Tribune*, September 3, 2019. https://www.chicagotribune.com/business/ct-biz-obstetrics-closing-hospitals-labor-delivery-20190903-kgdgsq2ai5a71mhmyzvago44gi-story.html.

Schultz, Jaime. "Reading the Catsuit: Serena Williams and the Production of Blackness at the 2002 US Open." *Journal of Sport and Social Issues* 29, no. 3 (2005): 338–57.

Schwartz, Marie Jenkins. *Birthing a Slave: Motherhood and Medicine in the Antebellum South*. Cambridge, MA: Harvard University Press, 2010.

Sears, William, and Martha Sears. *The Attachment Parenting Book*. New York: Little, Brown, 2001.

Seelinger, Lani. "Elizabeth Warren Tackles Maternal Mortality with a Plan That Prioritizes Black Women's Health." *Bustle*, April 25, 2019. https://www.bustle.com/p/how-elizabeth-warren-tackles-the-opioid-epidemic-in-her-latest-policy-plan-17855802.

Sehgal, Parul. "In a Raft of New Books, Motherhood from (Almost) Every Angle." *New York Times*, April 24, 2018. https://www.nytimes.com/2018/04/24/books/review-mothers-jacqueline-rose.html?hpw&rref=books&action=click&pgtype=Homepage&module=well-region&region=bottom-well&WT.nav=bottom-well.

Shapiro, Lila. "What the Job of a Sensitivity Reader Is Really Like." *New York Magazine*, January 5, 2018. https://www.vulture.com/2018/01/sensitivity-readers-what-the-job-is-really-like.html.

Sharpe, Christina. *In the Wake: On Blackness and Being*. Durham, NC: Duke University Press, 2016.

Siff, Andrew. "MTA Chair: We Never Phoned Family of Young Mom Who Died in NYC Subway." *NBC New York*, March 27, 2019. https://www.nbcnewyork.com/news/local/mta-mom-subway-fall-condolences-mistake-freddy-ferrer-andy-byford/1565164/.

Simmons, Ann M. "The Quiet Crisis among African Americans: Pregnancy and Childbirth Are Killing Women at Inexplicable Rates." *Los Angeles Times*, October 26, 2017. https://www.latimes.com/world/global-development/la-na-texas-Black-maternal-mortality-2017-htmlstory.html.

Smith, Mychal Denzel. "A Grief Observed." *New Republic*, June 22, 2017. https://newrepublic.com/article/143001/grief-observed-emmett-till-trayvon-martin-power-pain-Black-mourning.

Southall, Ashley, and Nikita Stewart. "They Grabbed Her Baby and Arrested Her. Now Jazmine Headley Is Speaking Out." *New York Times*, December 16, 2018. https://www.nytimes.com/2018/12/16/nyregion/jazmine-headley-arrest.html.

Stack, Carol. *All Our Kin: Strategies for Survival in a Black Community*. New York: Basic Books, 1983.

Stewart, Nikita. "Jazmine Headley, Whose Child Was Torn from Her Arms at a City Office, Gets a Public Apology." *New York Times*, February 4, 2019. https://www.nytimes.com/2019/02/04/nyregion/jazmine-headley-nypd-arrest.html.

Strauss, Elissa. "Baby-Friendly Hospitals May Not Be So Baby-Friendly after All." *Slate*, February 25, 2016. https://slate.com/human-interest/2016/02/baby-friendly-hospitals-may-not-be-so-baby-friendly-after-all.html.

Strings, Sabrina. *Fearing the Black Body: The Racial Origins of Fat Phobia*. New York: NYU Press, 2019.

Strings, Sabrina. "Obese Black Women as 'Social Dead Weight': Reinventing the 'Diseased Black Woman.'" *Signs* 41, no. 1 (2015): 107–30.

Swan, Jennifer Hubert. "New YA Books Rewrite Old Cultural Scripts." *New York Times*, March 2, 2018. https://www.nytimes.com/2018/03/02/books/review/ya-women-of-color-clayton-adeyemi.html.

Taylor, Keeanga-Yamahtta. *From #BlackLivesMatter to Black Liberation*. Chicago: Haymarket, 2006.

Thayer, Zaneta. "Racism Hurts Your Health—and Your Children's Too." *New Republic*, January 27, 2015. https://newrepublic.com/article/120858/racism-has-intergenerational-effects-health.

Thomas, Angie. *The Hate U Give*. New York: Balzer and Bray, 2017.

Thomas, Latham. "America Was Already Failing Black Mothers." *Cosmopolitan*, May 14, 2020. https://www.cosmopolitan.com/health-fitness/a32320216/black-maternal-health-covid-coronavirus/.

Thompson, Krissah. "Michelle Obama and Beyoncé: Friends and Feminists." *Washington Post*, January 7, 2014. https://www.washingtonpost.com/lifestyle/style/michelle-obama-and-beyonce-friends-and-feminists/2014/01/07/3d31b9aa-77ad-11e3-af7f-13bf0e9965f6_story.html.

Thompson, Krissah, and Helena Andrews-Dyer. "Michelle Obama Just Ripped Up the Playbook for First Ladies." *Washington Post*, September 6, 2017. https://www.washingtonpost.com/lifestyle/style/michelle-obama-just-ripped-up-the-playbook-for-former-first-ladies/2017/09/06/3f2bc3f8-9280-11e7-89fa-bb822a46da5b_story.html.

Tindal, Brenda. "'Its Own Special Attraction': Meditations on Martyrdom and the Iconicity of Civil Rights Widows." In *ConFiguring America: Iconic Figures, Visuality and the*

*American Identity*, edited by Klaus Rieser, Michael Fuchs, and Michael Phillips, 257–76. Chicago: University of Chicago Press, 2013.

Tinsley, Omise'eke Natasha. "Beyoncé's *Lemonade* Is Black Woman Magic." *Time*, April 26, 2016. http://time.com/4306316/beyonce-lemonade-black-woman-magic/.

Toler, Lindsay. "Debate over Ferguson Shooting Finds Bizarre New Forum: Amazon Book Reviews." *St. Louis Magazine*, May 11, 2016. https://www.stlmag.com/news/ferguson-brown-mcspadden-amazon/.

Tucker, Daniel. "South Side OB/GYN Unit Closing amid Black Maternal Health Crisis." *Morning Shift*, July 1, 2019. https://www.wbez.org/shows/morning-shift/south-side-obgyn-unit-closing-amid-Black-maternal-health-crisis/1951c5ac-8050-47ae-bca1-71060c7f8e83.

Tucker, Sarah Yahr. "There Is a Hidden Epidemic of Doctors Abusing Women in Labor, Doulas Say." *Broadly*, May 8, 2018. https://broadly.vice.com/en_us/article/evqew7/obstetric-violence-doulas-abuse-giving-birth.

Turman, Jack. "Cory Booker and Ayanna Pressley Introduce Bill to Address Maternal Mortality." *CBS News*, May 8, 2019. https://www.cbsnews.com/news/cory-booker-and-ayanna-pressley-introduce-bill-to-address-maternal-mortality/.

Turner, Sasha. "The Nameless and the Forgotten: Maternal Grief, Sacred Protection, and the Archive of Slavery." *Slavery and Abolition* 2 (2017): 232–50.

Underwood, Lauren. "Let's Vow That No Mom Should Die Giving Life." *The Hill*, May 13, 2019. https://thehill.com/blogs/congress-blog/healthcare/443453-lets-vow-that-no-mom-should-die-giving-life.

Vacaflor, Carlos Herrera. "Obstetric Violence: A New Framework for Identifying Challenges to Maternal Healthcare in Argentina." *Reproductive Health Matters* 47 (2016): 65–73.

Valeii, Kathi. "Birth Needs a #MeToo Reckoning." *Dame*, June 18, 2018. https://www.damemagazine.com/2018/06/18/birth-needs-a-metoo-reckoning/.

Van Cleaf, Kara. "'Of Woman Born' to Mommy Blogged: The Journey from the Personal as Political to the Personal as Commodity." *Women's Studies Quarterly* 43, nos. 3–4 (2015): 254–56.

Vedam, Saraswath, Kathrin Stoll, Tanya Khemet Taiwo, Nicholas Rubashkin, Melissa Cheyney, Nan Strauss, Monica McLemore, Micaela Cadena, Elizabeth Nethery, Eleanor Rushton, Laura Schummers, Eugene Declercq, and the GVtM-US Steering Council. "The Giving Voice to Mothers Study: Inequity and Mistreatment during Pregnancy and Childbirth in the United States." *Reproductive Health* 16, no. 77 (2019). https://reproductive-health-journal.biomedcentral.com/articles/10.1186/s12978-019-0729-2.

Vega, Tanzina. "Infertility, Endured through a Prism of Race." *New York Times*, April 26, 2014. https://www.nytimes.com/2014/04/26/us/infertility-endured-through-a-prism-of-race.html.

Vixen. "Serena's Crip Walk Dance: Fun Celebration or Bad Message?" *Vibe*, August 6, 2012. https://www.vibe.com/2012/08/serenas-crip-walk-dance-fun-celebration-or-bad-message.

Villarosa, Linda. "Why America's Black Mothers and Babies Are in a Life-or-Death Crisis." *New York Times Magazine*, April 11, 2018.

Waggoner, Miranda. *The Zero Trimester: Pre-pregnancy Care and the Politics of Reproductive Risk.* Berkeley: University of California Press, 2017.

Wagner, John, and Mark Berman. "Trump Threatens to 'Send In the Feds' to Address Chicago 'Carnage.'" *Washington Post*, January 24, 2017. https://www.washingtonpost.com/news/post-politics/wp/2017/01/24/trump-threatens-to-send-in-the-feds-to-address-chicago-carnage/.

Waldman, Annie. "How Hospitals Are Failing Black Mothers." ProPublica, December 27, 2017. https://www.propublica.org/article/how-hospitals-are-failing-Black-mothers.

Walker, Alice, ed. *I Love Myself When I Am Laughing.* New York: Feminist Press, 1979.

Walker, Alice. *In Search of Our Mothers' Gardens: Womanist Prose.* New York: Harcourt, 1983.

Walker, Alice. "In Search of Zora Neale Hurston." *Ms.*, March 1975, 74–89.

Walker, Alice. "Taking Care of the Truth." March 2013. https://alicewalkersgarden.com/2013/03/taking-care-of-the-truth-embedded-slander-a-meditation-on-the-complicity-of-wikipedia/.

Walker, Ameena. "Here's What the NYC Subway Map Looks Like with Just Accessible Stations." *Curbed New York*, September 25, 2017. https://ny.curbed.com/2017/9/25/16363262/nyc-subway-accessible-stations-map.

Walker, Rebecca. *Baby Love: Choosing Motherhood after a Lifetime of Ambivalence.* New York: Riverhead, 2008.

Walker, Rebecca. "How My Mother's Fanatical Views Tore Us Apart." *Daily Mail*, May 23, 2008. https://www.dailymail.co.uk/femail/article-1021293/How-mothers-fanatical-feminist-views-tore-apart-daughter-The-Color-Purple-author.html.

Wallace, Alicia. "A Critical View of Beyoncé's 'Formation.'" *Black Camera* 9, no. 1 (2017): 189–96.

Wanzo, Rebecca. *The Suffering Will Not Be Televised: African American Women and Sentimental Political Storytelling.* Albany: State University of New York Press, 2009.

Ward, Jesmyn. *Men We Reaped: A Memoir.* New York: Bloomsbury, 2013.

Warren, Elizabeth. "Protect a Woman's Right to Choose." Accessed November 4, 2020. https://elizabethwarren.com/plans/protect-womens-choices.

Warren, Elizabeth. "Sen. Elizabeth Warren on Black Women Maternal Mortality: 'Hold Health Systems Accountable for Protecting Black Moms.'" *Essence*, April 30, 2019. https://www.essence.com/feature/sen-elizabeth-warren-Black-women-mortality-essence/.

Washington, Harriet A. *Medical Apartheid: The Dark History of Medical Experimentation on Black Americans from Colonial Times to the Present.* New York: Anchor Books, 2008.

Weaver, Caity. "Wait—Is Qai Qai America's Most Important Doll?" *New York Times*, January 17, 2019. https://www.nytimes.com/2019/01/17/style/qai-qai-serena-williams-alexis-ohanian.html.

Weinbaum, Alys Eve. *The Afterlife of Reproductive Slavery: Biocapitalism and Black Feminism's Philosophy of History.* Durham, NC: Duke University Press, 2019.

Wheaton, Sarah. "More from Michelle Obama on 'Pride.'" *New York Times*, February 20, 2008. https://thecaucus.blogs.nytimes.com/2008/02/20/more-from-michelle-obama-on-pride/.

Whittle, Andrea. "The 2016 Pirelli Calendar Breaks Tradition and Stereotypes." *Vanity Fair*, December 2015. https://www.vanityfair.com/culture/2015/12/2016-pirelli-calendar-amy-schumer-annie-leibovitz.

Wiegman, Robyn. *Object Lessons*. Durham, NC: Duke University Press, 2012.
Williams, Patricia J. *The Alchemy of Race and Rights*. Cambridge, MA: Harvard University Press, 1991.
Williams, Patricia J. "On Being the Object of Property." *Signs* 14, no. 1 (1988): 5–24.
Williams, Patricia J. "Spirit-Murdering the Messenger: The Discourse of Fingerpointing as the Law's Response to Racism." *University of Miami Law Review* 42 (1987): 127–57.
Williams, Rhaisa Kameela. "Toward a Theorization of Black Maternal Grief as Analytic." *Transforming Anthropology* 24, no. 1 (2016): 17–30.
Winston, Ali. "Eric Garner Death Was 'Not a Big Deal,' Police Commander Said." *New York Times*, May 16, 2019. https://www.nytimes.com/2019/05/16/nyregion/eric-garner-pantaleo-trial.html.
Winters, Joseph. "Rescue US: *Birth*, *Django*, and the Violence of Racial Redemption." *Religions* 9, no. 1 (2018): 21–36.
Wolf, Joan B. "Breastfeeding Isn't Always Best." *New York Times*, May 23, 2014. https://www.nytimes.com/roomfordebate/2014/05/22/the-politics-of-breastfeeding/breastfeeding-isnt-always-best.
Wolf, Joan B. *Is Breast Best? Taking on the Breastfeeding Experts and the New High Stakes of Motherhood*. New York: NYU Press, 2010.
Wolf, Joan. "Is Breast Really Best? Risk and Total Motherhood in the National Breast-Feeding Awareness Campaign." *Journal of Health Politics, Policy and Law* 32, no. 4 (2007): 595–636.
Wong, Alia. "Cities Aren't Built for Parents." *Atlantic*, February 1, 2019. https://www.theatlantic.com/family/archive/2019/02/cities-arent-built-for-parents/581845/.
Wortham, Jenna. "Racism's Psychological Toll." *New York Times*, June 24, 2015.
Wu, Katherine J. "Study of Coronavirus in Pregnant Women Finds Striking Racial Differences." *New York Times*, July 10, 2020. https://www.nytimes.com/2020/07/10/health/coronavirus-race-pregnancy.html.

## Index

Abdur-Rahman, Aliyyah, 2
abolitionist, 25, 179
abortion, 18, 97
abundance, 29, 113-14, 119, 130
academy. *See* university
accounting: in white maternal memoirs, 140-42, 151, 157
activism: Black motherhood as platform for, 7-9, 15-16, 19, 25, 121, 137, 165, 177, 180-84; breastfeeding, 27, 34, 25, 38, 42-43; feminist, 20, 140; obstetric violence and, 78-83. *See also* Black Lives Matter (BLM); Mothers of the Movement
adoption, 151
aesthetics, 6, 12; of Black breastfeeding, 32, 35, 36, 57-68; Black feminist, 60; of Black Lives Matter, 20, 22; Black maternal, 29, 62, 104-9, 111-12, 117, 126, 128-30, 159, 162; Black queer, 129; of birth, 28, 92, 95, 96; of crisis, 50, 60, 134; maternal, 135, 138, 141
affect: of black breastfeeding gap, 39-40; Black maternal, 7, 10, 105-6, 112-15, 119, 121, 185; of Black maternal friendship, 126; of crisis, 12, 15, 175; of doulas, 29, 91; in maternal memoirs, 136, 138, 139, 140, 141, 142, 147, 158, 163. *See also* ambivalence; anger; anxiety; apathy; calm; compassion; ecstasy; ecstatic; grief; hope; joy; love; maternal feelings; pain; pleasure; rage; sorrow; suffering; vulnerability; worry
African women: representations of, 39, 58, 60-63; traditions of, 86
"afterlives of slavery" (Hartman), 13, 16, 19

Akubilo, Adaora, 31-32
Alexander, Elizabeth, 113, 183-84
Allers, Kimberly Seals, 36, 37, 40, 42, 56, 67-68, 195n36
ambivalence: in Black maternal memoirs; 147, 149, 150, 152, 153, 156, 204n16; around institutionality, 26; in white maternal memoirs, 136, 138-40, 142, 147
American Academy of Pediatrics (AAP), 21, 43-44, 47, 49, 54-55
American College of Obstetricians and Gynecologists, 11
Andre (interlocutor), 167-68
Andrews-Dyer, Helena, 175, 177
anger, 9, 39, 40, 114, 147, 165
antiBlack, 3, 5, 21, 109, 136, 137; misogynistic violence, 16, 34, 76, 93, 111, 146-47; obstetric violence, 8, 6, 11; violence, 20, 23-24, 57, 73, 144, 148, 166, 168, 175, 181, 185
anticipation of loss, 3, 122, 136, 142, 152, 154-55, 158-59, 175
antimedical, 27, 71, 92-94
anxiety, 17, 118, 136, 151, 163
apathy, 39, 40, 123
apolitical, 9, 24-25, 104-5, 109, 114-15, 117-21, 139; Beyoncé as, 118-20; Michelle Obama as, 104, 109, 170; Serena Williams as, 114-15, 117, 120
Arbery, Ahmaud, 9, 179, 184
Argentina, 78
*Argonauts, The* (Nelson), 135, 139-41
Ashé, Qiddist, 70
Association of Black Psychologists, 53

"attachment parenting," 49
Audrey (interlocutor), 99
Austin, Nefertiti, 134, 135
Australian Open, 129
*Australian Sunday Telegraph*, 111
autonomy, 93, 128, 148; birth, 72, 92, 100; bodily, 6, 18, 48, 70, 79 83; sexual, 6, 79, 68
Azarenka, Victoria, 116

*Baby Love: Choosing Motherhood after a Lifetime of Ambivalence* (R. Walker), 137–38, 148–54
Baby-Friendly hospitals, 27, 37, 41, 43
Baby-Friendly USA, 37
"baby reading," 49
"baby wearing," 49
bailout efforts, 25–26
Baldwin, Kate, 134
"ban the bag," 41
banality: of crisis, 13; of life, 65; of maternal life, 140–41, 157
Barr, William, 191n92
Bass, Margaret, 43, 196n71
beauty, 31, 59, 62, 104, 113, 129, 140, 144
*Becoming* (Michelle Obama), 122, 138, 169–70
"bereaved Black mothers" (Lawson), 8
Berlant, Lauren, 13–14, 15, 39, 50–51, 77–78
Bey, Marquis, 118
Beyoncé, 25, 29, 103, 104–7, 118–26; as apolitical, 118–20; birthday of, 105, 122, 123, 124–25; Black Lives Matter and, 104, 117–19; Grammy performance of, 104, 119; "Formation" and, 105, 118–20, 124–25; "Freedom" and, 121; *Homecoming* and, 105, 122; *Lemonade* and, 104, 117–18, 121, 123–26, 137, Mothers of the Movement and, 107, 125–26, 137; MTV Video Music Awards and, 121; "Sorry" and, 105, 122, 123–24; Super Bowl half-time show and, 104, 118–19; as political, 117–20, 123, 125; rebranding, of 117, 119–20
biological reproduction, 151–53, 154
birth: "bad," 91–92; disparities in, 2, 3–4, 6, 10–13, 21–22, 35–36, 55, 71, 75–76, 79; as exceptional, 73, 95–99; "good," 91; home, 93; long, 92; medicated, 78, 80, 82, 91–97; natural, 92; as ordinary, 98–99; as patriarchal, 27, 72; plan, 27, 96–97; slow, 91; as transformative, 27,72, 83, 90–92, 94–100, 152–53; unmedicated, 27, 91–92, 94–96

birth equity. *See* reproductive justice
birth justice. *See* reproductive justice
birth rape, 78, 79, 80–81, 83
birthwork, 27, 35, 70–78, 80–83, 176–77; professionalization of, 74, 85–91; training, 7, 69, 71, 74, 83–91, 177. *See also* doulas; lactation consultants; midwives
"Black anti-will" (Williams), 43, 51
Black boys, 3, 6, 26, 175
Black breastfeeding. *See* breastfeeding
Black Breastfeeding Week, 36, 67
Black breasts, 32, 34, 36, 38–39, 43, 50, 53, 56–59, 61–68
"Black excellence," 103
Black feminism: activism, 175–77; aesthetics of, 60; as anti-institutional, 26, 28, 34, 100, 137, 176; on Black domesticity, 157; Black maternal memoirs and, 134, 144; Black motherhood and, 4, 5–7, 16–20, 154, 160, 175, 178, 184–85; breastfeeding and, 27, 32, 35, 36, 43, 68, 177, 184; commodity, 130; doulas and, 72–73, 99, 100, 177, 184; ethics of, 4; as fugitive, 34, 137, 176; institutions and, 20, 26–28, 100–101, 176–77; power and, 176; as praxis, 6, 19, 27, 32, 34, 68, 71, 99; reproductive justice and, 4, 6, 16, 18, 20, 25, 27, 68, 71–73, 100; romanticization of, 28, 34, 100, 176; the state and, 4, 27–28, 32, 34, 71, 100–101, 175–77, 184; on the stranger, 160; the university and, 26–27, 176; on visual culture, 59
Black girlhood, 154, 158, 167
Black gold, 29, 36, 39, 41, 43, 50, 56–59, 62, 67, 68
Black life: advocacy for, 10, 50, 180; birthing, 22, 26, 119, 175, 184; Black motherhood and, 20, 22, 26, 50, 56, 59–60, 100, 105, 119, 130, 149, 159, 182, 183, 184; breast milk and, 28, 29, 32, 34, 35, 38, 39, 56, 59–60, 62, 65, 68; commodity of, 130; disposability of, 9, 23, 37, 118; doulas and, 70–72, 74, 80, 91, 99, 101; precarity of, 5, 32 43, 50, 56, 68, 71, 95, 149, 153; protecting, 34, 56, 60, 68, 70, 74, 80, 99, 101, 105, 130, 156; surveillance of, 23; violence and, 23, 26, 37, 38, 71, 75, 95, 99, 159, 182
Black Lives Matter (BLM), 20–26, 148, 154–55, 165, 179–83; Black maternal memoirs and, 135–36, 138; Black motherhood and, 7, 20–22, 25–26, 38, 175, 181–83; era, 4, 6, 12, 32, 50, 163, 174; soundtrack, 117–19

Black Mamas Bailout, 25–26
Black Mamas Matter, 7
Black Maternal Health Caucus, 11
Black men, 6, 22, 26, 175
Black Mothers' Breastfeeding Association, 42
Blackness: doula training centered in, 86; estrangement and, 159; obesity and, 51–52; proximity to, 106, 109, 117, 120, 124
"Black normal" (Edwards), 130
Black studies, 78
"Black women did it first," 176
"Black women magic," 117, 176,
blame, 39, 40
Bland, Sandra, 22–24
Bliss, James, 28
Bloomberg, Michael, 41
bodily autonomy. *See* autonomy
body: of Beyoncé, 105–6, 119; Black, 160; Black male, 22; Black maternal, 5, 8, 12–13, 15–16, 21–22, 57, 60, 68, 73, 75, 100–101, 106, 138, 161, 175, 177; Black perinatal, 20, 76, 105, 175, 182–84; Black pregnant, 73, 106, 129, 177; of Black women 27, 50–53, 82, 109, 117, 147; as lifegiving, 26, 60–63, 73, 140–41, 158, 175, 184; maternal, 139–43, 158; of Michelle Obama, 108–9; of Serena Williams, 103, 109, 111–14, 117, 129, 124; racial stress on, 20–22
body mass index (BMI), 51–52, 54
Booker, Cory, 11
Bordo, Susan, 51
Bradley, Mamie Till, 8, 165
brand management, 106, 117, 127; Beyoncé and, 117, 119–20; Michelle Obama and, 107, 109, 128–29; Serena Williams and, 109, 111, 115, 117
breastfeeding, 27, 37–38, 40–50; as anticapitalist, 47–48; Black: 27–28, 29, 32–43, 50, 52–68, 117; class and, 46, 194n18; economic benefits of, 47–49; health benefits of, 44–47, 49; immunization from 44, 49, 53, 56, 58, 68; gap, 32, 34–41, 43, 50, 53, 57, 68, 76; as natural, 32, 41, 44, 49, 57–62; non-, 29, 32, 34–35, 38, 50; obesity and 36, 43–44, 50, 52–55; patriarchal power and, 48; public health and 35, 36, 37, 41–46, 50, 52–55; the state and, 32, 34, 36, 38, 40, 41, 43, 50, 52–53, 68; unwilling, 35, 38, 50, 52
breast milk, 28, 32, 35–36, 38, 41–42, 46, 49, 56, 59, 63. *See also* Black gold; liquid gold

breast pumping 35, 46, 48, 64
Brianna, 89, 92–94
Bridges, Khiara M., 18, 188n17
Briggs, Laura, 5
Brooklyn Defender Services, 174
Brown, Caroline, 107
Brown, Elspeth H., 59
Brown, Michael, 22–23, 126, 164–67

caesarean section. *See* C-section
Callie, 159, 161–63
calm, 113, 114, 119–20
Camille (interlocutor), 96
Campt, Tina M., 59
capitalism, 47–48, 88, 139; anti, 94; bio, 17; medical, 80, 92–94; non, 47
carceral: desire, 179; feminism, 28; intimacy, 59; space, 184; violence, 25, 26
care: Black breastfeeding and, 56–67, 60, 62; Black feminism on, 19–20; Black studies on, 78; doulas and, 71–72, 75, 84, 90–91, 99–101; maternal, 136 137, 151–52; non, 6, 63, 64, 82, 175; women's studies on, 78
*Carpool Karaoke*, 122
Carr, Gwen, 3, 106, 121. *See also* Mothers of the Movement
Carter, Blue Ivy, 124, 130
Carter, Gloria, 124
Carter, Shannon K., 49
Castile, Philando, 9, 22
Castile, Valerie, 9, 106, 165, 184. *See also* Mothers of the Movement
"catalytic crisis" (Cusk), 139
"catching a baby," 70, 73, 99
catsuit, 111–12, 115, 117
"causes célèbres," 174–75
celebrity: Black maternal, 104–6, 109, 115, 117, 120–31, 170; citation, 121–26. *See also* Beyoncé; Michelle Obama; Serena Williams
Centers for Disease Control and Prevention, 74, 76
Charleston, South Carolina, 24
chestfeeding, 192n4
Chicago: birthworkers in, 29, 70, 73–76, 86; gun violence in, 74–76
Chicago, Judy, 146–47
Chicago Birthworks Collective, 74
Chicago Doula Project, 74

Index · 237

*Chicago* magazine, 70
Chicago Volunteer Doulas (CVD), 74
Childbirth and Postpartum Professional Association (CAPPA), 85, 89
Chocolate Milk Mommies, 56, 57–58, 62
choice, 4, 18, 38, 68
Christian, Barbara, 26
"churning," 174
cisgendered women, 192n4
"cite Black women," 176
civil rights movement, 7
"civil rights widow," 164–66
class, 6, 46, 51, 152, 155, 164, 194n18
Clinton, Hillary, 5, 24, 25, 108, 120–21, 164
Clinton Global Initiative, 41
Cohill, Lakisha, 56–63
Cole, Haile Eshe, 12
collective. *See* communal
Collins, Patricia Hill, 7, 19, 154
colostrum, 35
Combahee River Collective, 101
commodity: Black feminist, 130; of Black life, 130; of Black maternal pain, 5, 137, 169; of Black motherhood, 136; of birth, 72
Commonwealth Fund, 76
communal: Black breastfeeding, 57–63; Black birthing, 95, 98; Black motherhood, 19–20, 114, 119–20, 125, 127, 134, 147, 155, 158, 164; with nature, 138, 163; travel, 161
community property, 19, 158, 168
compassion: Black maternal desires for, 124, 157; Black mothers as worthy of, 5, 8, 13, 14, 35, 36, 184, 185; from birthworkers, 85–86; from corporations, 31, 41–43; from the state, 39–43, 55; and obligation, 39, 42
compassionate conservativism, 39
confession, 141
Congressional Black Caucus, 50
"controlling images" (Collins), 5
Cook County Sheriff's Justice Institute, 74
"cooked to the bone," 171
Cooper, Amy, 179–80
Cooper, Brittney, 121, 122–23, 126, 127
Cooper, Christian, 179–80
Cooper-Jones, Wanda, 9, 184
corporations, 130, 154, 180; breastfeeding and, 32, 34, 36, 42, 68; crisis and, 175; doulas and, 87–88; logics of, 32, 34, 41, 68, 87

corporeal, 51, 107, 113, 119, 140, 145, 149, 151–52; effects of racism on, 21, 56; excess, 43, 111
COVID-19, 29, 179–83
creativity, 130, 131, 137, 138, 144–45, 147–48, 150–51, 154–55, 159
crip walk, 124
crisis: against, 29, 57, 105, 134, 136, 153, 158–59, 169, 171; Black breastfeeding in, 29, 32, 34–35, 43, 184; Black feminism and, 4, 28, 184; Black maternal aesthetics and, 57–68, 105, 134; Black maternal health in, 3, 71, 91, 115; Black maternal politics and, 7, 15, 26; Black mothers in, 4–6, 10–16, 57, 95, 105, 174–75, 177, 180–81, 184; catalytic, 139; doulas as mitigating, 71, 73, 76, 83, 90–91, 98, 100, 184; logics of, 20, 26; maternal memoirs and, 134, 137, 139, 153, 158–59, 169, 171; maternal mortality, 74–76; obesity, 43, 51; as ordinary, 13–14; rhetoric of, 4–6, 15, 68, 78, 101, 176; temporality of, 12–13, 16, 20, 32, 36, 43, 50, 73, 77, 134, 175; US political life in, 14, 180, 182; visible through, 4, 12, 16, 83, 137. *See also* breastfeeding; COVID-19; obesity
C-section, 6, 27, 79, 81, 87, 91–92, 97, 177, 180
"cultural congruence," 156
Cuomo, Andrew, 11, 198n7
currency: of Black death, 12; of Black feminism, 25; of Black maternal celebrity, 123, 126; of Black mothers, 4–5, 9, 16, 25, 104, 175, 180, 184; of Black suffering, 12, 15, 39, 164, 175; of crisis, 15; US Left, 4–5, 20, 175
Cusk, Rachel, 135, 139–40

daughter, 149, 166: mother and, 134, 136, 137, 143–47, 149–54; un-becoming, 149–53, 159, 171. *See also* sister
Davis, Dána-Ain, 6, 19, 71–72, 79, 82, 92, 198n1
Davis, Jordan, 24
*Deadspin*, 116
death: black, 7, 12, 19, 22–24, 26, 60, 118, 119, 120–21, 126, 171, 179–80; of black children, 3, 6, 8, 22, 25, 26, 106, 118, 120, 126, 138, 165–66; black infant, 10–12, 90; black male, 8, 9; black maternal, 1–3, 6, 10–12, 15, 20, 22, 26, 73, 76, 90, 177, 180–84; proximity to, 5, 138, 163, 171, 174, 185; slow, 13–14, 50–51

238 · Index

death-world, 3–4, 37, 38; daughterhood as, 149; hospital as, 16, 76, 93, 177; outside of home as, 136; university as, 176
"defend the dead" (Sharpe), 22–23, 183
del Castillo-Hegyi, Christie, 47
demedicalize birth, 72, 99
Democratic debates, 3, 5
Democratic National Convention, 5, 24, 164
desire, 151–52; Black feminist, 26–28; Black maternal, 7, 68, 106, 157, 170, 175–76; feminist, 27, 82,
deviant: Black mothers as, 4, 13, 43, 57, 67, 114, 185
Devon (interlocutor), 193n11
Dickson, E. J., 181, 207n2
Diehl, Jessica, 112
"The Dinner Party" (Chicago), 146–47
dispossession, 160, 162
dissemblance, 16
diversity: in publishing, 135–36
domestic: Black, 67, 130, 137, 155–15; maternal life, 139; Michelle Obama as, 109; private life, 127–28
donation of breast milk, 41–42
Douglas, Delia, 109
doulamatch.com, 87
doulas: clients of, 71, 74, 77, 79–81, 87, 89–90, 95–96, 99; "community service" of, 101; corporate logics and, 87–88; as "independent contractors," 71; "low-tech" work of, 84–85; as medical missionaries, 71–72, 90; as paraprofessionals, 27, 83–84, 89–91, 100; pro bono programs, 71, 74, 86, 99, 200n48; professionalization of, 74, 85–91; radical work of, 71–73, 81, 84–85, 89–90; in the room, 71–73, 76–77, 80–81, 83, 95, 99; standardization of, 84, 88–90; the state and, 11, 26–27, 29, 71 73–74, 83–85, 90–91, 100–101, 176; training of, 7, 35, 69, 71, 74, 83–91; as transformative, 28, 70–73, 84, 90–92, 97, 99–100; visibility of, 72, 82, 89, 99–101
Doulas of North America (DONA), 85, 87, 89
duCille, Ann, 26
Dungy, Camille, 133–34, 138, 159–64, 171
Dunlop, Scott, 80–81
Durbin, Dick, 11

Earley, Brian, 110
ecology: collective, 161; time, 138

ecstasy, 151–52, 153–54, 185
ecstatic, 134, 137, 149, 151–52, 158, 171
Edwards, Erica R., 130
Elkin, Lauren, 135
embodied: ambivalence, 149; Black motherhood, 4, 6, 16, 73, 94, 114–15; effects of racism, 10, 20–22, 32, 56, 155, 177; knowledge, 72; motherhood, 143, 154
empire, 130
employment discrimination, 116–17
empowerment, 7, 16, 19, 56–57, 60, 63, 72, 94, 112, 142, 158
"empty the milk in the bottle," 54
endurance, 94–95, 138, 167–68
environmental racism, 71, 99
epidural, 72, 92, 94, 180
eros, 139–40
erotic, 67, 129–31, 139
estrangement, 153, 159, 161–63
"evangelism," 42
Evers-Williams, Myrlie, 165, 166
excess: Black life as, 9, 56, 109, 114, 149; corporeal, 43, 52, 111; flesh, 36, 50, 59, 115; sexual, 113; weight, 51–52
exposure: in white maternal memoirs, 140–41, 156

fabulous, 107, 114, 127, 129–30
Faith, 85–86, 95
family: Black, 17, 19, 25–26, 31, 60, 62, 117, 137; life; 127–28 portrait: 58–59, 62, 125. *See also* communal
fashion, 112, 129–30
fat phobia, 51
fecundity, 104, 114, 119, 129
Federal Council on Medicine in Brazil, 79
Fed Is Best, 47
Feldstein, Ruth, 8
feminism: on birth rape, 80–81, 83; on breastfeeding, 48; carceral, 28; ethic of, 143; governance, 28; and institutions, 27–28, 82, 91, 100; and Left politics, 91; maternal life-writing and, 137, 139, 148, 150, 153; on maternal politics, 7; on reproductive justice, 18, 82, 97; on reproductive labor, 140; political currency of, 104; on violence, 82; white, 28, 137, 139, 147; and women's health movement, 72. *See also* accounting; ambivalence; exposure; feminist birth industry

Index · 239

feminist birth industry, 27–28, 78, 83, 91, 96, 100
Ferguson, Missouri, 22–24, 164–65, 168
fertility: Black maternal celebrity and, 103, 104, 114, 169; hyper-, 169
First Lady portrait, 124–25
Fleetwood, Nicole R., 59, 109
flesh: Black female, 51, 117; Black male, 106; Black maternal, 4, 26, 36, 38, 43, 55, 56, 62, 67, 83, 175–76, 183–84; excess, 36, 50, 59, 115; maternal, 92, 143
Floyd, George, 9, 22, 24, 179, 184–85
food desert: breastfeeding gap as, 37
"food oppression" (Freeman), 38
foot soldier, 71, 78, 83–84, 100
"Formation" (Beyoncé), 105, 118–20, 124–25
formula: economic cost of, 46, 47; health risks of, 44, 46; hospitals and, 34, 40–41; industry, 36, 43, 44; as "junk food," 38; the state and, 40–41, 43, 44
fragility of Black life, 32, 50, 56, 68, 73, 106, 152
freedom: Black, 156; Black domesticity as, 157–58; Black feminism on, 6, 16, 18; in Black maternal politics, 7; -dream, 178; loss and, 153; maternal, 141, 144, 147–48, 149, 153
"Freedom" (Beyoncé), 121
Freeman, Andrea, 34–35, 38, 39, 40, 60, 189n56
French Open, 111–12, 116
Friedman, Vanessa, 104
friendship, 29, 105–6, 121–27, 130
fugitive: Black feminism as, 34, 137, 176; Black women's creativity as, 144; doulas as, 34, 84, 85, 91
fullness, 54
Fulton, Sybrina, 25, 106, 126, 135. *See also* Mothers of the Movement
futurity, 59, 114, 112, 123, 131, 153, 158

Gap, 31–34, 57
Garner, Eric, 3, 5, 22–23, 121, 126
Garner, Erica, 121
Garrett, Roberta, 139, 141
Garschi, Mishana, 17
Garza, Alicia, 23
genius, 145, 176
Geronimus, Arline T., 21–22
Gibson, Otis, 111
Gillibrand, Kristen, 3, 4, 5

Giuliani, Rudolph, 118
Givhan, Robin, 111
glamour, 29, 106, 127, 129, 130
"A Good Hike" (Dungy), 133–34
Goodson, Malaysia, 1–3, 5, 28, 174–75, 181, 184
Grammys, 104, 119
Grand Slam, 110
grief: anticipated, 136, 155: Black maternal, 3, 7–10, 19, 24, 107, 121, 126, 130, 175, 184–85: Black maternal memoirs and, 134, 136–39, 145, 147–48, 154, 159–66, 168–71; respectable, 24, 164–66
ground zero, 26, 43, 53, 174–75, 182
Grumet, Jamie Lynne, 49
*Guidebook to Relative Strangers: Journeys into Race, Motherhood, and History* (Dungy), 133–34, 138, 159–64
Gumbs, Alexis Pauline, 19, 154
gun violence, 69–70, 74–76, 99, 121
Gurley, Akai, 22, 23

Hallstein, D. Lynn O'Brien 142
Hamlin, Françoise, 7
Harris, Kamala, 3, 5
Harrison, Laura, 41
Hartman Saidiya, 143, 189n43, 189n56
Hartzell, Stephanie, 134
Hays, Sharon, 46, 204n24
Headley, Jazmine, 173–75, 181
Health Connect One, 74
Healthy Moms and Babies, 74
"helicopter parenting," 158
heritability, 17
heroism: Black feminist, 28; Black maternal, 1–4, 62–63, 174, 176
heteronormative, 60
heterosexuality, 59, 62, 112, 122, 143–44, 167
Higginbotham, Evelyn Brooks, 16
Hine, Darlene Clark, 16
Hirsch, Marianne, 147
history: claiming, 162–63
Hochschild, Arlie, 204n23
Holloway, Karla FC, 19, 168
home, 136, 140, 154, 157, 170; mothers as, 143; world as, 162, 164
*Homecoming* (Beyoncé), 105, 122
homeless, 160
hooks, bell, 157

hope, 122, 148
hospitals: Black-serving, 10; breastfeeding and, 27, 34, 41, 47; as death-worlds, 16, 76, 93, 177; violence of, 14–15, 16, 26, 80, 93–94, 95, 175, 184. *See also* Baby-Friendly hospitals; Jackson Park Hospital; Northwestern Medicine Women's Hospital; University of Chicago Medical Center; Woodhull Medical Center
*Hours, The* (film), 160–61
human, the, 160
humanity, 156, 160, 166
human rights, 18
Hurricane Katrina, 118–19
Hurston, Zora Neale, 145

identity categories, 148
"identity knowledge" (Wiegman), 78
Illinois Bureau of Maternal and Infant Health, 74
Illinois Maternal Infant and Early Childhood Home Visiting Program, 74
Illinois Maternal Mortality Review Committee, 73
Imani (interlocutor), 80, 82, 89–90, 91, 93, 94, 97–98, 99
immunization: from breast milk, 44, 49, 53, 56, 58, 68
"The Impact of Racism on Child and Adolescent Health" (AAP), 55
indigenous traditions, 60
infertility, 134, 138, 169, 171
injury, 5, 15, 82, 100, 139, 152, 155, 157, 178; collective, 161
innocence, 79, 154, 157
*In Search of Our Mothers' Gardens* (Walker), 137, 141–42, 144–48
institutional: anti-, 26, 28, 34, 100, 137, 176; Black feminism, 20, 26–28, 100–101, 176–77; feminism, 27–28, 82, 91,100; heterosexuality, 143; medicine, 4, 27, 32, 34, 37, 62–63, 74, 76, 81, 90, 93, 100, 115, 175, 178, 181, 184; motherhood, 16, 142–43, 154; reproductive justice, 18, 20, 27, 100; violence, 15
"intensive mothering" (Hays), 46, 49, 204n24
interconnected, 159, 161, 163
interiority, 16, 67, 113, 127, 148, 157
intersectionality, 18, 20, 28

"in the room," 72–73, 76–77, 80–81, 83, 95, 99
"in the wake" (Sharpe), 130. *See also* Christina Sharpe; "wake work" (Sharpe)
intimacy, 62; celebrity citation and, 122, 124–25, 163, 164; doulas and, 83, 89, 90, 95–97; in friendship, 90, 121, 127; motherhood and, 137, 139, 142, 147, 151, 163; strange, 134
invisibility: of Black breastfeeding, 35, 57; of Black mothers, 1, 10, 19, 174; of reproductive labor, 140–42; of the stranger, 160
Isaac, Amber Rose, 181

Jackson, Danielle, 11
Jackson, Dylan B., 55
Jackson Park Hospital, 75
Jasmine (interlocutor), 87, 97
Jay-Z, 118, 123, 137
Joanne (interlocutor), 87
Johnson, Angela, 35, 39
Johnson, Corey, 174
Johnson, Kecia R., 55
Johnson, Rita Henley, 37
joy, 103, 114, 121, 122, 126, 127,
Jung, Courtney, 27, 40, 42, 193n11
"junk food" (Freeman), 38, 52, 55
juridical, 14, 78–79, 82, 182

Kaepernick, Colin, 24
Kantor, Jodi, 104
Kelly, Robin, 11
Kelley, Robin D.G., 9
Kelso, Donna, 110
Killen, Kimberly, 134
*Killing the Black Body: Race, Reproduction, and the Meaning of Liberty* (Roberts), 17–18
killjoy (Ahmed), 161
King, Billie, 112
King, Gayle, 122
kinship. *See* communal; friendship
Kirk, Rosalind, 35, 39
Knowles, Tina, 104, 119, 124
Knowles-Carter, Beyoncé. *See* Beyoncé
Kopf, Dan, 46
Kukura, Elizabeth, 78

lactation consultants, 26, 27, 35, 37, 43, 46, 48, 53, 57, 70, 74, 85, 88–89, 176
lactivism, 27, 42, 194n28

"Ladies Night" (advertisement), 44
La Leche League, 192n4
La Revolución de las Rosas, 79
Latch On, 41
Latin America, 79, 83
Latinx, 182
Lauren (interlocutor), 35, 69–70, 74–75
Lawrence, Christie, 75
Lawson, Erica S., 7
Lawson, Tina, 104
Leibovitz, Annie, 103, 112–14
Left politics. *See* US Left
*Lemonade* (Beyoncé), 25, 104, 117–18, 121, 123–26, 137
Let's Move, 50, 104, 122
Liang, Peter, 23
lifework: birthwork as, 70, 74, 82
life-writing: Black maternal, 134, 135, 147–48, 149, 163, 171
Lights, Zion, 81
Lindsey, Treva B., 125–26
liquid gold, 32, 35–36, 44, 49, 54
literary studies, 134
Logan Correctional Facility, 74
*longue durée*, 17
Lordi, Emily, 138, 169
"lose your mother" (Hartman), 17, 143
loss: anticipated, 3, 122, 136, 142, 154, 168, 171; Black maternal friendship and, 126–27; Black maternal politics rooted in, 9, 107; Black motherhood and, 19, 107, 125–26, 139, 166–68; doulas and, 97–98; through infertility, 134, 138, 170; maternal memoirs and, 134, 136, 138–39, 142, 144, 147, 153–54, 166–68, 179–71; through miscarriage, 134, 138, 170; shared, 106, 121
"Lost Mothers" (ProPublica and NPR), 10
love, 26, 72, 99, 101, 143, 147, 199n12; unconditional, 149–50, 153, 162, 167
#LoveOnTop, 57
Lynda, 69, 77, 81

"magical thinking" (Alexander), 184
Mahmee, 115
Make America Great Again, 108
"Marketing Michelle" (Brown), 106–7
"marketplace" (Wanzo), 15
Markle, Meghan, 126

Martin, Tracy, 135
Martin, Trayvon, 23, 25, 56, 118, 125–26, 137, 165
Martucci, Jessica, 34, 47, 193n11
maternal feelings, 142–44,
maternal memoirs: accounting in, 140–42, 151, 157; ambivalence in, 136, 138–40, 144, 147, 149, 150, 152, 153, 156; Black, 29, 128, 133–39, 144–71; Black lives matter and, 135–36, 138; canon of, 135, 137, 138, 142, 145, 150, 169; capitalization of, 136, 148; crisis and, 134, 137, 139, 153, 158–59, 169, 171; exposure in, 140–41, 156; mother-daughter relationships in, 134, 136, 137, 143–47, 149–54, 166; the self in, 136, 139–40, 143, 145, 147, 149–54, 157, 158–60, 162, 169–71; white, 134–44, 147–48, 151, 157. *See also specific maternal memoirs*
Maternal Morbidity and Mortality Report, 73
maternity leave, 111, 116
"matrophobia," 143–44
Maximizing Outcomes for Moms through Medicaid Improvement and Enhancement of Services (MOMMIES Act), 11, 73
McBath, Lucy, 24–25, 106, 206n103. *See also* Mothers of the Movement
McClain, Dani, 137–38, 154–59
McKinney, Chelsea O., 34, 37
McKittrick, Katherine, 37
McSpadden, Lezley, 106, 135, 138, 154, 164–68, 191n98
Meadows-Fernandez, A. Rochaun, 31, 182
Medicaid, 11, 71, 74
medicine and the medical: anti-, 27, 71, 92–94; apartheid, 78, 101; capitalism, 80, 92–94; racism, 3, 5, 21, 37, 55, 57, 64, 78–79, 93, 175, 182; temporality, 92–94; violence, 6, 14, 22, 26, 76, 92–93, 95, 184
Medolac Laboratories, 41–42
memoirs. *See* maternal memoirs
mental health, 46, 55, 78, 99
#MeToo, 154
Miami police union, 118
midwives, 11, 27, 35, 57, 70, 82, 85, 86, 88, 93
Miriam (interlocutor), 87–89
miscarriage, 125, 134, 138, 169–71
misogyny, 5, 16, 34, 76, 80, 93, 111, 130, 146–47
molecular effects of racism, 10, 20–22, 32, 56, 155, 177
Momigliano, Anna, 48

Momference, 177
"mom-in-chief," 104, 108, 109, 129, 148
Moore, Demi, 103
moore, madison, 129-30
"More Life" (Chambers-Letson), 3, 7, 114, 170, 175
"A More Perfect Union" (Barack Obama), 148
Morgan (interlocutor), 86
Morgan, Jennifer, 17
Morgan, Piers, 118
mortality rates: Black maternal, 3-4, 10-13, 21-22, 29, 56, 70-71, 73-74, 76, 82, 90, 93, 180; Black infant, 4, 10-13, 19, 35, 76; racism as cause of, 4, 21, 56; state response to, 11, 27, 71, 73, 83, 100
motherhood as institution, 16, 142-43, 154
mothering while black, 136-37
Mothers and Offspring Mortality and Morbidity Awareness Act (MOMMA Act), 11, 73
Mothers of the Movement, 5, 24-26, 106, 107, 120-21, 125-26, 134, 137, 164-65
*Mrs. Dalloway* (Woolf), 160
MTV Video Music Awards, 121
Muñoz, José Esteban, 151-52
Muslim, 108
Muzik, Maria, 35, 39

naming, 162-63
National Bail Out Collective, 25-26
National Breastfeeding Awareness Campaign (NBAC), 44-45
National Institutes of Health, 52
National Public Radio (NPR), 3, 10, 39
native lands (Rich): mothers as, 143-44
natural: birth, 92; breastfeeding as, 32, 41, 44, 49, 57-62; hair, 118; mothering, 134, 137-38, 158, 171; world, 58-62, 133-34, 138, 163-64
Navratilova, Martina, 110
Nelson, Maggie, 135, 139-41
New York, 1-3, 173-74, 179-81; breastfeeding programs in, 52-53; doula programs in, 11, 71, 74
*New Yorker*, 108, 109, 169
New York Police Department, 173-74
*New York Times*, 3, 21, 23, 34, 42, 54, 104, 110, 112, 113, 118, 120, 129, 136, 174, 180
neoliberalism, 86, 97
Nike, 107, 112

nonbinary, 192n4
nonbreastfeeders, 29, 32, 34-35, 38, 50
noncare, 6, 63, 64, 82, 175
nonconsent, 78, 79, 81, 82
nonindictment 5, 23-24, 106
nonplace, 12-13, 16
nonprofits, 71, 74, 100
nontime, 12-13, 16
non-US place, 12-13, 14
normalcy, 127-28
#NormalizeBreastfeeding, 56-57, 63-67
Northwestern Medicine Women's Hospital, 75
"Notes toward a Politics of Location" (Rich), 142-43
nursing parent, 192n4
nurture, 36, 56, 57, 60

Obama, Barack, 107-8, 122, 148, 169-70
Obama, Malia, 127-28, 170
Obama, Michelle, 29, 50, 55, 104-9, 121-25, 127-29, 148, 169-70; as apolitical, 104, 109, 170; as political 104, 108-9, 138, 170; rebranding, 107, 109, 128-29
Obama, Sasha, 127-28
obesity: Black women and 10, 43, 50-56; breastfeeding and, 36, 43-44, 50, 52-55; epidemic, 43, 50-53, 102. *See also* Let's Move
obligation. *See* compassion: and obligation
obstetric violence, 3, 6, 11, 22, 27, 70, 78-80, 92, 95, 100, 180; Latin America and, 79, 83; as ordinary, 12, 78; and reproductive justice, 20, 57; as state violence, 7
*Of Woman Born* (Rich), 137, 141-44, 147-48, 154, 189n55
Ohanian, Alexis, 112, 116, 128-29
Oliver, Mary, 163
Olutola, Sarah, 123-24
Olympics, 104, 124
"One Child of One's Own" (Walker), 137, 141-42, 145-48, 149
openness, 159-60
*Oprah Magazine*, 129
ordinary: black breasts, 64-67; birth as, 83, 98-99; life, 127-30; birth violence as, 81, 83; conditions of the, 4, 13-14, 77-78, 174, 182; death as, 24; violence, 78, 168
Organic Law on the Right of Women to a Life Free of Violence, 78

Index · 243

origins: mothers as, 143–44
O'Rourke, Beto, 13
Osaka, Naomi, 110–11
Oshun, 104
othermothers (Collins), 19–20, 156
Ounce of Prevention Fund, 74

pain, 15, 175; birth, 94–95; Black maternal, 8, 138, 155; Black motherhood as symbol for, 4, 6, 65, 78, 125–26, 137, 175; collective, 161
Pantaleo, Daniel, 191n92
paraprofessional, 27, 83–84, 89–91, 100, 184
*partus sequitur ventrem*, 17
patience, 80, 83, 92
paternity leave, 116
pathology: of Black breasts, 57, 59, 62, 67–68; of Black fathers, 60; of Black motherhood, 4, 6, 15, 22, 56, 149, 174–76, 184–85; of Black women's bodies, 43, 52–53; non-, 14
patriarchy and the patriarchal, 10, 27, 48, 60, 72, 124, 130, 139, 142, 144, 146, 154, 157
Patterson, Randy, 86
"peace officers," 173
Peters, Ronald Trey, 9
Philly Loves Breast-Feeding, 194n26
Phu Thy, 59
Pinto, Samantha, 106, 134, 166, 202n57
Pirelli calendar, 113
Pitocin, 80, 180, 207n2
PJ (interlocutor), 80
playful, 106, 107, 121–22, 126–27, 130–31
pleasure, Black maternal, 106, 117, 122, 127, 149, 151–52
police violence, 22–23, 26, 29, 70, 118–19, 121, 164, 167–68, 173–74, 179, 182
political, the, 106, 120; Beyoncé and, 117–20, 123, 125; Michelle Obama and, 104, 108–9, 138, 170; Serena Williams and, 112–13, 117, 120, 123–24, 129
political subjectivity: Black maternal, 8–9, 22, 105, 120–21, 148, 154, 167
postpartum, 10, 11, 54, 67, 79, 90, 95, 99, 106, 112, 115, 117, 129, 140, 177
poverty, 4, 10, 21, 23, 51, 54, 167, 173–74
precarity: of Black life, 32, 36, 43, 56, 62, 144, 166; Black maternal aesthetic and, 29, 134, 149, 152–53 155; of Black motherhood, 4,

20, 73, 166, 168; of breastfeeding gap, 37; economic, 171, 176
Pressley, Ayanna, 11
Preventing Maternal Deaths Act, 11
privacy: Black familial, 127–28, 166; Black maternal, 8–9, 107, 127–30, 156–58; of Black women, 16; of domestic life, 127, 137, 140, 156. *See also* public/private
ProDoula, 85–88
progress narratives, 15, 17
psychic, 14, 55, 73, 97, 114, 151, 152; Black maternal capacities, 29; bond, 58; costs, 167, 177; needs, 70; nutrition, 49, 68; pain, 82, 95; pleasures, 149; strength, 113; violence, 56
public health, 6, 10, 21–22, 68; Black feminism and, 68; on breastfeeding, 35–37, 41–46, 50, 52–55; doula training and, 11; crisis, 179, 182; medical racism and, 56; on obesity, 50, 51–55, 104
public/private, 8–9, 133, 159, 142, 195n32
publishing industry, 135–36, 139, 148; diversity in, 135–36
Purtill, Corinne, 46

Qai Qai, 129
queer: aesthetic: 129, motherhood, 25, 89, 139; survival, 130
quiet, 113–14
Quiney, Ruth, 139–41
quotidian: Black maternal life, 140, 142, 154–55, 157–58; breastfeeding as, 64; fabulous, 130

racial science, 51–52
rage, 7, 9–10, 118, 136, 147, 165
"raise the dead" (Holland), 183
Rankine, Claudia, 103
Rauner, Bruce, 73
Reaching Our Sisters Everywhere, 40
rebranding. *See* brand management
redemption, 109, 114, 117, 164
Reddy, Nancy, 135
redress, 77, 78–79, 81, 82, 83
Reed-Veal, Geneva, 24, 106. *See also* Mothers of the Movement
refusal: Black breastfeeding imagined, 37, 43, 50–52; Black maternal, 15, 29, 105, 146, 149–50, 152–53, 163; of respectability, 134, 171

relationality, 4, 39, 49, 105, 121–22, 126–27, 131, 139, 147, 159, 167, 168
representation: of Black breastfeeding, 31–32, 35–38, 49, 57–68; of Black maternal friendship, 126–27; of Black maternal refusal, 137, 146, 152; of Black motherhood, 15–16, 20, 36, 119, 130, 136–37, 148, 175, 177, 180; of Blackness, 160; of ecstatic motherhood, 151; self-, 57–68; of Serena Williams, 103, 110–14, 123, 129
reproductive freedom. *See* reproductive justice
reproductive justice: Black feminists and, 4, 6, 16, 18, 20, 25, 27, 68, 72–73, 100; breastfeeding and, 68; doulas and, 70–73, 84–87, 89, 100; institutionalization of, 18, 20, 27, 100; movements, 18, 23, 25, 181; the state and, 27, 100, 180; on violence, 23, 57, 78, 82, 180
reproductive labor, 48, 140–42, 157
reproductive rights. *See* reproductive justice
resilience, 19, 20, 154
respectability politics, 9, 16, 24, 114, 166, 171; grief and, 164–65
responsive feeding, 54
*Rest in Power: The Enduring Life of Trayvon Martin* (Fulton and Martin), 135
*Rest in Power: The Trayvon Martin Story* (documentary), 137
Rice, Tamir, 22, 23
Rich, Adrienne, 137, 141–44, 147–48, 154, 189n55
rights: language of, 16, 82–83
risk mitigation, 43–44, 46–47, 50, 51–56, 62, 68, 93
Roach, Shoniqua, 157, 202n57
Roberts, Dorothy, 17–18
Robinson, Marian, 128
Roeder, Amy, 3, 12
Roitman, Janet, 14
Rosenblum, Katherine Lisa, 35, 39
Rosin, Hanna, 42, 48
Rowland, Kelly, 124
royal family (British), 126

sacred, the, 96, 114, 119, 133, 151, 157, 159
Salazar, Julia, 181
Samantha (interlocutor), 83–84, 89
sanctuary, 20, 157–58, 170
satiety, 36, 49, 52, 54
Save Black Women (commission), 11

"say her name," 175
"say their name," 22
Schumer, Amy, 113, 181
Sears, Bill, 48
Sears, Martha, 49
"second shift" (Hochschild), 140, 157
segregation: geographic, 37, 74; medical, 37–38
Sehgal, Parul, 135
self in maternal memoirs, 136, 139–40, 143, 145, 147, 149–54, 157–60, 162, 169–71
self-fashioning, 106, 120
sensuality, 29, 51, 55, 107, 121, 129, 130, 149, 152
"sentimental political storytelling" (Wanzo), 15
sexiness: maternal, 129–30
sexual: anti-, 129; autonomy, 6, 68, 79, 83; excess, 36, 39, 62, 68, 113, 120; subject, 119; violence, 17, 80–81
Shange, Ntozake, 123
Sharapova, Maria, 124
Sharpe, Christina, 190n87, 199n12
Sheridan, Susan, 142
"She the People" forum, 2
shield, 127–30, 156, 158
Shire, Warsan, 123
Simmons, Ann M., 10
Simmons, Vanessa 63–67
Sinclair, Ravae, 79
sister: daughter as, 146–47, 150, 153
SisterSong Women of Color Reproductive Justice Collective, 18
slavery, 13, 16–19, 35, 43, 146,
slow death (Berlant), 13–14, 50–51
Smith, Mychal Denzel, 136–37, 165
"social dead weight" (Strings), 51–52, 55
social media, 42, 56, 57, 62, 63, 104, 117, 129, 173, 181, 192n12, 208n6
solidarity, 72, 85, 100, 106–7, 121, 126, 130, 180
Solinger, Rickie, 18
Sontag, Susan, 39
sorrow, 7, 9, 19
"Sorry" (Beyoncé), 105, 122, 123–24
Spain, 79
Special Supplemental Nutrition Program for Women, Infants, and Children (WIC), 27, 38, 40, 53
spectacle, 4, 12, 24
"spirit murder" (Williams), 56

Index · 245

spiritual: abuse, 78; birth as, 83, 84, 88, 91, 92, 94, 97, 98; calling, 24, 119; communities, 58, 85, 92, 98; empowerment, 16; labor, 14, 29, 84; mothering, 88, 92, 98, 119, 134, 137, 138, 151, 155; natural world as, 60

"spoiled identities," 141

Stack, Carol, 154, 190n71

state, the: Black breastfeeding and, 32, 34, 36, 38, 40, 41, 43, 50, 52–53, 68; Black feminism and, 4, 27–28, 32, 34, 71, 100–101, 175–77, 184; Black motherhood and, 11, 17–18, 27, 29; biopolitical, 4; bureaucracy, 11, 173–74; as compassionate, 39–43, 55; doulas and, 11, 26–27, 29, 71 73–74, 83–85, 90–91, 100–101, 176; formula and, 40–41, 43, 44; racial, 8; reproductive justice and, 27, 100, 180; violence and, 5, 7, 20, 22–24, 26, 71, 118–20, 125, 148, 163, 168, 170, 175, 181, 182, 184

state of emergency, 13, 70, 76, 77, 134

"state of exception," 13

Stewart, Felicia R., 134

"strange intimacies" (Nash and Pinto), 134

Street, Cordielle, 181

stress: of Black mothering, 56; of racism: 10, 20–22, 32, 56, 155, 177

Strings, Sabrina, 43, 51–52

stop and frisk, 19

#StopMedolac, 42

stranger, 159–62; Black feminism on, 160; unbecoming, 159, 171

strength, 60, 62, 94–95, 113

suffering: Black maternal, 4, 5, 12, 21, 100, 164, 175; collective, 161; currency of, 12, 15, 39, 164, 175

Summit on Obesity in African American Women and Girls, 53

Super Bowl half-time show, 104, 118–19

surveillance, 23, 24, 39, 48, 67, 117, 121, 160, 168, 175, 184

survival, 7, 26, 93, 130, 147, 155, 157, 184

Sydney, 89, 93–94, 97

symbol: of Black child, 68; of Black mothers, 1, 3–7, 16, 20, 22, 68, 100, 174–76, 180–81, 183–84; of Blackness, 52; of Black women, 52, 100, 176

"Tales from a Black Girl on Fire, or Why I Hate to Walk Outside and See Things Burning" (Dungy), 163

taxonomy of violence, 76–77, 82–83, 91

Taylor, Breonna, 22, 179

Taylor, Keeanga-Yamahtta, 22, 23

"telling the truth," 141, 166–68, 171

*Tell the Truth and Shame the Devil* (McSpadden and LeFlore), 135, 138, 164–68

temporality: of birth, 83; of Black motherhood, 4, 12, 138, 147, 148, 150; of crisis, 12–13, 16, 20, 32, 36, 43, 50, 73, 77, 134, 175; medical, 92–94; of obstetric violence, 80; of slavery, 13, 17; of urgency, 12–14, 20; of white motherhood, 140

tenderness, 57, 59–60, 62, 65, 99, 143, 147

tennis, 109–12, 115, 116–17

third pandemic, 29, 181–84

Thomas, Latham 182

#1000BlackGirlBooks, 136

Thurgood Marshall Civil Rights Center, 164

Till, Emmett, 8, 165, 166

*Time* magazine, 49, 122

Tindal, Brenda, 165

togetherness: Black Motherhood and, 19, 57–60, 131, 146, 155, 163, 168; doulas and, 73, 82–84, 87, 89–92, 95, 98, 100

*toi* (interconnection between self and other; Williams), 160

ToLabor, 85

tranquil, 114, 120, 134

*Transgender Health*, 192n4

transgender parents, 192n4

transmisogyny, 130

transphobia, 5

trauma: against, 134, 138–39, 153, 155, 157, 159, 178, 185; Black infant, 36; Black maternal, 14–15, 39, 56, 62, 77–78, 82–83, 93, 136, 165–66, 168–71, 175, 178, 185; Black maternal friendship beyond, 122, 126–27, 130; Black maternal politics rooted in, 9, 20, 164; Black maternal relationality through, 106, 121; Black motherhood as symbol of, 3–6, 16, 26, 65, 100, 139, 155, 164–66, 175, 177–78; collective, 161; of mother-daughter relationship, 150, 152–53

travel, 161–62

Trayvon generation, 183–84

tropes, racialized, 39, 42, 51

Trump, Donald, 5, 107–8, 148, 154, 169 196n60

Truth, Sojourner, 146
Turner, Sasha, 18–19

un-becoming: daughter, 149–53, 159, 171; mother, 149; stranger, 159, 171
universal, 105, 109, 115–17, 120
universe, 98, 146, 154, 160, 162
university, 26–27, 176
University of Chicago Medical Center, 75
"unmothering" (Freeman), 16, 18
US Department of Health and Human Services, 44–45
US Left, 3, 4–5, 6–7, 12, 13, 14–15, 18, 32, 38, 91, 175, 184–85
US Open, 110–11, 116, 122, 123
US Right, 5, 168
utopia, 111, 154–55

vaginal birth after cesarean (VBAC), 91, 97
*Vanity Fair*, 103, 112–14
Varnam, Emily, 78
Venezuela, 78
vessels: Black women as, 119, 175
Villarosa, Linda, 3, 10, 12, 13, 21
violence: Black motherhood as site of, 15–17, 20–22, 37–38, 43, 65, 93, 95, 120, 138, 146, 150, 155, 174–75, 178; love and, 167; quotidian, 56. *See also* antiBlack; anticipation; Black life; birth rape; carceral; gun violence; hospitals; institutional; medical; obstetric violence; ordinary; police violence; reproductive justice; sexual; the state; taxonomy of violence; white supremacist
visibility: of antiBlack violence, 8, 24; of Black breastfeeding, 62, 68; of Black breastfeeding gap, 43, 57; of Black death, 8, 15–16, 24, 26, 82; of Black life, 3, 6, 163; of Black maternal aesthetics, 106, 111; Black maternal celebrity, 124, 127; of Black maternal memoirs, 134–35, 137; of Black mothers, 4–8, 12, 15–16, 20–21, 106, 120, 137–38, 148, 160, 175, 185; of doulas, 70, 72, 82, 89, 99, 101; of maternal ambivalence, 140, 150; medical violence, 7, 14, 15, 83, 184; of reproductive labor, 140–42
visuality, 20; Black breastfeeding and, 32, 35–37, 46, 49, 57–68; Black maternal celebrity and, 113, 119, 123, 125

vulnerability: Black feminism and, 34; of Black life, 4–5, 36, 39, 56, 62, 68; Black maternal celebrity and, 106, 117, 129; of Black mothers, 3, 67, 73, 83, 89, 181, 184; collective, 134, 161; motherhood and, 142, 151–53, 159; in writing, 142, 154

"wake work" (Sharpe), 199n12
Waldman, Annie, 10
Walker, Alice, 137, 141–42, 144–50, 153
Walker, Rebecca, 137–38, 146–54, 158–59
Wallace, Alicia, 103, 107
"wanting," 157
Wanzo, Rebecca, 15
war on drugs, 19
Warren, Elizabeth, 2–3, 4, 5, 108
*Washington Post*, 31, 111, 122, 124, 125, 177
Washington, Sha-Asia, 180–82, 184
"weathering" (Geronimus), 21–22, 56
Weinbaum, Alys, 17
Weiss, Marisa, 44
welfare: queen, 188n17; state, 40, 51
*We Live for the We: The Political Power of Black Motherhood* (McClain), 137–38, 154–59
Wells, Julia, 7
We Need Diverse Books, 136
wet nurses, 36, 42, 43
White Coats for Black Lives (WC4BL), 21
White, Hattie, 124
White House, 124, 127–28
white supremacist, 24, 108, 130; patriarchal violence, 10, 154
Williams, Desiree, 181
Williams, Michelle, 124
Williams, Patricia J., 43, 56, 160–62
Williams, Serena, 29, 103, 105–7, 109–17, 121–24, 126, 128–29; as apolitical, 114–15, 117, 120; body of, 103, 109, 111–14, 117, 124, 129; catsuit and, 111–12, 115, 117; drug testing of, 116–17; as political, 112–13, 117, 120, 123–24, 129; rebranding of, 109, 111, 115, 117
Williams, Venus, 109, 113, 122
Willis, Deb, 59
Wilson, Darren, 22, 23, 165
"wily patient" (Bridges), 188n17
Wimbledon, 116
Winfrey, Oprah, 122
Winters, Joseph, 109

wisdom, 63, 94, 108, 119
witness, 39, 84, 85, 91, 125, 145
Wolf, Joan, 44, 46–47
womanist, 144–45
womb: Black, 175, 184
"women's folly" (Walker), 145–47
women's studies, 78, 176
Woodhull Medical Center, 180–83
Woolf, Virginia, 160
World Health Assembly, 196n60

World Health Organization (WHO), 38, 40, 51
world-making, 72, 137, 158–59
worry, 151–52, 161
woundedness, 9, 56, 100, 152, 156
Wright, Jeremiah, 148

Yanez, Jeronimo, 9
Yoruba, 104

Zimmerman, George, 23

www.ingramcontent.com/pod-product-compliance
Lightning Source LLC
Chambersburg PA
CBHW070324240426
43671CB00013BA/2358